KREMLIN WINTER

Also by Robert Service

The Bolshevik Party in Revolution:
A Study in Organisational Change

Lenin: A Political Life
Volume One: The Strengths of Contradiction
Volume Two: Worlds in Collision
Volume Three: The Iron Ring

The Russian Revolution, 1900–1927

A History of Twentieth-Century Russia

Lenin: A Biography

Stalin: A Biography

Comrades: A History of World Communism

Trotsky: A Biography

Spies and Commissars: Bolshevik Russia and the West

The End of the Cold War: 1985–1991

Russia and its Islamic World:
From the Mongol Conquest to the Syrian Military Intervention

The Last of the Tsars: Nicholas II and the Russian Revolution

ROBERT SERVICE

KREMLIN WINTER

Russia and the Second Coming of Vladimir Putin

PICADOR

First published 2019 by Picador
an imprint of Pan Macmillan
The Smithson, 6 Briset Street, London EC1M 5NR
Associated companies throughout the world
www.panmacmillan.com

ISBN 978-1-5098-8303-5

1 3 5 7 9 8 6 4 2

A CIP catalogue record for this book is available from the British Library.

Typeset by Palimpsest Book Production Ltd, Falkirk, Stirlingshire
Printed and bound by CPI Group (UK) Ltd, Croydon, CR0 4YY

Visit **www.picador.com** to read more about all our books
and to buy them. You will also find features, author interviews and
news of any author events, and you can sign up for e-newsletters
so that you're always first to hear about our new releases.

To Adele
and
to Oscar, Carla, Lara, Dylan, Joely, Keira, Phoebe and Kai

Contents

FRACTURE

MANAGEMENT

POWER

AMBITION

List of Illustrations

1. Putin at his inauguration ceremony in May 2012 (AFP / Stringer)
2. Prime Minister Dmitri Medvedev (YURI KADOBNOV / Contributor)
3. Nikolai Patrushev, Security Council secretary and foreign-policy hawk (Alexei Nikolsky / Contributor)
4. Igor Sechin, Rosneft's boss and Putin's multipurpose hard man over many years (TASS / Contributor)
5. Sergei Lavrov, Foreign Affairs Minister (Mikhail Svetlov / Contributor)
6. Alexei Kudrin, long-term Finance Minister, friend of Putin and subsequently a permitted critic of official economic policy (Bloomberg / Contributor)
7. Vladislav Surkov, one-time manipulator of multiparty politics on Putin's behalf. Now his emissary in eastern Ukraine (Mikhail Klimentyev / Contributor)
8. Viktor Yanukovych, Ukrainian president until 2014 and a flagrant accumulator of personal wealth through office (Sergei Guneyev / Contributor)
9. Yevgeni Primakov, failed contender for the Russian presidency in 2000 and an early promoter of 'multipolarity' in world affairs (Sergei Guneyev / Contributor)
10. Mikhail Kasyanov, Putin's earliest prime minister and subsequently one of his fiercest critics (Mikhail Japaridze / Contributor)
11. Boris Nemtsov, unrelenting political enemy of Putin until he was assassinated in 2015 (Epsilon / Contributor)
12. Alexei Navalny, leading current critic of the Putin administration (FREDERICK FLORIN / Contributor)
13. 'March of Millions' protest poster, Moscow, June 2012 (Russian Subject Collection, Hoover Institution Archive)
14. Opposition giant puppet model of Putin as footballer for the Party of Scoundrels and Thieves (Russian Subject Collection, Hoover Institution Archive)
15. Navalny on stage at an evening rally in his Moscow mayoral campaign, August 2012 (Russian Subject Collection, Hoover Institution Archive)
16. Pussy Riot release-demand poster, 2012 (Russian Subject Collection, Hoover Institution Archive)

Acknowledgements

On a windy day at Lingfield Park races in 2015 our son Owain suggested backing an unfancied Irish bay gelding by name of Putin. He was putting up the idea, I discovered, for no other reason than that he wanted to hear me shouting 'C'mon, Putin!' in the final stretch. The gallant horse disappointed its backers that day, finishing fifth in a field of nine.

The better-known Putin has yet to enter an electoral race without possessing a boiler-plated guarantee of victory, and he and his administration constitute the core of the chapters that follow. I came to this project after serving as a witness in the *Berezovski* v. *Abramovich* trial in 2011–12 and the Litvinenko public inquiry in 2015–16. No one at those proceedings was left in doubt about the deep entanglement of the internal and external factors in Russia's politics. Nor was it possible to remain unconscious of the dangers and opportunities in Russian public life as well as of the balance between its volatilities and immobilism.

I also benefited from advice given by some of those who have had an influence on Russian affairs at the highest level. I am especially indebted to Catherine Ashton, Toomas Hendrik Ilves, Henry Kissinger, Roderic Lyne, Michael McFaul, Vadim Prokhorov, Jean-Arthur Régibeau and Radek Sikorski, whom I thank for sharing their experiences in politics, diplomacy and the law.

Colleagues at the Hoover Institution, Stanford and St Antony's College, Oxford have kindly looked at sections of the book: I am grateful to Roy Allison, Michael Bernstam, Paul Chaisty, Charles Hill and Amir Weiner for this help and for our many productive conversations. I also owe a debt of thanks to Luke Harding and Roderic Lyne for reading particular chapters. At Stanford it was helpful to exchange ideas on contemporary Russia with John Dunlop, Paul Gregory and David Holloway. For a book of this kind, it was essential to read as widely as possible and I appreciate advice offered by Timothy Garton

Ash, Joerg Baberowski, Peter Duncan, Chris Gerry, Robin Milner-Gulland, Philip Hanson, Dan Healey, Thomas Henriksen, Beka Kobakhidze, Svetlana McMillin, Andrew Monaghan, Keith Sidwell, Maciej Siekierski, Steve Tsang and Alexandra Zernova.

My wife Adele Biagi and friends Bobo Lo and Liz Teague read the entire draft. At Picador, Georgina Morley did the same. They all made copious, persuasive suggestions for improvements and had reservations about the book's analysis: I hope that the final version deals adequately with them.

A technical point merits emphasis. Putin lies at the core of the chapters even though he is far from being the sole originator of trends in Russian politics at home and abroad. His speeches and interviews are a crucial primary source. Available online in some abundance, they permit us to direct a sharp focus on what he thinks and does – or at least on what he wants others to believe that he thinks and does. The translations on his presidential website, however, are not always reliable, which is why I have usually supplied my own attempts.

The copiousness of public statements, however, does not disguise the fact that Putin's Kremlin is more secretive than Yeltsin's ever was. Unfortunately several recent accounts contain sheer speculation dressed up as certainty, and it is important to recognize that there are many known unknowns in Russian current affairs and, probably, an even greater number of unknown unknowns – and Western analysis, and any policy that is developed from it, needs to be rooted in the ground of what can be duly authenticated. Russia is too important to have its politics exaggerated, over-simplified or turned into a fantasy.

Much of the research for this book was done in the Hoover Institution Archives and Library. It was a matter of surprise and pleasure to examine so many valuable holdings on contemporary Russia, from the giant Putin puppet (see image 14) and the in-house FSB journal *Sluzhba bezopasnosti* to the piles of Opposition pamphlets. My stays at Hoover were enabled by support from the Sarah Scaife Foundation, to which I express my warmest thanks. I am grateful to Hoover Institution Director Tom Gilligan and Library and Archives Director Eric Wakin for their indispensable assistance. Thanks also go to my literary agent David Godwin for his unstinting help.

Adele and I have had our lives enriched by our grandchildren. This book is dedicated to her and to them, not forgetting their parents.

Robert Service
April 2019

Introduction

In March 2012 Vladimir Vladimirovich Putin was returned as president in the Russian election. It would be his third term in the supreme office and his second coming to the peak of power, and he was determined to seize back the initiative by pushing Russian policy, external and internal, back into the framework it had in 2008, when constitutional law prohibited him from immediately standing again for the presidency – a problem he solved by handing over the office to his protégé Dmitri Medvedev on the understanding that he himself became prime minister.

The four years of Medvedev's presidential term had nevertheless been a frustrating period for Putin, who had to sit back while Medvedev adjusted some of his cherished policies. When Putin resumed the presidency, he reverted Russia's foreign policy to a stance of confrontation with America. He promoted social traditionalism in Russia. He reinforced the political and security institutions. Putin and his team were avowed conservatives and militant nationalists who aimed to spread Russian influence beyond the country's borders. They would tolerate no challenge to Russia's power and prestige from the other states of the former USSR. America's attempts to expand its influence would meet with resistance. The Russian armed forces would exploit their renewed capacity to impose Moscow's will and a campaign of propaganda would begin to win hearts and minds around the world for Russia's cause. Putin had started on this path in his first and second terms. On resuming the presidency, he intended to complete the journey.

When in 2000 Putin had initially inherited power from Boris Yeltsin, he reduced the arena of democratic and civic freedom. He loosened the reins on the security agencies. He licensed an official cult of his greatness. Until 2004 he entertained the idea of partnership with America, but he objected to the continuing American armed intervention in Afghanistan and the Middle East and also to the anti-authoritarian revolutions in Ukraine and elsewhere. He tightened the Russian state's grip on its society and economy and he threw down a challenge in world politics. During the Medvedev presidency, he nursed a determination to wind the clock back to his own kind of policies once he retook the supreme office. His electoral victories in 2012 and 2018 gave him ample chance. In 2024, when he is again scheduled to step down, he will be seventy-one. Nobody knows whether, by then, he will have decided to amend the country's constitution and enable himself to stand for a fifth term.

Russian domestic and foreign policies evoke a mixture of fear, respect and admiration around the world. There is a sustained barrage of hostile commentary about Putin and his administration, citing a sequence of assassinations, cyber-crimes, quasi-imperial pretensions and military aggression.[1] Pro-Kremlin commentators are few (though Donald Trump is one of them), but there have been several attempts to put the anti-anti-Kremlin arguments which commonly designate Russia as the victim and omit mention of Russia the victimizer.[2] The two sides frequently fail to take each other's arguments seriously. One camp takes it for granted that nothing good can come out of Russia and that no improvement in the current situation is conceivable; the other emphasizes the unwarranted harm done by foreigners to Russia without taking account of Russian self-harm – or at least the harm done by the Kremlin.

If we are to move beyond polemics, it is crucial to examine how Russians feel and think about their country and the world – surely a prerequisite for judgement regardless of whether one lauds or criticizes Putin and his administration. Even the critics – I am one – must recognize that Russia has a lively society simmering with zest and potential. Although Russian affairs have taken a menacing pathway, there have always been alternative routes that many of its citizens have wanted to pursue. They and their leaders, however, are at one in feeling a strong resentment about the way that they and their people have been dealt with by the West. Though millions of Russians dislike the harsh, corrupt ways of their rulers, there is also a widespread opinion that the Putin administration has restored dignity and authority to the country. Like most states, Russia has much diversity in the attitudes of its people. Its ruling group has made a strategic choice to restrict civil rights and challenge America. Even so, Russia is still not as unfree in politics, the media and IT communications as China, Saudi Arabia or North Korea. Though it would be foolish to count upon a complete transformation of Kremlin policies even after Putin leaves power, the option of permanent no-change is unrealistic. Even if it takes decades, change will happen, and the rulers know they can never take the patience of the Russian people for granted.

For years after the USSR's collapse in 1991 it was usual to regard Russians as perennial losers. Their economy and armed forces were in tatters. They had given up control of eastern Europe and found themselves dispossessed of the other fourteen republics of the former Soviet Union. But when Putin became president in 2000, a rise in revenues from oil and gas exports benefited the economy, and the new administration followed up the invasion of Chechnya in 1999 by stamping hard on political opposition across Russia. Between 2003 and 2005, when 'colour revolutions' took place in favour of democratic accountability in Ukraine, Georgia and Kyrgyzstan, and the Americans pursued their plans to install an anti-missile defence system in east-central Europe, Putin began to confront Washington. President Barack Obama, the Democratic politician who succeeded George W. Bush in the White House in 2009 and announced a 'reset' of America's Russian policy, failed to improve the climate. Frost turned to ice in 2014 when Putin sent his army to occupy Crimea.

Dominant opinion in the West blames Putin, the Russian leadership or even Russia as a whole. Russians themselves have undergone a steady restriction of their political and civil rights and have experienced their country's increasing pariah status. Yet Putin is still popular in Russia after nearly two decades in power. His percentage rating admittedly fell to the low sixties in 2018, well down from its peak in 2015 after he had annexed Crimea, but it remains at a level that most of the world's leaders would envy.

Putin and his team have intentionally disrupted the order of world politics – this is not a secret: they admit as much themselves. They have also set about neutralizing political opposition, media criticism and public protest in Russia by fair means or, more usually, foul. But how has this happened without provoking greater unrest at home? What is the role of the security agencies and what part is played by TV channels, press and the internet? Indeed, what kind of political order exists in Russia? Does it merely wear the apparel of democracy without being democratic? Is it really an autocracy and, if so, is it individual or collective in nature? But why is there so much repression and corruption? Why has Chechnya suffered such brutalization? Moreover, what factors led Putin to decide on the annexation of Crimea in 2014 and the intervention in the Syrian civil war? Or to license covert interference in the politics of America and the European Union? And what is the significance of the Chinese card in Russian hands?

These are tantalizing questions that intersect and complicate each other. One view is that America and the European Union could have proceeded with greater restraint and circumspection; other observers heap the blame on Putin. As we shall explore, Putin was never likely to be an enthusiast for democracy or an easy partner of America even though he gave a different impression in his first presidential term. Nevertheless, there is also a need to attempt a ranking of Putin's personal responsibility and the sheer pressures of the Russian political and economic order. This is not a straightforward task because he has actively sought to minimize leaks from his administration. But is Putin himself perhaps less a gaoler than a detainee of the political order that he has helped to create? And how much is it the case that Putin and the ruling group, including security officials and big businessmen as well as ministers, gave a peculiar harshness and durability to their policies?

How long Russia's current stability will last is unpredictable, and many questions arise about the Russian future. How strongly ensconced in power is the current ruling group? What is the balance of force and persuasion in its methods? Can the Kremlin take public opinion for granted? Has the West mishandled the Russian leadership since the fall of communism? Is there a new Cold War? If so, is it as dangerous as the old one? What is the link between Russia's internal and external policies? This book is intended to lay out how to fill the space between those who see the Putin administration as more sinned against than sinning and those who find it hard to believe that anything good will ever emerge from Russia.

IMAGE

1. FATHER TO THE NATION: THE PUTIN CULT

Millions of Russians think of Vladimir Putin as a patriotic son of Russia who rose to the heights by talent and effort and who lifted up his country with him. He occupied the presidency for the first time at the start of the millennium and won his fourth term by an electoral landslide in March 2018. His United Russia has a majority in the upper and lower houses of the Federal Assembly – the Federation Council and the State Duma. He controls the government, security agencies and armed forces. And he is internationally recognized, too, *Forbes* magazine having named him the world's most powerful man in 2017 and again in 2018.

The Russian authorities have created a political cult in his honour and at his behest. A Moscow pre-school primer tells children about the great figures in Russian history, starting with the founder of the Romanov dynasty Tsar Mikhail. Peter the Great is highlighted as well as Nicholas II, who abdicated in March 1917. The little book alludes to no other leader since the early twentieth century leader until it reaches Putin. Lenin, Stalin and Gorbachëv pass without comment. Putin is celebrated as someone whom Russians should admire as one of the country's great rulers.[1] Wherever you go in Moscow, there are pictures of him. Newspaper kiosks sell his posters. TV daily news programmes carry items about him to the exclusion of all other politicians. The opposition press contributes to the phenomenon by reporting on his latest pronouncements. No other Russian political leader comes near to attracting the same amount of attention. Public life orbits round him.

Putin emphasizes the ordinariness of his Soviet boyhood in which he learned to look after himself in the back streets of St Petersburg – or Leningrad as it was known from 1924 until 1992. He advertises his university education in the law.[2] He is a fitness fanatic who for decades competed as a judo master. He emphasizes his recent passion for playing ice hockey. He speaks warmly of his family; but since 2013, when he and his wife Lyudmila divorced, he has ceased to mention her and focused instead on his late parents and his two daughters. He remains pleased that the KGB chose him as a recruit soon after he graduated from Leningrad State University. He also stresses that his later meteoric rise to the highest echelons of the Russian political elite came as a surprise. He had belonged for a mere two years to the Kremlin's charmed circle of influence when in July 1998 President Boris Yeltsin made him director of the Federal Security Service (FSB), which was the successor agency to the KGB. In August 1999 he became Yeltsin's new prime minister and at New Year 2000 Yeltsin shocked the Russian public by stepping down and nominating him as acting president.

It was a vertiginous upward trail. Putin has told of how he havered when Yeltsin offered him the premiership, saying he had him in mind as the next president. Like everyone in Russia, Putin knew how capricious Yeltsin was. In the blinking of an eye, Yeltsin might easily turn around and fire him. How, anyway, was Putin to obtain privacy and security for his family? If he accepted Yeltsin's invitation, how would he cope with being rocketed into prominence? While life and work were good for him as the FSB director, why take on a new job with such precarious prospects?[3]

Putin's uncertainty was understandable. But his tale of diffidence is also part of his act to reinforce the image of a leader who is modest and lacking in personal ambition. At the presidential election in March 2000, he claimed that it was a sense of duty that impelled him to stand. Putin was then an unknown quantity for most Russians, and his backers worked to build his reputation as a young, decisive politician in contrast with the departed Yeltsin. He personally piloted a plane to Chechnya to give credence to the picture. Mostly, however, he left it to others to talk up his virtues. A biography, *First Person*, quickly appeared, which underscored his humble origins. More details have come from Putin's subsequent recollections. One of his grandfathers, Spiridon Putin, worked as a cook in Petrograd (as St Petersburg had been renamed in 1914 to give it a less Germanic image in time of war) before the communists seized power in 1917. Spiridon must have welcomed the October Revolution because he was soon employed in the Kremlin kitchens. Later he got a job at one of Joseph Stalin's dachas, a coveted position in a period when most people were scraping round to feed themselves.[4]

It was providential for Spiridon that he stayed on a lowly rung of the ladder of the Soviet order. If he had been any higher, his physical proximity to Stalin might have endangered him in the Great Terror of 1937–8 when most of the regime's public figures were executed or sent to a labour camp on the dictator's orders. But nobody bothered about an obscure cook.

Putin's father, also Vladimir, was drafted into the Red Army after the USSR entered the war against the Third Reich in 1941. He served with distinction in a forward unit, joining in operations behind German lines on the Leningrad front. President Putin has mentioned the hard times that his parents endured after the war, and he took part in the 'Immortal Regiment' parade in 2015 with enthusiasm. This popular annual event is held in the big cities on Victory Day, 9 May, and family members walk in procession holding up photos of parents or grandparents who fought in the Second World War. At the end of 2015 in a publicized meeting, Putin's political adversary Gennadi Zyuganov, the communist party leader, felt moved to congratulate him, saying, 'You, moreover, took part holding a portrait of your father, a victorious hero. It seems to me that it would be very important for securing unity in society, and it would then be possible to bring many projects and programmes to fruition.'[5]

Putin replied warmly. And after he told Zyuganov to ask whatever questions he liked, 'Mr Zyuganov' praised Putin for his realistic analysis of international politics and called for 'solidarity in society' in the struggle against international terrorism. He also offered friendly advice in advance of the commemoration of the 1917 centennial:

> It will soon be the centenary of [the] February [Revolution] and the centenary of [the] Great October [Revolution]. Unfortunately, to much regret, a wave of anti-Sovietism and Russophobia exists which destroyed the USSR and gave birth to great disputes.
>
> We ought to think about this and sign up to some kind of 'pact' between 'Whites' and 'Reds' and between all the state's patriotic forces which would allow us to come to these dates as a united people, which is what happened recently with Crimea and Sevastopol, whose return had a consolidating effect on society.

Adversaries in the political arena, Zyuganov and Putin momentarily found common cause in their Russian patriotism, and Putin was pleased that his old rival was treating him, if only for this once, as father of the Russian nation.

Putin had snatched some of his guiding ideas from Zyuganov and other political rivals. Russia's politicians have had to adapt their public messages in the light of the fundamental changes in the country since the fall of the Soviet Union. Every party that seriously sought power had to devise a vision of the future that would appeal to modern Russians. The Communist Party ditched key features of Marxism-Leninism. Abandoning interest in the international labour movement, it became a vehicle of patriotism, military assertion and welfare economics, and Zyuganov seldom uttered the name of the man who founded the USSR: Lenin. Vladimir Zhirinovski, the Liberal-Democratic Party leader, adjusted his thinking with the same flexibility as Zyuganov. But whereas Zyuganov lamented the disintegration of the communist administration, Zhirinovski shed no tears. Instead he highlighted Russian nationalist values and argued for the use of force against any foreign state attempting to demean Russia's global status.

Putin, however, outflanked them by wrapping himself in the flag of a militant patriot, and by this and other less salubrious means he ensured that they continued to lose every presidential and parliamentary election.

He had resigned from the Communist Party in August 1991 after the coup against President Mikhail Gorbachëv. The conspiracy was led by KGB Chairman Vladimir Kryuchkov and supported by several of the leaders in the party and governmental hierarchy. The plotters fumbled their effort, and Gorbachëv was soon freed from house arrest in Crimea. But he never recovered all his old powers and the USSR collapsed at the end of the year, leaving Yeltsin as president of an independent Russia. By then Putin was working for the St Petersburg mayor and democratic politician Anatoli Sobchak, who had once been his law lecturer. When Sobchak had invited him to join his team, Putin at first demurred on the grounds that it would not help Sobchak if it became known that the team included an officer of seventeen years' standing in the KGB's external service. But Sobchak wanted enforcers who could help him run the city, and Putin was not the only person he recruited from a security agency background – indeed the mayor's office was stuffed with young former secret-service officers.[6]

Putin later downplayed his past rank of KGB lieutenant colonel:

> I ... wasn't a top Soviet official, I wasn't a party functionary, I wasn't a Politburo member, I didn't work in the provincial party committees. Essentially, though I worked in the intelligence services, I was

an ordinary citizen of the Soviet Union to the extent that an intelligence officer can be thought of as ordinary.[7]

He obviously wanted no taint of the mistakes by the communist leadership to affect his personal reputation.

He was not reticent about his past employment. When summar-
izing his thinking, he showed distinctly greater fondness for the
security agency than for the party:

> I did not join the party only because I had to, and I can't say that
> I was such a communist in my ideas, but nevertheless I was very
> careful in my attitude to it . . . Unlike many functionaries, I did
> not throw away my membership card, I did not burn it. I don't
> want to criticize anyone now – people could have various motives
> and their behaviour is their own business. The Communist Party
> of the Soviet Union fell apart; I still have my membership card
> somewhere or other.[8]

To this day he uses the lexicon that he learned in the secret service.
For instance, when addressing ministers and others who were
obstructing an official economic plan, he lost his temper with them
and spat out the remark that 'the saboteurs are sitting in this very
room'.[9] On other occasions he has spoken with affection about his time
in the KGB. One of his boasts was that he had an underdeveloped sense
of danger – the official file on him noted this as a defect.[10] Quite how
nostalgic Putin feels about his intelligence agency days is exemplified
by his surprise visit to his old boss Lazar Matveev on his ninetieth
birthday in May 2017. Matveev, living in quiet retirement in south-east
Moscow, was the KGB *rezident* in Dresden where Putin was posted in
the second half of the 1980s. Putin brought gifts of a presidential watch
and a copy of the Communist Party newspaper *Pravda* issued on the
day of Matveev's birth in 1927.[11]

He used to avoid appearing sentimental for fear of giving the
impression of weakness. Over the years, he has unfrozen somewhat.
Revealing recently that his father died two months before he became
prime minister in September 1999, he recalled how the old man on his
hospital bed said to the medical staff, 'Look, here comes my president.'[12] While acknowledging that he has risen high in public life, Putin
frequently stresses his ordinary upbringing. Since first occupying the
presidency he has also identified with the Orthodox Christian faith.
The sincerity of his belief has been called into question because he has

sometimes fumbled his words and gestures during church services. Nevertheless he affirms the religious pulse inside himself and recounts how his mother had him baptized in Leningrad in defiance of the communist authorities and their policy of militant atheism. The act of baptism turned out to involve an astonishing coincidence. The priest conducting the ceremony was a certain Father Nikolai. Years later, in conversation with Russian Orthodox Church Patriarch Kirill, Putin ascertained that Kirill was the son of that very same priest.[13]

Putin is protective of the privacy of his daughters Maria and Yekaterina. In 2013 foreign reports identified Maria as living in the Netherlands. Putin countered that none of his family was resident abroad. (Reportedly Maria had returned to Russia in the interim.) Both daughters, he insisted, are Moscow residents pursuing a 'normal life' without involvement in politics.[14] He stated that he made time to see each of his children at least once a month.[15] Describing them as 'ordinary' individuals with jobs in education and science, he denies they would ever behave like 'princes of the blood'. In June 2017 he let slip that he has two grandchildren, one of whom was at kindergarten while the other was a babe in arms.[16]

One aspect of Putin's character is unusual for a son of Russia. He rarely drinks alcohol and when he accepts a glass of wine at official occasions, he sips rather than gulps. Tea is Putin's favoured beverage.[17] When Yeltsin was filmed sitting at a table that was laid with a teacup and saucer, people laughed because he had a well-known weakness for vodka. With Putin, it is no charade and his rejection of alcoholic spirits has won him wide approval, especially with Russian women, many of whom have suffered at the hands of hard-drinking husbands. In 2002 the female electronic-dance duo Singing Together (Poyushchie Vmeste) had a hit single with 'A Man Like Putin', a song that contained the chorus,

> Someone like Putin who'll be a tower of strength,
> Someone like Putin who won't take to the drink,
> Someone like Putin who won't disrespect me,
> Someone like Putin who won't walk out on me.

For many Russian women, he was the kind of man with whom they would like to share their homes.

In 2015, after stories spread of illness, his spokesman Dmitri Peskov assured everyone that the president was so strong that he risked damaging people's hands when offering his greeting.[18] Though there were credible rumours that Putin had back problems, he has generally kept himself fit with daily workouts on the exercise equipment at his official residences. When he took up ice hockey at the age of sixty, he enjoyed competing on the rink in front of a cheering crowd.[19] For his summer vacations, he flew to picturesque parts of the Russian Federation, where he was filmed riding and fishing, sometimes stripped to the waist for the benefit of the cameras. In 2011 his aides arranged for him to try scuba diving in a Black Sea archaeological resort, but his reported discovery of some ancient remains was a set-up job that even Peskov had difficulty in laughing off. But it is all part of a public relations campaign to show Russians that their leader is in blooming health, unlike his predecessor, who was a medical wreck during his later years in power, and even Gorbachëv succumbed to exhaustion. Putin has no intention of tumbling into a situation where his subjects want rid of him because of ill health.

Although, like some of the tsars, he encourages Russians to tell him of their local grievances, there is an unwritten rule that they refrain from criticizing any general defects in current governance. In a TV phone-in show in April 2016, women working in the Ostrovnoi fish-processing plant on an island off the east coast of Siberia complained about not having received their wages since the previous October. A shocking story of corruption and exploitation emerged. Shikotan is an isolated place where the labour force felt like slaves. Putin's face expressed horror, as if he had never imagined that such things could arise in Russia. Within minutes a caption appeared on the screen to the effect that a criminal case had been started.[20] Next day the enterprise director appeared on site clutching a bagful of wages and blaming the bad fishing season for the delay. Sakhalin Province Governor Oleg Kozhemyako flew to the island to allay any notion that the authorities would try and hush up the situation.[21]

The clear inference was that if anyone could improve the lives of ordinary Russians, it was their president. In October 2014 Vyacheslav Volodin, then serving as Putin's first Deputy Chief of Staff, declared his motto: 'While there's Putin, there is Russia. Without Putin, there's no Russia.'[22] Two years later Putin gave a show of modesty by diverting attention to the annals of European history, 'It was the famous French "Sun King" Louis XIV who said that he was France, but this of course is an incorrect thesis.'[23] Countries, he explained, were bigger than their rulers – and Putin sensibly denied that he and Russia were one and the same. He returned to the topic a few weeks later when he remarked that he only attracted attention because he was an elected national leader and that his experience in Russia was something that occurred in other countries.[24] Volodin had probably tried to prepare the scene so that his president could enjoy warm applause without appearing to have invited flattery. But flattery is precisely what Volodin and others were organizing for him. They wanted him to receive public reverence, which he strove to accept with regal impassivity.

Though he is self-possessed when appearing on television, he can become cantankerous when faced with any journalist he senses is hostile or incompetent. Megyn Kelly, NBC's star presenter, looked forward to a gentle reaction after she had showered him with compliments in hosting one of the St Petersburg International Economic Forum sessions in June 2017. She had misjudged him. As soon as she put awkward questions in the TV interview, he snarled about her elementary ignorance.

Sometimes reporters go too far in the opposite direction. Overexcited young Russian television presenters in particular have shown a propensity for sycophancy. In 2015 an exchange with Maria Sittel that went as follows was broadcast on television:

> **Sittel:** Vladimir Vladimirovich, wouldn't you like to clone yourself or assemble an army of lookalikes?
> **Putin:** No.
> **Sittel:** . . . Ah, but our bureaucrats in Russia won't acknowledge anyone else but you.
> **Putin:** I've already answered. Let's move on.[25]

This was enough to make at least some of the audience squirm with embarrassment, and Putin showed he agreed by brushing aside Sittel's flattery. His brusqueness was a clever ploy. He rightly assumed it would serve to enhance his aura of power and dignity.

It was the same when a TASS news agency reporter, Andrei Vandenko, tried to wheedle him into agreeing to places to be named after him:

> **Vandenko:** It's not necessary to proclaim an autocracy. You only have to point your finger and tomorrow it would be possible to bring back the Gulag. Or, for example, [we could have] a cult of the individual so that there would be a Vladimir Putin Street. A group has recently been formed [in the Urals] to rename a road as Sacco and Vanzetti Street, after the Italian anarchists who were sent to the electric chair in America. They

surely have nothing to do with the Urals. But Vladimir Vladimirovich [Putin] does. He didn't deliver the country over to ruin in the 1990s but instead brought a halt to the excesses of the bandits and the oligarchs, and so on and so forth . . . What do you reckon about all this?

Putin: I think that people are doing this for good and decent motives.

Vandenko: And such impulses will exist in every Russian town if you were merely to twitch an eyebrow.

Putin: I understand. But it's too early [for leaders] to raise up monuments to each other. And I have myself in mind. What's necessary is to keep on working and it will be for future generations to evaluate the contribution of each individual to Russia's development.[26]

Then, emotion took over:

It's completely obvious that Russia, for me, is my entire life. Not for a single second can I imagine myself without Russia. I've previously talked about how they traced my family's genealogy in the archives. They came from a village not far from Moscow, 120 kilometres away, where my forebears lived from the seventeenth century and throughout all those centuries went to one and the same church. And I feel my own connection with the Russian soil and the Russian people, and I could never live anywhere else but Russia – but Russia of course can get by without people like me. Russia has a lot of people.[27]

It was a display of modesty and patriotism intended to enhance his status among fellow Russians.

He stresses how hard he works for them. On one rare occasion he even claimed that this involved a life of some personal danger. He spoke about the risk of assassination in the course of a series of interviews with American film director Oliver Stone between 2015 and 2017, which were broadcast on both American and Russian television. Stone, a veteran critic of United States administrations, uses the roundabout methods of interrogation of the 1970s American fictional TV detective Columbo, which was how he inveigled Putin into discussing the incidence of violent attacks on politicians. Stone remarked that Cuban leader Fidel Castro – another of Stone's famous interviewees – claimed to have avoided death fifty times through keeping direct personal control of his bodyguard. Putin surprisingly failed to repudiate Stone's comment that five attempts had reportedly been made on his life. When Stone commented that plots against the lives of politicians have tended to succeed if the killer was infiltrated into the guard unit, Putin looked straight at the camera and stated that he had confidence in the men who looked after his safety and that he was not minded to interfere as Castro had done.[28]

Whether or not there really were five attempts to kill Putin, at least one incident is well attested. It took place in February 2012 when Adam Osmaev, a Chechen 'volunteer', led a plot to bomb the motorcade in which Putin was travelling. Osmaev escaped across the border into Ukraine. Russian security forces tracked him down and made two unsuccessful efforts to shoot him in Kyiv, which is the only reason his activity became public knowledge.[29] Russia's authorities continue to avoid discussion of assassination attempts, presumably in order to discourage ideas about mounting any more. In saying this to Stone, perhaps Putin was dropping his guard for a moment – or maybe he felt like piquing the world's curiosity. Or he could have made the story up in the interest of accentuating his importance.

Such was his grip on the country's politics that in December 2017, when announcing his intention to stand in the following year's presidential election, he did not allow his name to go forward as candidate for United Russia; nor did he attend the ceremony to register his candidacy. This nonchalance continued. As when he stood for the presidency in 2000, 2004 and 2012, he behaved as if it was beneath his dignity to engage in political campaigning. In his few campaign speeches he spoke in airy terms about what he would do to secure Russia's future. He made no reference to opposing contenders by name. He wished to convey the message that he had a country to run and no time to waste on politicking. He totally ignored the barbs that Russian critics threw at him. If anything, moreover, he liked being denounced by foreigners because it served to increase his popularity among Russians. He gave no sign of considering a change of direction in policies. What he had done, he implied, was a source of pride for him. He performed as father to the nation and left it to others to deliver the plaudits. Throughout the 'campaign' he knew that he would win the election in a landslide.

Those of his opponents who might have constituted a competitive threat had already been eliminated from the contest. In particular, crowd orator and media activist Alexei Navalny was barred from standing after a conviction for embezzlement. When challenged about this at a press conference, Putin snapped back:

> I assure you that the authorities have been afraid of nobody and are still afraid of nobody. But the authorities must not be like a bearded peasant idly picking out bits of cabbage from his beard and watching the state turn into some muddy pool where oligarchs go fishing and pull out the goldfish for themselves, as was the case in the 1990s or as still happens in Ukraine today. Do we want Russia to become a copy of present-day Ukraine? No, we do not want that and we won't allow it![30]

This is a president who takes pride in his efforts to clean up the polluted pool of Russian politics. He dismisses Navalny as belonging to the type of politician who can only cause chaos.

Ever since emerging on the highest public stage, Putin has been convenienced by the removal of real and potential rivals. Back in 2000, when he offered himself for election for the first time, leading opponents such as Moscow mayor Yuri Luzhkov and ex-prime minister Yevgeni Primakov were undone by televised revelations about their financial trickery and poor health respectively. The charismatic liberal Boris Nemtsov was assassinated in 2015. Mikhail Kasyanov, who left the premiership in 2004, had his reputation shredded in 2016 when a video was shown on television showing him having extramarital sex with a female political assistant.

The approved list of candidates in 2018 included socialite and TV chat-show presenter Xenia Sobchak, who was the daughter of Putin's late mentor in St Petersburg, Anatoli Sobchak. Standing for the Civic Initiative Party, she censured Putin's policies, reserving her barbs for criticism of the Syrian military intervention. She knew that she could never beat Putin on election day. As she neatly put it, the casino always wins against the gambler.[31] The Communist Party fielded a fresh candidate, Pavel Grudinin, who was general director of the Lenin State Farm. Its usual nominee, Zyuganov, had lost so many elections that he decided that it was time for someone else to stand. Grudinin performed impressively enough for the worried authorities to leak information that he had a Swiss bank account and that his son owned property in Latvia. Against all of them stood Vladimir Zhirinovski, who represented the Liberal Democratic Party in the presidential polls for a record seventh time. While Sobchak was young and glamorous and Grudinin a suave communicator, Zhirinovski was his antique buffoonish self. TV coverage inordinately favoured Putin. In the candidates' televised debates, from which Putin absented himself, the squabbling exchanges enhanced no one's reputation.[32]

The disqualified Navalny called on his supporters to boycott the ballot booths, but this appeal had little impact. The authorities took no chances and organized a campaign about the duty of all citizens to cast their votes. Although Putin was coasting to a certain triumph, he wanted to avoid a low turnout and the accompanying adverse publicity.

On 3 March 2018, in a nod to electoral normality, he appeared at a Saturday rally in the Luzhniki stadium. When, six years earlier, he had stood forth as a presidential candidate, he had recited stanzas from Mikhail Lermontov's poem on the battle of Borodino in 1812 between the Russians and Napoleon's Grande Armée before asking the crowd whether they loved Russia. He now repeated this patriotic ploy but with a different question: 'We are a team, right?' A tidal surge of cries – 'Da! Da! Da!' – came back at him. Though some in his audience had been paid to attend and others were put under pressure by their employers, there was no denying the collective response on the day. Putin started a chant of 'Rossiya! Rossiya!' and then led the way in singing the national anthem with the vast crowd. Nobody failed to notice his delight.[33]

Speaking to the Federal Assembly on 1 March 2018, Putin continued to focus on raising national morale. There were few policy initiatives except for a promise to introduce a minimum wage to lift millions out of poverty. He painted a vista of continual general improvement in health care, housing and transport during his years in power. He skipped over the need to deepen the rule of law, to widen political freedom or to lessen social inequality. Putin dedicated the longest part of his speech to the armed forces – he seldom misses a chance to emphasize his position as commander-in-chief. When announcing Russia's new nuclear missiles that could hit any global target, he invited viewers to suggest names for them. When he waved to signal the order for screens to display the pictures of each new weapon, he was a picture of glee.[34] His performance combined menace with a distinct lack of taste but he had – rightly – calculated that army drumbeats would appeal to the parts of Russia's electorate that he was courting.

Putin is presented by the TV channels and the loyal sections of press and radio as embodying the best features of life in Russia. His instinct as a ruler is to be simultaneously distant from and near to his people, both exceptional and ordinary. He is the public face of the Kremlin's ruling elite. In the eyes of most foreigners, he embodies all things Russian. He presides with aplomb over political life. He delivers speeches, grants interviews and takes part in television phone-ins. He invites Russian reporters to follow him around. He is the focus of the great official ceremonies. As head of state he confers awards for outstanding services and achievements. He is a walking, talking national cult.

2. IMAGINING RUSSIA: A VISION FOR THE RUSSIANS

Putin's administration devotes much time and energy to the task of purveying a national vision that placates and excites the Russian people. They understand the priority of persuading Russians that they are committed to bringing them a better life. But they do not go about this task in a selfless fashion. The administration and its most influential supporters set out a vision that had wide appeal while also bolstering their own interests. Political self-service lies at the foundations of their efforts.

At a time when most citizens still struggle with the changes that flooded over them after the end of the communist order, Putin – like Yeltsin before him – is keen to assure fellow citizens that a radiant future awaits them. He speaks in elevated tones, 'Russia is a country that has chosen democracy for itself by the will of its own people.'[1] He tells the Russians that they no longer have anything to apologize for. Their country, he tells them, is a model of decency and peaceful intent. He warns that malign foreign elements have conspired to produce a picture of Russia and its rulers that is the opposite of reality. He depicts Russophobia as a confection built on prejudice and lies that contributes to the dangerous volatility of global order. Though his message is targeted at fellow Russians, it is also one that he wants to resonate around the world.

Putin claims to be different from all those Soviet communist general secretaries who imposed their ideology on the Russian people:

> It is up to all of us, to our entire society – both the so-called neo-Slavophiles and the neo-Westernizers, both the statists and the so-called liberals – to work together to formulate common developmental goals. We need to break the habit of only listening to like-minded people and unhesitatingly rejecting any other point

of view with malice and hatred. You can't toss around the country's future like a football, booting it into the air and plunging us into rabid nihilism, consumerism, criticism of absolutely everything, or gloomy pessimism.[2]

But this chariness about telling the Russian people what to think lacks credibility. In fact, Putin and his public relations advisers are ardent advocates of their values and want fellow Russians to adhere to them.

After returning to the presidency in 2012, Putin increasingly advocated the virtues of 'tradition', railing against the 'permissive' cultures of Europe and the United States. For Putin, societies come to grief when their rulers abandon ancient customs:

Today the norms of ethics and morality are being revised in many countries, wiping away national traditions and the distinctiveness of nationality and culture. Society is now being asked to provide not only a healthy recognition of everyone's right to freedom of conscience, political views and a private life but also an obligatory recognition of the equal value – strange as it may seem – of good and evil, concepts which clash. Such a destruction of traditional values 'from above' not only produces negative consequences for societies but is also fundamentally anti-democratic.[3]

He identified the Middle East as a blatant example of the harm that such ideas caused:

In recent years we have seen how attempts to impose a supposedly progressive model of development on other countries have in practice resulted in regression, barbarity and immense bloodshed. This is what happened in a whole number of countries in the Middle East and North Africa. This is the dramatic situation that presented itself in Syria.[4]

Rulers are said to imperil their people when they abandon tradition. He depicts Russia as the one powerful country to hold a torch for custom and decency:

We know that the world has more and more people who agree with our position of support for traditional values which for millennia have constituted the spiritual, moral foundations of civilization for every people: values of the traditional family and of genuine human life including the religious life, not only material but also spiritual life – which are the values of humanism and the diversity of the world.

This, of course, is a conservative position. But, in the words of Nikolai Berdyaev, the meaning of conservatism is not that it prevents movement forwards and upwards but rather that it prevents movement backwards and downwards, into chaotic darkness and a return to a primitive state.[5]

Russians, in Putin's estimation, have held to their ancestral values regardless of who governed them: 'Even with all the well-known costs, the level of morality both in tsarist Russia and in Soviet times acted as a very meaningful scale and criterion for people's reputation at place of work, in society and in daily life.'[6]

Putin denies wishing to change the Russian people. For him, their worthiness is axiomatic, and he ridicules the utopianism of Lenin and his successors in trying to transform the outlook of ordinary Russian men and women through violent revolution. Putin's attitude can be seen as an echo of the kind of mindset that prevailed in many European countries undergoing 'nation-building' in the nineteenth century when poets, musicians and folklorists joined efforts with political activists to unify their own people by eulogizing their national virtues. But those were countries that, to a greater or lesser extent, would turn into nation states. 'Russia' before 1917 was not a nation state but an empire whose government had to take account of the experiences and sentiments of many subject nations. This obligation remained after October 1917, when the communists, with their internationalist creed, seized power. The Kremlin leadership is making up for lost time. Whereas Yeltsin was half-hearted in playing the nationalist card, Putin regularly throws it down on the table and misses no chance to praise the instincts and attainments of Russia's men and women.

His courting of their approval also carries a note of ethnic nationalism. This is dog-whistle politics: he wants Russians to know that he will always protect their interests. But he cannot say this openly, for fear of giving unnecessary offence to the other national and religious groups – and he certainly rejects ideas of 'racial purity'.[7] He has repeatedly called on citizens to treat each other with tolerance regardless of ethnicity, faith or political doctrine. His requirements are stability and harmony:

> This means that liberals have to learn to talk with representatives of left-wing views and, conversely, that nationalists must remember

that Russia from its very inception was formed specifically as a multi-ethnic and multi-confessional country. Nationalists must remember that by calling our multi-ethnic character into question and by starting to exploit the matter of Russian, Tatar, Caucasian, Siberian or any other nationalism and separatism, we are starting down the road of destroying our genetic code. Essentially, we are beginning to destroy ourselves.[8]

Such a formulation camouflages the fact that Putin and his administration, while displaying a pronounced favour for ethnic Russians, do not refer to themselves as nationalists. They walk the walk without talking the talk.

Yet Putin still stresses Russia's shared European heritage when it suits him. He has the chameleon's capacity to change colour according to each shift in circumstance in which he finds himself. When talking to the European Commission president José Manuel Barroso about the Islamist threat to the continent, he asked, 'How many are we?' By 'we' he meant the Christians, seeking to draw a line between Christianity and other ways of life and governance such as in China or the Islamic world.[9] Putin said all this when he still hoped that the rest of Europe would sympathize with his armed reduction of Chechnya. More recently he has put an emphasis on Russia as the friend of the world's Muslims and on the choice of China as a strategic partner. He adjusts his ideas according to current political convenience, but always gives salience to the theme of Russian national distinctness.

One of Putin's most fervent advocates, the chairman of the Duma's Education Committee, Vyacheslav Nikonov supports the same school of thought when expounding his concept of Eternal Russia. Nikonov has called himself a 'hereditary politician' by right of being the grandson of the notorious Soviet Foreign Affairs Minister Vyacheslav Molotov, but his views would have horrified his grandfather, who barbarically crushed Russian traditions in the course of Stalinist agricultural collectivization and Stalin's Great Terror. Nikonov, however, is going with the flow of contemporary Russia. Like others in the ruling elite, he assures Russians that their past is glorious and that they have nothing to learn from abroad.[10] He celebrates Russian national peculiarities. He claims that Russians have always been unusually lacking in materialistic attitudes and that they are exceptional exponents of tolerance and peacefulness. Noting that Russia has usually been ruled by an unelected leading group, he sees this as a source of pride. He derides political oppositionists who denounce the existence of a bloody dictatorial regime while knowing full well that 'they can go off to their dachas after saying that, and not to [prison in] Siberia'.[11]

Nikonov differs from the extreme conservative Alexander Dugin, who brags of having developed a conceptual scheme that constitutes an advance beyond the main currents of modern social theory – liberalism, Marxism and fascism. His Fourth Political Theory is, in fact, a dangerous rag bag. Russian civilization, he trumpets, has consistently had militarism at its foundations, 'War is our mother.' He expresses certainty that more wars are Russia's fate, and is gleeful about the prospect.[12] He predicts that liberalism is about to fade away as did Marxism and fascism. He ridicules Putin for calling Russia a European country. His own starting point is that Russia constitutes a self-contained civilization, situated geographically between Europe and Asia. Dugin sponsors what he calls neo-Eurasianism. When Westerners demand respect for the principles of tolerance, they supposedly are engaged in an attempt to subvert age-old Russian values. Only by following its own special path, according to Dugin, can Russia avoid ruin – and he repeatedly predicts ruin for the West itself.[13]

Dugin's crazed effusions overlap at key points with the thrust of arguments by Putin's supporters such as Nikonov and Lavrov. All of them, including Putin, are nationalists of a kind that denounces rampant globalization, liberalism and progressive social thinking. But Dugin has expressed sympathy with the philosophy espoused in the United States by Steve Bannon, a founder of Breitbart News and Donald Trump's 'chief strategist' until August 2017, and Bannon's team helped to publish an English translation of Dugin's main work, *The Fourth Political Theory*.[14] Dugin held a chair in the Department of the Sociology of International Relations at Moscow State University until 2014 when his extremist opinions led to public protests. He had been giving vent to his angry disappointment that Putin held back from annexing eastern Ukraine. But despite his travails, he continues to receive air time on Moscow TV channels. This is less surprising than it may appear. It is one of Putin's techniques to allow his associates and sympathizers to rant and rave, leaving him appearing to be a sober statesman. Though Dugin has become an opponent and fills the air with nationalism, he constitutes no serious political threat to the Kremlin leadership.

There is a consensus among nationalists in supporting traditional social values. They were united in anger in February 2012 when the

female rock group Pussy Riot staged one of their guerrilla performances in the Cathedral of Christ the Saviour. Pussy Riot sang out
against both Putin and the Orthodox Church hierarchy. They were
arrested and convicted of 'hooliganism motivated by religious hatred'.
The episode increased the disgust with which Putin was regarded
around the world. The sentence of two years' imprisonment was a
wholly excessive punishment to which the performers reacted with
stoicism and dignity. But the Western media had not taken account of
the fact that Pussy Riot had deliberately chosen a prominent place of
Christian worship in which to commit an act of blasphemy involving
foul language. If they had done the same thing in Canterbury Cathedral, the public sympathies would have been on the side of the clerical
custodians of the building. Russian leaders were banking on the fact
that most Russians would agree that political protests were out of place
on sanctified ground.

The Kremlin leadership also stresses the importance of traditional
families. Putin keeps silent about the collapse of his own marriage. He
talks in general terms about the sort of society he envisages but clearly
wants couples to have more children than has recently been the norm.
In his second presidential term he declared:

> Yet another general national problem is the low birth rate. The
> country has more and more families that have only one child. We
> have to raise the prestige of motherhood and fatherhood and
> create conditions that are favourable to the bearing and bringing
> up of children.[15]

This remark flowed from anxiety that Russia's shrinking population
will create difficulties for welfare and economic output in future generations. Putin also has it in mind – like Kremlin rulers over several
decades – that whereas the ethnic Russians had a birth rate in serious
decline, the non-Russians in the Russian Federation – the Muslims in
particular – continued on average to have a large number of children.

As to how a family should live its life, Putin has said little beyond
open disapproval of parents who beat or slap their children. But he is
against active state interference in private matters. What happens at
home, should stay at home.[16] If he has opinions on the best relationship
between spouses, on feminism or on how to bring up one's offspring,
he has yet to share them with the public. The State Duma, however, was
less restrained in February 2017 when it passed a law to decriminalize
physical domestic abuse. Feminist groups complained in vain about

the licence this gives to archaic patriarchy. But then Putin is not a 'new man' in the contemporary Western style. When he and his then wife Lyudmila met the US National Security Advisor Condoleezza Rice he joked about her efforts to get fit: 'Yes, Lyudmila is learning ballet. She is dancing *Swan Lake*. Of course, if I tried to pick her up, I would be a dead swan.'[17] And once, when asked whether he ever gets down and moody, he retorted, 'I'm not a woman, so I don't have bad days.'[18] These were the words of an unreformed, unabashed Russian male. Among his associates, they evidently still pass as being normal and acceptable.

Putin's attitude to relations between men and women attracts little commentary from abroad. Not so his remarks on same-sex relations. He and his political friends have no patience with the advocates of homosexuality. In 2012 Railways Minister Vladimir Yakunin said that Western enemies of Russia had spread gay propaganda in order to bring down Russia's birth rate and make Russians vulnerable to easy manipulation.[19]

Yakunin saw homosexual activism as a national security question. Putin has never gone as far, but is plainly uncomfortable about the entire topic. Putin shook his head when Oliver Stone asked whether he would be comfortable about sharing a sports club communal shower with a man who was known to be gay. Grinning, he explained that he would not want to 'provoke' such an individual.[20] People of a traditionalist frame of mind, including those in Russia, may have seen nothing untoward in what he said – they may even have admired Putin's frankness, but it was a rare misjudgement if he was trying to gain the sympathy of a liberal Western audience. As were his attempts to justify his remarks by saying that he simply wants to prevent gay activists from proselytizing among the young and innocent, an offence under Russian law since 2013. He added that same-sex marriages conflict with the interests of society since they will not produce children.[21]

Foreign criticism was vehement, including from singer and gay-rights advocate Elton John. This had a comical upshot when John received a phone call from someone purporting to be Putin inviting him to Moscow. It was a prankster who made Elton John look silly as the newspapers picked over the banalities that he and 'Putin' had exchanged. The real Putin soon found himself being asked by reporters to explain his standpoint. Under pressure, he declined to specify whether he thought that gays were born or made, but he rejected any imputation of anti-gay discrimination, stressing that homosexual activity was not illegal under Russian law, in contrast with the situation in seventy other countries. He also pointed out that, by contrast, certain Islamic countries had laws that applied capital punishment in cases of homosexual activity. As president he opposed the Orthodox Church's appeal for the recriminalization of homosexuality and emphasized the constitutional separation of church and state.[22]

Putin wants people to appreciate his moderation, and the ruling group paint their Russia as the bringer of peace and decency and deplore what they see as scurrilous images of the country. If only other nations followed the Russian example, they suggest, there would be no wars. Putin has even complained about being misunderstood before an audience of invited foreign visitors:

Russia has no intention of attacking anyone. The whole thing is laughable . . . It is simply inconceivable, stupid and unrealistic. Europe alone has 300 million people, all being NATO members. Together with the USA this is probably a total population of 600 million. Russia currently has only 146 million. It is simply laughable to bring up the subject. No, people are anyway using all this in pursuit of their political aims.[23]

He has continued to insist that Russia's ambitions are both modest and benign, in the facing of increased global dangers:

If we don't create a coherent system of mutual obligations and agreements and if we don't build the mechanisms for resolving crisis situations, the signs of global anarchy will inevitably grow.[24]

He voiced these thoughts in front of a foreign audience only months after ripping up the Budapest Memorandum and annexing Crimea. If foreigners have suspicions about military ambitions, they should lay them aside. Even Russia's deadliest armaments should cause no alarm:

Brandishing nuclear weapons is the last thing to do. This is harmful rhetoric, and I do not welcome it. But we must proceed from reality and from the fact that nuclear weapons are a deterrent factor that ensures world peace and security worldwide. They cannot be considered a factor for any potential aggression, because it is impossible and would surely mean the end of our entire civilization.

But the absolutely clear thing is that nuclear weapons are a deterrent factor and many experts believe that if the world hasn't experienced great armed conflict in more than seventy years since the end of the Second World War, one of the reasons is the possession of nuclear weaponry by leading countries. It is still important that the non-proliferation framework for nuclear arms and their delivery vehicles should be observed and that all the nuclear powers should take a very responsible attitude towards their nuclear status. Russia will follow this line despite any statements that could be made in the heat of a polemic. But let me repeat that at the government level Russia will always treat its nuclear status very responsibly.[25]

This is the vision that Kremlin leaders offer for Russian life in the twenty-first century. It is intended both to soothe and to stimulate. The ingredients blend celebration and optimism with a menacing commitment to neutralize those whom the administration designates as the enemies of Russia at home and abroad. The Kremlin assures the Russians that its vision is the one best fitted for their country's needs and customs in an ever more turbulent world.

3. TSARS, COMMISSARS AND AFTER: THE NEW OFFICIAL PAST

Russians talk more often about food prices, welfare and salaries than about history. In this they are no different from most other peoples. But the twentieth century was a troubling period for generations of their families, and every Russian leader seeking public support has to supply an account of the past that enough citizens find plausible and appealing. They need to feel that the Putin team will end the era of traumas and enable them to benefit from the opportunities ahead.

Putin knows that tutoring the public imagination is not something he could do alone. Not least because what he learned about the history of the twentieth century during his time at Leningrad State University came only from compulsory courses in Marxism-Leninism. As a result, once he took office, he sought help from well-informed consultants, even including fierce critics of the Kremlin's policies such as Alexei Venediktov, editor-in-chief of the Ekho Moskvy radio station and a former history teacher. After communism was consigned to the dustbin, the ruling elite looked for lessons it could learn from the annals of tsarism. When the baffled Venediktov asked Putin why he would choose to talk to someone who opposes the official political line, Putin quipped that he was willing to discuss things in private with enemies but drew the line at traitors.[1]

Another surprising source of advice was the veteran crusading anti-communist and former political prisoner Alexander Solzhenitsyn. Putin frequently met with Solzhenitsyn, even awarding him one of the prestigious State Prizes not long before his death in 2007.[2]

Such encounters enable Putin himself to appear as a man of culture, a man with an inquiring, if not an altogether open, mind. They also allow him to parade his patriotic fervour, for example in 2013 when he mentioned that he agreed with Solzhenitsyn's call for an increase in the Russian population.[3] Putin predictably cribs many of his ideas from conversations and leaves it to his speech writers to find the best quotations from Russia's intellectuals for use in his oratory. But it is worth noting that he has a distinct preference for sources who are dead and unable to answer back.

Putin and other Kremlin leaders continually pillage history for help with the present. They are nimble marauders, plundering only those items that will serve current political purposes. But like the Vandals who sacked Rome in 455, they find their thinking affected and impregnated by what they discover in their loot.

Their favourite aphorisms are by distinguished Russian authors who affirm the values of leadership, patriotism and the collective will, preferably with a smattering of contempt for the West. As well as Solzhenitsyn, Putin likes to quote the Christian émigré philosophers Ivan Ilin and Nikolai Berdyaev.[4] While Solzhenitsyn helped revive Russian literature after decades of battering by Marxism-Leninism, Berdyaev, banned from publication by the Soviets, was a master of Russian philosophical prose. Ilin's philosophical writings constituted an act of aggression on the language, although his political articles are succinct and punchy, but Berdyaev, who in his long life moved from liberal Marxism to liberal individualism, is useful only in small snatches. Solzhenitsyn helpfully despised Western decadence and called for Russo-Ukrainian unity as well as a firm hand at the levers of Kremlin power. Only Ilin has all the features that Putin is after. Ilin was a lifelong nationalist enemy of Marxism and the USSR. As an émigré in Weimar Germany, he welcomed the rise of Nazism as the antidote to Soviet communism. If Russian leaders are going to applaud his patriotism, they have to observe silence about his enduring support for aspects of European fascism. But Ilin helpfully warned against Western schemes to break up 'Russia', and he saw Ukraine as part of the Russian patrimony. He wished for a strong leader at the head of a national dictatorship. It is easy to imagine why, under Putin, he has been endorsed as an intellectual authority. In 2005 Ilin's remains were repatriated from Germany and reinterred at Moscow's Donskoi Monastery in a solemn ceremony led by Patriarch Alexi II.[5]

Putin's treatment of Ilin reflects the interests and purposes of the ruling group.[6] Following the route pioneered by Yeltsin, he laments those periods when the Russian people – or its discontented elements – resorted to violence, which disastrously diverted the country's course of development. As both an ex-communist and anti-communist, Putin deprecates the entire idea of armed revolution. 'What we need now,' he believes, 'is evolution.[7] He argues that Russia has come nearest to fulfilling its potential when Russians have lived in peace under stable rule.

He has no animus against the Romanov dynasty that governed for over three hundred years. He applauds the tsars who made Russia into a great power and in April 2015 proclaimed, 'I would remind you [. . .] of the words of Alexander III, our emperor, who said that Russia has only two allies: its army and navy. And in his parting words to his son [the future Nicholas II] he then said that everyone is afraid of our vastness.'[8] In November 2016, when unveiling a statue of Alexander III outside Crimea's old Livadia Palace, Putin quoted tsarist Finance Minister Sergei Witte, who said that the emperor achieved peace at home and abroad 'not by making concessions but by righteous and unshakeable firmness'. The Crimean statue is the eighth of Alexander III erected while Putin has been in power. Putin also remarked that Tsar Alexander had fostered a spurt of industrial growth and was a kindly sponsor of the arts.[9] This cloaked the damage that Alexander III did by harshening the cultural censorship and reversing many of the social reforms of the 1860s. The frieze below the statue base shows the novelist Fëdor Dostoevski and the chemist Dmitri Mendeleev. Russian schoolchildren could have told Putin that Dostoevski and Mendeleev produced the bulk of their greatest work before Alexander III came to the throne in 1881.[10]

Another of Putin's heroes from the Romanov era is Pëtr Stolypin, who served as Nicholas II's prime minister from 1906 to 1911. When opening the Federal Assembly in October 2016, Putin remarked: 'More than a hundred years ago, addressing the State Duma deputies, Pëtr Arkadevich Stolypin said, "We all must unite and agree our efforts, our obligations and rights to support the historic supreme right of Russia: to be strong."'[11]

Stolypin was a reforming conservative whose ambition was to restore the status of a great power to Russia and immunize it against the threat of renewed internal insurgency. In December 2013 Putin told the Federal Assembly that local government agencies should emulate the achievements made in Russia before the First World War and paid tribute to the changes introduced by Stolypin to land ownership and to the structure of industry.[12] Stolypin is famous for trying to enable the emergence of a class of individual smallholders in the villages, but as events were to show, most peasants were hostile to his agrarian reform – and it is difficult to know what Stolypin did to change the empire's industrial structure.

But this is hardly the point. When talking about history, Putin and his speech writers have contemporary politics at the front of their minds. Public approval, not objective historical plausibility, is the goal.

It was in this spirit that Putin, in his annual presidential address to the Federal Assembly on 1 December 2016, heralded the centenary of the February and October Revolutions of 1917:

> This is our common history and we need to treat it with respect. This is something that the outstanding Russian and Soviet philosopher Alexei Losev wrote about. 'We know the thorny road our country has travelled,' he wrote. 'We know the long and exhausting years of struggle, want and sufferings, but for a son of the Motherland, this is all something of his own kin, something inalienable.'
>
> I am sure that the absolute majority of our people have precisely this attitude towards their Motherland, and we need history's lessons primarily for reconciliation and for strengthening the social, political and civil consensus that we have managed to achieve today.
>
> It is unacceptable to drag the splits, anger, grudges and bitterness of the past into our life today, and in pursuit of political and other interests to speculate on the tragedies that affected practically every family in Russia, no matter what side of the barricades our forebears were on. Let's remember that we are a united people, one single people, and we have only one Russia.[13]

For Putin, the downfall of the Romanov monarchy and the communist seizure of power a few months later were a double blow that led to tragedy at every level of society. In a speech earlier in 2016, Putin had deplored the gruesome murder of the Romanovs in a Yekaterinburg cellar in summer 1918:

> Everyone used to denounce the tsarist regime for its repressions. But what did the establishment of Soviet power begin with? Mass repressions. I'm not talking here about the whole scale of them but simply about the most blatant example: the annihilation and shooting of the tsarist family including the children. There could have been some ideological grounds for the liquidation, I suppose, of potential heirs. But why did they kill Dr Botkin? Why kill the servants – people generally of a proletarian background? What for? The reason was to cover up the crime.[14]

Though Putin exploits historical episodes for political purposes, he is genuinely interested in the fate of the Romanovs. On his state visit to London in June 2003, Foreign and Commonwealth Office officials witnessed his excitement when they presented him with a volume of declassified documents, including several which touched on this episode. Until then he had been a bored and uncommunicative visitor to the British capital.[15]

For Putin, it is vital that people should remember the many other horrors that followed the October Revolution:

> We never used to give this a second thought. All right, they were struggling against people who were fighting Soviet power with arms in their hands, but why kill the priests? In 1918 alone three thousand priests were shot and ten thousand in a ten-year period. In the Don region, people were drowned in their hundreds under the ice of the river. When you think about it, and when new information appears, you start to evaluate many things in a different way.[16]

Putin has had no good word to say about Lenin and takes notable exception to the constitution that he imposed in 1922:

> If you're a historian, you must know that Stalin at that time formulated the idea of the autonomization of the future Soviet Union. According to this idea, all the other subject parts of the future state had to enter the USSR on the basis of autonomy with entirely broad authority. Lenin criticized Stalin's position and said it was an untimely and wrong idea.

Putin's conclusion was damning:

> And so he, Lenin, campaigned for the state – the Soviet Union – to be formed on the basis of full equality with the right of secession from the Soviet Union . . . And this was the time bomb under the edifice of our statehood. Quite apart from the fact that they fixed borders and territories for ethnic groups within an essentially multinational state, the borders were also drawn up arbitrarily and nor were they generally decided on a rational basis. For instance, what was the pretext for handing over the Donbass to Ukraine? The idea was to increase the percentage of the proletariat there so as to have greater social support there. Sheer madness, wasn't it?[17]

In the Soviet period Lenin was feted as the man who 'gathered the lands' back together after the disintegration of empire in 1917. This

cuts no ice with Putin, who denounces Lenin's constitutional settlement as ill-considered, capricious and disastrous.

Under Putin, church and state have demanded respect for the
White commanders who fought the Red Army and its communist
leadership in the civil war that followed the October Revolution. The
remains of General Anton Denikin were brought back to Russia in
2005. Statues were erected to Admiral Alexander Kolchak in St Petersburg and Irkutsk. Films about the White cause were produced and
proved popular. Many commentators represented the Whites as valiant
fighters and patriots.[18]

The communist leadership has long since ceased to attract praise.
Lev Trotsky was both reviled and neglected in official Soviet accounts,
and though he is no longer overlooked by Russian scholars, he
continues to be treated severely. Joseph Stalin, as usual, provokes
controversy. No decent Russian condones the Great Terror of 1937–8,
but not a few public figures contend that his role in industrializing
Russia and defending it against the Third Reich was indispensable –
this is one of the Communist Party's remaining tenets of its old
Marxist-Leninist credo. History remains a ground of conflict and Putin
has trodden it carefully. About one essential matter, Stalin's mass
repressions in the late 1930s, he speaks bluntly:

> Stalinism is associated with the cult of the individual and mass
> violations of the law, with repression and camps. There is nothing
> like this in Russia today and, I hope, never will be again. Our
> society is simply different now and would never allow it. But this
> does not mean that we should not have order and discipline. It
> means that all citizens of the Russian Federation, regardless of
> their official position, must be equal before the law.[19]

At the same time, while Putin recognizes the horrors of Stalinism,
he firmly denies that it was the worst phenomenon of the twentieth
century. The Third Reich deserves greater condemnation:

> First of all, of course, it is impossible to put Nazism and Stalinism
> on the same plane because the Nazis directly, openly and publicly
> proclaimed one of their policy goals as the extermination of entire
> ethnic groups – Jews, Gypsies and Slavs. For all the ugly nature of
> the Stalin regime, for all the repressions and for all the deport-
> ations of entire peoples, the Stalin regime never set itself the goal
> of exterminating peoples, so the attempt to put the two [regimes]
> on the same footing is absolutely without foundation.[20]

This gave rise to speculation that Stalin might be about to receive posthumous rehabilitation, which was heightened in 2015 when a ten-ton statue of him seated alongside Winston Churchill and Franklin D. Roosevelt was installed outside the Livadia Palace in Yalta, where they had met in February 1945 to discuss the post-war political and territorial settlement in Europe. Sergei Naryshkin, the State Duma chairman at the time, unveiled the monument to the strains of the Russian national anthem. Zurab Tsereteli's sculpture had been rejected by the Ukrainian government ten years earlier, when Yalta had been governed from Kyiv. After the Crimean annexation, however, the Kremlin wanted to celebrate the Yalta Conference, although there were protests from the Crimean Tatars, whose ancestors Stalin had forcibly deported from the peninsula in May 1945.[21]

Despite these glimmerings of approval, Putin had no patience with Stalin's policies in eastern Europe in the late 1940s. The forcible exporting of communism, Putin insisted, was a terrible blunder:

> After the Second World War we tried to impose our own development model on many eastern European countries, and we did so by force. This has to be admitted. There is nothing good about this and we have to hearken to this today. Incidentally, this is more or less how the Americans are behaving now as they try to impose their model on practically the entire world, and this too will end in failure.[22]

Admitting that wrongs were done by Russia while insisting that the Americans are the current worst culprits is a very characteristic approach. Putin also knows that most Russians, aside from rabid neo-Stalinists, are unlikely to object to his conclusions.

He is always circumspect when speaking about Nicholas II. Reverence for the Romanovs is widespread in post-communist Russia, and when in 2017 a film was released about the affair between the future tsar and the ballerina Matilda Kshesinskaya, there was immediate protest about the erotic content. Few Russians are more devoted to Nicholas's memory than Duma deputy Natalya Poklonskaya, who served as Crimea's Prosecutor-General immediately after the Crimean annexation. She joined others in demanding an inquiry as to whether the film was anti-Russian and anti-religious. This led to a counter-reaction from another film director, Stanislav Govorukhin, who was also a Duma deputy as well as the former chair of its Culture Committee. Faced with this dispute, the Ministry of Culture took the safe road of equivocation. On 15 June 2017 the film's director, Alexei Uchitel, complained to Putin about how his film was being treated. Putin's response was that, though he respected Uchitel's career and his patriotism, Poklonskaya had the right to express her opinion. It is important to Putin that dialogue is at least seen to be encouraged and that he avoids becoming personally embroiled in divisive historical debate.[23]

His comments about Lenin might once have been jarring to the millions of Russians who were brought up to revere the USSR's founder. But times have changed and there is little risk of controversy so long as Putin avoids anything as drastic as removing Lenin's mummified corpse from the Red Square mausoleum.

In 2016 Putin showed his deftness at the opening of an exhibition at the Yeltsin Centre in Ekaterinburg. The curators had annoyed nationalists by failing to describe Lt General Andrei Vlasov as a traitor. Vlasov, captured by the Germans on the Eastern Front in 1942, persuaded himself that he could fight on the German side in pursuit of the liberation of Russia from the grip of Stalinism. Towards the end of the war, he revolted against the Germans. This did not save Vlasov from Stalin's vengeance and he was hanged in Moscow in August 1945. But what was Putin's opinion?

> There's nothing special in the fact that a discussion is opening up: this is a normal phenomenon. Some take a favourable stance, some hold more liberal views on the continuing events and on the prospects for development, some are of conservative, traditional views. We have always had our blood-and-soil patriots (*pochven-niki*) and our Westernizers. Some people regard themselves as blood-and-soil patriots. But at the present time when we are remembering the events of 1917, and when we are about to mark the centenary of the revolutionary events in 2017, we must advance towards reconciliation and rapprochement, and not towards rupture and the stirring up of passions.[24]

This measured response was designed to secure a calm, reasoned discussion of Russia's troubled past. He did not succeed, and the nation's history continues to be fought over. But Putin benefits from appearing to stand outside the fray.

Foreign attitudes to that history irritate Putin enormously. The endless fascination with Joseph Stalin in the Western media causes particular resentment. He notes that 'dictators' of other nations seldom attract the same attention. Oliver Cromwell's bloody career is over-looked and a statue of him stands outside the Houses of Parliament in Westminster. The body of Napoleon, who rampaged across Europe with his conquering armies, is venerated in Les Invalides in Paris. Yet Stalin is demonized. For Putin, there is no mystery about the reasons. The West's political establishment wants a stick with which to beat Russia and the Russians, and nothing is handier than the record of the long-dead Soviet dictator.[25]

When they are not waving a stick, they engage in a game of mockery that is equally aggressive. In 2018 the Ministry of Culture banned Armando Iannucci's black comedy *The Death of Stalin*. Culture Minister Vladimir Medinski did not dwell on the film's elementary mistakes about the names of people and institutions. Offence was taken at the scornful tone adopted for so baleful an episode, and perhaps behind everything was the belief that foreigners should keep their noses out. Medinski has turned himself into the administration's song-bird on historical subjects. A prolific author even after occupying ministerial office in 2012, he sought to wash the Russian and Soviet past clean from denigration. He defended Russians under tsarism against charges of indolence, drunkenness and thievery.[26] He did this so vigorously that several professional historians concluded that he did protest too much.[27] And his most successful book alleged that foreign authors had wrongly highlighted the rape of German women by Soviet soldiers in 1945.[28]

Putin has often suggested that the USSR was a complex phenom-enon. He has mixed emotions about the people's experience of communism in the decades after the October Revolution. There were benefits in the centrally planned economy, and he has praised the Soviet Union's advances in health care, education and the expansion of the military-industrial sector that enabled the victory over the Third Reich.[29] He shows respect to surviving veteran communists. He held conversations with Vladimir Kryuchkov, who led the August 1991 coup against Gorbachëv. In 2014 he awarded the Order of Honour to Kryuchkov's fellow plotter Marshal Dmitri Yazov. In February 2019 he commended the courage and professionalism of the Soviet armed forces in the USSR's war in Afghanistan.[30]

But he has never endorsed the communist political system or over-looked the weaknesses of its economic institutions. He is not nostalgic about communism but is bitter about the break-up of the USSR, which in April 2005 he described as 'the greatest geopolitical catastrophe of the [twentieth] century'. His remark is widely misunderstood. He did not at all regret the passing of Soviet communism but rather the consequences of its disappearance: the mass poverty of the 1990s, the rise of the so-called oligarchs and the dislocation of families separated by the new borders.[31] Even so, he was guilty at the very least of hyperbole; for he entirely ignored other events that might be thought to deserve a higher ranking as catastrophic. Among them, surely, would be the onset of the two world wars in 1914 and 1939, Hitler's rise to power in 1933 and the Chinese Revolution of 1949. Not to forget Russia's own October 1917 Revolution.

Putin's preoccupation with the Soviet Union's disintegration has a distinctive focus: he hates the fact that millions of citizens of Russian nationality found themselves cut off from Russia in the fourteen other newly independent foreign states – he once went as far as calling this a 'humanitarian tragedy', adding:

> I would like to repeat my argument that the Russian people became the biggest divided people in the world, and that is absolutely a tragedy. And this isn't to mention the socio-economic dimension when as a result of the collapse a social system fell apart and an economy crumbled – the previous one had been ineffective but when it fell apart, it led to the impoverishment of millions of people, and that's also a tragedy for real people and real families.[32]

In Putin's eyes, demographic separation and societal dissolution were twin features of the same outcome. This attitude was not something that he dreamed up after he came to power. He believes that although things were bad under communist rule they were much worse after the communists fell from power. He sees the 1990s as the national nadir, when an 'epidemic of collapse' took hold in the Russian Federation.[33] He been saying as much since the early 1990s, when he was a middle-ranking local politician whom nobody tipped to end up climbing to the peak of Russian power. It would seem to indicate that this is a heartfelt opinion.[34]

Russia's relations with Estonia, Latvia and Lithuania are another sensitive spot. These countries regained their independence with the disintegration of the USSR at the end of 1991. Though they had proclaimed their own freedom, the signing by Yeltsin of accords with the Ukrainian and Belarusian presidents in December was the decisive step. The three presidents simultaneously agreed to the formation of a

Commonwealth of Independent States that all fifteen of the USSR's constituent republics would be invited to join. This projected regional grouping would be looser than anything that Gorbachëv would have found acceptable, which is exactly what Yeltsin wanted. But although the Commonwealth of Independent States was duly formed in 1992, its collective purposes were persistently undermined by its members' wariness about Russia's wish to dominate them. Estonia, Latvia and Lithuania refused point-blank to join. Similar difficulties affected the Collective Security Treaty Organization, which Russia initiated in the same year to fulfil military and other security needs. The only countries that agreed to join at the outset were Armenia, Kazakhstan, Kyrgyzstan, Tajikistan and Uzbekistan, and all of them were wary of becoming vulnerable to Russian pressure.

Visiting Hamburg in February 1994, Estonia's President Lennart Meri made a speech denouncing the USSR's illegal annexation of the Baltic States in 1940 and again in 1944. Meri described how he and his family, along with tens of thousands of Estonians, were deported to Siberia. Putin, who at that time was an official in the St Petersburg mayor's office and was on a work trip to Germany, happened to be present in the audience. Despite being an obscure Russian official, he rose from his seat and theatrically stormed out of the hall.[35] For him, evidently, the Red Army's wartime operations and Stalin's geopolitical decisions should be venerated. He had no patience with Baltic leaders who denied that the USSR liberated them after expelling the Third Reich. He was deaf to Meri's point that Estonia became a captive nation under Soviet rule.

Sometimes, moreover, Putin finds it difficult to distinguish between the Soviet Union and the Russian Federation, as when he told the Federal Assembly in March 2018:

> After the collapse of the USSR, Russia, which in the Soviet period was called the Soviet Union – or Soviet Russia as it also known abroad – lost 23.8 per cent of its territory if we're talking of our national frontiers, 48.5 per cent of its population, 41 per cent of gross general product, 39.4 per cent of industrial potential (nearly half of our potential, I would underline), 44.6 per cent of its military potential in connection with the break-up of the USSR armed forces among the former Soviet republics.[36]

This was a truly slippery comment. Putin contends that it is only foreigners who confused the USSR with the Russian Federation. In fact, he does exactly the same thing himself. Russia suffered no loss of territory when the Soviet Union disintegrated. Not a square yard. The newly independent country emerged with its borders intact and in 2014 used armed force to widen those borders at Ukraine's expense.

Unlike many fellow Russians, Putin has not blamed Gorbachëv or Yeltsin for the way that the country emerged from communism. He prefers to emphasize the difficulties that they faced. In a *Time* magazine interview in 2007, the American reporter remarked that Putin was not a 'president-revolutionary' like Yeltsin. Far from being irritated, Putin agreed:

> I nevertheless consider that he and Gorbachëv anyway did what I surely could not have done. They took the step towards the destruction of a system that the Russian people could no longer endure. I'm not convinced I would have been able to decide on such a step. Gorbachëv took the first step and Yeltsin completed the transition, which I believe was an historic and very important one for Russia and the Russian people. They – and above all Yeltsin, of course – gave Russia its freedom: this is an absolutely unconditional historic achievement of the Yeltsin era.[37]

Putin too has a mission to change everything for the better, but he wants to do it in his own fashion and bring the cycle of Russia's traumas to an end once and for all.

4. YEARS OF HURT: PICTURING NATIONAL HUMILIATION

The Russian people were bruised by the shifts in international relations after 1991. The USSR had been one of the two superpowers. The earth shook wherever the Soviet leadership walked, and the Kremlin was widely respected. Where respect was lacking, fear filled the space. Yeltsin sought to integrate the new Russia in the world order as a normal, cooperative, constructive great power. This was always going to be an uphill struggle when the Russian Federation had a ruined economy, a shattered administration and a demoralized army. Independence was accompanied by fallen pride.

Resentment can grow like a tumour in countries that endure such a reversal of fortune. Millions of Germans in the 1920s burned with anger at how their governing elites had allegedly stabbed Germany and its armed forces in the back and brought about defeat in the First World War. And after the Second World War, when financial exigency compelled the British to give up their imperial territories, umbrage was taken about the loss of global power and prestige. When governments fail to compensate for such emotional disturbance, awful consequences can flow. This was among the reasons for Adolf Hitler's rise to the German chancellorship in 1933; and though the United Kingdom did not crumple into political extremism, the after-effects of the end of empire continue to be registered. The USSR lost the Cold War. Though Gorbachëv and Yeltsin asserted that there was no victor, they failed to dispel the national feeling of humiliation among countless Russians. It was a sentiment that Putin and his contemporaries shared at the turn of the millennium. In Britain and France this state of mind is called a post-imperial syndrome. What Russia has been experiencing is not just a post-imperial but also a post-superpower syndrome. Nobody should underestimate the intensity of these feelings.

Like Putin, many Russians regret the post-1991 reality that, when they cross from the outermost Russian provinces, they find themselves in foreign countries such as Ukraine or Kazakhstan. For centuries they have been told to delight in the achievements of the Russian Empire and the Soviet Union. Nowadays they have a special term for the states that were formed when the USSR fell apart: 'the near abroad' – a sign that they do not think of Ukraine or even Uzbekistan and Estonia as being quite as foreign as Greece and France. When Britain, France and other European powers relinquished their empires, their colonies were overseas. The Russians had an empire made up of neighbouring countries, a fact of geography that makes it difficult for them to forget about the imperial loss. In the 1990s the Russian Federation went through a prolonged economic recession. Most Russians, except for the tiny minority that benefited from the privatizations, were floored by poverty and were indignant that Moscow, the capital of a motherland that had been one of the world's superpowers, became a waiter at the tables of global diplomacy.

Putin was not the first Russian president to object to American global policy. Yeltsin had complained to President Bill Clinton about the difficulty he had in calming Russian public opinion after America's military intervention in the former Yugoslavia. Debate in Russia grew red hot in early 1996 after Clinton ordered the bombing of Bosnian Serb forces. This happened at a time when Yeltsin was engaged in his campaign for re-election to the Russian presidency. When he appealed for Western leaders to appreciate his problems he was ignored, and NATO war planes continued to attack targets in Bosnia.[1] It was a lesson for Russia about its diminished status in world politics. Russia might have inherited the USSR's seat on the United Nations Security Council, but the reality was that America and its allies placed no curbs on their behaviour. When Yeltsin offered Moscow as the site for Yugoslav peace talks, he was brusquely disregarded. Little consideration was shown about Yeltsin's need to enhance his international prestige and shore up his standing in Russia.[2]

Yeltsin was also caught inside the force field of Western financial pressures. The International Monetary Fund closely supervised what was done with the money that was lent to Moscow. The Russian media reported on Yeltsin's inability to reject external demands. Inside the ruling elite there was mounting disquiet about the country's humbled condition. The wars in former Yugoslavia were a television spectacle. The Russian people watched and were horrified. Yeltsin himself grew agitated and explained his concerns privately to Bill Clinton. The Partnership for Peace arrangements between Russia and NATO, inaugurated in 1994, had failed to deter the Americans in March 1999 from welcoming Poland, Hungary and the Czech Republic into NATO membership. This happened shortly before Yeltsin stepped down from the presidency, and it was Putin who had to deal with the consequences.

At first Putin handled the situation calmly and sought to improve Russia's dealings with America. But when the relationship foundered, he would look back in anger:

> First, in the mid-1990s there were the [air] strikes against Belgrade. Essentially, this was aggression . . . This was barbaric, simply barbaric. All the more so because it was done by ignoring the UN Charter and nobody sanctioned it. When confronted with this, people immediately started saying that things were outdated and change of some kind was needed.

Between March and June 1999, America and its allies bombed Serbia into submission without approval from the United Nations Security Council. The military campaign was in reaction to the brutal Serbian persecution of the Muslims of Kosovo, an enclave in Serbia's south. Serbia's defeat resulted in President Milošević's fall from power in Belgrade, and for the Russian authorities the episode marked a disruption of such order as existed in Europe after the Cold War.

And for Putin, Serbia was not the sum total of American misbehaviour:

> Things got worse with the events in Iraq. Did the UN sanction the operations in Iraq? No! And beforehand there were operations in Afghanistan in 2001. Yes, we all know the tragedy of September 11 2001, but, even so, under existing international law, an approach should have been made to the UN Security Council and an appropriate resolution should have been received from the start. No.
>
> Then came Iraq. Then the resolution was passed on Libya. No. Everyone's an expert here and knows and has read the resolution on Libya. What is written in it? A no-fly zone there. But what kind of no-fly zone was it if they began to conduct airborne missile strikes against [Libyan] territory? They crudely distorted and violated the UN Charter.
>
> And then came Syria.[3]

He also defends Yeltsin against Western accusations of drunken incompetence:

As soon as he raised his voice in defence of Yugoslavia, he immediately turned into an alcoholic and a generally disreputable
person in the eyes of Westerners. Everybody suddenly discovered
that Boris Nikolaevich liked a drink. But was it really any secret
beforehand? No, and it did not hinder his contacts with the
outside world. As soon as it became a matter of defending Russian
interests in the Balkans and Yeltsin talked openly about it, he
turned almost into the West's enemy.[4]

This, according to Putin, was why the Americans 'set the dogs' on
Yeltsin, and he had no intention of becoming their next quarry.[5]

He is convinced that Russia's international difficulties can be traced
to the United States' handling of the collapse of the USSR:

The need was to carry out a rational reconstruction and adapt the
system of international relations to the new realities. However, the
United States in my opinion, having declared itself the winner
of the 'Cold War', self-confidently saw no need for this. And instead
of establishing a new balance of forces, which is the necessary condition for order and stability, they took steps that produced a sharp
and deep imbalance.

The 'Cold War' ended. But it did not culminate in the conclusion
of a 'peace' with clear and transparent agreements on the observance
of existing rules and standards or on the creation of new ones. This
created the impression that the so-called victors in the 'Cold War'
had decided to pressurize the situation and bring the entire world
under their control to suit their interests. And if the existing system
of international relations and of international law and the system of
checks and balances got in the way of achieving this objective, this
system was declared worthless, outdated and in need of immediate
removal.[6]

He omitted to explain how anyone could have stopped Milošević's
butchery of ethnic Albanians in Kosovo except by force.

Hating to appear weak, Putin only rarely complains publicly about
how the world handles Russia. But just occasionally he lets rip, as in an
interview with Germany's *Bild* magazine on 5 January 2016, when he
was asked about European security. In response, Putin denounced the
eastward expansion of NATO beyond Germany. He referred to confidential transcripts of Gorbachëv's Moscow conversations with German
politicians in 1990. Putin said that there had been no proper agreement
on how to end the Cold War and the East–West division in Europe and

that there should be no increase in the number of NATO members. Discarding the fact that Gorbachëv never got this in writing from President George H. W. Bush or Chancellor Helmut Kohl, Putin implied that Russia had been cheated by subsequent Western decisions.[7]

Turning to earlier history, however, Putin has acknowledged that Stalin made a gross error in forcing through the communization of eastern Europe in the late 1940s and rejects the idea that the Reds came to the Baltic States as conquerors as much as liberators. Entirely missing from the Kremlin's account is any acknowledgement that America and its allies did not push Estonia, Latvia and Lithuania into applying for NATO membership. The three countries shared an unenviable history. In 1944 the USSR brutally annexed all of them, and memories of 'Russian' imperialism were vivid for their politicians and peoples, who sought security guarantees against Russia's potential expansionism. The same attitude prevailed in Poland and other countries of central and east-central Europe, which the Soviet Union had held in political thrall after the Second World War. Throughout the 1990s worries persisted about Russia's potential to become a threat to all its neighbours. The fact that Russia, a nuclear power, was seen as being led by a dangerously volatile drunk added to the anxiety. This may have been harsh on Yeltsin, who rarely added to global tensions, but it was understandable that many countries in the region took a jaundiced view of Russian professions of good faith – and such countries continually called upon the Americans to let them join NATO.[8]

Clinton hesitated to comply for fear of offending or undermining Yeltsin. The Germans were equally reluctant.[9] But a process began in 1999 that would come to a climax in 2004 under George W. Bush. Though both Clinton and Bush believed that the American interest lay in rendering the eastern half of the continent secure for American power and American business, it was governments from Tallinn to Sofia that supplied the decisive impetus for NATO's enlargement. They had to surmount German vacillation before agreement could be reached.

Putin tried to seem unbothered by the rush to join NATO. This was his stance even after 2004, when his hopes for a partnership with the United States had ended. Behind the scenes, though, Russian diplomats had always taken a different line. When Slovakia pressed to enter the alliance, its diplomats received a frosty reception in Moscow. Sergei Prikhodko, who had acquired influence in the making of foreign policy under Yeltsin and Putin, rejected Slovakian assurances that no hostility towards Russia was implied. Scorning Bratislava's protestations, Prikhodko warned that Slovakia would be regarded as an 'enemy country' if it insisted on joining the American-led military alliance.[10] The Russians also used rough language in their talks with Estonia, Latvia and Lithuania, countries they regarded as belonging to a special zone of interest because they had been part of the USSR. The fact that Putin hardly ever makes public mention of them is not a sign that he does not bother about them. Rather, the reverse: his reticence is a manifestation of acute disquiet.[11]

But Russian leaders in the early 2000s saw that unless they declared war, they could not halt the process. Slovakia joined NATO along with the so-called Baltic States and others in 2004. Albania and Croatia were admitted in 2009, Montenegro in 2017. If Putin did any growling, he kept it to confidential meetings of fellow Russians. But the hurt felt in the Kremlin was real, and the blame was placed upon the Americans.

Putin is also exercised by what he perceives to be the active help given by America to anti-Soviet and anti-Russian international terrorist organizations since the 1980s:

> In their time they sponsored Islamist extremist movements to fight the Soviet Union which were battle-hardened in Afghanistan. From them grew both the 'Taliban' and 'Al-Qaeda'. The West, if it didn't support, did at least close its eyes [about this] and I would say it really did give support in the form of information and political and financial assistance for international terrorists to penetrate Russia – we have not forgotten this – and the countries of the Central Asian region. Only after horrific terrorist attacks were committed on the soil of the United States itself did there grow an understanding of the common threat of terrorism.[12]

In 2001, nevertheless, the Russians had agreed to the Americans using Karshi-Khanabad in southern Uzbekistan as a base from which the United States air force could send bombers to attack the Taliban in Afghanistan. The Russian leadership saw this as an altruistic gesture that Washington repaid with ingratitude.

But, again, this is a squint-eyed way of looking at the situation. Uzbekistan was supposedly an independent state, free from Russian interference. But Russia expected the whole of ex-Soviet central Asia to be in its privileged zone of influence and the Russian sanction for the Khanabad facilities suited the interests of Russia's own security. The

Taliban remained a menace long after the Soviet military withdrawal from Afghanistan in 1989. In the years that followed the security service reported that Chechen jihadists were being trained in Afghan camps as the Taliban lent support from afar to armed jihad in the Russian Federation. When the Americans indicated their ambition to wipe out the training camps, Moscow was delighted. Putin, his special services and his Defence Ministry were content for someone else to eliminate terrorists who might be intending to return to Chechnya.[13]

Nevertheless, the Kremlin also claims that Washington is scheming to break up Russia. As early as 2004 Putin implied that the Americans were conniving in the growth of jihadism on Russian territory:

> Some people want to tear a fat, tasty piece of the pie from us. Others are helping them. They help them because they think that Russia, as one of the world's great nuclear powers, still represents a threat to them. This, for them, is why the threat needs to be removed.
>
> And, of course, terrorism is only an instrument to attain these objectives.[14]

Little noticed at the time, Putin's remark was a sign of a serious willingness to challenge America.

Security Council Secretary Nikolai Patrushev, the ex-KGB officer who ran the FSB from 1999 to 2008, declares the Americans have held on to the Cold War military doctrine that built confrontation into their planning.[15] He argues that America's rulers want to seize the incomparable natural resources of Russia's outlying regions. Though Putin has not gone this far in public, he does contend, drawing on his experience as FSB director in 1998–9, that the West provided 'complete support of separatism and radicalism in the North Caucasus'.[16] The international dimensions of terrorism are a murky subject. Andrei Kovalëv, who served on Russia's Security Council until 2001, has recalled that the Russian security agencies pushed for schemes to fund Islamist jihadi groups in Western countries.[17] Since that time, efforts have been made to establish a cooperative framework for combating terrorism in Russia and the West. But Putin still bears a grudge about Western activity and sets his face against further external interference.

The Russian ruling group habitually thinks and talks in terms of enemies, threats and confrontations. Nor is this the monopoly of intelligence professionals.[18] Sergei Glazev, one of Putin's leading economic advisers since July 2012, enjoys making anti-American tirades. It was the United States, he contends, that was behind the 1991 accords to break up the USSR. With typical hyperbole, he charges that the Americans are conducting a 'hybrid world war' against Russia by means of their control of the global banking system. He maintains that Washington exploits its mastery in information technology to exert what he calls cognitive control over the Russian economy. He adds that America is developing Ukraine as a base for a projected armed onslaught on Russia and pulling the European Union along with it.[19] Glazev even declares, as if no corroboration is required, that it was the United States which dragged Russia into the wars in Ukraine and Syria.[20]

Looking at the past, Glazev opines that Alexander I and Nicholas II made the cardinal error of partnering the United Kingdom when it plainly made no sense for Russians to go to war against Napoleon's France or Kaiser Wilhelm II's Germany.[21] His analysis ignored the elementary fact that in both 1812 and 1914 Russia confronted enemies who were bent on conquering Russian territory. But Glazev remains untethered to requirements of historical plausibility. His goal was to steer the policies of the Russian Federation far away from cooperation with the treacherous United States, which in his eyes has taken the place of perfidious Albion. Suspicion pervades the Kremlin, and America remains the object of their undiluted mistrust. It is a preoccupation that has turned into an obsession.

American leaders have, however, given momentum to that mindset. Putin bridled at President George W. Bush's decision in 2002 to construct an anti-ballistic missile shield against Iran with facilities in Poland, Romania and Turkey. By 2007 Putin had had enough and announced that the Intermediate Nuclear Forces Treaty of 1988 no longer suited Russia's national interests. This, the first great agreement on arms reduction leading to the end of the Cold War, was a landmark in the history of European international security. Putin did not follow this up by altering official policy, but the fact that he had signalled a readiness to do so is significant – and the relationship between Russia and America worsened.

Putin also objected to what he saw as American instigation of the upheavals in Georgia, Ukraine and Kyrgyzstan between 2003 and 2005. He denied that it was Georgians, Ukrainians and Kyrgyz themselves who undertook the so-called 'colour revolutions' in their countries. For Putin, American secret services and American finance lay behind them. It was wounding enough that America's zone of influence now covered almost the entire former Eastern Bloc in Europe, but when the Americans seemed to be interfering in Russia's 'near abroad', the pain was even sharper. Criticisms of the Russian invasion of Georgia in 2008 by Bush and Secretary of State Condoleezza Rice strengthened opinion in the Russian leadership that America was seeking to poke its nose into other people's affairs.[22]

On first entering the White House in January 2009, President Barack Obama spoke of a wish to move away from the diplomatic disputes with Russia. His Secretary of State, Hillary Clinton, had her doubts about Obama's intended 'reset' in policy. So too did Secretary of Defense Robert Gates and Moscow Ambassador John Beyrle. But Clinton gave Obama's policy a try. In March 2009 she met Russian Foreign Affairs Minister Sergei Lavrov in Geneva and presented him with a red button mounted on a yellow plastic box marked 'reset'. It was a light-hearted occasion. Unfortunately Clinton was reliant on advisers whose Russian was less than idiomatic. The translation used for 'reset' was *peregruzka*, which means 'overload'. Lavrov spotted the mistake but nonetheless accepted the gift with a gracious chuckle, which encouraged some hope for an improvement in relations.

In London later that month, Obama had his first meeting with President Medvedev, who had taken office in May 2008, and found him open to his ideas on the reset.[23] A former lawyer from the St Petersburg city administration, Medvedev had formed a bond with Putin in the 1990s. A proficient administrator, he became Putin's Chief of Staff in 2003 and first deputy prime minister in 2005. He was known for his emphasis on the need for the rule of law and for the protection of the rights of small and medium-sized start-up companies. Bland and well mannered, he appeared cut from a different cloth from most of Putin's other cronies. Obama saw a glimmer of hope for a further improvement in relations with Russia and in July 2009 paid a visit to Moscow, where he made little reference to American anxieties about the extent of human rights abuses in Russia. He also announced the suspension of stage four of Bush's cherished anti-ballistic missile shield in east-central Europe. Though Obama did not scrap the entire programme, even Putin, who was prime minister at the time, conceded that the Americans had made a 'correct and brave' decision. When Putin tried to lecture Obama about the chaos of the 2003 Iraq war, the American president threw him back on his heels by pointing out that he had opposed it from start to finish.[24]

By March 2010 the way was clear to make the next reduction in Russian and American nuclear weapons arsenals, leading to the 2011 New Strategic Arms Reduction Treaty. The Russians seemed to have some confidence in Obama's good intentions. In May 2010 Russia and China agreed to the American proposals for United Nations sanctions against Iran in reaction to Tehran's intensified nuclear development programme. Five years later, after agreement was reached with Iran to forestall the militarization of Tehran's scientific research, the Americans lifted those sanctions, but declined to call off their shield programme. Putin took this badly, implying that the United States was being hostile towards the Russian Federation. He and other Kremlin politicians were also irritated that American administrations reserved their worst rebukes for Russia while garlanding with praise the nearby leaders of Azerbaijan and Kazakhstan.[25] Everyone knew that Baku and Astana were not havens for the rule of law. What is more, Washington let off Beijing with cursory reproaches for its human rights abuses while censuring Moscow. Putin saw only hypocrisy in America's talk of ideals. In reality, he believed, the Americans were picking on Russia out of self-interest: their purpose was to remove their powerful challenger in global affairs while dressing it up as a matter of principle.

Putin stands firm by his vision of the national interest. In 2016 he snapped at German interviewers who asked whether Russia had made any errors in foreign policy in the previous quarter of a century: 'Yes, it's made mistakes. We failed to make our national interests clear, and we should have done this from the start. And if we'd done that, perhaps we would have had a more balanced world.' When the interviewers inquired further whether his country had failed to articulate its interests, he replied, 'Absolutely.' Pressed by a German scholar in the same way in 2017, he replied: 'The most important mistake on our side in relations with the West was that we trusted you too much.'[26]

Do the Russian authorities genuinely believe all that they say about the malign intentions of Western powers? When Security Council Secretary Patrushev calls up the spectre of American ambitions to shatter the Russian Federation, is he speaking from conviction? When Putin maintains that America has been fomenting the jihadi insurgency in the North Caucasus, is this based on credible reports? He frequently accuses the Americans of stoking up trouble, recently claiming that he remonstrated with President George W. Bush about the covert support that the American administration gave to active jihadis. According to Putin, he personally handed over a list of names of CIA intelligence agents who were operating on missions to help armed terrorist groups in the Russian Federation. He has playfully added that the records of the Bush–Putin conversations must exist in files held in Washington and that, at any rate, 'George' would be able to remember. Putin recorded that the CIA's response was to say that it had every right to have contacts with 'the Opposition' and would continue to do so.[27]

If we take Patrushev and Putin at face value, the Kremlin has become a depository for imagined slights and threats. Yet people who have private conversations with Russian politicians and generals find that they concede that NATO offers no direct military threat to Russia – and the proof of their sense of security in the mid-2000s was that they had moved the bulk of their armed forces from their western to their southern frontiers.[28] The Kremlin leaders used to know the difference between their own rhetoric and geopolitical reality. But rhetoric, when it is repeated year after year, can turn into a credo that distorts analysis and produces serious misjudgements. It is not that the leaders are wrong to think that nations tend to pursue their own interests at the expense of the outside world. Nor are they mistaken in their belief that Russia has been regarded with deep suspicion in many countries. But in assuming the worst of America and preferring confrontation to negotiation, the Putin administration has taken this to a self-harming extreme.

5. LONG LIVE RUSSIA! ACHIEVEMENTS AND PROSPECTS

Putin knows that his plans for Russia will remain ineffectual unless he can inspire the nation. When he first came to power, he was quick to realize that the Russian people longed to feel better about themselves; it was his job to assist in this process.

As in Soviet days, the Kremlin identified sport as an instrument of its purposes and Putin personally helped Russia's bids to become a host country for global competitions. With his lifelong passion for judo and his personal workout regime, he was well qualified to head the Russian campaign to host the Winter Olympics in January 2014 and the FIFA World Cup in summer 2018. In both, he was triumphant. Funds were released for Russians to give an impressive account of themselves in the projected events. Training facilities were renovated, and there was excited speculation about what the Russian skiers and skaters might achieve at the Sochi Winter Olympics. Putin revealed that 214 billion rubles were spent on the preparations – 100 billion of which came from the state budget with the balance from private investors.[1] A new railway was tunnelled through the mountain that separated the city from southern Russia. New motorways were built. The city's old sanitary system, which spewed its sewage into the Black Sea, was upgraded. Sochi would present a dazzling achievement to the visiting world.[2]

Putin attended the opening ceremony, and used the opportunity to share his vision of the Russian past, present and future. Perhaps he would have liked to be one of the torch-bearers at the moment when the Olympic flame reached the city, but he had had to welcome the International Olympic Committee dignitaries. The torch had, however, been carried by both Minister of Defence Sergei Shoigu and Foreign Affairs Minister Sergei Lavrov, a keen footballer who said he wanted to get his diplomats to lose 'their double and triple chins'. Whatever happened, official Russia was going to be prominent throughout.[3]

Stage designers, directors and choreographers had received an assignment to outdo the displays at previous Olympics. Whereas the organizers of the London 2012 summer games drew attention to the achievements of the British National Health Service, the Sochi planners celebrated what the Russian people had done to defeat the Third Reich. Every year since 1945, on 9 May, Russians had held a parade on Red Square to commemorate their forebears who drove the Wehrmacht back to Berlin and crushed Nazism. The original scheme for the Sochi opening ceremony was to place on each seat an envelope with the photograph, name and date of birth of a Soviet citizen who had perished in the Great Patriotic War. It had also been planned to hold a minute's silence in the stadium, but when the IOC got wind of this, it intervened to stop the Russians from so blatant an attempt to politicize a sporting occasion.[4]

Nonetheless, there was jubilation at the opening ceremony on 7 February 2014. Above the stadium, in the gathering darkness, were hoisted five gigantic artificial snowflakes which miraculously turned into the rings of the Olympics logo. Everything went well until one of the snowflakes failed to alter shape. This did nothing to spoil the festive atmosphere because the chortling spectators responded with applause.

Everything else followed without a hitch. A ballet based on Tolstoy's *War and Peace* was performed, focusing on early nineteenth-century aristocratic life – no merchants, soldiers or peasants were included. Not even a tsar. The Russian Empire's history was sanitized and the tensions that tore it apart in 1917 smoothly glossed over. The next scene, using the same tranquillizing technique, dealt with the October Revolution. No reference was made to Lenin or Trotsky. There was a vague impression of basic changes in society, but there was no allusion to what the communist seizure of power was about. Even Stalin's violent policies for economic transformation at the end of the 1920s received anodyne treatment. But there were gasps of surprise when the enormous model of a bright red locomotive appeared in the sky above the arena while a dance ensemble on the ground imitated train wheels in relentless motion. No allusion was made to the cost in famine and blood of Soviet industrialization. No hint was given of the Great Terror of 1937–8. It was as if Stalin's purges and labour camps had never happened.

The obliqueness continued in the portrayal of the Second World War – perhaps the organizers were deferring to the International Olympic Committee and its ban on overt politicization. Of the gruelling battles against the Wehrmacht, there was no suggestion. Instead the performers, men and women, acted out a tableau in static poses of intense suffering. Simple and understated, this was the ceremony's most poignant scene.

The post-war decades were brigaded into a single period. Whereas tsarism had been illustrated in blue and the revolutionary years in red, everything after 1945 was a blaze of white (which meant that all three colours of the national flag had been highlighted by the end of the evening). Carefree boys and girls wore neckerchiefs of the Pioneer organization and frolicked to bubble-gum pop music. A limousine of Soviet manufacture was driven round the set with its occupants leaning out of the windows and waving to all sides of the stadium. No hint appeared of the material privations in the late 1940s or of the political and social repression that outlasted Stalin's death in 1953. The implicit message was that ordinary Russians had a gay old time once the war was over. Food, fun and prosperity were presented as the common experience of citizens of the USSR. Love – rather than Revolution or Cold War – was the motif that underpinned the whole montage and the word itself was shone up into the night air in enormous lettering. Communism was blanked from view and the final scene came to its boisterous, tuneful end as in a Broadway musical (or, indeed, a Stalinist musical of the late 1930s).

The evening as a whole told a story of Eternal Russia, the Russia whose continuities outweighed any temporary rupture. There was no allusion to the efforts needed to bring the communist era to a close and lay the foundations of a market economy. Smooth, gradual change was suggested as the key to happiness and progress. Though Putin was only an onlooker, he had signed off on a production in which every dance and melody expressed Russian dignity and Russian joy.

This was the prelude to a Games where Russia's competitors won a sackful of medals. The victories were merrily reported by the country's TV channels. Earlier there had been criticism in sections of Russia's press about the awarding of construction contracts worth billions of dollars to Putin's friends and associates. Abroad, there had been forecasts that foreign activists would carry out public protests against recent anti-gay-rights legislation, but these did not materialize. The games passed off peacefully. The Russian security forces had been put on the alert to prevent terrorist outrages – the Kremlin was nervous not just about the terrorism that had recently shaken other countries but also about the fact that Sochi is close to the Caucasus mountain range, where groups of Islamist terrorists continued to operate. Official precautions proved effective and the Olympics took place without serious incident either in the athletes' residential quarters or on the ice rinks and ski slopes.

The biggest commotion at the games had nothing to do with sexual policy or bombs but with the refereeing of an ice hockey match between Russia and the United States. The tournament was still at the group stage on 15 February 2014, and Putin and prime minister Dmitri Medvedev had come to watch one of their favourite sports in hope of a Russian victory. The match came close to causing a diplomatic incident. With the score tied at 2–2, play went into extra time and the Russians hit the back of the American net to break the stalemate. But the referee disallowed the goal because the posts had been incorrectly positioned. The watching Russians might possibly not have minded so much if the referee had not been an American – an extraordinary mistake on the part of the international authorities. As the partisan crowd booed with gusto, TV commentators asked how an American referee had received charge of a contest involving the United States. When the Americans won the penalty shoot-out, uproar broke out in the stadium.[5]

The next day Putin expressed regret that the goalpost problem had not been noticed earlier and left it at that. He must have realized that he would ruin his purposes at Sochi if dispute supplanted enjoyment, and he chose to ignore Obama's tactlessly hearty note of congratulation to the American hockey squad.[6] By the end of the Olympics, the Russian competitors had carried off thirteen gold medals, eleven silvers and nine bronzes. The Moscow media boasted that this put the country at the top of the rankings and well ahead of its nearest competitors, Norway, Canada and the United States. Less was said about the way that the Russian Olympic Committee had helped to achieve this result by securing the naturalization of Korean-born speed-skater Ahn Hyun-Soo and American-born snowboarder Vic Wild – between them they won five golds and one bronze. But no rule was broken in recruiting them and the Russian Olympic Committee was behaving no differently from several other national committees.

Victorious Russian competitors were granted a reception at the Kremlin, where they were given magnificent cars and large cheques. Millions of rubles were reserved for those who had brought honour to Russia. Defence Minister Shoigu presented Ahn Hyun-Soo with a medal 'for strengthening the fighting commonwealth'. Somehow the skater's athletic prowess was seen to exemplify the militancy that the authorities wished to promote in every corner of the country. The vehicles were from the top of the German Audi range – a concession to the idea of foreign superiority that was out of joint with the leadership's patriotic preoccupation.[7]

Opposition politicians, abetted by newspapers such as *Novaya gazeta*, exposed the waste and fraud that accompanied the Sochi games contracts.[8] They were disappointed because most Russians remained pleased with the image of their country that the games had spread round the world. But at the end of the year, a scandal erupted about systematic doping practices throughout Russian elite sport. Regulations had been flouted in preparation for the Sochi Olympics. The political establishment had put such pressure on the organizers to produce an all-conquering team that they had introduced performance-enhancing drugs for their athletes. The Russian Ministry of Sport at first denied the allegations, but after the World Anti-Doping Agency (WADA) activated its investigations, the evidence became compelling and laid bare the scope of Russian official connivance. WADA employees recounted that the FSB had threatened them during work at Russia's drug-testing laboratories. As more abuses came to light, the Russian whistle-blower, Grigori Rodchenkov, director of Russia's main anti-doping lab, fled the country and went into permanent hiding in the United States. The quest for sporting triumph ended in turmoil and, in 2016, Russia's entire squad was suspended from the Rio de Janeiro Summer Olympics. Russians could compete only as individuals and after securing personal drug-free accreditation from independent authorities.

Putin was furious. This public shaming of Russian athletes was yet another operation in the West's propaganda war. But the facts of the case were ultimately undeniable, and the Russian authorities agreed to remove from office those individuals whom WADA implicated in doping activity. Putin declared there to be no place for performance-enhancing drugs in sport, but he still managed to put this in his own defiant fashion:

> At the moment we are facing a relapse into political interference in sport. Yes, the forms of such interference have changed but the essence remains the same: to turn sport into a tool of geopolitical pressure and use it to shape a negative image of countries and peoples. The Olympic movement, which plays a colossal role in unifying humanity, yet again could be on the brink of a split.[9]

Russia's self-respect would be salvaged by an athletics competition in Moscow at the same time as the Rio Olympics. Even individuals who had been banned for doping offences were allowed to take part. Putin again attended to present the prizes. But it was not until September 2018 that WADA lifted its ban on Russian participation in the Olympic movement, and even then the decision to reinstate Russia incurred much international criticism. The mud still stuck.

Formula One motor racing, however, caused Putin no problem, and a grand prix was held at the new Sochi Autodrome in October 2014. As with the Winter Olympics earlier in the year, no expense was spared to put on a great Russian show for the visitors from abroad, another feather in Putin's cap. Britain's Lewis Hamilton won the race in a Mercedes, after which Putin appeared on television chatting with the drivers in the changing room and congratulating Hamilton at the prize-giving. The event was a triumph for Russia even though no Russian driver won a podium place. It was a hundred years since Russia had hosted an international grand prix, at a St Petersburg track. Global motor sport was returning to Russia, with all the pizzazz of super-expensive cars, global brand advertising, leggy models and international celebrities. And Formula One's organizers compliantly avoided drawing anyone's attention to events a few miles away in recently annexed Crimea.

FIFA's decision to hold the summer 2018 Football World Cup competition in Russia was also a political victory for the Putin administration. The government supplied lavish funds to renovate the Luzhniki stadium in Moscow, where the final would be held. New stadiums were designated for construction in cities as far apart as Kaliningrad on the western Baltic and Yekaterinburg in the Urals. As host nation, Russia – which saw itself as an old 'soccer power', automatically qualified for the group stage. Despite standing at seventieth in the global rankings, hope grew that the Russian team would show its prowess on the pitch. Ministers in Moscow were eager to bring credit to the country by being seen to look after the visiting teams and their supporters. TV shows prepared public opinion in Russia for a summer of sporting excitement.

The tournament yielded many surprises, including the progress of the home team beyond the group stage into the quarter finals. Their muscular and unhistrionic playing style appealed not only to Russian fans but also to television viewers around the world. The stadium cities gave the foreign supporters a friendly reception and in Moscow a gigantic screen was erected on Red Square for the benefit of both Russians and visitors from abroad who lacked match tickets. And, unlike 2014, Putin did not subsequently invade a foreign country.

But it was not just great sporting events that revived national pride. In 2008 Russia won the Eurovision Song Contest, held that year in Belgrade. Full-voiced and emotional, Dima Bilan performed 'Believe' with panache and his victory was the climax of several previous contributions – along with Sweden, Russia has had more top-five finishes in the twenty-first century than any other country. The annual event is popular with the public, and Russian television refrains from using the tone of mild ridicule in its presentation that has become conventional on live television in Britain and Scandinavia. In 2012 the Russian broadcasting authorities chose a group that had all Europe talking since every member was a grandmother. Hailing from the village of Buranovo in the Udmurtian republic, they dressed as the ordinary rural women that they were. They had formed a breezy ensemble whose song 'Party for Everybody' was designed to raise funds to repair the local church. The Buranovo Grannies won the hearts of millions, despite being pipped for victory by the Swedish entry, and showed European viewers that Russian society was more diverse and attractive than most of them had assumed.

Putin and the leadership also celebrate science and the arts. On Russia Day in June 2014, he awarded State Prizes to a number of worthy citizens for careers that had enhanced national well-being, among them Mikhail Piotrovski, Hermitage Museum director in St Petersburg, Gennadi Krasnikov for his company's semiconductor technology, the writer Valentin Rasputin for his stories that kept alive the flame of Russian peasant traditions, and Viktor Zakharchenko, director of the Kuban Cossack Choir. The leading ethnographer Valeri Tishkov, whom Kremlin rulers from Gorbachëv onwards have consulted about the country's complex ethnic relations, was also recognized.

It is rare for State Prizes to go to Russian politicians. Putin is wary of praising any of them unless they are safely dead, and even then he is sparing with eulogies. In 2014, however, he made an exception for Yevgeni Primakov, who at various times had served under Yeltsin as head of the foreign intelligence service, Foreign Affairs Minister and prime minister. Primakov had made his peace with Putin despite the fact that Putin's presidential campaign team had used dirty tricks to jostle him into withdrawing from the 2000 election. He was in declining health, and Putin wanted to honour him while there was still time. In 2016, two years after Primakov's death Putin paid tribute to the part he had played in shaping Russian foreign policy.[10] It was Primakov's concept of multipolarity – the idea that the world was essentially multipolar, not unipolar – that Yeltsin had referred to in a meeting with China's President Jiang Zemin in April 1997. Yeltsin and Jiang had subsequently agreed to work towards 'multipolarization'.[11]

Putin had himself consulted Primakov before meeting Henry Kissinger in 2009. Primakov explained that while a multipolar world was already a reality, the difficulty was that many US leaders thought and acted as if it was a unipolar one.[12] At the same time Henry Kissinger and Zbigniew Brzezinski were urging the American political establishment to abandon the triumphalism that had underpinned the assumptions of some policy-makers in Washington since the 1990s. Both Brzezinski and Kissinger argued that the other great powers would insist on reserving the right to protect perceived interests in the countries on their borders.[13] Putin celebrated Primakov as an original Russian thinker and inaugurated the annual Primakov Readings, which are intended to foster the kind of discussion of international affairs that he and Primakov endorsed.[14]

Patriotic pleasure in Russian achievements and Russia's potential brought the two politicians together. In discussing the notion of a multipolar world, Putin stresses the right of all countries to freedom from American control. But there is a sleight of hand in the way that he handles these ideas. He fails to mention that the multipolarity notion implies that the small number of great powers in the world dominate the multitude of weaker adjacent states. Putin is implicitly philosophizing about Russia's right to dominate. While accepting that Russia lacks the capacity to compete with the United States as a global superpower, Putin wants acceptance of Russia's right to a dominant regional influence. He focuses on the fact that many of the countries that claim to be free are not free at all. As allies of one great power or another, they find themselves treated as 'vassals'. Alliances, he maintains, are a fig leaf covering the subordination of the several to the single mighty power. Russia has broken away from any such subservience and is one of the few states round the world that is genuinely sovereign and independent.[15]

When Putin puts on a swagger, he wants to encourage Russians to believe that the days of national resurgence have begun. He increasingly insists that Russia's interests and preferences should be considered in global deliberations. Russia has a permanent seat in the United

Nations Security Council and will use its veto powers whenever
America seeks decisions at variance with the Kremlin's orientation.

He repeatedly declares that no other country's citizens are as free
as they are in Russia. To foreign criticism of government interference
in the media, he simply notes the vast number of TV stations and asks
whether it would be possible for the authorities to control the content
of their programmes.[16] Putin deals with reports of political repression
by declining to discuss them. In his view, conditions in Russia ought to
be the object of universal envy. When noting the troubles unleashed
worldwide by Muslim jihadi terrorists, he maintains, overlooking the
many periods of armed conflict, that Russia has cohabited peacefully
with Islam for centuries. The vast majority of Russian Muslims are
neither immigrants nor the offspring of immigrants but belong to
long-established communities. He boasts that the country's Muslims
know no other motherland than Russia.[17] Although there is a grain of
truth in this suggestion, it ignores the fact that Russia's Muslim citizens
have memories of official persecution of their religion. But in his
mission to convince everyone that Russia deserves plaudits, not disparagement, this does not bother President Putin.

Faced with criticism, Putin is generally quick to defy global, or at
least Western, opinion. Film director Oliver Stone counselled him that
if he wanted foreigners to believe in the then forthcoming 2018 elections, he should permit the activity of international monitors. This was
the nearest that Stone got to criticizing systematic political fraud and
Putin's part in it. Putin was unimpressed. It was not for the Russians, he
snapped, to justify themselves before the world's gaze and he had no
intention of submitting his country to the indignity of such inspection.[18]

Turning to Russian progress, he talks of a reduction of the national
debt from a high of 92 per cent of gross domestic product to under 13
per cent in 2017. He contrasts Russia with the United States, where the
debt is 100 per cent.[19] He recalls that when as prime minister in 1999
he restarted the Chechen war, Russia was still in economic difficulties
and he had to discuss ways to relieve the financial pressures with the
International Monetary Fund, which would only postpone the Russian
loan repayments if he agreed to halt the military operation. For Putin,
this was a step too far. He was pacifying Chechnya by armed force, and
no foreign agency was going to hold him to ransom.[20] The surge in
hydrocarbon prices that started at the very end of the twentieth century
enabled Russia to pay off its huge foreign obligations as well as those of
the other ex-Soviet republics, including even the $16 million that

Ukraine owed. Agreeable relations were later resumed between Russia and the International Monetary Fund, and Putin expressed pleasure in the Fund's activities in several Russian regions. But the breakdown of political trust between Russia and the Western powers that followed led to the withdrawal of the Fund's assistance. Putin regretted the turnabout but denied that it crippled Russian prospects.[21]

He and his fellow rulers also show off about the gigantic projects that they have undertaken. The national rail network, essential to hold this vast country together, has undergone substantial modernization. One recent achievement is the new Sapsan high-speed line built in collaboration with the Siemens company between Moscow and St Petersburg. It now takes less than four hours to travel the four hundred miles, and a further link has been added to the Volga city of Nizhni Novgorod. The government has allocated funds to raise at least five Russian universities into the world's top hundred in the global ratings. There is fierce competition for official backing for the so-called 5-100 Project. In 2012 Putin announced the Kremlin's determination to see this through to fulfilment, and already the leading academic institutions in Moscow and the provinces have recovered from the sorry condition that characterized them in the 1990s. Huge hotels have sprung up in all the big cities. In Skolkovo, a town to the south-east of Moscow, sumptuous research facilities have been established to foster Russia's advance into the new age of information technology.

TV channels join in the refrain that the country is achieving feats of global wonder. Every daily schedule tells the Russian people that they are lucky to be alive today and that even greater accomplishments lie ahead. They themselves will be the engine of continuing national success and should be proud of themselves.

CADRES

6. BEHIND THE FACADE: PUTIN AS LEADER

The face that the Kremlin shows to Russia and the world wears a mask. The Putin cult is a case in point. Putin's denials that he was ever personally ambitious are unconvincing at best, and if he genuinely hesitated about accepting the premiership and acting presidency from Yeltsin, as he likes to maintain, this is unlikely to have been because of worries about his family's security.[1] But it is entirely credible that he would have thought hard about Yeltsin's enthusiasm for sacking his prime ministers, although he perhaps overdoes the trauma he experienced on first arriving in the capital: 'When I moved to Moscow from St Petersburg, I was shocked and astounded how many crooks there were gathered here, and their behaviour was so astonishing for me that I couldn't get accustomed to it for a long time.'[2] The idea that St Petersburg was entirely without corruption is laughable. Putin was not a political innocent. Yeltsin promoted him because he showed the toughness and loyalty that Yeltsin needed and he coped tenaciously with conditions in Moscow.

Yeltsin's chaotic mode of rule as his health deteriorated and his alcoholism took a grip was a source of disdain among the ruling elite. There had been an increasing trend for Yeltsin to appoint ex-KGB officials to high office to reduce the disorder around and below him – few of his advisers were averse to his taking a chance on Putin.[3] But the self-aggrandizement of leading businessmen – the 'oligarchs' – who profiteered from the country's natural resources was another matter. Some of these entrepreneurs had pushed their way into posts of political authority and proceeded to exploit their elevation, causing widespread resentment. Among them was the flamboyant billionaire Boris Berezovski, who had served as the Security Council deputy secretary and regularly boasted of the influence he wielded over Yeltsin, deaf to the rancour that this provoked.

The president's position grew ever more perilous. Two politicians, ex-prime minister Yevgeni Primakov and Moscow mayor Yuri Luzhkov, allegedly advised him to step down from office. The alternative, they allegedly warned, would be a worsening situation in the country that could end with him suffering the same fate as Romania's Nicolae Ceauşescu, who was summarily executed in 1989.[4] The account has never been verified, but when Primakov was prime minister – from September 1998 to May 1999 – he certainly upset Yeltsin with a series of independent moves. Among them was Primakov's overture to parties in the Duma, including the communists, for an accord to halt the ongoing pressure to impeach Yeltsin for 'treason'. Yeltsin was the butt of multiple charges. He was blamed for shattering the Soviet Union in 1991, using lethal force to disperse the Russian parliament in 1993 and failing to defend the national interest against NATO. Primakov called for a respite from endless polemics and for compromise on economic policy. Yeltsin suspected that Primakov had his own designs on the presidency.[5] Tensions mounted to the point that Yeltsin sacked him in favour of first deputy prime minister and Internal Affairs Minister Sergei Stepashin, but in August 1999, when Stepashin purportedly refused to guarantee that there would be no judicial proceedings against the Yeltsin family after he retired, Yeltsin replaced him with the FSB's Putin.

Yet the appointment was a surprise, and not only in Russia. Putin was an unknown quantity for the average Russian, but then so were several of his predecessors. What also took many people aback was the fact that someone from the FSB was being appointed to the second highest office in the land. But Putin's elevation was in keeping with how Yeltsin operated. Yevgeni Primakov became prime minister some years after spending half a decade as director of the Foreign Intelligence Service; Sergei Stepashin, who maintained friendly links with the KGB in the Gorbachëv period,[6] took the premiership after heading the Federal Counter-Intelligence Service and then the Ministry of Internal Affairs.

One important fact that has escaped attention is that the FSB was being courted by those who wanted to succeed Yeltsin. Moscow mayor Yuri Luzhkov and St Petersburg Governor Vladimir Yakovlev, two of the leaders of the new All-Russia-Fatherland Party, placed articles in the agency's in-house magazine *Security Service* (*Sluzhba bezopasnosti*).[7] The country needed to be run in a more orderly fashion and a consensus was forming about how this should be done. Stepashin, when he was Minister of Internal Affairs, had written to Primakov, then prime minister, to rant about the thievery that was bringing Russia to the brink of 'catastrophe'.[8] All of them talked about the need for a renewal of honesty in public affairs. Whether they were sincere in this is doubtful, but they certainly aimed to shore up the foundations of central institutions and stamp on the current disorders. Stepashin and Primakov were not alone. All-Russia-Fatherland was formed by a merger of the two main 'patriotic' parties. Its aim was to challenge the liberals as well as the communists and the political far right at the December 1999 Duma election. It was a party that drew on support from regional leaders with a guiding belief that liberalism, insofar as it had been tried in Russia, had served to enable massive economic fraud. It also alleged that communism had proved its total bankruptcy as a method of rule.

FSB Director Putin shared this outlook. Unlike Primakov, though, he had tactical finesse and avoided upsetting Yeltsin. He also charmed Berezovski and other business moguls who might obstruct his advance, and Berezovski began to talk of him as a protégé: he did not appreciate that Putin was never going to do as he was told.

Yeltsin had his reasons for looking after the FSB leadership. Having come to power as an enemy of the Soviet KGB, he began to see that the remodelled security services could help him to strengthen his political authority. As his own popularity fell away, Yeltsin's democratic commitment took second place to his efforts to cling on to power. He also found the security services a useful counterweight to the tycoons pushing for policies in their personal interest. By schooling and tradition, moreover, FSB personnel think of themselves as indispensable to the country's well-being. Before the late 1980s they had played a subordinate role to the Soviet Communist Party in the USSR, but from 1991 they felt they had been left alone to save the Russian Federation from itself. Even many of those who resigned from security agencies for careers in the private sector kept in contact with them. Some helped to establish private guarding companies offering protection to businesses. Yeltsin in his fitful way realized that eliminating corruption from the heights of government was desirable, and it was this that was behind his increasing tendency to appoint former KGB officials to the new agencies that oversaw administrative affairs. The resurrected secret services were becoming a state with the state.[9]

Like others in the Kremlin elite, Putin sensed that time was running out for Yeltsin. Disquiet at the influence wielded over him by big business reached a peak. Private profiteering seemed to have supplanted governance in the national interest. The economy had been in deep recession since the late 1980s – as it happened, an abrupt recovery was about to ensue as the result of a rise in the world market price for oil and gas, but this was not yet clear to most members of the Russian leadership. In foreign policy, Bill Clinton pressed Yeltsin into accepting the bombing of Belgrade in 1999 after Serbian President Milošević carried out ethnic cleansing of Albanians from Serbia's Kosovo enclave.[10] Yeltsin complained to Clinton of the sleepless nights he endured as a result of the phone calls he had to take from Russian politicians expressing their outrage.[11]

Kosovo became a pinch point. The same had happened in July 1914 when Nicholas II declared war on Austria-Hungary in defence of Serbia. It was not that the tsar was notably solicitous about the plight of Serbians, but rather that he had given way to Austria-Hungary and Germany in earlier diplomatic tussles. Russian conservative and liberal opinion had had enough and brought their pressure to bear in the Duma and the press. But whereas Nicholas would have gone to war regardless of pressure – he too had had enough – Yeltsin was not going to fight Clinton over former Yugoslavia or anywhere else. Nevertheless, American military operations in the Balkans in defiance of Moscow's wishes had agitated Russian communist, nationalist and conservative opinion for years. Though most Russians had not shown any particular sympathy with Serbia, the Kosovo question affronted Russia's national dignity. Throughout the 1990s, Russians had watched as the Americans successfully pushed for the world to accede to their foreign-policy demands. Events in former Yugoslavia seemed to exemplify global politics since the disintegration of the USSR.

The indirect effect was to shine a bright light on what was felt to be wrong with Russia's internal situation. The focus was on thieving businessmen, corrupt officialdom and a scorned president who was no longer fit for high office. The Russian people searched for an end to their woeful financial and employment conditions. The scene was set for political explosion and social disturbance. 'Kosovo' suddenly united public opinion and brought these troubles to centre stage.

As Yeltsin began to despair of reversing the public mood, he took the drastic decision to make Putin his successor. This was patrimonial politics: as president, Yeltsin thought it his right to hand the job on to his latest protégé. When he told Clinton about his plan, he promised that Putin was well informed and intelligent, with a strong understanding of democratic principles and the necessary toughness to lead Russia.[12] He also endorsed Putin's war in Chechnya, warning Clinton about the dangerous spread of jihadism throughout Europe. Though Putin was in daily political charge of the military campaign, its planning predated his premiership and had Yeltsin's approval. As early as March 1999 Putin as FSB director had conferred with Internal Affairs Minister Stepashin and Defence Minister Igor Sergeev about the military reoccupation of the Chechen territories. The pretext for the war was an explosion in apartment blocks in Moscow and three other cities in September 1999. Though Putin was later accused of engineering the outrage, there were reasons to think that it was instigated by Yeltsin's close relatives and political advisers – known widely as The Family – who saw these machinations and a short, victorious war as crucial to the administration's survival.[13]

Putin's genial demeanour, moreover, was reassuring to the leaders of big business – Berezovski, for example, had faith in Putin, unlike his view of Primakov or Luzhkov. Primakov's crusade against economic crime had induced Berezovski to take the precaution of staying abroad for several months. On his return, it was clear that he wanted a firm hand in the Kremlin when Yeltsin stepped down, and he became one of Putin's supporters. It was in this atmosphere that, on New Year's Eve 1999, Yeltsin suddenly announced his retirement, automatically making Putin the acting president.

Putin was then still an unknown in the eyes of the Russian public. When appearing on television in his new role, he was bright and brisk. His aim was to say nothing that might agitate people before the presidential election in March 2000. Although he talked modestly about himself in public, he was possessed of an intense personal ambition. He was determined to transform and dominate the way that Russia was ruled. Generally he kept quiet about his thinking on the subject, although in summer 2008 he let slip to US Secretary of State Condoleezza Rice: 'Russians have always been at their best when they have been ruled by great men. Peter the Great, Alexander II. Russia needs a strong hand.'[14] Putin has governed in the same spirit. He had little democratic experience. Until he first stood for the presidency he had never – not once – offered himself as a candidate at an election at any political level. Not even in his time in St Petersburg politics in the early 1990s. It was to Yeltsin that he owed his ascent of the slippery ladder of public office in Moscow as he became first director of the FSB, then prime minister and finally the acting president. He was accustomed to working inside a political machine that insulates itself from public pressure. His career has been an authoritarian ruler's dream.

In Putin's first presidential term between 2000 and 2004 there was a soft aspect of Russian foreign policy that has long since disappeared. Tactical pliability, however, was accompanied by a cynical view of international relations that he took pains to disguise. Even today he remains reluctant to give a frank exposition of his beliefs about global politics, fearing that he might cause concern to the Russian electorate. As much as he can manipulate their votes, it makes no sense for him to alienate them unduly. In the margins of his speeches, however, he displays a belief that amoral motives underlie the actions of the world's leaders as they compete for influence. Harshness and even brutality, he thinks, are integral elements of statesmanship. Although he is mostly courteous at joint press conferences with foreign presidents, he can also lose his temper. He assumes that rival powers have no interest in Russian security or prosperity and will do down Russia at the first opportunity. In politics, dog eats dog.

On coming to power, as we shall see in later chapters, he carried out important economic reforms to deepen the foundations of Russian capitalism.[15] He also balanced accommodation to America and NATO with renewed national assertiveness. He spoke of Russia as a European country. He made no objection to the American request for airbase facilities in Uzbekistan before the invasion of Afghanistan. He continued Russia's quest to join the World Trade Organization. Like Yeltsin, he suggested that the Kremlin might even apply for member-ship of NATO. But the velvet glove of conciliation concealed a steel fist. Whenever Western leaders spoke of human rights abuses in Russia, he cut them short. Criticism of the war in Chechnya made him fractious and he insisted that no foreign leader had the right to define the Russian national interest. The UK's prime minister Tony Blair, who was the first foreigner to befriend him, was also the first to feel the lash of his tongue at a press conference. However much Putin on other occa-sions smiled at American and European leaders, he brooked no trespass onto his international agenda. They were given to understand that Russia would steer its own course.

When in September 2004 Chechen terrorists occupied School No. 1 in Beslan in North Ossetia and killed captive parents and chil-dren, he suggested that there was international connivance behind the massacre. By then his patience with America had been snapped by

George W. Bush's initiative in 2002 to introduce a new anti-missile defence system to eastern Europe and his support for the 'colour revolutions' in Georgia and Ukraine in 2003. America morphed into being Russia's official enemy number one.

This situation changed somewhat in January 2009 when Barack Obama entered the White House and announced his wish to 'reset' ties with Russia. There developed a second period of mutual accommodation, made easier by the fact that Medvedev rather than Putin was president for four years from May 2008. Much was quickly achieved. With American assistance, Russia secured membership of the World Trade Organization after years of applying in vain. A New Strategic Arms Reduction Treaty was signed, committing Russia and America to reducing their strategic nuclear warheads to 1,500 each. There was agreement also to establish a US–Russia Bilateral Commission, which would create working parties to seek an end to a range of chronic disputes between the two countries. In 2011 Obama reduced general military expenditure by 10–15 per cent by means of a bipartisan agreement in the US Congress.[16]

Putin was not alone in being irked by Medvedev's conduct of public affairs. Those who cherished the old Soviet traditions were annoyed that Medvedev remained seated to greet the 9 May Victory parade on Red Square – the custom was for the head of state to stand and salute. Medvedev was sometimes impulsive in the way he issued his presidential decrees. Technological lobbies resented how he poured money into his pet programme at Skolkovo while starving the funding available for the reputable science institutions in Novosibirsk and Zelenograd. He boasted of turning Moscow into a world financial centre. The reality in 2013 was to be that Russia languished in 130th place as a banking market – below even Botswana – in the global rankings.[17]

Disquiet was also felt about Medvedev's actions in foreign policy. With the onset of the 'Arab Spring', Libya collapsed in turmoil and its ruler Muammar Gaddafi violently suppressed the street demonstrations. Medvedev spoke of Gaddafi's loss of legitimacy and accommodated Western powers in discussions as to how to end the bloodshed in Tripoli and Benghazi. France, followed by the United Kingdom, decided to impose a no-fly zone. Secretary of State Hillary Clinton pushed Obama to support them. Obama, however, laid down a preference for approval by the United Nations, and he was lucky that it was Medvedev rather than Putin who was Russian president at the time. Medvedev told US Vice-President Joe Biden that Russia would not get in the way of air strikes. These were the days when Gaddafi looked likely to march on Benghazi and massacre every rebel in his path. In the vote at the UN Security Council on 17 March 2011, the Russian and Chinese ambassadors abstained, which left Western powers with a mandate to impose a no-fly zone over Libya to protect civilians from Gaddafi's war planes.

Medvedev had never had much time for Gaddafi, about whom he talked with contempt in the presence of Americans.[18] But as events unfolded, the French and British, with American intelligence support, started a bombing campaign that went beyond the framework of the UN Security Council mandate. Medvedev refrained from criticizing the Western powers. As the crisis intensified, he sacked the Russian ambassador in Tripoli for continuing to write disapproving reports on the military action.[19]

The measures on Libya angered the large part of Russia's elite and electorate that wanted its president to flex his muscles in international affairs. The rift widened between president and prime minister. Putin made a public comparison of Obama's Libyan action with Bush's war in Iraq, 'Where is the logic and the conscience? There's nothing of either. There are already victims among the civilian population, on whose behalf the bombing strikes are supposedly being made.'[20] This annoyed Medvedev, who spoke on television a few hours later in favour of the Security Council's decision. Foreign policy was meant to lie on the Russian presidency's exclusive table, and Medvedev objected to Putin picking up his cutlery. Western leaders showed a preference for Medvedev over Putin. Many leading Russians felt the same. Political advisers such as Vladislav Surkov and Gleb Pavlovski supported Medvedev in the hope of a more liberal pattern of governance than Putin would provide – Pavlovski warned that the leadership could not afford complacency about the possible shifts in public opinion.[21]

Medvedev felt inspirited to canvass for support in commercial circles for his plan to stand again at the presidential election of March 2012. As Medvedev probed the possibilities, Putin did the same on his own behalf. Patron and client got ready for the competition. The only question was whether they would contend against each other at the polls or seek a prior decision from the country's ascendant elite as to which of the two should stand as its candidate.

The Medvedev option collapsed with the first breath of wind. In July 2011, Medvedev called a meeting of twenty-seven leading businessmen and asked point-blank whether they would back him. A shuffling of feet occurred in the audience. The billionaires had not forgotten how Putin had dealt with business moguls Vladimir Gusinski, Boris Berezovski and Mikhail Khodorkovski. Gusinski had been forced to sell up most of his assets, including the NTV television station that had regularly criticized Putin, before fleeing the country in 2000. Berezovski had continued to put up a struggle, so Putin called him in for a discussion. When Berezovski said he was minded to move into 'public opposition', Putin faced him down, 'Well, all right, that's your business!'[22] By the end of 2000, after recognizing that Putin held all the cards of power, Berezovski concluded that it was best for him to go into foreign exile. Khodorkovski stayed behind and maintained the challenge to Putin and in 2003 paid the price of being arrested. Two years later he was sentenced to nine years' imprisonment. The other business magnates learned the new rule book, and those of them who sat in Medvedev's audience in 2011 were averse to risking their fortunes or freedom by entering the political fray. If Medvedev wished to contend for the presidency, he would have to go ahead without their blessing. They themselves would only spectate.[23]

Putin chafed with impatience while waiting to return to the highest office. Whenever he thought Russia's purposes were being thwarted, he reacted like the KGB officer that he once had been. His truculence in international affairs came as a shock to those who had been impressed by his friendly overtures to the West during his first presidential term.

They should not have been surprised. He was only applying to foreign policy the same ruthlessness he had shown in internal politics. In Russia he had suppressed democratic aspirations whenever they threatened the requirements of the Russian ruling elite. He had accepted the formalities of democracy on sufferance while restricting its influence in practice. Kremlin leaders showed indifference when investigative journalists were assassinated in Russia. The Presidential Administration repeatedly rigged the laws governing national elections. Chechnya was subjected to armed occupation and then handed over to Akhmat and Ramzan Kadyrov, willing Chechens not known for their civilized manners. Whatever Putin's foreign policy had been in the year 2000, he had already decided to impose severe political order, and the effects were bound to leach their toxicity into international affairs. The symptoms were obvious as early as 2004, when he reacted badly to Ukrainian elections that brought a leadership to power which sought friendship with NATO and the European Union and cooled relations with Russia. The prospect of an alternative model of governance on the Russian frontier was the last thing that Putin was going to tolerate, especially if the Ukrainians adopted democracy and the rule of law.

His patriotism, mistrust and mercilessness are the characteristic qualities of an intelligence officer. Russia's secret services survived the collapse of the Soviet order better than any other institution, and Putin showed his resolve during his tenure as FSB director in 1998–9 to raise their level of morale and efficiency. When he addressed the State Duma in November 1998 and took questions from the floor, he was frank about what he thought the security institutions required and deserved. He only half-joked: 'Nobody with the exception of State Duma deputies loves the Federal Security Service. That's why everybody obstructs it.' He tried to foster a changed attitude to the FSB and asked the Duma for support. He wanted a pay rise for his officers and demanded more of them be recruited. He advocated legislation to enable the FSB to conduct its investigations without hindrance. This was essential, Putin stressed, for the intelligence agencies' capacity to keep the country safe.[24]

He boasted that his officers were engaged in a process of constant self-reform which had raised the level of their many services. He described an established pattern whereby they were assigned posts inside the Presidential Administration and ministries to facilitate their impact on current discussions.[25] The FSB was integrated into the organs of daily governance and influenced every sector of public life. Russia in his estimation had not yet resolved its key problems. Privatization had been conducted in an 'incorrect' fashion with the result that in places such as the port of Novorossiisk, on the Black Sea coast, 'there emerged an owner who began to take command of state property, created his own security service and subjugated and brought state institutions under his control'. Putin deliberately spoke only about a single city: he knew it would be a serious tactical error if he caused business leaders at the national level to tremble. Only later did they discover that he meant what he said far beyond the Novorossiisk quayside.[26]

Putin did tell the Duma, however, about what the FSB had done to prevent the illegal export of Russian natural resources. He disclosed that his officers had succeeded in getting hold of many wrongdoers abroad – he already endorsed the freedom of Russia's security services to conduct extraterritorial operations (this activity was not framed in Russian law until 2006). He denounced the 'criminalization' of the regional elites throughout Russia, where organized crime groups had penetrated public life and were manipulating politicians. He complained about the extent to which Russia's internal republics had insulated themselves from the fiscal system operated from Moscow. Putin called for measures to put a stop to the flight of Russian capital abroad. In his opinion, profits made at home should stay at home and not vanish into foreign bank accounts.[27]

He would say nothing yet about wresting back government control of those of the country's natural resources that had been privatized, chiefly delivered by Yeltsin into the hands of a small group of business moguls known as the oligarchs in return for their support in the 1996 presidential election. But like millions of other Russians, Putin believed in the requirement for greater state regulation and this had been a key theme of the doctoral dissertation he submitted at the St Petersburg Mining Institute in 1997.[28] (It is common for Russian politicians who are on the make to manufacture an academic status for themselves.) But he refrained from dealing with the topic when standing for the presidency, mindful not to put the 'oligarchs' on their guard.

The years he spent inside the secret services have improved his ability to dissemble and sharpened his impatience with opposition. He hates being contradicted. Those who thwart him are poking their fingers into a wasps' nest. This does not, however, mean that he never asks for expert advice, especially on how to handle the economy. Even so, the consultations can become fiery. The economist Andrei Illarionov frequently visited Putin at his dacha at Novo-Ogarëvo, but when Illarionov intruded his opinion that the 1999–2000 war in Chechnya constituted a crime, Putin angrily debated with him for half an hour. Neither convinced the other, and although Illarionov continued to work for Putin and economic reform, they never discussed Chechnya again.[29]

There were also fireworks at an encounter with selected journalists in 2008, when *Ekho Moskvy* columnist Arkadi Dubnov inquired about the fate of Mikhail Khodorkovski, the oil magnate who had been Russia's richest man before his trial and incarceration. 'Vladimir Vladimirovich,' Dubnov asked, 'tell us why you hate Khodorkovski so much.' Such bluntness disconcerted his colleagues, who knew that the businessman had refused Putin's demand for entrepreneurs to stay out of politics. Putin exclaimed, 'Yes, but he was up to his elbows in blood!' Without batting an eyelid, Dubnov came back at him, 'How come? Vladimir Vladimirovich, what was it they condemned him for? Why did they condemn him for tax crimes?' Putin growled, 'Well, don't you know about this? They drag themselves with bags of cash into the procurator's offices and the courts!' Dubnov made a final jibe, 'So is this what we get as the result of your eight years in power?' At this point a fellow reporter tugged at Dubnov's jacket to stop the exchanges, 'Arkadi, pack it in. What on earth are you up to?'[30]

As the others kept up the pressure with questions about Khodorkovski, Putin flew into a rage. Dubnov was now watching, rather than interrogating. Putin, he could see, 'truly believed and had convinced himself that [Khodorkovski] was a murderer and that he was up to his elbows in blood'. Until then Dubnov had assumed Putin had been playing a role. But he was soon convinced that Putin was holding Khodorkovski in gaol because he genuinely held him guilty of complicity in murder.[31]

Dubnov may be right, but it is also possible that Putin was drawing upon his KGB training to use outrage as a tool when he was failing to get his way using the power of argument. Russian politics are a rough school that trains its practitioners in personal hardiness. Putin brags that he grew up in a tough environment. Speaking to foreign guests in October 2015, he confided, 'You know, here's something I'd like to say. Fifty years ago I learned one rule on the streets of Leningrad: if a fight is inevitable, be the first to attack.'[32] In discussion he is practised at adopting an alarming tone. Perhaps as a result of his judo coaching, he aims to catch people off balance. But he has also learned when to be more moderate in talking to leaders from abroad, because he has discovered from experience that asperity wins him no prizes. Most foreigners who come into his presence have heard of his reputation and try to avoid annoying him. His fits of temper are notorious. But no sooner has he lost self-control over some disagreement in international affairs than he is speaking in a tranquil manner on another topic. One moment he is like a torrent and the next like standing water.[33]

If he grew up that way, it was also exactly how the KGB trained him. His fellow recruit in Leningrad and later political appointee Vladimir Yakunin has written about the schooling that promising young intelligence recruits received:

> The ability to read body language, to read all of the signs that other people communicate unconsciously, has been a great advantage in my subsequent career. And, conversely, I can use my demeanour almost like an instrument to help me persuade and

manipulate. We were taught how to subtly change the expression of our eyes, the tightness of our skin, the cast of our jaws: at times I can be all soft and full of laughter, at others I can be like a beast, but I never lose control of my emotions.[34]

Yakunin recalls that Dale Carnegie's American bestseller *How to Win Friends and Influence People* was on the KGB's training curriculum. When in 2005 Putin made him head of the Russian railway network, he found this coaching in chameleon-like behaviour helpful when negotiating with foreigners. Putin, too, is able to adapt his mood and manner to suit each fresh environment.

Part-gargoyle and part-charmer, he won the admiration of President George W. Bush, who in June 2001 announced that after staring into Putin's eyes, 'I was able to get a sense of his soul'. At first, Bush had found Putin heavy going because he had come with a stack of prepared talking points. To a man who valued Texan informality, this was uncongenial. But then they discovered that they shared an interest in the Bible.[35] Bush was not to know that Putin had been advised by an American contact to advertise his Christian faith as a negotiating ploy.[36] When Bush took a trip to St Petersburg, Putin took him out to his residence and showed him the private chapel that he had built in the grounds.[37] Most importantly, in 2001, Putin had shown that he understood the enormity of the September 11 terrorist attack on New York's World Trade Center by being the first head of state to call Bush to express his condolence and offer active cooperation.

While Russia's dealings with America were deteriorating in the mid-2000s, Putin remained courteous in meetings with Bush, and he and Obama called each other Vladimir and Barack.[38] Yet foreign leaders know him as someone who listens intently to the opposite side's argument. Germany's Chancellor Angela Merkel has acknowledged his willingness to hear her out when they disagree, and they keep up a dialogue even in times of international stress.

Despite this, Putin still has the reputation of a carnivore prowling among herds of unsuspecting ruminants. His friendly banter can swiftly give way to anger when he feels seriously baulked and he creates an alarming environment if he feels the need. On one of José Manuel Barroso's many visits to Russia, the European Commission president was looking forward to having a relaxed evening at Putin's presidential dacha. Barroso, who had flown to Moscow from Kazakhstan, expressed admiration for the dinner that his Russian hosts provided. Putin stormed back at him, pretending to be shocked at the disrespect he was showing to President Nursultan Nazarbaev. It was confected outrage. Putin wanted to discomfit Barroso so as to gain the upper hand in the negotiations that they were about to undertake.[39] This was far from being the nastiest recorded case of how he probes points of weakness. In 2007 he brought Koni, his black Labrador, into a meeting with Angela Merkel at the Sochi presidential residence. It is widely known that she is nervous of dogs, having been bitten by one in her youth. Trying to shake her up and take advantage came naturally to Putin, judo master and ex-KGB officer. And in his male-chauvinist fashion, he assumed that a frightened woman would yield to his political requirements.

But Merkel gave him his comeuppance when she told reporters, 'I understand why he has to do this – to prove he's a man. He's afraid of his own weakness. Russia has nothing, no successful politics or economy. All they have is this.' It was an outburst untypical of a German chancellor who values discretion. Putin had set out to humble her and she paid him back in language he would understand.[40] Russian TV stations refrained from reporting what she said. Russians evidently were to be shielded from witnessing her scathing assessment of Russia's achievements with Putin at the helm.

Publicity is certainly given, however, to meticulously preparing for meetings, making it a point of honour to master his daily brief. He himself has bragged that he typically reads entire policy documents rather than abstracts,[41] and has surprised foreign interviewers with his command of Russian economic statistics or of Russia's diplomatic considerations. Admittedly there have been those who have queried this, as when the reporters Konstantin Gaaze and Mikhail Fishman cited unnamed Kremlin officials who said that he spent only fifteen minutes a day on documents, being more interested in his exercise machines and the swimming pool.[42] But most observers tell of a perfectionist who constantly tries to improve his political skills. He will never become a great orator. But this does not bother him so long as he can make an impact as a pugnacious if monotonous speaker. He once quipped that he was being coached in rhetorical technique, then had to deny this when people failed to understand that he was joking.[43]

He has always appreciated the importance of public image. When working in the St Petersburg administration in the early 1990s, he took the unusual step of commissioning a TV documentary about his work.[44] Years later he told media editors, 'It's better not to be chewing in front of the cameras.' He explained that broadcasters would exploit the slightest visual faux pas.[45] On rising to the presidency, he worked at grooming himself in public relations. When in November 2000 he met Prime Minister Blair in Moscow, he asked about how to improve his image. Blair's team included some of the world's doyens in media manipulation, and Blair was famous for his ease with audiences and his actorly flair. Putin listened avidly to how the British did it. His zeal to learn from Western experience stretched to asking Blair to send over a team of consultants to Russia to advise on how to reform the Russian civil service.[46]

Putin recognized that he was capable of huge misjudgements. In August 2000 he had incurred widespread disapproval of the way that he handled news about the disaster in the cold waters of the Barents Sea when the entire crew of the *Kursk* nuclear submarine perished. Putin complacently refused to interrupt his summer holiday. He was by nature and instruction an enemy of sentimentality: KGB officers were meant to adopt an impassive demeanour. The Russian public saw things differently: Putin was president and it was his duty to help the country to deal with the pain. His popularity plummeted. It was ten days before he understood the damage done by his inactivity and went in person to the Vidyaevo naval base. There he met hundreds of bereaved family members, who lost their tempers with him in full view of the TV cameras. This was not so much an embarrassment as sheer humiliation. But rather than blame the naval high command for years of negligence, he castigated the Russian media for their investigations into the tragedy and hit out at media owners who were living safely in their plush Mediterranean villas.

But he learned from this episode. After *Kursk*, he always visited scenes of outrage or spoke on television to condole with victims and threaten wrongdoers with punishment. When terrorist atrocities took place at Moscow's Nord-Ost Theatre in 2002 and two years later at Beslan's School No. 1 he was immediately shown supervising the security operations. Experience might have changed his practice, but his temperament and attitude remain the same.

In discussion, Putin is remarkably decisive and sticks fixedly to his decisions. He is comfortable when explaining them on TV to the Russian public. Years of power have lent him an aura of self-confidence. Once he has marked out and expounded his line of thought, he sits back holding the arms of his chair. His calmness somehow accentuates his inner energy. He is animation in human form and careful viewers can observe the frequent movement of his feet. He moves his head towards TV presenters or interviewers to make his points, often raising the right hand in a fist. His fingers move restlessly on the edge of his table. He is not a fidget but rather he aims to demonstrate that his policies alone can deal with the recurrent crises in world politics. He speaks rapidly, clearly, articulately. He rations levity to a minimum. He expects to be in charge and reacts to dissent with a cannonade of assertions. Impassivity gives way to anger. In an instant the gentle ruler shows himself an irascible autocrat.

Some have contended that the facade of competence conceals a degree of psychological insecurity. One of his former advisers, the so-called political technologist Gleb Pavlovski, whom he consulted about internal political strategy until April 2011, tells of having witnessed at least one crisis of self-confidence:

> In the spring of 2010, Putin fell into a kind of depression, which was very noticeable. He even began to speak badly – he would read from pieces of paper. There was an uncertainty, a lack of confidence, when he appeared in front of people. He didn't look into the camera, which is not like him. A doubt appeared in his mind about his own decisions, and about the people he was working with. He began to change. He decided that they were all doing something not quite right, everyone was making wrong decisions, including Dmitry Medvedev. And he had no influence over that. So a kind of a fear deepened in him.[47]

Pavlovski voiced regret that Putin dealt with his doubts by retreating further into himself and handling those around him with distrust.

Whatever the truth of this, Putin is unmistakably sensitive by temperament despite having the hide of a pachyderm about his policies. It has been suggested that, at five feet six, he has feelings of awkwardness about his height. When Tony Blair and Putin stood side by side at their first press conference, Blair towered over the Russian president. Putin did not make the same mistake twice. At subsequent sessions with the press he arranged for there to be a gap between him and any tall foreign leader, and it was rumoured that his team procured a concealed step for him to mount.[48] It has also been asserted that special arrangements were made when Putin was filmed alongside Oliver Stone in their series of TV interviews. Allegedly Stone fixed the lighting so as to disguise his own much taller stature. In fact the two of them were recorded together without special effects. There was nevertheless a piquant scene when Putin, taking his American interviewer to an ice hockey game in which he was going to play, emerged from the changing room in full kit beaming with enthusiasm – and Stone exclaimed, 'Mighty Mouse!'[49]

This was not a remark Putin's people judged appropriate to include in the interview transcripts. The affable Stone had voiced a touch of condescension. What was published instead was the exchange between the two men after the game when Putin inquired whether Stone had had a good time. Stone said yes and asked whether Putin felt exhausted. Putin shrugged this off, 'No, everything's fine. I'll try to get some sleep and restore my strength.'[50] The edited volume presented Putin as a steely ruler. This was not a fiction: Russia had produced some rulers of steel in the previous century and Putin is the latest in the line, on and off the ice rink.

7. LOYALTY AND DISCIPLINE: THE KREMLIN TEAM

Many in Russia and abroad picture Putin as a kind of contemporary tsar or party general secretary. He wields unmatched authority, an authority that has risen since his return to the presidency in 2012. The mechanisms of power remain firmly clasped in his hands. As Russian president he has extensive formal powers. He appoints and can dismiss the prime minister, the cabinet, the chairman of the Central Bank and the highest judges. He has the right to dissolve the State Duma and announce fresh elections. His annual address to the Federal Assembly lays down the guiding principles for Russian's external and internal policies. His rulings settle disputes inside the government. He controls foreign policy and approves national military doctrine. He chairs both the Security Council and, since 2014, the State Commission for Military-Industrial Issues.[1] He is the supreme commander-in-chief of the armed forces, a puissant monarch.

Yet there were always limits to the dominance that even Russia's mightiest leaders – Ivan the Terrible, Peter the Great and Joseph Stalin – could exert in practice. Rulers had to build an effective team round them. Tsars plucked their ministers mainly from the high aristocracy until the nineteenth century, when they increasingly turned to other levels of society for talent. Under communism there was a reversion to an even older way of choosing an entourage whereby each general secretary promoted associates who had been with them for most of their career. Personal loyalty was the principal demand. This has been likened to a clan system – a comparison that makes a degree of sense except that communist 'clans' did not mainly involve ties of blood. Gorbachëv was unusual in being reluctant to elevate long-term friends and associates to prominence, while Yeltsin had a compulsive habit of firing his own appointees almost as soon as he had welcomed them to office. Putin has reverted to a more traditional style of Russian rulership, however, maintaining a stable team in the top tier of the Kremlin leadership. Authority and riches are showered on his favourites, from whom he requires unconditional allegiance in return.

This system already existed at lower levels of power before Putin first became president. Networks of patrons and clients were a feature of the Soviet system of rule even under Stalin, who strove in vain to break them up by means of his bloody purges.[2] The persistence of administrative clanship was itself a reaction to the flow of arbitrary orders from on high. Officials needed a network of patronage for protection. When the USSR began to fall apart, the incentive to hold close to friends and acquaintances grew stronger and it was felt at every level of Russian society as the uncertainties of life increased in the 1990s. While state institutions weakened, people needed alternative ways of bringing security to their lives. Putin was known for his loyalty to both his bosses and his subordinates – this was one of the characteristics that attracted Yeltsin's attention. He felt comfortable with such a system. Informal networks were often the only means of getting things done in an environment where bureaucratic formalities congested the administration. Putin, like other officials who had to cope with the chaos that preceded and followed the collapse of the USSR, had no intention of reforming this pattern of governance.

However, when Putin took over, he inherited a political system that was rife with factionalism. Prime ministers and their cabinets had appeared like passenger liners out of a sea fog, only to disappear when Yeltsin took against them. Putin's aim was – and remains – to eliminate the chaos from Russian politics. Stability and order were and are his priorities. Yeltsin left him with a situation where there were ceaseless disputes between the upholders of state power and the proponents of democratic rights and liberal economics, and each side was itself divided.[3] When leading opponents went up against each other, it was Putin alone who could arbitrate. He inevitably annoys the losers with his rulings, but he knows he cannot please everyone and is also aware that being thus above the fray consolidates his supremacy. Disputants do not express public discontent. Liberal economic voices have not entirely disappeared, but they are weak and becoming weaker. Even so, there is a degree of impatience with him among those security officials who have grumbled about Putin's reluctance to complete the job and eject every liberal from all the ministries.[4]

At times, disputes between the various intelligence agencies have threatened to disrupt their effectiveness, at which point Putin generally steps in as moderator. But devolving authority to fellow leaders fosters a competitive and dynamic environment. Putin knows that so long as he can keep the pot simmering, he will remain master of the kitchen.

Though he has increasingly bestowed favour on the secret services, he does not display automatic beneficence towards his old KGB comrades. In 2013 when calling on Vladimir Yakunin to rescue the building work that was behind schedule for the Sochi Winter Olympics, he cautioned him to avoid 'irrevocable mistakes'.[5] This was a mild version of the tradition begun by Joseph Stalin, who set near-impossible targets while threatening dire punishments for failure to fulfil his five-year plans. Construction at Sochi was completed at a frantic tempo. Like Stalin, Putin also warned his subordinates not to try to fool him with false displays. He aimed to deter the 'Potëmkin village' syndrome, which was named after Prince Grigori Potëmkin, conqueror of Crimea in 1783, who allegedly tricked Catherine the Great into believing that he had already established prosperous Russian peasant colonies along the banks of the river Dnieper when she visited the region. The problem facing Yakunin was that asphalt supplies had run out in southern Russia. He knew that Putin would be angry if he discovered that inferior substitutes had been used in the construction of the new mountain highway. Like a communist functionary from the old USSR, Yakunin ranted and raved to lay hold of the asphalt and complete the project before the president arrived to inspect it.[6] Up and down the ladder of command there are leaders who know how to intimidate – and Putin sits on the top rung and sets the authoritarian tone.

In quieter times, Putin has listened to a plurality of viewpoints. If big decisions are required on Russian economic development, he pulls in the main contending advocates and lets them argue their corner. Former Railways Minister Yakunin tells of a session where the respective merits of state subsidies and the free market were debated. He himself argued for higher railway tariffs while Finance Minister Anton Siluanov spoke up to protect his balanced budget. Yakunin shouted, 'You are the Minister of Finances, so you should at least be familiar with all four rules of arithmetic, not just addition and subtraction!' The outburst drew a reprimand from Putin for discourtesy.[7]

Putin restricts the discussion to a small informal group inside the ruling elite – and the talk can obviously become heated.[8] His confidants are associates of long standing who accept that he alone will make the ultimate decision. Everybody knows that once a policy is settled, Putin will not countenance a review of the reasoning behind it. Like a military commander, he issues abrupt orders and demands instant action, his favourite saying being 'Look into it and report' or simply 'Report!' Behind the scenes no one except for a few trusted friends is allowed to contradict him.[9] In public the discipline is total, and none of them dares to cut across him. When US Ambassador Michael McFaul attended meetings with Putin and other Russian leaders, it was as if Putin was the team manager and the rest were his players. Even Patrushev, who was his friend and superior in the KGB hierarchy before 1991, consistently deferred to the president.[10]

Through the expanding Presidential Administration Putin issues decrees on all manner of topics. Chief of Staff Anton Vaino, who has been in post since 2016, shoulders a gruelling work load. The government itself is topped by the Council of Ministers, headed since 2012 by Medvedev, who was given the post when he stepped aside for Putin to reoccupy the presidency. Putin has the right to dismiss the entire cabinet, but he knows he can rely on Medvedev to deal with the business of government within the framework of approved policies. Friction between the two men has stayed within manageable limits. Medvedev has accepted his defeat at Putin's hands in the previous year and even when he was president, Medvedev only rarely spoke out against Putin's policy preferences, and even then he did not name him.[11] In subsequent years Medvedev has kept his lips sealed: he knows this is a requirement of survival and reappointment to the post.

Putin's supremacy is consolidated by the fact that successive elections for over a decade have given United Russia, the political party he founded, a majority in the State Duma, the lower house of Russia's parliament. In 2016 Putin secured its compliance with his purposes by moving his Deputy Chief of Staff Vyacheslav Volodin across to the Duma, where he became its chairman. Many sensitive matters, moreover, are handled at the Security Council's weekly sessions, with Putin as its chairman and Patrushev as its secretary.[12] The secret services have a huge importance, as does the Ministry of Finances. Russia has a sprawling edifice of institutions held together by an understanding of the general line that has been laid down by Putin in consultation with the rest of the ruling cabal. It also coheres because all the team's members understand that the potential consequences of disunity are dire. They did not come to power by a free and fair electoral process and are on permanent alert for signs of public discontent. The Kremlin elite has to present itself as a disciplined vanguard.

Like Brezhnev in the 1970s, Putin assigns the box seats of power to proven loyalists. A remarkable number of holders of high office are friends from his Leningrad youth or former colleagues in the city's KGB or the mayor's office. Inside the ruling group they are known as the Piterskie (for St Petersburg, the name the city reverted to in 1991).[13]

Prime Minister Dmitri Medvedev was Putin's legal adviser when he served as St Petersburg's deputy mayor. Nikolai Patrushev is another old KGB hand. Sergei Ivanov, his Defence Minister between 2001 and 2007 and his Chief of Staff till August 2016, had known Putin since their time in the KGB. Igor Sechin, executive chairman of the oil company Rosneft, worked as Putin's personal assistant in the St Petersburg mayor's office after leaving the Main Intelligence Directorate (GRU) of the armed forces.[14] Sechin was deputy chief of Putin's Presidential Administration until 2008 and was heavily involved in the seizure of Khodorkovski's assets in 2004. He was also deputy prime minister while Putin was premier. FSB Director Alexander Bortnikov began his career in the Leningrad KGB and rose to the top FSB job in 2008 when President Medvedev removed Patrushev on grounds of ill health and moved him across to become Security Council secretary, a post he continues to hold. Sergei Naryshkin, born and bred in Leningrad, trained as a radio engineer. Famously averse to publicity, he has declined to talk about his recruitment to the KGB and later to Anatoli Sobchak's St Petersburg mayor's office. He is unusual in the ruling elite for his gentle manner and intellectual demeanour. He likes to 'advise' rather than give noisy orders.[15] From 2008 he was Medvedev's Chief of Staff in the Presidential Administration. In Putin's third presidential term he became chairman of the State Duma, a post he held until 2016, when Putin made him the Foreign Intelligence Service director.

Until 2000, officials who had had careers in the 'power agencies' made up half the list of the hundred most influential Russians, meaning that Putin had a corpus of useful supporters as soon as he became president. By December 2007, it is reckoned, about seventy of the top hundred public figures belonged to this category – and a career in the secret services continues to be an asset for entrance into public life.[16]

He regularly tests the people he appoints, and culls those who fail those tests. Although his St Petersburg former comrades are efficient administrators, few of them had the expertise to lay the brickwork of a market economy. Putin is committed to capitalism and knows that specialist knowledge is required to smooth the conditions that banks, factories, railways, communication networks and trade require. Alexei

Kudrin, Finance Minister from 2000 through to 2011, is one of the few with a professional training in finance. When confronted by another of Putin's confidants who objected to his line on economic policy, Kudrin rasped out, 'Stop arguing with me, I'm a professor!'[17] Kudrin was in ministerial office throughout the lengthy period of Russian economic expansion from 2000 – and he stood out against ministers, officials and advisers who wanted even greater state control than Putin permitted. Lobbyists for the armed forces and security services regarded Kudrin as public enemy number one.

But a world-class economy cannot be founded on one man, and in May 2001 Putin called upon a Yeltsin favourite, Mikhail Kasyanov, to work as his first prime minister. Like Kudrin, Kasyanov was committed to free-market ideas and the rule of law and wanted to eliminate bureaucratic interference in entrepreneurial activity. He later wrote that Putin also chose him because he had no personal ties to any of the 'oligarchs' in big business. As an ex-director of the FSB, Putin knew who was beholden to whom.[18] In return, Kasyanov received the assurance of Putin's support in pointing economic policy in the direction of reform.[19] Kasyanov also recalled Putin's plan for how they would work together:

'On his side there was only one condition, which was never to trespass on his "turf". The presidential turf covered the agencies of coercion and internal policy. Internal policy above all involved interaction with political parties and work with the regions.' Putin promised that he would never dismiss the government without giving a public explanation or having a very serious reason.[20]

This account is a collector's item. In the Gorbachëv and Yeltsin years, Russian politics were a leaking bucket. High-ranking individuals rushed to publish their recollections after leaving office, keen to explain why they resented the way they had been treated. Some, though, made a case for their ex-leader. While Putin has been in office, as both president and prime minister, reticence has become obligatory. It took a brave spirit such as Kasyanov, who was fired as prime minister in February 2004, to spill the beans.

When he took office, Kasyanov was initially satisfied with the demarcation of functions between president and prime minister. They cooperated productively even though Kasyanov was aware that Putin insisted on keeping the upper hand; Putin had the prerogative of choosing whichever ministers he wanted whereas Kasyanov could only appoint their deputies. At the start, Putin was restrained, leaving

Kasyanov to manage the huge tasks of economic reform while he focused on Chechnya and his own electoral prospects. Kasyanov was able to liaise with Putin's Chief of Staff, Alexander Voloshin, to ensure that there were no misunderstandings. He had ready access to Putin himself and was able to resist ministerial appointments that he did not like.[21] Even when there were personnel changes at the Defence Ministry, a 'coercive' institution if ever there was one, Kasyanov felt free to recommend Lyubov Kudelina as Deputy Minister – and he recorded that Putin and Kudelina got on famously. For a while the relationship between president and prime minister seemed to be a harmonious collaboration that would advance the cause of reform, at least in the economy.[22]

But Putin was put out by Kasyanov's habit of thinking for himself in discussions of policy. Kasyanov argued against the arrest of businessman Khodorkovski. He expressed annoyance with Putin's decision to appoint an individual without economic qualifications, Alexei Miller, to head Gazprom. Kasyanov saw no reason to avoid consorting with opposition politicians including the liberal Boris Nemtsov – and he did this in full view of all those gathered at the World Economic Forum at Davos in Switzerland.

Putin decided to remove him from the premiership by offering to make him Security Council Secretary instead. He was still willing to trust him with a big job outside the cabinet, even one that dealt with the FSB. Kasyanov rejected the proposition and turned Putin down on two occasions. Putin came back just once more, 'Listen, I've never previously offered something to anyone three times.' But Kasyanov dug his heels in, 'Please don't imagine I'm some strange creature of wonder. I'm not playing up or indulging in games. In my life I've climbed up all the rungs from simple economist to premier. There's only one rung I've not climbed, just one official position, but that's the one that you occupy.'[23] Putin's next idea was for Kasyanov to stand as mayor of Moscow in the next election. This time Kasyanov gave the offer some consideration until he had an encounter with Yuri Luzhkov, the incumbent mayor, who told him things about the job that definitively put him off – what they were, Kasyanov has never disclosed. Putin kept at it, suggesting that Kasyanov should take charge of the Inter-State Bank of the Commonwealth of Independent States. The answer yet again was no because Kasyanov believed that Russia's priority should lie in constructing links with the European Union. At this point, Putin stopped making friendly gestures.[24]

In their final discussion Putin threatened to crush Kasyanov if he engaged in oppositional activity – and dredged up the rumours that Kasyanov had taken bribes when he was Minister of Finances in the 1990s. When Kasyanov retorted that Putin knew this was rubbish, Putin reminded him that there was no smoke without fire, and advised Kasyanov to bear this in mind.[25] Kasyanov did the opposite and became one of the Opposition's leading figures. But when he dared to challenge Putin's protégé Medvedev in the 2008 presidential election, the Central Electoral Committee rejected his candidature. Pushed to the margins of political affairs, Kasyanov still caused trouble for Putin, and in April 2016 Russian television carried a grainy film of the married Kasyanov having sex with the much younger political activist Natalya Pelevina, which did lasting harm to his reputation.

Kasyanov was remarkable for leaving office and then formally joining the Opposition. More typical was Kudrin, who, after resigning from the Finance Ministry, accepted a post outside the cabinet as head of a research tank and as dean of studies back at St Petersburg State University. He and Putin were old Leningrad friends – it was Kudrin who had recommended his transfer to Moscow in 1996. Kudrin had long believed that 'a liberal policy can only be a tough one'.[26] He endorsed Putin's moves against the 'oligarchs', including the arrest of Khodorkovski.[27] But from 2004 Kudrin's patience was strained by the growing expenditure on the armed forces. He also had personal ambitions. The final straw had been Putin's decision to nominate Medvedev as the next prime minister when, as everyone expected, he himself won the 2012 presidential election. Until that moment Kudrin had hoped to get the job. In an angry reaction he criticized Medvedev's policies at a New York conference and said he would not serve in a cabinet under him. Medvedev took his chance to dispatch a rival and, in a televised session of governmental business, demanded Kudrin's resignation. Kudrin stepped down after consulting Putin, who evidently told him that he had only himself to blame.[28]

But Kudrin was no Kasyanov. Though he attended Opposition rallies to protest electoral fraud in late 2011, he got over his mini-rebellion and ceased to criticize the Kremlin leadership in personal terms. He and Putin remained in contact, and they have appeared in public together, politely exchanging opinions about where Russia is heading economically. In spring 2016 Putin commissioned Kudrin to write up his ideas. This was a clever move in that it effectively neutralized open criticism inside the ruling group past and present as well as putting limits on the victory of the enemies of economic liberalism. Putin barred Kudrin's report from publication, but did not prevent him from circulating a redacted milder variant on the internet: economic liberalism is muffled but not silenced.[29]

Kudrin's intellectual sparring partner in economic policy is Sergei Glazev, who has the least typical of backgrounds for a team member. One of Yeltsin's early ministers, he resigned from the Russian government in September 1993 when Yeltsin peremptorily dissolved the Supreme Soviet. He then joined the Communist Party of the Russian Federation. Very much the advocate for state intervention, Glazev is also a strident nationalist who believes that since the fall of communism Russia has been subjected to 'colonization by Western capital'.[30] In 2004 he even stood as an independent candidate against Putin in the presidential election. In those days he saw Putin as the champion of the liberal wing of Russian economic thought and called for a return to state subsidies, central governmental control and a loosening of monetary policy.[31] But as Putin's policies swung steadily towards state economic control, Glazev saw him in a different light. Old differences were forgotten, and the odd couple started to work together.

Glazev argued for Russia to follow the Chinese economic model and abandon any idea of copying American precedents.[32] He pointed to the huge US national debt, a debt that is projected to grower ever more huge. He also stressed that the United States' share of global output is falling. He assured everyone that the United States and the European Union are heading for chronic decline.

He was far from complacent about Russia's future. He stressed that Russia was economically falling behind America. In his opinion, the Chinese would be the best strategic partners for the country's regeneration. He urged the Kremlin to ensure that Russian business should seek links with China and the three other BRICS countries, Brazil, India and South Africa. Russia's focus, he argued, should be on building up its own Eurasian Economic Union so that it might head a regional bloc made up of friendly countries of the former Soviet Union.[33] Glazev maintains that China's history shows the wisdom of avoiding excesses of privatization.[34] Whether Chinese economic development would have succeeded without heavy reliance on private enterprise is a matter of doubt.[35] For years he had proposed regenerating Russian manufacturing by making government credits more widely available over a sustained period. Putin signalled his assent in a decree on 7 May 2012 that committed the cabinet to a long-term objective of creating

25 million highly skilled jobs by 2020. A rise in productivity was the key priority. Ministers would help by trying to increase the share of investment to 27 per cent of gross domestic product by 2018.

This involved a scaling back of Kudrin's sovereign wealth initiative. Whereas Kudrin had worked to build up funds against the day when hydrocarbon prices might plunge on world markets, Glazev argued against depositing revenues in profitable foreign funds and for advancing finance to Russian companies. Glazev and others have contributed ideas for a programme for state capitalism that supplied the groundwork for Putin's current policies. Putin began to cite Glazev with enthusiasm. No doubt Glazev is also congenial to Putin because of their shared passion for the idea of a Eurasian Economic Union. Whereas Kudrin pushed for an improved linkage with the European Union, Glazev looks for opportunities in the 'near abroad' and recommends a strategic partnership with China.[36]

Putin has employed others who, like Glazev, have had no prior connection to him. He has shown enduring favour to fellow sports enthusiast Sergei Shoigu, who was Yeltsin's Minister of Emergency Situations from 1991. Shoigu, half-Tuvan and half-Russian, became popular for his activity during episodes of natural disaster and terrorist outrage in Russia. In 2012 Putin made him Defence Minister. In the same way, Putin has stuck by Sergei Lavrov, who has been the Foreign Affairs Minister since 2004. Lavrov is an unusual member of the Putin team in so far as he was actually trained for the profession – diplomacy – in which he finds himself today. Another thing that marks him out from most ministers, the athletic Shoigu aside, is his love of sport. Lavrov is a Moscow Spartak fan who still plays football – quite a distinction for someone born in 1950. There is a touch of the old diplomatic world about him as he laments the fact that even he is not allowed to smoke a cigarette in his own ministry.[37] Lavrov started as a Soviet diplomat in Sri Lanka and was then the Russian Federation's ambassador at the United Nations. Both Shoigu and Lavrov know that adherence to Putin's line of policy is an absolute prerequisite for survival in office.

The same rule holds for survival at the highest level of big business. The time has passed when tycoons were able to exercise a domineering public influence. Putin clawed back state control over large sectors of Russia's natural resources. In some instances, direction came to be supplied by the officials-turned-businessmen whom Putin appointed to leading positions in Moscow television companies and the state-controlled energy and transport corporations. Not all such appointments met with acclaim. In 2016 a Bloomberg reporter asked Putin about the lengthy tenure of Alexei Miller at Gazprom. Why, he asked, did he remain in post after Gazprom had tumbled from being one of the world's top ten biggest companies to a pitiful 198th place? Putin replied that Gazprom consistently satisfied the demands of Russia's consumers.[38]

Yet the Kremlin's ruling elite is not monolithic. German Gref, the executive chairman of Russia's largest savings bank, Sberbank, is a former Deputy Minister of Finances. Known to be an economic liberal, he found work in the government uncomfortable. He has since been awarded a happy second career running one of the largest public funds. Arkadi Dvorkovich, the current head of Russian Railways, once served in the Presidential Administration. He was strongly associated with Medvedev. Dvorkovich's proven competence and discretion were enough to keep him in post until after the 2018 presidential election. Putin demands loyalty above every other qualification. He also expects his appointees to work hard in their posts. No one is promoted to a sinecure, even though the material rewards of office can be huge and usually are. Everyone knows the score and Putin reciprocates by showing them loyalty. Both sides keep a watchful eye and stick to the informal rules. The Putin team has become ever more united in the image that they – and Russia – present to the world.

Putin, however, does not expect his team to be timid. Truculence is almost a requirement of membership, and Putin licenses his team to say what he thinks but cannot voice in public. He chooses people who like to play rough. He wants to make Russia feared as a dangerous, unpredictable force in international relations. This has left space for Security Council Secretary Patrushev to act as his attack dog. When serving as Duma Speaker, Naryshkin made several crude anti-Western remarks but he quietened down in 2016 when Putin appointed him as Foreign Intelligence Service director. Patrushev has never stopped barking. He blamed the United States for attempts to destroy the USSR and then the Russian Federation. He contended that a succession of American politicians starting with Zbigniew Brzezinski in the 1970s had deliberately worked to undermine the Soviet economy, and that President Reagan in the 1980s had arranged to reduce the world market price for oil so as to wreck the USSR's budget. After destroying the Soviet Union, the Americans purportedly strong-armed the International Monetary Fund into imposing loan conditions that hobbled

Russian economic development. According to Patrushev, Chechnya had fallen under the West's control in the 1990s. The United States had also tried to annihilate South Ossetia and was behind the recent political turmoil in Ukraine.[39]

Patrushev expected Russo-American tensions to increase. American experts were predicting a crippling global shortage of energy, food and water – and Russia had vast resources that the Americans coveted.[40] Having dismantled the Soviet Union, Patrushev argued, the Americans arrogantly expanded NATO to the Russian borders and gulled Ukrainians into trusting that life would improve if they accepted the Western embrace. He called on people to learn a rudimentary fact, 'Without Russia, Ukraine simply won't be able to develop successfully.'[41]

A Security Council secretary who sees American conspiracies everywhere illustrates the crudity of official thinking about foreign policy. Patrushev's vision is an extreme variant of Putin's world view, and Putin plainly does not feel the need to disavow him, far less to sack him. Paranoia about 'enemies' at home and abroad is a characteristic of most members of the Putin team. Not that all of them share it. Kudrin continues to hold a candle for a more 'liberal' policy of engagement with America and for a less state-centred programme for the economy. But Kudrin lost the factional struggle in the Kremlin and the security lobby triumphed. Almost all the members of the Putin team are shock troops who are drilled exclusively in the tactics of forward movement. They are attackers. The positions of those in the front rank have undergone much rearrangement since Putin first occupied the presidency, including his own, when he stepped down to become prime minister in 2008. He continues to reshuffle and renew his key personnel.

Kudrin was exceptional in holding on to the Ministry of Finances for as long as eleven years, but though everyone in the vanguard has moved at some time from one post to another, the changes have seldom been convulsive. The firing of Kasyanov was one of the exceptions. Putin sticks by his frontline commanders and fosters an atmosphere of solidarity.

In 2005 Vladislav Surkov, serving as Deputy Chief of Staff in the Presidential Administration, put this with gusto in a speech to leading businessmen: 'We believe in the national elite. I emphasize the word "national".' He noted that Russian entrepreneurs travelled a lot abroad. He urged them to support Putin's objectives by becoming more than just an offshore aristocracy. He called for the creation of 'a new political class'. His desire was for politicians and businessmen to come together in ruling Russia for its own good. The geostrategic thinker Sergei Karaganov had put it in stark language in 2000: 'The country is in an impasse: if the ruling class doesn't find within itself the strength to carry society to a change in power and the model of development, Russia is doomed to decay and collapse.'[42] In the winter break of 2013–14, as regional governors and leading officials of United Russia prepared to enjoy themselves, they received an unexpected gift. Vyacheslav Volodin, then head of the Presidential Administration, had sent them books to read. Among them were Berdyaev's *The Philosophy of Inequality* and Ilin's *Our Tasks*.[43]

If a new political class is to emerge, it must acquire a collective sense of purpose. Surkov had expressed a sense of urgency for unity in action without pressing works of the intellect on fellow politicians. Times were changing, as Volodin's Christmas present showed. Fresh mortar had to be patched into the wall for Russia's rulers to feel confident about its solidity. The job is only half done and complacency is not in order.[44]

8. LIFE AT THE TOP: NO EMBARRASSMENT OF RICHES

The Kremlin has turned anti-Western discourse into the main ingredient of its ideology, served up as the country's staple fare while its leaders celebrate traditional values that are said to mark off Russia from the menacing, condescending, decadent West. Yet these same leaders are unable to resist the allure of the West themselves. This dichotomy took some years to be disclosed. After instigating the USSR's collapse, Boris Yeltsin avoided referring to 'the West' because he wanted Russia to be welcomed into a global community of states.[1] Along with his ministers and the new business elite, he even admired the Western style of life. But the political difficulties of securing approval saw Yeltsin's popularity dip, and he concluded that he should pay greater attention to national sensibilities. In the early 2000s Putin too stressed that Russia is a European country; but as relations with America deteriorated, this soon gave way to the habit of baiting the Western powers and condemning Western culture. Leading public figures talked up Russia's past, present and future.

Whatever they say in public, however, the dominant elite in politics and business retains its fondness for things foreign. The 'new Russians', whenever possible, deposit their income in Western banks in New York and London or in secretive offshore funds. Periodically the Russian government urged everyone to repatriate their money, and Putin looked askance at individuals choosing dual citizenship while working or living abroad. When the authorities in Cyprus offered a Cypriot passport to the billionaire Viktor Vekselberg, therefore, he turned it down: it was obvious to him that such a move would be deemed unpatriotic. His fellow billionaire Oleg Deripaska, though, apparently took the risk of accepting one.[2] Deripaska was taking a gamble, but he was a businessman and at least it was not against the law for businessmen to stash away their profits abroad. For ministers and state officials it was a different matter. From May 2013 it was forbidden for them, and even their spouses or under-age children, to hold overseas accounts or other financial instruments.[3] Putin wanted the money that members of his administration earned at home to stay at home. National economic development was the supreme goal.

Russian money, however, stayed abroad in huge quantities and was sheltered in the world's financial capitals, especially London. In the 1990s Cyprus supplanted Crimea as a favourite spot for sunny vacations, but soon the entire northern shore of the Mediterranean was full of rich Russian visitors. In the winter months whole Alpine villages become Russian resorts. Many of the richest Russians send their children to British private schools. They buy up sumptuous residences in Western capitals. Back in Russia they purchase limousines, internal décor for their dachas, haute couture and domestic IT appliances from suppliers in the West. The wealthiest of them fly Western rock stars such as Elton John to Moscow or the Black Sea coast to entertain them on their birthdays. Materialism lies deep in the ethos of rulers who oscillate between flaunting their wealth and concealing it. In April 2015 Putin himself declared an income equivalent to less than $120,000 and ownership of two modest apartments as well as a shared garage.[4] In April 2017 he claimed to have been paid a salary worth only $150,000 and to possess an apartment of 77 square metres, a plot of land covering 1,500 square metres, a garage and three cars, all of them of Russian manufacture.[5] The number and whereabouts of Putin's bank accounts still elude definitive scrutiny.

The leading liberal politician Boris Nemtsov exposed Putin's penchant for luxury, though, by pointing to the twenty palaces, villas and other official residences at his disposal – ten times as many as the American president. Nine of the palaces, moreover, have been built since 2000. The Novo-Ogarëvo 'dacha' is two storeys high and has saunas, an aviary, swimming pool, helipad and stables.[6] Nemtsov wrote also of the super-yacht *Sirius* and a Mercedes-Benz S600.[7] Though he could not accuse Putin of holding these items as personal property, he argued that he had made other illicit gains by exploiting the advantage of high office and that ordinary Russians were picking up the bill. Putin sports expensive watches, and photographers with powerful lenses have zoomed in on his Lange & Söhne Tourbograph timepiece. He also possesses a Blancpain, a Bréguet Marine and a Patek Philippe. None of these are state property. His watches are so luxurious that Russian newspapers have run articles on them.[8]

Nemtsov held back from alleging anything that he had not witnessed or could not verify through documents, but Sergei Koles-. nikov, who had worked with Putin in Leningrad in the 1990s, refused to stay quiet. On 21 December 2010 he wrote an open letter to President Medvedev alleging that Putin, at the time holding prime ministerial office, had been diverting state funds for the construction of a personal palace near the Black Sea at the tiny settlement of Praskoveevka in the Krasnodar region to the south-east of Crimea.[9] How was it, Kolesnikov asked, that Putin could afford such a project on his salary? He also queried why gas pipes and electricity cables had been laid to the palace at state expense. For Kolesnikov, who continued his charges in the Russian national press after Medvedev refrained from replying to his letter, this was an additional sign of gross corruption at the highest level.[10]

Kolesnikov claimed to have been present at a meeting with Putin at his country house outside Moscow when the issue of the Black Sea palace was raised directly, and recounted that the Russian president had ordered deputy prime minister Igor Sechin to deal with it. Soon afterwards, according to Kolesnikov, Sechin called him in for a discussion of the details. According to Kolesnikov, he had many other meetings where Mr Putin's instructions for fittings and furnishings were discussed with a senior FSB officer. More usually, he says, Putin passed on his preferences through his friend Nikolai Shamalov, Kolesnikov's business partner, who, Kolesnikov maintained, 'didn't seek to justify it: he considered that whatever the tsar decided, it wasn't our business to discuss it . . . There was a tsar – and there were slaves, who didn't have their own opinion.' All this remained secret until Kolesnikov, disgusted by the vast expenditure, broke off ties with Shamalov. 'I hadn't worked fifteen hours a day for ten years,' he exclaimed, 'to build a palace!'[11]

Kolesnikov added that the finances for all this had been channelled through Putin's project to provide Russian hospitals with new equipment, to which several Russian business leaders, including the oil, nickel and aluminium magnate (and Chelsea Football Club owner) Roman Abramovich, had made sizeable donations. Kolesnikov had imported the medical equipment and his company obtained large discounts on the supplies. Millions of dollars, he contended, were acquired in this fashion, with much of the saved cash ending up in offshore companies – without the donors' knowledge – for use in other projects. These allegedly included investments in some of Russia's

ailing industries such as shipbuilding – projects which Kolesnikov says
he discussed directly with Putin. A great proportion of the funds,
Kolesnikov recorded, was siphoned into 'Project South', the code name
for the palace outside Praskoveevka.

Putin's spokesman Dmitri Peskov was swift to reject the whole idea
that Putin had any connection with the project.[12] He said that Praskoveevka was owned by other unnamed individuals and that Kolesnikov
was conducting an outrageous attack on Putin's reputation – and in any
case the property was to be reported in 2011 as having been resold to
a reclusive billionaire, which bolstered Peskov's argument.[13]

No further evidence came to light to prove or disprove Kolesnikov's
original charges, and Peskov treated the matter as closed. This did not
stop the political opposition from continuing to condemn Putin for his
friendships with several super-rich businessmen. One of them is
Gennadi Timchenko, a Russian based in Finland since 1999,[14] who has
been close to Putin since his St Petersburg days and amassed a huge
fortune through his oil export activity. Other old friends who have
become extremely wealthy include Arkadi and Boris Rotenberg and
Yuri Kovalchuk. Whereas Putin's supporters saw nothing wrong for a
president to have a cordial relationship with entrepreneurs, his enemies
diagnosed an epidemic of corruption that enables cronies to gain privileged access to state-owned assets and make huge profits with no
special skills or effort. The suggestion is that they transmit a portion of
their winnings to Putin.[15] Each side argued that the other lacked the
necessary corroboration. But by 2014 the mutterings in the opposition
media had embarrassed Putin into making public defence of his
Petersburg chums. It was unfair to charge Timchenko, the Rotenberg
brothers or Kovalchuk with illegality, he argued, because they did not
make the bulk of their money in the crooked 1990s: each of them had
earned his money legally.[16]

This only confirmed suspicions that, if they were not super-wealthy
under Yeltsin, then it must have been Putin's patronage that enabled
their spectacular success. Putin's fondness for the life of the moneyed
elite was observed by US Ambassador Ronald Spogli, who in January
2009 wrote from Rome about the closeness between Italy's prime
minister Silvio Berlusconi and Putin. Berlusconi believed, according to
Italian acquaintances, that Putin was drawn towards him as a fellow
'tycoon'. Whenever they met, the two exchanged lavish gifts.[17] (After
falling from power and into disgrace, Berlusconi went on sending
Putin birthday presents – in 2017 a duvet with a photoprint of them

standing together.[18]) In 2003 Putin had taken his family on holiday to Berlusconi's private Sardinian villa, where his host shielded him from Russian reporter Natalya Melikova's questions about the rumours of an illicit affair. 'I don't hold with journalists who push their snotty nose into the private doings of other people,' Berlusconi said, mimicking firing a rifle.[19]

Some estimates put Putin's real assets at a staggering $40–50 billion, a figure that the Panama Papers published in 2016 appear to corroborate. But suspicion is not the same as proof – and Putin's spokesman Dmitri Peskov dismissed the accusations as tittle-tattle. Journalists have been more effective in tracing the source of wealth for his daughters Yekaterina and Maria.[20] As Moscow's opposition press has noted, many sons and daughters of Kremlin leaders can be found in cushy positions in big business, and it seldom seems that their entrepreneurial qualifications have got them there.[21] Their material success is typical of the new political elite that has featherbedded the next generation of their families. Yekaterina made the most of her father's contacts and became head of the National Intellectual Development Foundation. She and her partner possess a large residence in Biarritz overlooking the beach.[22] The current ruling group have joined a fledgling aristocracy without passing through a stage of mercantile endeavour, and expect to hand on their lifestyle and privileges to their offspring. They are the new upper class.

Navalny and his Fight against Corruption Foundation have also had greater success in chasing down the wealth accumulated by Putin's entourage, possibly through contacts in the Kremlin motivated by disgust, personal ambition or factional calculation. Using drone technology, activists made videos of the sumptuous residences that Security Council Secretary Patrushev and Prime Minister Medvedev were building for themselves. Navalny published the images online, starting with Patrushev's country palace. Pointing out that nothing in the FSB director's career had involved commerce, he asked where Patrushev and his wife had got the money for such a towering edifice.[23]

The Fight against Corruption Foundation also published evidence about Medvedev's multiple financial schemes. Navalny accused Medvedev of taking bribes and raising sweetheart loans from wealthy businessmen to buy his several palaces, yachts and vineyards around the country. To cap it all, volunteer investigators photographed what they called Medvedev's 'secret dacha', lying close to the secluded settlement of Plës in Kostroma province near the banks of the River Volga.

This was a fabulous mansion standing in grounds of two hundred acres on the old Milovka estate with a six-metre-high metal perimeter fence.[24] Though Medvedev could keep snoopers off his land, the drone photography revealed a luxurious estate including three helicopter pads, some swimming pools and a boating pier.[25] This time Navalny had gone too far. If he could finger Medvedev, he might be able to embarrass Putin. The authorities arrested twenty of the Foundation's employees, and seized papers and cash from its offices.[26]

But the Fight against Corruption Foundation survived. In 2018 it acquired the latest quadcopter drone and flew it over deputy prime minister Igor Shuvalov's palatial residence at Skolkovo outside Moscow. A wood screens the building from public view, and Shuvalov ensured that a new 'elite' apartment block was prohibited from having windows facing his property. As Navalny remarked, even Buckingham Palace and America's White House were visible from nearby.[27]

But towards such attacks the Kremlin has a hide of leather. Former Railways Minister Vladimir Yakunin exemplifies the insouciance:

> We created monsters during that era [of the 1990s]; and we fed them, too. They became fat and strong off Russia's flesh and blood. When today I hear how some officials in the Putin administration are being criticized for corruption, for having improperly obtained two million rubles, I want desperately to remind them that tens of trillions were stolen during the 1990s: 'appropriated' by the so-called Democrats and Liberals, shapeshifters who lauded the state one moment, and the next were demanding that it should be reformed out of existence. They were the men who were lionized in the West because by making all the right noises about introducing a market economy they were perceived to be behaving correctly.[28]

Yakunin, one of the Russian super-rich, was ignoring the main point. Rather than face up to the corruption in public life since the turn of the millennium, he targeted the scandals of privatizations in the Yeltsin period, and the West's approval of Yeltsin's financial management – when the Western press at the time had been full of reports on fraudulent insider dealing.

Waste and graft abounded during the preparations for the Sochi Winter Olympics. Nemtsov and his colleague Leonid Martynyuk produced a booklet attacking Yakunin, champion of the project, for having amassed a fortune from it. Putin's childhood friends Arkadi and

Boris Rotenberg were also accused of benefiting inordinately. The booklet queried the very rationale for holding an international skiing and skating tournament in a subtropical climate: 'There is no doubt that no one in Sochi plays ice hockey, goes skating or does figure skating. You can't name a single biathlon competitor, skier or figure skater who comes from Sochi.' Stadiums would predictably stand empty once the Olympics competitors departed. The permanent running costs of the infrastructure would remain huge. Harm to flora and fauna would be irreversible. Nemtsov and Martynyuk accused Putin of handing out juicy contracts to his friends and ignoring due procedure and the national interest.[29] Martynyuk was briefly arrested, and Yakunin issued a writ for three million rubles alleging defamation of the Russian Railways company that he ran.[30] Martynyuk fled to New York.

Putin loathes to be taken to task about high-level fraud. In November 2014 he shrugged off a finding by Transparency International, the global anti-bribery campaign organization, ranking Russia only 136th out of 170 countries in rooting out corruption, questioning whether the research was impartial. But he did not try to deny that Russia was riddled with corruption.[31]

On 15 June 2017 he grew tetchy with Danila Prilepa, a teenager who was in the TV audience for a live phone-in. Prilepa put up his hand: fraudulent 'bureaucrats and ministers in the country's government', he remarked, 'have not been a novelty for a long time', and the occasional showy arrests failed to result in practical improvement. Putin, he went on, was 'undermining the confidence of citizens'. The youngster's boldness caught the president off guard: 'Danila, you read out the question: did you prepare it earlier or did someone suggest it to you?' Putin was all but accusing the youngster of bad faith. But Danila kept his nerve: 'It was life itself that prepared me for this question.' At that point Putin realized that he was making a poor impression. At last he squeezed out a smile and whinnied, 'Well done, young fellow! [*Molodets!*]' before taking the heat out of the occasion by describing the various steps the authorities were taking to pursue wrongdoers.[32]

Prilepa had pulled off his coup by disguising his purposes until the last moment. He knew how the show's management did checks on audience members and telephone callers to prevent embarrassment for the president. He also was careful to avoid accusing Putin of personal corruption, only of being ineffective in rooting out corruption. He must have known that if he pressed any further his life could take a severe turn for the worse. But Prilepa was a hero for what he did.

He was not alone that day. The TV producers also failed to censor some of the text messages appearing at the bottom of the screen during Putin's Q&A. A flavour of the impertinent questions is given here:

> Putin, do you really think that the people fall for this circus with its planted questions?

> When are you going to go off and retire? Alexander Chulkov, Perm.

> Three terms of the presidency are enough!

> How much longer are we going to hear: 'There's no money but be patient.' Elena Valentinovna (pensioner).

> The whole of Russia thinks you've sat on 'the throne' too long.[33]

One texter strayed into counter-revolutionary territory, 'Why all this game of elections? A total waste of money and a thieving of the votes! Bring back the Tsar!' Whether this was genuine exasperation or a satirical jibe is unclear, but it was definitely an affront to presidential dignity.

Most of the other text messages, however, showed no hostility to Putin. There was even a query as to why the summer had been so cold. Apart from the lapse with Danila Prilepa, Putin had reason to feel pleased with a polished performance.

He tries to maintain the same environment for his leading associates. When in 2016 a reporter asked whether he approved of Igor Sechin, Rosneft's chairman and a former deputy prime minister, taking the *Vedomosti* newspaper to court for revealing the immense fortune he had acquired, including a residence of staggering opulence at Barvikha on Moscow's outskirts, Putin replied that the press should respect personal privacy and changed the subject. The court, however, found that Sechin's privacy had been invaded.[34] The sole consolation for *Vedomosti* was that its reporters got off with a light fine and Sechin's demand for damages was rejected.[35]

Putin pleaded for calm in discussing the verdict – a request authoritarian rulers often make when people are raising objections to authority – and implied his approval of its requirement for *Vedomosti* to destroy all copies of the offending edition and remove it from their website. For him, the important thing was for Kremlin leaders to be able to enjoy their assets safe from prying eyes.[36] Throughout the Putin years, the leadership could assume that wealth gained in office would remain untouchable.

There have been a few scandals, as when in 2002 the Railways Minister Nikolai Aksënenko had to resign, accepting moral responsibility for the widespread fraud under his aegis. But Aksënenko was someone who had been in post in Yeltsin's time – even considered as a candidate for the premiership. Putin was firing someone who did not belong to the new inner core. Even then, the Prosecutor-General refrained from taking Aksënenko to court: ministers caught committing some criminal offence faced nothing worse than being asked to quietly leave the building. By the time Aksënenko died in 2005 Putin had weeded out other ministers of undependable loyalty, and police and courts sat on their hands as his appointees continued to amass personal fortunes. When the judicial system did come into play, it was because the decision had been taken in the Kremlin. When the net was spread out to trawl for dishonest officials, it caught only the small fry. Procurator-General Yuri Chaika shamefully admitted that even when fines were imposed, they were rarely collected: only a thousandth was paid of what was owed.[37]

In 2012 the press got wind that Defence Minister Anatoli Serdyukov had been caught filching from the public purse, after a raid by Investigative Committee police on the apartment of Serdyukov's mistress Yevgenia Vasileva, who was a director of the Oboronservis company that managed real estate properties for the Defence Ministry. Serdyukov was caught there in his dressing gown. Vasileva and others were charged with having siphoned off $100 million to bribe state officials and fund a lavish lifestyle for themselves. Although Serdyukov was fired from his post, he continued to benefit from his close connection with Putin's St Petersburg friends: in late 2013 Putin revealed that Serdyukov would not face criminal charges. 'Well, what of it?' he added. 'Are we now saying that he doesn't have the right of employment anywhere?'[38] Medvedev went further, stressing that Serdyukov had been 'rather effective' as Defence Minister. Serdyukov felt safe to ignore the Investigative Committee's inquiries.[39]

But in November 2016 Oleg Feoktistov of the FSB sensationally organized the arrest of Minister of Economic Development Alexei Ulyukaev on a charge of bribery. Feoktistov led the Sixth Directorate responsible for inquiries into high-level corruption.[40]

The move would never have been made but for the brute insistence of Igor Sechin, Putin's veteran associate who ran the Rosneft oil company. Sechin arranged with Feoktistov to set up a 'sting' at a meeting with Ulyukaev in Rosneft's Moscow offices. Sechin handed over a package worth \$2 million, it was alleged, which Ulyukaev greedily accepted as the agreed bribe in return for ministerial approval of Rosneft's purchase of the huge Bashneft oil company. When Ulyukaev stepped outside for his waiting car, FSB officers took him into custody. Under interrogation, Ulyukaev protested his innocence, contending that he thought that Sechin had been handing him a present of wine or sausages.[41] Kremlin politics are played for high stakes, and campaigns against corruption are often a masquerade for cliques in public life to mount covert attacks on each other[42] – the ruling group fight among themselves like cats and dogs for influence. But Ulyukaev's subordinates could not believe he would have been stupid enough to extort a bribe from one of his inveterate enemies.[43]

Sechin was a ferocious political beast who had already played it rough over the question of Bashneft's ownership. In 2014 he had brought a money-laundering case against the billionaire Vladimir Yevtushenkov, whose real 'crime' was his refusal to sell Bashneft to Rosneft. Yevtushenkov was put under house arrest, and Bashneft was taken out of his control, even though the Moscow arbitration court found the criminal charges against him had no validity.[44] Ulyukaev was Sechin's next target. As Minister of Economic Development he had held up Rosneft's acquisition of Bashneft, and Sechin was angry and impatient for resolution in his own favour.

Sechin's motive was political as well as commercial. For years he had advocated state economic control, while Ulyukaev, a trained economist who had spent the late 1990s criticizing the stalling of reforms, proposed further liberalization.[45] He had been one of the leading members of Russia's Democratic Choice, a party led by the liberal former acting prime minister Yegor Gaidar. Sechin hated liberals and quasi-liberals; he also fought ruthlessly anyone who got in the way of his commercial interests. Everyone in the cabinet knew what he was like. But Ulyukaev was said to be no saint either. It was complained that his annual income of over \$1 million vastly exceeded his governmental salary, and that he ran an illegal offshore bank account through other family members.[46] But this formed no part of the court case, which was about Ulyukaev's behaviour that day in the Rosneft offices: with his long experience of the wiles of Russian public life, was Ulyukaev likely to have grubbed a kickback from someone like Sechin?

Whatever the truth of the matter, Ulyukaev's arrest left several other members of the uppermost elite feeling uncomfortable. If he could disappear into custody, who might be next? Evidently there were those who grumbled about the way things had been handled: when in August 2017 Feoktistov was fired, there was speculation that the Kremlin had slackened its determination to act against financial wrongdoing at the highest level.

But Ulyukaev still had to answer the accusation against him in open court. There had been nothing like this in Putin's entire period in power: for the first time a high-ranking member of the Kremlin elite was being hauled before judges instead of being permitted to resign with minimal fuss. As the start of judicial proceedings approached, Putin apparently asked Sechin to arrange an 'amicable' settlement.[47] Usually people did as the president bade them, but Sechin wanted total victory, and pressed for a judicial verdict. Having sent in his written testimony, however, he quixotically called for the wheels of justice to roll onward in his absence, replying to three successive summonses that his Rosneft duties demanded uninterrupted attention. It was as though it was beneath his dignity to submit to cross-examination – a grandiosity that came naturally to someone who considered himself exempt from the obligations of mere citizens.

The court case came to a sudden end on 15 December 2017 when Ulyukaev was found guilty and sentenced to nine years in a penal colony. The verdict seemed to come as a complete shock to him. Disquiet was voiced as to whether justice had been done. 'Terrible, unjustified verdict,'[48] tweeted ex-Finance Minister Kudrin. Although Kudrin did not mention Sechin by name, during Kudrin's tenure at the Finance Ministry there had been no love lost between them. In 2014, three years after Kudrin had to leave office, Sechin still had it in for him, accusing 'the Navalnys, Nemtsovs and Kudrins' of acting as agents provocateurs against the interests of the Russian economy.[49] Whereas Ulyukaev had paid a heavy price for being a vulnerable economic liberal, Kudrin remained the president's friend and adviser, while Putin's other great friend Sechin, had been permitted to devour the lesser prey, Ulyukaev. The affair had implications far outside the courtroom: in its war of attrition against the champions of private enterprise the state-power lobby had won another battle.

But for once Putin voiced criticism of Sechin.[50] This was unusual, since he prefers to keep his disagreements in house. Sechin had thwarted his efforts to keep the settlement of disputes inside the ruling elite. The growing trend was for courts, not only in Moscow but also in London, to replace the violent spats that had marred the conduct of commercial business in Yeltsin's time. Putin had also seen the Ulyukaev case as a chance to persuade the Russian people that the authorities were entrenching the rule of law. But Sechin's antics had shown that at least one member of the inner elite could still treat due legal process with disdain and behave as if the rules were for others. Judicial progress in Russia had a long way to go.

9. ECONOMIC FIST OF STATE: HOLDING THE 'OLIGARCHS' TO ACCOUNT

Putin is the luckiest of Russian rulers. In his wildest dreams he could not have had a better year than 2000 to enter the presidency. From the mid-1980s until almost the end of the century, the global price for hydrocarbons had been in uninterrupted fall. Gorbachëv came to power when oil prices started to collapse; Yeltsin had to cope with inadequate fiscal returns from the export trade. In mid-1999, exactly when Putin became prime minister, the trend went into reverse and continued upwards through to mid-2014, and providence blessed Putin with a buoyant budget.

He had watched with disgust how under Yeltsin the leaders of Russian big business had tried to redraw the contours of politics. He and his supporters had no intention of suffering the same indignity. In July 2000, two months after the presidential inauguration ceremony, he invited nearly two dozen business leaders to the Kremlin. Seated at a vast round table, he started calmly. For a few minutes some of those gathered were deluded into thinking he wanted to treat them as his equals. But the dry, matter-of-fact delivery and the frequent pauses soon signalled something less friendly. The atmosphere turned icy. When Putin wanted to emphasize a point, he lowered his eyelids or pursed his lips. His phlegmatic gestures showed he was in no hurry. State interests, he announced, would regain the priority they had lost after 1996, when Yeltsin had had to allow the 'oligarchs' control of large swathes of Russia's natural resources in return for their support in the presidential campaign. Putin was getting his audience to realize that he would brook no defiance. He was the master in his new house.[1]

There had been plenty of hints of Putin's intentions in his dissertation at the St Petersburg Mining Institute in 1997, and in his reports as FSB director in 1998–9.[2] His first prime minister, Kasyanov, was firmly in favour, and Kudrin at the Finance Ministry had long believed that the only way to establish a dynamic market economy was by strengthening the powers of central government. He had said as much in the late 1990s, at a time when businessmen like Berezovski were rampaging through public life.[3]

Putin had no intention of renationalizing the economy. He understood the necessity of encouraging private enterprise if Russia was going to recover its position as a world power. But the business tycoons had to know their place. They also had to pay their taxes. If he was to bring stability and efficiency to the country's governance, he needed a larger and more dependable stream of revenues than was available when the average Russian tycoon thought fiscal obligations were something that only applied to others.

After the humbling of Gusinski, Berezovski and Khodorkovski in 2000–4,[4] everyone knew the rules of the game had changed. This, Putin argued, was all for the benefit of the Russian people. Taxes raised meant welfare expanded, and businessmen had to be brought down to earth so the government could secure its finances. When he criticized the tycoons of trade and banking, he always had particular individuals in his sights. Not once did he focus on his own appointees, such as Sechin at Rosneft or Miller at Gazprom: Rosneft and Gazprom lie inside regular state control, and their leading personnel can be replaced at his whim (as indeed happened to Yakunin at Russian Railways in 2015). Independent entrepreneurs, however, are fair game. They operate in an economy where they depend on Putin and his ministers to approve their licences and dole out contracts. Their autonomy from government is only partial. When the Kremlin finds fault with some particular deal the business concerned can soon become the butt of political anger.

An example of this came in 2009 when, as prime minister, Putin toured a derelict factory in Pikalëvo, 160 miles west of St Petersburg, in the company of businessman Oleg Deripaska, who controlled the shares of the conglomerate that owned it. Mass lay-offs had devastated life in the town, and the protests caused a traffic jam that stretched over 250 miles. Putin assured everyone that he understood their feelings. With the TV cameras on him, he turned on Deripaska. Why, he demanded, had the regional authorities failed to make the necessary investment? He ordered Deripaska to sign an agreement on the spot to resume production – here was a contract already prepared. Deripaska signed, but Putin pretended he could not see the signature. Deripaska wrote out his name again. 'Give me my pen back,' muttered Putin. The Russian TV news channels broadcast the whole spectacle.

Whether it led to an improvement in the local economy is doubtful, and there is little sign that Deripaska stumped up the promised funds, even though he continued to enjoy a close association with Putin and other Kremlin leaders. The little drama at Pikalëvo had been arranged merely to propagate the image of Putin as the protector of ordinary employees.[5]

The handling of Deripaska was mild in comparison to the fate of American businessman and investor Bill Browder. As the chairman of Hermitage Capital, Browder had famously overseen the largest inflow of foreign funds into the Russian economy. But in so doing he fell foul in 2007 of those in the ruling elite who resented his success in their country and retaliated by levelling tax-evasion charges against him. Their aim was also to get hold of the Russian assets he had accumulated. Browder, however, was made of strong stuff: his grandfather Earl had led the Communist Party of the USA before Stalin removed him, and mental toughness had been handed down through the generations. Most of Russia's successful businessmen had exploited loopholes in fiscal legislation, and Browder was reputedly no different.[6] He had reason to feel that he was being singled out for persecution: until then he had been known as a supporter of Putin's leadership – had never criticized his policies. In 2003–5 he had even endorsed the chasing down of Khodorkovski, seeming to accept, like others, that the Russian authorities were genuinely interested in comprehensive reform of Russian business governance.[7]

Browder saw things differently when influential Russians turned the heat on him. Rather than submit to legal threats, and rolling over to accept a dent in his finances, he fought back through the courts, even Russian courts.

In 2008 the police arrested Browder's lawyer, Sergei Magnitski. Browder's protests – by then he was working abroad – made no difference. Magnitski was held in Moscow's Butyrki prison, where he was denied adequate medical attention for gall stones, pancreatitis and a blocked gall bladder. After nearly a year of maltreatment he died an agonizing death. A Kremlin-appointed human rights council confirmed he had experienced physical assault. An indignant Browder lobbied Washington for sanctions against those Russian officials regarded as complicit in bringing the case against his lawyer. In late 2012 President Obama signed into law the Magnitsky Act, which blackballed them from entering the United States or using the American banking system.[8] In Russia, the powerful figures with links to Russian government and policing agencies continued to enjoy their victory over Browder and to blacken the name of Magnitski. Indeed, in 2013 there was a bizarre trial of the deceased Magnitski, which revived a gruesome ancient precedent. The result was never in doubt: Magnitski was found guilty of tax evasion. At a further trial, Browder was sentenced in absentia to nine years' imprisonment.[9] He had already lost millions of dollars through the collapse of Hermitage Capital. But the Russian authorities, who were striving to encourage foreigners to invest their funds in the country, suffered greater long-term damage when potential investors drew the conclusion that Russia was no longer a safe bet.[10]

Like Browder, businessman Boris Berezovski stayed away from Russia and never ceased to publicize the iniquities of Russian governance. In 2003 Berezovski received political asylum in the United Kingdom. Seldom questioned in the 1990s about his own business ethics, he appeared frequently on BBC news programmes and at British student gatherings to denounce Putin as the devil incarnate. He also financed anti-Kremlin activity in the former USSR. To Putin's annoyance, he intervened in Ukrainian politics by making funds available to the Opposition that in 2004 won the so-called 'Orange Revolution' in Kyiv and elevated to the presidency Viktor Yushchenko, who had campaigned to free the country from subordination to Russia. Berezovski, still a rich man, bought tapes that threw suspicion on Putin for meddling improperly in Ukrainian affairs, and released them for public attention.[11] He also gave Alexander Litvinenko – a Russian former intelligence officer who fled Russia in 1999 after accusing Putin of illegal activity when FSB director – financial support that enabled him to live comfortably in north London and send his young son to a prestigious private school.

'We need to use force to change this regime,' Berezovski told the Guardian newspaper in 2007. 'It isn't possible to change this regime through democratic means. There can be no change without force, pressure.'[12] When asked whether he was fomenting revolution in Russia, he replied, 'You are absolutely correct.' Pressed to describe the measures he was taking, Berezovski went on, 'If one part of the political elite disagrees with another part of the political elite – that is the only way in Russia to change the regime. I try to move that.' He refused to give the names of his contacts, explaining that they would be murdered if identified. Berezovski insisted that he was providing his 'experience and ideology' to people in the political elite and advising on 'my understanding of how it could be done', adding, 'There are also practical steps which I am doing now, and mostly it is financial.'[13] This bombast – there is no sign that he was in touch with the elite's members – could only invite trouble from Moscow. Already a marked man, Berezovski stood in plain view and dared the Kremlin's rulers to come after him.

In 2011 Berezovski started proceedings in London's High Court to demand restitution of the money he'd lost through the forced sale of his main Russian companies to Roman Abramovich. Abramovich offered Berezovski a large settlement out of court, but Berezovski had resolved to regain all he had surrendered. His case now rested on the allegation that it had been Abramovich, not Putin, who had been the prime mover in forcing him to sell up his assets in Russia at knock-down prices. This represented a complete about-turn: until then Berezovski had ranted against Putin's diabolical powers; now he was suddenly alleging that Putin had been putty in Abramovich's hands.

Berezovski behaved as though winning over any British judge would be as easy as obtaining asylum from the Home Secretary. His confidence was unquenchable: unlike Abramovich, he insisted on speaking in English in court, which put him at a disadvantage under cross-examination and prevented him putting his case with complete lucidity. The mid-morning breaks saw him more intent on swaggering round the foyer than on focusing on how to present a solid argument; he seemed to enjoy sitting alongside his Chechen bodyguards and glowering at hostile witnesses.[14] The contrast with Abramovich, who had let his lawyers prep him about how to behave in court, was marked. Abramovich answered the questions put to him without prevarication.

These were high-stakes proceedings. Putin's former Chief of Staff, Alexander Voloshin, came to the United Kingdom to testify on Abram-ovich's behalf. Voloshin was a busy man who had become a director of Yandex and sundry other large Russian companies after leaving the Presidential Administration: his appearance at the High Court was a sign of Putin's determination to trounce his leading enemy abroad.

While the case rumbled slowly to its conclusion, Berezovski continued his political offensive. In January 2012 he sent a letter to Patriarch Kirill of the Russian Orthodox Church. 'Help Putin come to his senses,' it pleaded. 'Deliver the voice of the people to him. And when Putin hears you, take power out of his hands and hand it over to the people peacefully, wisely and in a Christian fashion.' This was the product of a mind that had lost touch with the realities of public life in Russia. The patriarch ignored the request.[15]

As well as the vacuous claim that power in the Kremlin after Yeltsin's retirement lay not with Putin but the businessman Abramovich, Berezovski had also accused Abramovich of swindling him in business deals, but he had no proof because, even in his own version of events, the deals in question had been done verbally. In court, he had made a bad case worse, frequently contradicting himself and making allegations that were easy to refute. In August that year Judge Elizabeth Gloster found against Berezovski.

Having failed to prepare himself for the possibility of defeat, he walked from court in a state of shock. 'I'm absolutely amazed what happened today,' he explained outside on the pavement. 'I'm surprised completely.' His voice ringing with resentment, he told reporters, 'Sometimes I had the impression Putin himself wrote this judgment.' With that he sped off in his chauffeur-driven limousine, which had often been seen illegally parked while the case had been going on.[16] Now he faced the ruinous costs of the whole trial. As his money ran out, so did his verve. Concluding that his public career was over, he wrote three miserable letters to Putin in which he admitted his mistakes and sought permission to return home.[17]

In March 2013 Berezovski was found hanging by his belt in the bathroom of his Ascot residence in the Surrey countryside. The inquest recorded an open verdict. Some of his friends doubted it was suicide. But if it was a hit job, no clues appeared as to the killer's identity or paymaster.

Now only Khodorkovski remained of the 1990s business tycoons who continued to oppose Putin from abroad, Gusinski having become politically inactive. Khodorkovski, settled in western Europe following his release from Siberian captivity in December 2013, did win a court ruling in The Hague for the restoration of $50 billion to himself and other Yukos oil company shareholders, but this was turned down on appeal. He remained wealthy enough to subsidize the Open Russia Foundation to promote the cause of freedom for Russia.

With Khodorkovski never achieving Berezovski's international impact, Putin seemed to have confirmed his reputation as the 'terror of the oligarchs'. But this was only half true. The term had been repurposed from its dictionary definition of someone belonging to a small ruling group and now characterized any big businessman of Russian nationality. While Putin had cut down Gusinski, Berezovski and

Khodorkovski, it was never his ambition to remove all the many super-rich entrepreneurs from Russian public life. In fact he encouraged them to play a part in it. Some, with Putin's assent, became members of the Federation Assembly, and Roman Abramovich was elected governor of Chukotka in eastern Siberia.[18] Putin was not against opulent entrepreneurs, only those who challenged the ruling group's authority and policies. Owners and directors of the great companies could enjoy their superflux of income, and so could cabinet ministers.

Indeed, they were frequently found side by side. In February 2018 an opposition video featuring Alexei Navalny included the Instagram account and memoirs of 'sex guru' Nastya Rybka (real name Anastasia Vashukevich), who had surreptitiously filmed her experiences on a yachting trip to Norway two years earlier. Along with other young women, she had been paid to spend time on board. Rybka videoed businessman Oleg Deripaska on his yacht – the same Deripaska who had been the butt of Putin's staged anger in Pikalëvo – as he sat on deck talking with deputy prime minister Sergei Prikhodko.[19] This shaming material was compounded by a drone flight over an estate outside Moscow where Prikhodko, despite having held posts in government at far from enormous salaries, was shown as possessing a mansion of 1,540 square metres, as well as sumptuous apartments in the capital. Nor was it easy to explain, noted Navalny, how Prikhodko's wife had accumulated so much money and property, unless Prikhodko was on the take from businessmen like Deripaska.[20]

Since Putin had, as prime minister in 1999, demanded the resignation of Prosecutor-General Yuri Skuratov after a video showing him engaging in illicit sexual intercourse, Navalny asked why no action was being taken against Prikhodko.[21] Both Deripaska and Prikhodko meanwhile issued robust denials of all the allegations made against them.[22]

The controversy died away. Navalny had never truly imagined that his campaign would succeed. He knew that Russia's economy at its commanding heights operates in a framework of state capitalism. This means that no great corporation can flourish without active political support. Private companies and state-owned or state-controlled companies coexist and both kinds have to maintain good relations with the government – and if that fails, then with Putin. Deripaska is a billionaire entrepreneur who knows how to stay in official favour. The rivalries between privateers like Deripaska and statists like Sechin turn to unity, in any case, when it comes to what they consider is their right to cream off huge personal incomes from their businesses. And while Putin prefers them to keep their fortunes invested in Russia, he has to make it worth their while. When state contracts are on offer, therefore, they expect and receive first bite at the cherry.

Their place in the queue was inadvertently made more secure by the West tightening economic sanctions on Russia, deepening the country's dependence on native capital. To that extent Putin was not just the giver of orders and dispenser of job appointments: the economy relied on the willingness of 'oligarchs' – the old compliant ones and the new ones he had promoted – to help him make Russia great.

It is a paradox that while Putin is master of Russia and can cull the herd whenever one of its bulls snorts at him, his political fortunes are linked to the country's prosperity. As yet the Russian people have accepted their fate under Putin with remarkable quiescence, but Putin and his ministers cannot take the situation for granted, and though he can humiliate Deripaska, as he did in 2009, his own prospects are entwined with the degree of consent he can obtain from him and the other billionaires. This is the price of his apparent autocracy, and he has never been unwilling to pay it. He needs the 'oligarchs' just as much as they need him. Putin understands which side his bread is buttered.

10. START AND STOP REFORMS: PERKS FOR THE FEW, COSTS FOR THE MANY

Putin has always known that history will judge his long period of rule by the extent to which Russia modernizes its economy. A constantly stated goal, it must nevertheless not conflict with his geopolitical strategy. Initially, when Russia and America were cooperating, he endorsed a wide-ranging programme of reforms that had proved beyond Yeltsin's capacity to enact. Putin and Kasyanov, his first prime minister, committed themselves to overdue measures of fiscal reform, judicial reform, agrarian reform, pension reform, banking reform, tariff reform, housing reform, natural-monopolies reform – and it was Kasyanov's job to oversee their passage through the State Duma and their implementation.[1]

Both knew this to be a Herculean task. It was all very well to snatch back control of those natural resources grabbed by Berezovski and other private entrepreneurs. The greater task was to create an advanced economy. Most Soviet scientific institutes and nearly all factories had for decades been uncompetitive on the global stage, and Yeltsin had involuntarily officiated over Russia's de-industrialization. As America's Silicon Valley invented and diffused its products of information technology, the Russian economy became an avid purchaser. Russia had trouble in becoming a producer, far less an exporter, even of sophisticated manufactured goods. The advanced capitalist countries, which now included some in east and south-east Asia regarded until recently as 'underdeveloped', were now pulling ahead.

Kasyanov kept the floodgates unlocked for as long as he enjoyed the president's approval and support, and together they set about implementing change sector by sector. Although the Constitution of 1993 guaranteed the right of private ownership of land, Yeltsin had proved unable to get the State Duma's approval for a full legal enactment. Putin and Kasyanov picked up the baton and, despite rancorous debate in the Duma, secured assent to a Land Code.[2] Kasyanov also secured the passage of a new Labour Code: it was not perfect, but nevertheless replaced the many obsolete laws of the communist era.[3] The reform of the pensions system, another contentious matter, Kasyanov resolved by drawing together the leaders of all parties of both houses of the Federal Assembly to produce an agreed national scheme to reduce people's dependence upon the state.[4]

In 2001 the government introduced a flat rate of income tax of 13 per cent, lowering corporation tax from 35 to 24 per cent, and lightening taxes on small businesses, too – all on the basis that a lighter fiscal load would make individuals and companies more amenable to cooperation with the authorities.[5] A consolidated new fiscal law was introduced in December 2003 and applied retrospectively against Mikhail Khodorkovski's companies. Kasyanov himself saw this involved some unfairness, perhaps even illegality, but the higher goal was to achieve a stable, predictable fiscal framework for business and government, which justified overruling Khodorkovski's protests.[6] Khodorkovski's arrest delivered sharp proof that the political leadership's patience had run out. Tax receipts swelled as Russia's corporations, who until then had customarily minimized their fiscal contributions, accepted the new regime, the petrochemical giants Sibneft and Lukoil leading the way. The revenues that accrued to the Finance Ministry allowed the government to manage its finances with more assurance.[7]

The scope of economic reform widened as Putin and Kasyanov looked at the Russian budget's heavy reliance on oil and gas exports, a degree of dependency, advisers argued, that was no way to secure the status of a great power. In sketching out his own perspective, Putin used uncharacteristically abstract language:

> Of course, the most important task is to shift our economy on to an innovative path of development. It's not a simple matter to do this even with high energy prices, when in general it's easier to achieve a positive result. It's difficult enough to switch the basic monetary flows to that sector because that requires the creation of the most favourable conditions for the development of the processing branches of production.[8]

He and his fellow rulers have assimilated the truism that any country aspiring to modernity has to do more than offer for sale what can be physically mined from its territory. They know that Russia must develop a strong base in advanced civilian technology.

Talking up Russia is Putin's passion. He now contends that the Russian IT industry has become globally competitive in the production of software, and is gaining strength in the hardware sector.[9] Whether it has done more than supply the country's Defence Ministry, however, is doubtful. Putin was more convincing when he sounded an alarm:

> As regards the fact that we have exhausted the opportunities for extensive growth in connection with high energy prices – that is also true . . . It is not just a question of high prices for oil. Favourable or unfavourable external conditions still depend on the state of our partners' economies. For example, oil prices might be high, but those of metals can fall because there is reduced demand for metals on the world market. And this is a very fundamental factor that triggers a whole chain reaction. The demand for coal falls and so on. A smaller volume of goods is conveyed, the transport sector begins to suffer – there is a whole chain that is involved. External economic factors therefore for the moment remain favourable, but already they also cannot be said to be completely favourable.[10]

He was speaking in 2013; just over a year later the prices for oil and gas plummeted, and the Russian budget went into a downward spiral.

Economic reformers have had posts in all Putin's cabinets, but had to fight their corner against ministers speaking for the military and security lobbies. Putin held the ring. When dispute appeared intractable, he stepped in to adjudicate, and sometimes was willing to annoy the champions of state intervention.[11] The marketeers, known to their enemies as neo-liberals, argued the case for reducing political interference in the economy, enhancing the rule of law and improving conditions for start-up businesses; the interventionists recalled the havoc that overmighty entrepreneurs had wreaked during the Yeltsin presidency. Marketeers, moreover, have a reputation for never having got their hands dirty with real work, whereas interventionists are regarded as overzealous practitioners of the command style of administration. Both claim to have the interests of the Russian people at heart. The lobbyists for private enterprise can point to the personal greed displayed by the advocates of state ownership and control; their opponents accuse the leading businessman Anatoli Chubais, a frequent spokesman for the private sector, of a callous attitude to the Russian poor.[12]

Victory has increasingly accrued to the statist lobby, but the struggle goes on. Even after being forced out of the cabinet in

September 2011, former Finance Minister Kudrin continued to canvass for his alternative strategy. In April 2013 he took part from the floor in Putin's 'Direct Line' TV programme, issuing a warning that the continuing rise in wage levels lessened scope for the overdue turnaround in the economy. In Kudrin's opinion, there was a need for labour productivity to grow at a faster rate than wages and salaries. Putin rejected this argument, describing Kudrin as having been the finest Finance Minister but not the best minister on social questions.

'You know,' Kudrin retorted, 'I worked for a long time as the deputy prime minister and was responsible for the economy, but today's system of half-measures and half-reforms is not going to work and Russia won't break free from its oil dependence.'[13] He cautioned Putin against ignoring what both of them knew: that future economic success depended upon reducing the size of the state sector and liberating entrepreneurial initiative. That Putin has even allowed Kudrin to debate with him in this manner is a sign he is aware that state capitalism alone is too narrow a foundation.

Putin remained keen to decouple the Russian people from social welfare benefits in public transport, medicine, housing and utilities: he is almost American in his zeal to foster individual self-reliance. Under communism there was a system of universal material support, even though in comparison with advanced Western economies the USSR had a low standard of living. Putin followed Yeltsin in setting out to replace subsidies for utilities with monetary grants, though only cautiously, since the new grants were smaller than the subsidies. Ministers tried to accustom the electorate to reduced expectations of state welfare, aiming to make the Russian people less reliant on handouts and more self-supporting.[14]

Several benefits and entitlements inherited from the Soviet decades and maintained under Yeltsin had remained either free of charge or at heavily discounted rates, but on 1 January 2005 the government introduced further cuts, hitting certain groups in society hard: pensioners, veterans, the disabled, single parents and orphans. To ease the transition, the government offered financial compensation. The snag was that the new payments would be delayed for a month and fall short of the value of the welfare benefits that had been abolished. Street protests by pensioners turned into the biggest against Putin since the 2000 presidential election. Elderly bus and tram passengers were reported as having come to blows with drivers who, in line with the new rules, insisted on payment of fares. Roads were blocked by irate citizens of pensionable age; their actions spread to eighty out of Russia's eighty-five regions. Putin was receiving a lesson in the limits of his authority. He dealt with the embarrassment by blaming the government for misjudging how to implement the measure. Ministers introduced adjustments, and the police were instructed to avoid excessive force when dispersing the crowds; business moguls were easier to confront than an angry mob of the retired poor.[15]

The debacle pushed Putin in September 2005 to proclaim four new 'national programmes' in housing, social welfare, agriculture and health care, to be overseen by Medvedev, first deputy prime minister at the time. The idea was to assure the electorate that the authorities still had its interests at heart. Acknowledging that overzealous economic liberalization held dangers for war pensioners, Putin promised to tread softly in moving away from the old benefit system. He rejected the advice from Kudrin:

> We disputed about this for a long time, and I told him, 'Alexei, you won't be able to do this right and it won't work out.' He said, 'No, we'll succeed.' We know what came of this. We had to pour out money to deal with the problems and shoulder great socio-political expense. To be frank, I had thought this would be the outcome. But really, if we had done nothing about it, public transport would surely have come to a halt in several regions because the number of people using subsidized tickets in several regions is much greater than the number of people who paid the full fare . . . . But why am I saying this? Because tough action in the economic sphere regardless of consequences in the social sphere isn't always justified, especially in our country, where our citizens' incomes are still very modest.[16]

This was the president speaking as Father of the Nation.

But Putin had not forgotten the advice Kudrin had given him. When he tried to tempt him back into the government, Kudrin refused, unless Putin changed economic strategy. 'He's a butterfly,' joked Putin. 'He doesn't want to work. As soon as he feels things getting heavy, he spreads his wings.'

Kudrin hit back:

> Today we do not have a programme for freeing our economy from its dependence on oil, a programme where we would put everything in its due place in proper measure: money, institutional and structural reforms and the role of the regions. That's the

problem, Vladimir Vladimirovich. I am not ready to oversee other, inertial processes and manual administration. I want to be involved with real work.[17]

No longer a minister, but still a friend of the president and member of the uppermost elite, he felt free to speak his mind.

Together they had achieved much, both during Kasyanov's premiership and afterwards. Kudrin and Kasyanov had convinced Putin to take a long view on Russian policy. Economic Development and Trade Minister German Gref drew up a strategic plan through to 2010 and beyond. All of them agreed to prioritize paying off the enormous foreign loans contracted by the USSR and then the Russian Federation in the last two decades of the twentieth century, to free future generations from the financial burden that Gorbachëv and Yeltsin had left behind. Capital and interest would be paid off expeditiously, and eventually the rise in revenues from gas and oil exports made this possible. The important thing was to lay the groundwork for an accelerated regeneration of the economy that would end Russian dependence on foreign powers and banking groups. No longer, resolved Putin and his ministers, would they have to go cap in hand to the International Monetary Fund.[18]

At the same time they wanted to deepen Russia's integration in the world economy. Talks went on during Putin's first presidential term for entry into the World Trade Organization, which Kasyanov and Kudrin reasoned would lower the tariff barriers to Russian exporters. Progress was slowed by Russia's desire to protect its producers from being overwhelmed by a tidal wave of imports. By 2006, satisfactory terms appeared in sight, but important details proved intractable. When in 2008 there was a global financial downturn, Russian politicians expressed relief that Russia was not more integrated in worldwide commerce after all. 'We tried with all our heart to get into the World Trade Organization,' Putin told European Commission president Juan Manuel Barroso a year later, 'but fortunately you refused us admission.'[19] Nevertheless the economic liberals in the Russian ruling group did not give up. In 2012 Russia entered the World Trade Organization as its 156th member.[20]

This was achieved despite strong opposition from the Russian agricultural sector. Agriculture itself was undergoing a transformation, as government policy changed to promote large-scale farming. State credits and tax reliefs were provided, leading to a drastic surge in cereal production as commercial and financial interests got involved. For the biggest of the cereal producers, the World Trade Organization offered the prospect of low customs dues abroad and higher profits. Russia's dependence on foreign wheat was reversed, and the country rose to become one of the world's leading exporters.[21] Even foreign direct investment began to flow into the countryside. Dairy and vegetable farmers, however, were terrified by the prospect of foreign imports. Their representations were ignored.

So, too, were those of Russian manufacturing. Putin had set himself the goal of integration in the world economy, and fobbed off those – including Sergei Glazev, who became his official economic adviser in 2012 – who called for protectionist policies until such time as Russia could see off the international competition.[22]

In the early 2000s Kasyanov and Kudrin fended off calls to expand the military budget, pushing instead – Kudrin's legacy as Minister of Finances – the idea of putting aside an ample portion of the growing oil and gas revenues into a Stabilization Fund. The idea was to copy other oil-producing countries like Saudi Arabia and Norway, which had established sovereign wealth funds to invest in foreign securities. High oil and gas prices, went Kudrin's thinking, could not be a permanent phenomenon, and he persuaded Putin to make savings in the current good years to prepare for the inevitable downturn. After paying off Russia's external debts, he wanted to prepare for the future. The Finance Ministry favoured US Treasury bonds, which gave guaranteed revenues, over the risk of buying shares in American corporations.[23] And if ever hydrocarbon sales tailed off again this Russian sovereign wealth fund would be an invaluable asset. This was a project for the restoration of national pride as well as a bulwark against the vagaries of world markets.

The policy outlasted the Kasyanov premiership and stayed intact through to 2007–8, when the global economic recession hit Russia. A malaise that had started with ill-considered schemes for house purchases in the United States had damaging consequences for the global financial system. There was nothing the Russian government could do to avoid an infection that now swept round the world. Companies, directors and employees were blighted. Putin and Medvedev alleviated the crisis by reaching into the sovereign wealth fund. For them, this was one of those emergencies for which it had been devised. Step by step they reduced the size of Kudrin's cherished legacy. In February 2008 Kudrin divided it into a Reserve Fund and a National Well-Being

Fund.[24] Whereas the Reserve Fund of $125 billion had been invested in low-risk foreign securities, the $32 billion in the National Well-Being Fund was established to support the welfare system.

In August 2008 the cost of invading Georgia intensified pressure on the budget. Primakov, who as leader of the Chamber of Trade and Industry usually supported the military, industrial and construction lobbies, warned of the need to prioritize both the rule of law and the protection of small business start-ups. He also wrote memoranda pointing out that foreign companies were hugely more dynamic than Russian ones, and that the privileges enjoyed by the country's big corporations had not fostered a good environment for industrial inno-vation. Norway's Statoil Hydro, for example, was eight times more productive than Lukoil and twelve times more than Gazprom.[25] But Primakov's intervention was brushed aside before the urgency of fore-stalling an imminent economic crisis. From 2013, the authorities ran down the Reserve and National Well-Being Funds to finance projects to improve transport, communications and other parts of the country's infrastructure.[26] Kudrin had protested in vain at the increase in mili-tary expenditure. His exasperation would be the background to his forced departure from the government in September 2011.

Several leading public figures had always objected to the stra-tegic course plotted by Kudrin and the Finance Ministry since 2000. They questioned the sense in maintaining the Reserve Fund and National Well-Being Fund and criticized their management. Sergei Naryshkin, who held a succession of high political posts before heading the Foreign Intelligence Service in 2016, had always disliked Kudrin's pet scheme.[27] Andrei Belousov, one of Putin's economic advisers, disliked the idea of Russian money being used to support the American economy.[28] He argued for all but 5 per cent of the Reserve Fund's assets to be made available for governmental contracts[29] – which, as Belousov knew, would have almost extin-guished the very point of having a Reserve Fund. For years Sergei Glazev had been arguing for more revenues to be dedicated to infra-structure projects. He and a growing group of consultants ramped up their demand to sweep away the vestiges of the laissez-faire policies that were Kudrin's legacy.[30]

With his own economic advisers divided, Putin had to feel sure that policy was based on reliable analysis, so on 6 November 2013 he convened a wide-ranging consultative meeting. After heated discus-sion it was decided to make a drastic switch in strategy. The new plan was to draw down heavily on the two funds, albeit without reducing them to extinction – Kudrin's dream still had life in it. Finance had to be released, the meeting resolved, to develop Siberia and the Far East and rebuild the main rail line between Moscow and Nizhni Novgorod. Large Russian private companies were to receive grants for taking part, and there would be state assistance to secure adequate capitalization for the Russian banking system.[31]

The Kremlin leadership did not confine itself to Russia's internal concerns. In December 2013 Putin consented to bail out Ukraine's President Viktor Yanukovych by buying $15 billion of Ukrainian Eurobonds to relieve pressure on Kyiv's loan repayments and end Ukraine's quest for membership of the European Union.[32] This was not the first time that the ambition for international influence and prestige triumphed over national economic self-interest. At the start of the twenty-first century, Russia had forgiven Iraq its vast debts, a sign of the renewed Russian desire to increase the country's influence and prestige beyond its borders. The subsidy to Yanukovych followed the same policy.

While all this was going on, the government looked for foreign direct investment. Ministers knew that if economic improvement was to accelerate, the country had to attract many more enterprises from abroad. The results were puny. The European Bank for Reconstruction and Development kept a tally of investments from abroad in countries emerging from communism. Central Europe and the Baltic States did best, registering $4,492 per capita in the two decades through to 2008. Ukraine recorded a mere $899, and Russia even less again at $304.[33]

This intensified calls from Russian economic liberals for a more stable legal environment. As the official commitment to state capitalism grew, Kudrin and his supporters warned that Russia was being driven down a cul-de-sac: instead of being opened up to the world economy, it was putting up political barriers. If the Russian government wanted an influx of foreign capital, it had to implement the rule of law. Global firms were unwilling to take the risks in establishing branches in Russia while concerns were rife about physical safety, judicial maladministration and political interference. Both foreign and economic policy had to be overhauled.

But by the end of Putin's first presidential term, he had abandoned his zeal for further reforms to the Russian state and society. New legislation tended to regulate only the lives of the poorer strata of society, while the rich remained a law unto themselves. Putin's appointees to the large corporations were allowed to be as arrogant and greedy as Berezovski and his contemporaries. Though Putin had disciplined unruly 'oligarchs', he was neglectful of the rights and needs of ordinary citizens.

FRACTURE

11. POINT OF DECISION: THE REACTION TO REVOLUTION IN KYIV

A seismic upheaval in world politics was registered on 27 February 2014 when masked Russian troops seized the parliamentary building in Sevastopol on Ukraine's Crimean peninsula. Other strategic sites were overwhelmed without serious resistance. A new government was proclaimed for Crimea. Its ministers held a referendum on independence, and used the favourable outcome to declare a wish for incorporation in Russia. On 18 March 2014 the Federal Assembly in Moscow voted to accept Crimea as a territory of the Russian Federation.

For Vladimir Putin it was axiomatic that Russians and Ukrainians share a single national identity.[1] His is a mindset that is centuries old. Admittedly, he has also talked in a more nuanced way: 'But we love Ukraine and I truly think of the Ukrainians as a fraternal people, if not exactly one and the same as the Russians and a part of the Russian people.'[2] Usually, though, he fudges the distinction between a Russian and a Ukrainian.

The Kremlin elite could only accept an independent Ukraine so long as no other state controlled its future and Ukraine regarded Russia as its most important partner. Alarm bells would ring in Moscow whenever Ukrainian politicians talked about applying for membership of the European Union or NATO. Putin and his entourage were especially sensitive to such sentiments: Russian politicians wanted to keep Ukraine as a zone of their special economic interest, and Russian big business felt the same. Russian commanders saw the Sevastopol naval base in Crimea as crucial for Russia's security, Sevastopol being venerated in Russian military annals for the sieges that took place in the Crimean War of 1853–6 and in the Second World War. Many ordinary Russians felt that Russia and Ukraine ought to stick together.[3]

Putin can hardly deny that millions of Ukraine's people speak Ukrainian rather than Russian. He points instead to those other millions who are Russian speakers, some of whom speak no Ukrainian. Bilingual citizens, moreover, can be found in every place in Ukraine, big or small, and the linguistic overlap between Russian and Ukrainian is extensive: a monolingual Russian and a monolingual Ukrainian can read each other's language, albeit imperfectly.

There are deep cultural links. The Russian Orthodox Church draws on a heritage founded in Kyiv in the ninth century, when the entities of 'Russia' and 'Ukraine' had yet to exist. The lands that now constitute Ukraine fell under Russian suzerainty in 1654 when Ukrainians threw off the Polish yoke and sought Russia's protection. Russia, Prussia and Austria chopped up Poland among themselves in the partitions of 1771–95. This resulted in still more Ukrainian communities becoming subjects of the tsars. It was an empire that had recently spread southward at the expense of the Ottomans and annexed Crimea and the surrounding region. The authorities in Russia's capital St Petersburg divided the conquered lands into provinces and encouraged the resident nobility to adopt the Russian language. Ukrainian schools were few. The Ukrainian tongue was spoken primarily by peasants. When Nikolai Gogol and other writers from Ukraine burst onto the literary scene, they chose Russian as their preferred language. The lasting result was that many Russians, including Putin, never accepted that Ukrainians were a separate people with their own nationhood.

Even so, the critics of Putin tend to overestimate Ukraine's national homogeneity and the longevity of its frontiers. Before the First World War the Ukrainian lands were shown on tsarist maps as provinces of the Russian Empire without reference to ethnicity, and the region where Ukrainian was the main language was officially called Malorossiya (Little Russia) – the authorities in St Petersburg wanted there to be no doubt about Russian dominance. This changed after the February 1917 Revolution, when the Russian Provisional Government took account of a rise in Ukrainian national assertiveness. But it was the Germans, not the Russians, who were the first to designate and demarcate a state called Ukraine, when they held peace talks at Brest-Litovsk with Lenin's communists, who had seized power in Russia in the October 1917 Revolution, only to find that Germany could and would overwhelm them unless they ceded sovereignty over Ukraine and the other western borderlands of the former Russian Empire.

Ukraine was for some months a puppet state, nominally independent but under German military occupation. With Germany's defeat in the First World War and the subsequent communist victory in the civil war, Lenin and Stalin had to decide what to do about the territories that Ukrainians inhabited. Against many objections from communist veterans, they decided to maintain a Ukrainian Soviet republic, albeit under Moscow's control. Yet they did not trust the Ukrainians to rule themselves unless the new Ukraine had a strong industrial sector, and consequently carved off Kharkov and the Don Basin from the Russian Soviet republic and transferred them to the Ukrainian authorities. The result was that millions of Russians found themselves resident in Soviet Ukraine. At the same time the communist administration encouraged the Ukrainian language to be taught in schools. Ukrainian speakers were promoted to public office. Despite it being a Soviet republic of mixed ethnicity, by the 1920s national confidence was taking hold in Ukraine. In 1929 that confidence turned into hatred and resentment when Stalin brutally imposed the collectivization of its farms. Mass famine followed in 1932–3. Stalin also restricted the use of the Ukrainian language in schools and the press. Great Russia was hailed as little Ukraine's elder brother. The entire experience only sharpened Ukrainians' feelings of hatred towards Moscow.

Then came the German invasion in 1941, and again the Ukrainians suffered appallingly. History brought nationhood cruelly to Ukraine. Putin draws a veil over this, and when he speaks of the sufferings Stalin inflicted, he picks out as 'the first and greatest victim' of repression not the Ukrainians but the Russians.[4]

When the fighting stopped in 1945 a redrawing of frontiers took place. Chunks of pre-war Poland were transferred to Soviet Ukraine, while post-war Poland received German lands east of the rivers Oder and Neisse, something Putin has cited to press the point that present-day Ukraine is an artificial creation.[5] After Stalin's death in 1953 his successor, Nikita Khrushchëv, who had once been his appointee as the leader of Ukraine's Communist Party, knew how bruised most Ukrainians felt by the rough treatment they had received at the hands of Moscow.

Khrushchëv's gesture to the Ukrainians was to transfer Crimea from the Russian to the Ukrainian republic. It also made equal sense from an economic viewpoint: water and transport went into the peninsula from Ukraine, whereas Russia was separated from Crimea by the waters of the Kerch Strait – something Russia has overlooked when highlighting the supposed capriciousness of Khrushchëv's decision. Putin too has reason to ignore the fact that the deed was done in 1954: Khrushchëv had not yet become the Kremlin's ruler, and required approval from the Soviet leadership.

In Khrushchëv's time the matter seemed of little moment, as Russia and Ukraine were part of the same communist multinational state. At any rate, Ukrainian sensitivities were not assuaged. Restrictions on national self-expression lasted into the late 1980s, and the political leadership in Kyiv was appointed and supervised by the Kremlin. Under Gorbachëv, Ukraine stayed troubled but quiet, still ruled by a communist elite for the most part appointed back in Brezhnev's time. This was how Gorbachëv liked it: he did not want trouble from Ukraine while he had his hands full with reform in Moscow.

Tensions between Russia and Ukraine grew as both moved towards independence. After the abortive August 1991 coup against Gorbachëv, some of the politicians close to Yeltsin travelled to Kyiv to scout the Ukrainian scene. They warned President Kravchuk to act with caution: if Ukraine unilaterally seceded from the USSR, they said, it would be unwise for Ukrainian leaders to regard the existing Russo-Ukrainian border as immutable. Some Russians of influence wanted Russia to take over the neighbouring parts of Ukraine where Russian speakers were in the majority and where Russian security interests were at stake. As things turned out, over the next few years the rulers of Russia and Ukraine avoided a clash as Yeltsin negotiated smoothly with Kravchuk and his successor Leonid Kuchma, despite a drawn-out wrangle over Russia's naval base in Sevastopol.[6] In any case, Russia and Ukraine were at the time both dependent on the West's financial assistance. The result in 1994 was an agreement known as the Budapest Memorandum, signed by Russia, Ukraine, the USA and the United Kingdom, under which the Russians and Ukrainians committed themselves to respecting each other's sovereignty and frontiers.

On this basis Ukraine gave up all its nuclear forces, which only increased Russian leverage on Ukraine's leaders, since Ukraine remained dependent on Russia for its fuel supplies. Whereas the Russian recovery from economic depression was difficult until the turn of the millennium, the Ukrainian budget remained a basket case, and Russian ministers took grim pleasure in publicizing their indulgence of Kyiv's failure to pay its gas bills on time, or even at all.

The election that brought Viktor Yushchenko to the presidency in Ukraine in 2004 was a turning point in Russo-Ukrainian relations, especially when Yushchenko talked about forming a close association with the European Union, with a view to perhaps even joining as a full member. There was also talk about applying for NATO membership. This horrified Russian ministers, whose preference was for Ukraine to enter a projected Eurasian Economic Union. Putin had long wanted to create a regional economic bloc that Russia could dominate, and regarded Ukraine as the most prized potential member. The stakes were high, and from the turn of the millennium the Kremlin's edginess about Crimea was voiced many times. With encouragement from Moscow, the Crimean Russian speakers pushed hard for their rights. Activists in Sevastopol demanded recognition of Russian as a state language and denounced Ukrainian nationalism and Kyiv's reverence for Stepan Bandera, who in the Second World War had fought for Ukraine's independence by collaborating with the Third Reich. They were proud of the Russian naval base in the city, and lauded Crimea as the cradle of Russian Orthodoxy.[7] The newspaper *Legendarny Sevastopol* declared that Sevastopol would never be divided from the Russian Federation – a strange notion when the city was separated from Russia by an agreed international frontier.[8]

At the Munich Security Conference on 10 February 2007 Vladimir Putin complained that the 'guarantees' made in 1990 against NATO's eastward expansion had not been honoured. While voicing annoyance at the presence of NATO forces on the Russian borders, he affirmed that Russians would refrain from reacting: too much force had been used in recent times. He called for international disputes to be referred to the United Nations.[9]

Putin's anger increased the following year when President Bush, exasperated by Serbia's renewed refusal to leave Kosovo's Albanians undisturbed, yielded to the Kosovan government's demand for complete independence. Ignoring Russia's inevitable objections, on 18 February 2008 the United States went ahead and granted recognition.[10] It could not have happened at a more sensitive time for US–Russian relations. At the beginning of the year the Russian Foreign Affairs Ministry had picked up that the Bush administration was entertaining the idea of admitting Ukraine and Georgia to NATO membership, if not immediately then at least by agreement on a Membership Action Plan (MAP). Secretary of State Condoleezza Rice had doubts about the prudence of such a step, and when she ran the plan by President Yushchenko in February at the Davos Economic Forum, it brought him near to tears: 'It will be a disaster, a tragedy, if we don't get the MAP.'[11] The US Ambassador in Warsaw, William J. Burns, reported that Russia's Foreign Affairs Minister, Sergei Lavrov, consistently stressed that this would be an expansionist step too far: the West had to understand the 'emotional and neuralgic' nature of the Ukrainian question for the Russian side. In any case, Lavrov had added, Ukraine's Russian-speaking citizens would most likely reject such a proposal, and then there could be civil war.[12] Discussions proceeded at the National Security Council in Washington. Bush continued to push for a positive response to Ukrainian and Georgian overtures: 'If these two democratic states want MAP, I can't say no.' The problem was that the other NATO countries were largely left out of these discussions until shortly before their leaders arrived in Bucharest in early April 2008 for the NATO summit, and even Bush had not taken a final decision in advance of leaving the United States.[13]

Germany's Chancellor Angela Merkel had never trusted Georgia's President Mikheil Saakashvili, and was disappointed by Ukraine's Viktor Yushchenko. Saakashvili, honey-tongued but impetuous, scared her with his willingness to provoke the Russians, while Yushchenko, who had won the 2004 election on a platform of democracy and outreach to the European Union, had failed to fulfil his promises. Moreover, Merkel and her Foreign Affairs Secretary Frank-Walter Steinmeier wanted to damp down the discussion inside NATO. The Poles took the opposite view, asking why Berlin was more anxious about Moscow than sympathetic to Moscow's past and potential victims. Merkel huddled with east European leaders speaking Russian, ironically the sole common language. The result was a compromise that involved less than the offer of a Membership Action Plan but something towards it. Rather than take a decision in Bucharest, the idea was to hold a meeting of foreign ministers later in the year, in the hope that this would soothe Russian anger.[14] It may have patched up cracks in NATO, but it would never appease Russia. No one was more aware of this than Merkel, who had assured Putin that Germany would withhold support for the American proposal.[15]

Putin aimed to poke a stick into the rolling wheel of NATO policy. He signalled his intention by arriving forty minutes late for his own speech to the summit. An atmosphere of nervous expectancy mounted in the hall. As Poland's Foreign Affairs Minister Radek Sikorski put it, usually the distinguished audience would have stalked off after being kept waiting even ten or fifteen minutes. They stayed in their seats because they wanted to hear the official Russian line on the most delicate item on their agenda.[16]

His words were full of menace. He denounced all talk of Georgia entering NATO, stressing that Russia had resisted the temptation to recognize Abkhazian and South Ossetian independence in response to America's recent recognition of Kosovo. His next words caused a shudder among his listeners. Any attempt to bring Ukraine into NATO, he warned, would place the country on 'the verge of extinction'.[17] His listeners were in deep shock. The speech was so incendiary that, to this day, Moscow has refrained from publishing it. Sikorski, however, asked the Russian Deputy Foreign Affairs Minister for a copy, which he later handed over to the Ukrainians, wanting them to know the danger that was facing them, and to encourage them to strengthen their military preparations.[18]

Putin's implied threat to invade and break up Ukraine – indeed, his whole combative performance – gave NATO leaders much cause for disquiet. In North America and across Europe the media carried vivid descriptions of his impact. But over subsequent days the story faded. It was as though Western politicians wanted to forget the unpleasantness and get on with other business. Putin was not their favourite politician, and the idea spread that his successor, Medvedev, was a more amenable public figure who, it was hoped, would strike a different posture in international relations on Russia's behalf. When Bush and Secretary of State Rice stopped talking about encouraging Georgia and Ukraine to join NATO Merkel appeared to conclude that the heat had gone out of the question. Only Poland's President Lech Kaczyński wanted to keep the pot boiling, but he failed to persuade anybody except Saakashvili, who was already convinced anyway.[19]

Russo-American tensions relaxed further when discussions seemed to indicate that, whatever he thought about NATO expansion, Putin had no strenuous objection to Ukraine becoming a member of the European Union. According to the president of the European Commission, José Manuel Barroso, the Russian leadership drew a distinction between military alliance and political and economic realignment: 'They were opposed to Ukraine's membership in NATO. But Putin has told me several times – so I'm not quoting second hand – that he would not have an objection in principle regarding membership of Ukraine to [sic] the EU Membership!'[20] What Barroso perhaps failed to understand – or ask about – was what terms of EU membership Putin would have found acceptable for the Ukrainians; but in any case it was the prevention of NATO's further eastward expansion that the Russian leadership had focused on. This was a period when Russia itself was negotiating on a number of levels for integration into bigger international commercial blocs, including the World Trade Organization. The Russians even explored whether they themselves might acquire some kind of associate membership of the European Union.[21]

But the geopolitical considerations did not change when Putin stepped down from the presidency, something Georgia's Mikheil Saakashvili overlooked when in August 2008 he moved troops into South Ossetia, which was part of Georgia but enjoyed a Russian security guarantee. US Secretary of State Rice had heard Putin ranting, 'If Saakashvili wants war, he'll get it. And any support for him will destroy our relationship too,'[22] and had tried her best to persuade Saakashvili to do nothing to provoke the Russians. 'You can't use force,' she had bluntly warned him in July. Putin had been dispatching forces into the Ossetian enclave for months. He had issued Russian passports to any South Ossetian who chose to apply. Saakashvili knew all this, but had decided that if he failed to assert Georgia's authority, South Ossetia would become a Russian province. When he put this to Rice, she issued her bleakest warning: 'No one will come to your aid, and you will lose.'[23]

Saakashvili offered tentative compromises to Moscow without changing his course. War clouds gathered, and Putin and Medvedev, who had succeeded him in May, thought the Americans should have done more to stop Saakashvili.[24] Seeing him as Washington's puppet, they could not believe that Rice could not have simply ordered him to be sensible. They also wanted to settle accounts with Saakashvili for his drive to become a NATO member, and now he was giving them the excuse they needed.[25]

Medvedev, facing the first international test of his presidency, ordered Russian armed forces over the Caucasus mountains on 7 August. The Georgian army was swiftly overwhelmed. Medvedev was convinced that more was at stake in the conflict than the protection of Ossetian rights: Georgia's liaison with the Western powers was regarded in Moscow as a serious challenge to Russia's interests. If it had not been for the Russian military operation, Medvedev believed, the Georgians would sooner or later have achieved NATO membership.[26]

President Nicolas Sarkozy of France involved himself for the European Union by flying to Tbilisi and seeking Saakashvili's assent for a ceasefire before the Russians advanced further. There was talk about the Georgian capital Tbilisi falling to them in the coming days. Saakashvili agreed, and Sarkozy sped off to Moscow to ask the Russian leadership to stop the fighting on their side.[27] Though Putin was prime minister at the time and no longer president, he talked publicly about the campaign and the merits of occupying Tbilisi. Buoyed by Russia's military victory, he exclaimed to Sarkozy that he was thinking of copying what the Americans had done to Saddam Hussein and 'hang[ing] up Saakashvili by the balls'.

Sarkozy, himself no stranger to a volatile temperament, urged him to think of the likely political outcome: 'Yes, but do you want to end up like Bush?' Putin calmed down, admitting, 'Ah, you've got a point there.'[28] Sarkozy secured a compromise for an end to the war. It was vaguely drafted and not as definite on Georgia's security needs as Saakashvili had asked, but he was in no position to refuse.[29]

Both Medvedev and Putin wanted the Western powers to understand their concerns about what they saw as Russia's legitimate interests. At the NATO summit, Putin had already issued a caution: Crimea, he stressed, had not been joined to Ukraine until an arbitrary decision taken by the communist leadership in Moscow in 1954. He went further: in Ukraine's southern region, he asserted, there were only Russians, no Ukrainians.[30] In reality, according to the 2001 census, Russians were three-fifths of the Crimean population; Ukrainians constituted nearly a quarter. It was preposterous too for Putin to deny the existence of large Ukrainian and Crimean Tatar minorities, and he must have realized that many in the audience – including Ukraine's President Yushchenko – knew he was spouting nonsense. Probably he just wanted to feel sure that he had got his strategic sensitivities about Crimea across. If so, he failed. Western leaders, with the notable exception of the Poles and others in east-central Europe, listened anxiously to the speech and then promptly forgot about it.

In subsequent public declarations Putin omitted to remind them. On the contrary, on 30 August 2008 he gave an interview to Germany's ARD television station in which he robustly rejected any idea that Russia was ever likely to infringe on Ukraine's sovereignty, bristling at the suggestion by the French Foreign and European Affairs Minister Bernard Kouchner that the Russian leadership might be contemplating an invasion of Ukrainian territory and the seizure of the port city of Sevastopol in Crimea. 'Crimea is not a disputed territory,' he sternly explained:

> There has been no ethnic conflict there, unlike the conflict between South Ossetia and Georgia. Russia has long recognized the borders of modern-day Ukraine. On the whole, we have completed our talks on borders. The issue of demarcation still stands, but this is just a technicality. I think questions about such goals for Russia have provocative undertones.[31]

The interview took place a few days after Russia ended its Georgian war. It was a time when the Kremlin was under severe international criticism, and Putin, like Medvedev, was trying to persuade the world that Russian armed forces had no further objectives in the former Soviet Union.

This remained Putin's public position. Having issued his threats in Munich and Bucharest, he put them aside. Perhaps he was encouraged by the return to the Ukrainian presidency in February 2010 of Viktor Yanukovych.[32] Yanukovych defeated rivals who wanted a continuation of the 'Orange Revolution' and imprisoned one of his leading critics, the businesswoman and ex-prime minister Yulia Timoshenko, on a charge of economic corruption. He cheered the Kremlin by speaking of the need to conciliate Russia even though he continued to engage positively with the European Union. Yet refraining from repeating his Munich and Bucharest performances had the baleful consequence of sedating the West. In diplomacy, what is left unsaid is often as important as what is spoken.

As prime minister Putin kept his attention on Ukraine, particularly when talking to Russians about Crimea. He encouraged Russian entrepreneurs to set up branches in Sevastopol.[33] Rich Russian businessmen had for years been buying up Crimean real estate and developing the region's seaside resorts,[34] a trend Putin applauded. An increase in Russia's economic presence would bolster the naval commitment at Sevastopol. While Crimea's Russian-speaking inhabitants voted mostly for politicians who wanted friendly links with Russia, the Tatar community, worried by the rise of Ukrainian nationalism in Kyiv, gave some of its support to Yanukovych on the grounds that he would look after them.[35]

All this pleased the Kremlin leaders as Yushchenko looked on with alarm. He had a definite preference for closer alignment with the European Union and NATO, and the lessons of the Georgian war led him to see Ukraine's security more than ever as depending on entry into NATO via a Membership Action Plan.[36] In both Moscow and Kyiv worried discussions continued as to what was being considered in the other capital.

Meanwhile the Kremlin addressed the question of Sevastopol. Russia's naval base with its 25,000 serving officers and sailors had been a matter of disquiet for Moscow since the mid-1990s, when Kyiv had claimed ownership of the entire fleet. But the naval oath to Russia retained its authority, and Kyiv realized its ambition was impractical because most of the forces would have mutinied. In 1997 Kyiv prag-matically agreed a division of the fleet between the two countries, granting Moscow a twenty-year licence to station its ships and troops at Sevastopol.[37] On coming to power President Yanukovych had agreed an extension of the Russian lease in April 2010 under the Kharkiv Accords, by a further twenty-five years, in return for a huge discount in the price Ukraine paid for Russia's oil. Altogether Russia had to stump up $40–45 billion for permission to use its Sevastopol facilities. Putin was livid. 'I would be willing to eat Yanukovych and his prime minister for that sort of money! No military base in the world costs that much!'[38]

Yanukovych had won the Ukrainian presidency on a pro-Russia ticket, a victory welcomed by the Russians for putting an end to Ukraine's 'Orange Revolution'. Yushchenko, the revolution's leader, had always lacked a majority in the Supreme Rada (the Ukraine parlia-ment), and had originally appointed Yanukovych as prime minister to establish a political balance. Though Yanukovych's rise now to presi-dential office cheered the Russian authorities, it was not to the point where they felt they could be complacent. Ukraine's politics remained volatile. Russian-language activists in Kyiv expressed fears that Ukrainian nationalists might pull off a coup with American assist-ance.[39] Smartly produced brochures appeared urging Ukrainians as a people to support moves to join the European Union and enter NATO.[40] And Yanukovych could lose another election, just as he had lost to Yushchenko in 2005. What is more, Yanukovych was a tough negotiator. He had not only driven a hard bargain for Russia's retention of its Black Sea naval facilities, but he had also resumed Ukraine's nego-tiations for associate membership of the European Union. He continually played off Moscow against Brussels, aiming to increase Russia's financial support by hinting that he might otherwise choose the European Union as Ukraine's partner. There was no guarantee the favourable line towards Moscow would endure.

This display of enthusiasm for the European Union led Brussels to explore ways of tempting Yanukovych to break with Moscow. Russia's reaction was to introduce a range of economic sanctions against Ukraine.[41] Predictable though this might have been, it naturally increased the standing of Ukrainian politicians who were more prin-cipled than Yanukovych in their desire to take the road towards Europe.

In autumn 2013 the European Union made a detailed offer to include Ukraine in a 'deep and comprehensive free trade area'. Putin saw a double economic danger in this. One possible outcome would have placed Ukraine in a customs union from which Russia would have been excluded; another would have provided the European Union with tariff-free access to the Russian economy, since there were no commercial barriers between Russia and Ukraine. Geopolitics were also in play. Putin hated the thought that Ukraine might move beyond the Russian orbit of influence. Foreign Affairs Minister Lavrov raised objections, calling for multilateral negotiations: 'We must work for a union of unions, an alliance of the EU and the Eurasian Union.'[42] Meanwhile the European Union kept up the momentum on preparing the ground for Ukraine to proceed to full membership at some future date. Reforms would have to be made involving free markets, sanctity of contract, political liberty, fair elections and the rule of law – all utterly incompatible with the prevailing conditions in Russia and the rest of the projected Eurasian Economic Union.

Inside the Russian government, deputy prime minister Igor Shuvalov had responsibility for nudging Ukraine into a tighter embrace. He went on a public relations offensive in Kyiv, and at the same time tried to convince European public opinion that the European Union had no reason for anxiety if Ukraine chose to enter the Eurasian Economic Union as Russia's partner.[43] But about one thing he was adamant: the Ukrainians had to opt either for the Eurasian Economic Union or the European Union. As Shuvalov put it, the customs arrangements of the two bodies were incompatible. This was his way of stressing that Russia would suffer from unrestricted Western economic competition if Ukraine joined the European Union while maintaining its existing free-trade regime with Russia.[44] From the Russian leadership's standpoint, the Ukraine-in-Europe proposal would be a Trojan horse inside Russia's walls.

Brussels underestimated the agitation it was causing in Moscow. Foreign Minister Lavrov got nowhere when he brought up the matter with President Barroso, who saw no problem in the European Commission's conduct. The Europeans had done nothing, Barroso reminded Lavrov, to impede the rapprochement between the Russians and the Chinese, so why, he asked, would the Russians want to interfere when the Europeans and Ukrainians chose to get closer.[45] In Barroso's opinion, expressed in late 2014, the European Union was innocent of the charge of recklessness:

> We were perfectly aware of all of the risks. I spoke with Putin several times, and he told us how important for him was the

customs union, the Eurasian [Economic] Union, and the specific role he saw for Ukraine. But should we have given up? Should we say, 'OK, Vladimir, Ukraine is yours, do whatever you want?' That is the logical consequence of what they are saying. That's perfectly unacceptable.[46]

Theoretically, if Ukraine were to acquire association status with the European Union, this could have the advantage for Russia that a cleansed political and economic order in Ukraine – one of the requirements for such status – would be able to meet its financial obligations. Kyiv would cease to disappoint its Russian creditors. But this was not how Moscow saw it. In Putin's opinion, the granting of association status to Ukraine would disrupt any chances of harmony between the two countries and damage the Russian economy. The Russians could have no confidence that if Ukraine moved into the European Union's orbit, it would not also eventually obtain membership of NATO. Putin could not appear to be weak in reacting to foreign threats. He was not as invulnerable to the vagaries of public opinion as he appeared, and he knew it.[47] Barroso refused to back off. When Lavrov raised objections with European Union negotiators, he hit a brick wall: 'It's none of your business.'[48] Putin was offended by the way Brussels was trying to speed up the talks with Ukraine: Russia, he was later to note, had had to spend seventeen long years negotiating its accession to the World Trade Organization.[49]

After 1991 it was in the interests of the Kremlin rulers for Ukraine to remain stuck in a morass of corruption: if Ukraine reformed with the rule of law now governing public life and business, the Russian people might want the same, and that would mean revolution and the end of Putin and his clique.

By December 2013, according to Kremlin officials, the Russian General Staff was already conducting contingency planning for a military operation.[50] But back in summer that year, it would seem, professional soldiers were already being asked whether they would be willing to fight in Ukraine, and those who demurred were released when their contracts expired.[51] The commanders were getting ready even before the politicians gave the go-ahead. But the politicians were already moving – or being moved. At the December Security Council Patrushev was pleased to hear Vladimir Konstantinov, the Speaker of the Crimean parliament, who was visiting Moscow at the time, let it be known that Crimea would readily 'go to Russia' if Yanukovych should be overthrown.[52]

On 29 November 2013 the Kremlin's worries suddenly faded when
Yanukovych announced his desire to come to an agreement with
Russia. Abandoning the understandings he had worked out with
Brussels, he was now plumping for Moscow's Eurasian Economic
Union.

Yanukovych would have been conscious anyway of the serious
trouble likely to arise in Moscow if Kyiv chose in favour of Brussels. He
had recently flown to Sochi for discussions with Putin at his presidential residence. It was a place of much symbolism: close to the
Russo-Ukrainian border, and to Yalta, where in 1945 Stalin, Roosevelt
and Churchill had planned the future of Europe. Putin was used to
having to pay for Yanukovych's compliance, and this time was no
different. When Yanukovych revealed his budgetary difficulties, Putin
agreed to advance $15 billion in credits. Yanukovych had stretched
Putin's patience to the limit and had obtained a financial bailout. Whatever words were exchanged, on the Russian side they were unlikely to
have been kindly. On his return to Ukraine, Yanukovych tried to
persuade his citizens that he had achieved a better deal than anything
that would be available from the European Union.

Putin was delighted, but only for a few days. Huge demonstrations
were held in Kyiv's Maidan and surrounding boulevards against Yanukovych's decision. He sent in armed police, but resistance only
increased as the young street protesters were bolstered by support from
western Ukraine, where hostility to Yanukovych and to Russia was
profound. Western politicians and media rushed to express their
support.

Putin rejected appeals from pro-Russia political groups in Crimea
for him to send more troops into the peninsula for the protection of
Russian-speaking inhabitants, even though it was put to him at a press
conference on 19 December 2013 that this was what the Russians had
done in 2008 in South Ossetia and Abkhazia. The reason for armed
intervention in those two enclaves, replied Putin, was not merely to
defend the Russian speakers but to restore order. He denied that
Crimea was in similar ferment, stressing that the Russian naval
garrison in Sevastopol ensured stability. He did, though, repeat his
warning that the Moscow authorities were not indifferent to the 'situation of our compatriots'. He also took a swipe at the European Union
for failing to act against Estonia, Latvia and Lithuania – EU member
countries – which discriminated against Russian residents who did not
speak the state language. But, Putin assured people, 'this absolutely

doesn't mean that we're about to flash our swords and put the troops in'. 'Complete rubbish,' he insisted. 'Nothing like this is happening or can happen.'[53]

Nevertheless, contingency plans were afoot. By the first weeks of February 2014, according to the anti-Putin newspaper *Novaya gazeta*, a memorandum was doing the rounds in the Kremlin's highest reaches with a proposal to occupy and annex both Crimea and eastern Ukraine in the event of Yanukovych's overthrow. The thinking behind it was that a coup in Kyiv would lead to an abrupt collapse of Ukrainian statehood and cause a division of the country between its western and eastern regions. Kyiv had fallen into the hands of football hooligans, criminals and fascists; Yanukovych was a broken reed, low in moral authority and resolve; his supporters were inadequate to the task of restoring order, and the European Union was aiming to swallow up the west of Ukraine in a 'geopolitical intrigue'. Several of Ukraine's 'oligarchs', the memorandum went on, were financing the Maidan disturbances, and they in turn were operating under the control of the Polish and British secret services. Russia, it was recommended, should take the initiative and arrange for the 'unification' of the Ukrainian eastern regions with itself.[54]

It's not known who wrote the memorandum, but the contents point to the kind of thinking widespread in both the governing elite and public opinion. At its heart is the presumption of external conspiracies against Russia and even against Ukraine. Many of Putin's public statements rested on the same assumptions.

As late as the end of January 2014, American intelligence saw no reason to warn of an impending political emergency.[55] But the street demonstrations grew fiercer and the Maidan area was still occupied by protesters. The threat to Yanukovych swelled with the arrival of activists from western Ukraine. Moscow media denounced them as fascists who denied the role of the Red Army in defeating the Third Reich. Yanukovych ordered heavy police action to quell the growing insurgency and licensed snipers to fire on demonstrators.

Repression, however, served to stiffen the protesters' resolve. US Assistant Secretary of State Victoria Nuland arrived in Kyiv and personally distributed food to those camped out on the Maidan, which only infuriated the Kremlin. Talk of an American conspiracy to foment trouble in Ukraine became common fare on Russian TV news broadcasts. Moscow urged Yanukovych to take decisive action, but in Kyiv Yanukovych could see that the situation might spin out of control if he ordered more repression. Negotiations had become essential to avert civil war.

With the European Union's consent, Poland, Germany and France offered to mediate. Foreign ministers Radek Sikorski, Frank-Walter Steinmeier and Laurent Fabius flew to Kyiv. Sikorski arrived on 19 February and, while waiting for Steinmeier and Fabius to join him, witnessed the brittleness of public order. He tweeted a photograph of snipers ready to fire down on demonstrators. On 20 February the three ministers met with Yanukovych and told him time had run out for him and that he must resign. Yanukovych turned pale, and he left the room to take a phone call 'from abroad'; in his absence his officials explained that the caller was in Moscow. Everyone knew this meant Putin. When Yanukovych resumed his place half an hour later he agreed to discuss the question of his departure. Though he would give no exact date, he said it would be by the end of the year. Russian support for him had evidently crumbled, and Putin had accepted the idea that Yanukovych had to go. There was agreement to bring Russian special envoy Vladimir Lukin into the talks, since it would be hard to work out a peaceful solution if Moscow was not involved.[56]

The three foreign ministers from the European Union, having Yanukovych's consent to act as intermediaries, established a base in the European Union embassy for talks that evening with the opposition leaders Vitali Klichko, Oleh Tyahnibok and Arseniy Yatsenyuk. They resisted the signature of an agreement before Yanukovych had acceded to their terms for the treatment of the Maidan protesters. Lukin help-fully proposed that both the Berkut security force and the demonstrators camped on the Maidan should cease to confront one another. At seven o'clock in the morning of 21 February agreement was finally reached for a formal signing ceremony at midday. Catherine Ashton, the European Union's High Representative for Foreign Affairs and Security Policy, indicated assent. The Obama administration did likewise. The Kremlin was the only fly in the ointment, refusing to allow Lukin to sign any agreement that did not envisage a reorganiza-tion of Ukraine on a federal basis. Even so, Putin did not act to block the agreement itself. Fabius had already left for a scheduled trip to China. This left Sikorski and Steinmeier to complete the job and sign alongside Yanukovych, Klichko, Tyahnibok and Yatsenyuk.[57]

The ceremony was arranged for 6.45 p.m. Yanukovych had made momentous concessions by promising to restore the 2004 Ukrainian constitution and give the Rada back all its old powers. New presidential elections would be organized no later than December 2014. Street confrontations were to cease and illegal weapons be surrendered.[58]

That evening Yanukovych spoke by phone to Putin and reported that he had steadied the situation. Putin was not reassured. 'But in any case,' he was to recall, 'I told him, "It seems wrong to pull the forces of law and order out of Kyiv."' 'Yes,' Yanukovych had replied: 'I understand that.' But he went on to say that he intended to stick to his prearranged programme and fly to Kharkiv to attend a conference. Putin could hardly believe his own ears: he urged Yanukovych to stay in Kyiv and restore law and order. But Yanukovych insisted on doing things in his own way. In desperation Putin himself turned to Obama, phoning him to extract a promise that Washington would continue to support the Kyiv agreement. It was the most Putin could achieve under such unstable circumstances.[59] His worries about Yanukovych were well founded: the Berkut security troops did not merely withdraw from the streets but pulled out from the central district altogether, and Yanukovych did nothing to bring them back. Overnight, he lost his grip on power.

A day later, Kyiv was convulsed by revolt. Putin's worst fears were realized, leading him to develop a lasting anger and contempt for Yanukovych: 'What a handsome fellow too!'[60] By then Yanukovych had decided to flee with whatever money and possessions he could take with him. Fearing for his life if the Ukraine's new authorities were to lay hands on them, Yanukovych picked up his suitcases and money and entrusted himself to Russians who were dispatched to bring him across Ukraine to Crimea.

A makeshift plan was agreed to meet Putin in Rostov-on-Don across the Russo-Ukrainian frontier.[61] Meanwhile a crowd broke into his residence outside Kyiv, and footage of abundant ill-gotten wealth was broadcast on state television. Documents retrieved from the presidential offices proved that Yanukovych had been ordering savage repression up to the moment of his flight. Yanukovych's feared police retreated from sight.

Suddenly Russia had 'lost' Ukraine. This, at least, was how Russian leaders and probably many ordinary Russians felt. In the Kremlin, anger followed astonishment as the administration tried to fathom why Yanukovych had not stayed and toughed it out. His flight had left a power vacuum, and no one could tell who would take over the presidency and government, except that it would be one of those who had confronted him. The Supreme Rada elected a cabinet led by Arseniy

Yatsenyuk. American and European politicians hastened to announce their support.

Russia's plans lay in ruins. The outcome Putin had sought to prevent through his speeches in Munich and Bucharest had become reality. Putin and his associates were hated in Kyiv, and the Ukrainian media freely exposed the depth of malfeasance and corruption under Yanukovych, who had treated Ukraine as his family's cash cow. Putin was living a personal nightmare.

12. THE INSEPARABLE PENINSULA: THE ANNEXATION OF CRIMEA

In the late evening of 23 February 2014 Putin attended the closing ceremony of the Sochi Olympics. There was a smile on his face. He was beaming with pleasure at the magnificent display in the stadium and at the facilities for the competitions.

The presidential plane had brought him just in time from Moscow, where that morning he had laid a wreath at the tomb of the Unknown Warrior.[1] Nobody looking at him had any inkling of the ominous decision about the Ukrainian crisis he had taken in the early hours, a decision reached with his closest confidants – Defence Minister Sergei Shoigu, Security Council Secretary Nikolai Patrushev, FSB Director Alexander Bortnikov and Presidential Chief of Staff Sergei Ivanov[2] – at his Novo-Ogarëvo residence, after the news that Yanukovych had fled Kyiv. Talks had lasted deep into the night. Putin later recounted:

> We finished around seven o'clock in the morning and I let everyone go and I went to bed . . . And on parting – I won't make any secret of this – on parting before everyone left, I told all my colleagues, and there were four of them, that the situation in Ukraine had unfolded in such a way that we were obliged to begin work for the restoration of Crimea to Russia. Because we can't abandon this territory and the people who live there to the vagaries of fate and fling them under the wheels of the nationalists.[3]

The decision was nothing less than to order Russian forces to overturn the Crimean regional government and expel Ukraine's forces from the peninsula.

All those present in Novo-Ogarëvo had links to the various security agencies. (Even Ivanov had served as Defence Minister before joining the Presidential Administration.) Prime Minister Medvedev, Foreign Affairs Minister Lavrov and Finance Minister Siluanov had not been invited, even though the significance of the situation stretched far beyond the military. If Putin chose to occupy the Crimean peninsula, he would be putting Russia's entire future onto a new, visible and dangerous track.

The consultations at Novo-Ogarëvo were eerily reminiscent of those at Party General Secretary Leonid Brezhnev's side in December 1979 when they considered the proposal to send the Soviet army into Afghanistan. Brezhnev was no longer well enough to oversee policy, but an inner group of the Party Politburo group, including Defence Minister Dmitri Ustinov, KGB Chairman Yuri Andropov, Foreign Affairs Minister Andrei Gromyko and Politburo veteran Mikhail Suslov, discussed with him the possibility of military intervention. The decision was then finalized without the holding of a full Politburo. The Chairman of the Council of Ministers, Alexei Kosygin, who had primary responsibility for the civilian sector of the economy, was not present. The main difference from 2014 was that the Foreign Affairs Ministry was represented in the person of Gromyko. It was a decision that led to appalling carnage terminated only ten years later when the Soviet army began its ignominious retreat.

Unlike the sickly Brezhnev, Putin was in full possession of his faculties. He still had to be sure that if he sent troops into Ukraine, he would be acting with due prudence. Patrushev had no doubts: the Russian army must be deployed without delay. Shoigu is said to have been cautious, perhaps because he recalled the disaster of Afghanistan. Another consideration may have been that it was he and not Patrushev who would be accountable for the Russian forces' performance.[4]

But Putin and the rest of the group also knew that Russia had not suffered unduly as a result of the Russian invasion of Georgia. George W. Bush had huffed and puffed but done little beyond suspending the activity of the NATO–Russia Council. No sanctions on travel or business were applied to any Russian politician, official or corporation. Nothing was done to assure the Georgians that they would eventually be able to acquire NATO membership.[5] But if Putin had gained confidence from this, he would have been sensible to reflect on one big difference between Georgia and Ukraine. Whereas Saakashvili had knowingly annoyed the Russians and ignored the cautionary advice of the Americans, the new authorities in Kyiv had already received encouragement from the European Union and America. Whereas in 2008 South Ossetia and Abkhazia had been turned into Russian protectorates, Putin now planned to annex the peninsula to Russia. The

Americans were likely to resort to non-military measures that would wreak harm on Russia. The Magnitsky Act of 2012 showed that an angered America was willing and able to retaliate. Putin was about to dive over a cliff with no assurance of calm and deep waters below.

Throughout 2013 the American intelligence services had picked up no signs of imminent invasion, though on 23 February 2014 Obama's National Security Advisor Susan Rice told NBC News that it would be 'a grave mistake' for Russia to invade Ukraine: a strange remark, unless she had heard that such a move was a possibility.[6] But if the Americans did know something, they did nothing about it. Yanukovych's over-throw and the new direction of politics in Kyiv anyway transformed the international situation. Whoever took power in the Ukrainian capital would hug close not only to the European Union but also to NATO. This would – or at least could – put the Sevastopol naval base in jeopardy, and with it national security. No Russian leader could survive the national shame of that. Ukrainian nationalists, prominent in the Maidan protests, would inevitably gain in influence. Russian speakers in Ukraine feared discrimination. Russia regarded its moves as being of existential importance.

Unless he had been dissembling (which cannot be discounted), Putin had had no long-matured plan to seize Crimea, but undoubtedly the disarray in Kyiv offered an unprecedented and possibly unrepeat-able opportunity to secure Sevastopol, the great port city that had been the cause of recurrent wrangling and expense since the fall of the USSR. The Russian navy had its own base in Sevastopol, and a crack contingent from the army and air force was ready for deployment from Russian territory. Russian armed forces had tanks and aircraft in numbers the Ukrainians lacked and which the NATO countries had put out of service in east-central Europe. Ukraine had insufficient conventional forces to stop Putin from overrunning as much of Ukraine as he wanted. An armed response from the Americans could be discounted. In the highly improbable case that Obama might consider firing missiles from American warships in the Black Sea, Putin was ready to put his nuclear forces on alert.[7] Crimea lay there for the taking. Putin decided to act.

On 27 February Russian troops, in disguise and wearing masks, occupied the Supreme Council of Crimea in Simferopol, before seizing strategic buildings across the peninsula. Sergei Aksënov, who led the Russian Unity Party and had often called for Crimea's incorporation in Russia, was elected prime minister by pro-Russian parliamentarians, who were admitted into the Supreme Council building by a cordon of heavily armed Russian troops. The vote was announced in violation of the Ukrainian constitution, which requires prior permission from Ukraine's president. One of Aksënov's first acts was to organize a referendum on joining the Russian Federation. With the police and television under control, he intimidated his political opponents. Tatars and Ukrainian speakers were wary about protesting. Meanwhile the government in Moscow affected to be uninvolved. The referendum result was a foregone conclusion. On 16 March, by a large majority, voters in Crimea opted to switch allegiance from Kyiv to Moscow.

Two days later, Putin came before the Federal Assembly in the Russian capital to propose approval of Crimea's accession. Red Square was ringed by troops reinforced by an OMON contingent brought in from Novosibirsk two thousand miles away. It was a frosty Moscow day. Inside the Kremlin precinct, politicians and other dignitaries queued to enter the Great Kremlin Palace. There was a mood of bright expectancy. A single parliamentarian, the maverick communist Ilya Ponomarëv, voted against Putin's proposal; his Duma status was quickly suspended and he took refuge in Ukraine.[8]

In Kyiv the mood turned decisively against Russia, even among citizens previously neutral or even pro-Russian. Putin could not have done more to enrage Ukrainian opinion. Ukrainian political leaders vowed to defend the country against further attack. Acting President Turchynov thought this might best be achieved by adopting a 'non-bloc' status for Ukraine: keeping itself free from alignment with either Russia or the European Union. The Secretariat of the Supreme Rada took the opposite position, drafting a law for Ukraine to seek full NATO membership.[9] The Rada repealed the 2012 language law allowing the provinces to embed Russian as one of the state languages.[10]

In the West there was horror at what Putin was doing. If he had counted on a repetition of Bush's limp reaction to the Russian war in Georgia, Obama quickly disillusioned him. Though the Magnitsky Act had initially been aimed only at the kind of low-level officials responsible for the torments that killed Bill Browder's lawyer, it set a precedent, and now President Obama imposed economic sanctions. On 15 March 2014 the UN Security Council condemned the Crimean referendum. China abstained, and Russia vetoed the decision anyway.

The Russian case never varied: that Crimea had been unfairly transferred to Ukraine in 1954, and that the persecution of Russian-speaking Crimean residents had compelled Russia to intervene so that a proper referendum could be held. Lavrov rushed back from a visit to Japan to take charge of Russian diplomatic efforts to justify the action in Crimea – having to quickly put aside his resentment at being left out of the original decision. The entire leadership united round official policy. When foreigners argued that the annexation breached the 1994 Budapest Memorandum, Lavrov would reply that Russia had merely agreed not to use nuclear weapons against Ukraine, blatantly overlooking the guarantee not to infringe territorial integrity.[11]

On 27 March 2014 the United States presented a motion to the UN General Assembly calling for respect for Ukrainian territorial integrity and denouncing the Crimean peninsula's annexation. The vote was carried by a huge majority.[12] China, Brazil, India, South Korea and Turkey and several other countries with large economies also refused to cooperate with American-led sanctions. Iran, too, rejected the Western line – Tehran was itself being sanctioned by the United States and saw no advantage in annoying the Russians, who as a result were not as comprehensively isolated as the Americans wanted. Nevertheless, American and other Western sanctions delivered a blow to Russian finances, and companies round the world with banking and commercial interests in the United States could not afford to ignore Washington's list of prohibited contacts, regardless of their own government's policy.

The only cheer for the Kremlin leadership was the patchiness of foreign condemnation. In November 2016 the United Nations General Assembly accepted Ukraine's resolution denouncing Russia as an occupying power, but seventy-six abstained, with both India and China voting against.[13] At the General Assembly in March 2017 Russia was again assailed by criticism, but this time eighty-two countries either abstained or declined to vote.[14]

By seizing hold of the tiny Black Sea peninsula, Putin had added less than 2 per cent to Russia's land mass, which already comprised a whole ninth of the world's earth surface. Crimea is a speck on the map of Eurasia, cheap to conquer but extremely expensive to annex and sustain. A more modern naval dock and base already existed at Novorossiisk on Russian territory to the east of the Kerch Strait.[15] Russia's strategic interests on the Black Sea did not depend exclusively on retaining Sevastopol, though Putin apparently thought they did. He now learned the price he was going to have to pay, as Ukraine cut off water, gas, oil, transport, salaries and welfare payments to the peninsula, compelling Russian ministries to plug the gaps. Putin vowed to complete the bridge across the Kerch Strait, the construction of which had been agreed between Presidents Medvedev and Yanukovych in 2010. Now Russia alone would undertake the project, despite the difficulty of raising foreign loans.

At a stroke, Putin had thrown away his recent gains in 'soft power'. He had forfeited the benefits of a normal partnership with the advanced Western economies. Inside the American political establishment, his action transformed those Democratic Party leaders who had been urging restraint in policy towards Russia into impassioned advocates of increasing the pressure on Putin. If Putin had not anticipated this reaction, he and his advisers were poorly informed.

Obama now provided equipment for the Ukrainian forces to defend themselves. But he stopped short of supplying advanced lethal weapons, to prevent the emergency turning into the Third World War. NATO policy in the Cold War had been the same: though America and its allies refused to accept the legitimacy of the USSR's annexation of Estonia, Latvia and Lithuania, they never did anything militarily to restore the independence of the Baltic States. The rest of eastern Europe lay under Soviet political control from soon after the end of the Second World War through to 1989. When Berlin workers rose in protest in 1953, NATO refrained from intervening; also when the Hungarians revolted in 1956, and when Czechoslovakia asserted its freedom in 1968. Usually the West complained and condemned communist repression, but then stood aside while it took place. Richard Nixon and Henry Kissinger went so far as to indicate Washington's willingness to share with Moscow a condominium over Europe.

This attitude faded during the years of Gorbachëv's rule and in the 1990s disappeared entirely after the USSR's collapse, but former US Secretary of State Henry Kissinger and others resuscitated it after the turn of the millennium when the Russian Federation began to assert itself, fearing the consequences of not allowing the Russians to stand up for their perceived interests. The Crimean events confirmed Kissinger in his opinion that Western policy had failed to achieve a due understanding of Russia's regional considerations. He criticized the European Union for its part in provoking the political emergency in Ukraine: in his opinion, Merkel and others had tried to turn Kyiv into a Brussels satellite. On 5 March 2014 he wrote in the *Washington Post* that they had underestimated the danger of restarting the Cold War by forgetting that for Russia Ukraine 'could never be just a foreign country'.[16] Even

Robert Gates, the former CIA director and Defense Secretary as well as a veteran foreign-policy hawk, came to believe that America and its allies had for too long ignored Russia's interests.[17]

Putin, of course, was of the same mind and, as he laid out his self-justification in subsequent months before world opinion, he argued that Russia had simply followed the precedent set by America in the former Yugoslavia, but without the shedding of blood:

> There was no war in Crimea. There were no bombing strikes, no military operations and no casualties. Not a single person perished. The only thing we did was to ensure the right of the people to obtain what they wanted, which by the way was in strict compliance with the UN Charter. We did literally almost the same as you did in Kosovo, only a little more.[18]

Speaking to an audience of invited foreign guests, Putin was running little risk of anyone pointing out to him the sharp contrast between Crimea and Kosovo. Whereas the Americans bombed Serbia into giving the Kosovars their freedom after Milošević had systematically brutalized them, the Russians 'liberated' Crimea in time of peace – no soldiers from Kyiv had been maltreating Russian people on the peninsula. Furthermore, America did not go on to colonize Kosovo or turn it into its fifty-first state. Russia reduced the Crimean peninsula to the status of an administrative entity, subject to rule from Moscow.

Putin's Crimean campaign had also put paid to his old argument that America was the single nation to infringe international law. Previously he had been fond of declaring that Russia stood for fixed borders, national sovereignty and peaceful resolution of disputes between states. The Crimean annexation showed otherwise: Russia was revealed as an expansionist bully. But Putin did not care about foreign criticism: he had put an end to months of uncertainty in the Kremlin. Crimea would return to Russia.

On 17 April 2014 Putin hinted that Russia's desires might not have been sated by the annexation of Crimea:

> The question is . . . how to ensure the legitimate rights and interests of ethnic Russians and Russian-speaking citizens in the south-east of Ukraine. I would remind you, using the terminology of tsarist times, that this is Novorossiya (New Russia): Kharkov, Lugansk, Donetsk, Kherson, Nikolayev and Odessa were not part of Ukraine in tsarist times. These were all territories handed to

Ukraine in the 1920s by the Soviet government. God knows, why did they do this?[19]

He was indicating a new threat to eastern Ukraine. The Donbass region was now in his sights. He was testing Obama's will, and probing to see how much he could get away with.

Fighting broke out in Ukraine's eastern region on 7 April, when hundreds of troops in green apparel burst into the Ukrainian security service buildings in Donetsk and Luhansk (Lugansk). The Donetsk People's Republic was proclaimed. Moscow affirmed that the fighters were local Russian-speaking volunteers, when in reality they were part of the Russian army, and their ultimate purpose was to bring about the incorporation of eastern Ukraine in the Russian Federation. Anti-Kyiv protesters swarmed onto the streets to support the military action. Guns found their way from Russia. The Ukrainian authorities deployed their army against the rebels. Town after town became a battleground.

Presidential elections in Ukraine produced a clean first-round victory for the businessman and politician Petro Poroshenko, on a platform of national pride and defence, and he issued a plea to Western powers for assistance. Ukrainian nationalism intensified, moderated only by the realization that Ukraine's armed forces were outgunned by the Russians. Obama withheld his support beyond the financial and diplomatic, but repeated his demand for Russia to withdraw its forces from both Crimea and eastern Ukraine.

On 17 July international opinion, already agitated, became apoplectic when the rebel forces near Shakhtarsk shot down a Malaysian Airlines passenger plane flying from Amsterdam to Kuala Lumpur. While Moscow blamed Ukrainian artillery, the evidence already pointed towards Russian responsibility. Western governments were unanimous in calling on the Kremlin to bring the war to a halt. As the investigation in eastern Ukraine proceeded and it became more and more difficult to brush away international criticism, Putin reacted carefully. While some of his spokesmen pinned the blame for the atrocity on Kyiv, Putin limited himself to querying the sense in sending a non-combatant plane over a war zone. He had learned from the mistake made in April 1983 by Soviet General Secretary Yuri Andropov in denying that his forces had brought down a South Korean airliner in Siberian airspace. Soon afterwards the truth had become irrefutable, and Andropov came to be seen abroad as a liar. As someone who cultivates the image of a hard but plain-speaking leader, Putin prefers others to do the lying.[20]

Such troops as Putin dispatched to fight proved capable of turning eastern Ukraine into a charnel house but never looked likely to defeat the Ukrainian army. Having realized that only a full-scale invasion would bring victory – something certain Russian public intellectuals, notably Alexander Dugin, were urging him to undertake to achieve the permanent annexation of Ukraine's entire south-east[21] – he endorsed a proposal for peace talks in Minsk. After the downing of the Malaysian airliner, Putin wanted a respite from the bad publicity, and negotiations would give the impression that the Kremlin was not being intransigent.

On 5 September a ceasefire was signed in Minsk between the Ukrainian government and rebel forces. This, was a long way, however, from a permanent settlement. The European Union's patience was exhausted: a week later it imposed a further set of economic sanctions against Russia. The aim was to hit the Russian economy at its rawest points, so the oil companies Rosneft, Transneft and Gazprom Neft were among those prohibited from raising capital in European markets. Measures were also reinforced to stop Russian banks from obtaining loans in the European Union. The list of individuals banned from travelling to Europe and accessing their assets was increased.[22] So severe was the harm to Russia's economy that Standard and Poor's, the credit ratings agency, downgraded the country's sovereign debt to near junk status.[23]

Fighting continued sporadically in breach of the ceasefire. President Poroshenko refused to buckle. On 14 November 2014 he drew a distinction between the Donbass and the rest of Ukraine:

> We will have work, they won't. We will have pensions – they won't.
> We will care for our children and pensioners – they won't. Our
> children will go to school, to kindergartens – their children will
> sit in cellars. They don't know how to organize or do anything.
> This, ultimately, is how we will win this war.[24]

His optimism was accompanied by defiance of Russia's attempt to reduce the country to splintered fragments. 'Ukraine must remain a unitary state,' he explained on 22 January 2015: 'there will be no discussion of Ukraine's European choice; and the sole state language is and will be Ukrainian.'[25] Putin's military operations were never enough to overturn the political leadership in Kyiv, but more than sufficient to stiffen Ukraine's resolve to stave off the Russian assault. Poroshenko presided

over a country with many internal divisions, but united by its commitment to national defence. In February yet another ceasefire was agreed
in Minsk after talks involving Belarus, France and Germany as well as
Russia and Ukraine. The Minsk Accords demanded fresh elections and
demilitarization in eastern Ukraine and an amnesty for all fighters.

The chances of success were poor, not least because Putin maintained that Ukraine was an artificial political construct. Western
Ukraine, he had publicly noted, was part of Poland before the Second
World War: 'What was Lvov if not a Polish city?' He now went further,
dredging up a legal problem that brought into question the very integrity of Ukrainian statehood. When Khrushchëv had transferred
Crimea to Ukraine in 1954, he had omitted to push the change through
the Russian and Ukrainian Supreme Soviets, but only through their
Presidiums.[26] Constitutionality, Putin was suggesting, had been flouted.
It was a dubious assertion, but he was correct insofar as the transfer
had taken place without a properly broad discussion: Crimea had been
shifted on the map through a perfunctory process overseen by the
Kremlin leadership.

Then Putin went on the attack, accusing the Western powers of
hypocrisy:

> Today we are talking about events in Ukraine, and our partners
> confirm the need to observe the country's territorial integrity.
> They say that all those fighting for their rights and interests in the
> east of Ukraine are pro-Russian separatists. Whereas those who
> fought against us in the Caucasus, including under the leadership
> of 'al-Qaida' – using its money and holding its weapons in their
> hands and even with al-Qaida militants taking a direct part in
> combat actions – were fighters for democracy. It's shocking but it's
> a fact. They talked to us about the disproportionate use of force.
> They said, 'How come you're firing from tanks and bringing up
> artillery: you can't do that, you can't do that!' And what about
> Ukraine? The aircraft and the tanks, the heavy artillery and the
> salvo systems. They've even used cluster bombs and ballistic
> missiles – it challenges all reason! Yet there's complete silence
> about the disproportionate use of force.[27]

His stance, of course, was that of a Great Russian nationalist, who
does not recognize Ukrainians as a people in their own right. 'I make
no distinction between Ukrainians and Russians,' he explained on
Russian TV. 'I think that we are one people. Someone may have a

different opinion on this, and we can discuss it. This is probably not the place to talk about it right now. But we are helping people, above all we're helping the Ukrainian people.'[28]

What he failed to accept was that his own actions had done more than anyone since Stalin to drive a wedge between the two peoples.

Putin claimed that foreigners were secretly involved in fighting on the side of Ukraine's government. 'We often talk of "the Ukrainian army, Ukrainian army"', he exclaimed in a speech to students at the St Petersburg Mining University, where in 1997 he had received his doctorate:

> Who is doing the fighting there? Yes, there are official units of the armed forces, but a large part of the fighting is carried out by so-called volunteer nationalist battalions. Essentially this isn't an army but a foreign legion – in this case a NATO legion which naturally does not pursue the national interests of Ukraine. It has entirely different goals which are linked to the achievement of geopolitical goals of containing Russia, which is absolutely not in the interests of the Ukrainian people.[29]

Suggesting that the fighters taking on the Russian army units in eastern Ukraine were not Ukrainian nationals could hardly be more bizarre.

He went on to justify his operation in Crimea on humanitarian grounds:

> These were [Crimean] people who were scared of the coup; let's be direct about this, they were shaken by the state coup in Ukraine. And after the coup in Kiev – and it was nothing but a coup d'état, however much they dressed it up: the extreme nationalist forces who were coming to power at that moment, and to a significant extent came to power, simply started to threaten people. And threaten Russian people and Russian-speaking people living in Ukraine in general and in Crimea in particular because there's a greater concentration of Russians and Russian speakers [in Crimea] than in all the other parts of Ukraine.
>
> What did we do? We didn't go to war, we didn't occupy anyone, we didn't fire our weapons, nobody perished as the result of events in Kiev. Not a single person. We used the armed forces only to prevent the more than twenty thousand troops serving there from interfering in the free expression of their will by the people living there. People went to the referendum and voted.

They wanted to be part of Russia. The question is: what is the nature of democracy? For me, what's important is not territory or borders but the fate of people.[30]

In other words, the Kremlin had done nothing wrong. Putin had seldom exploited sentiment so blatantly.

It was left to Foreign Affairs Minister Lavrov to put a pragmatic spin on things. Speaking to American reporters, Lavrov recalled that Yanukovych had signed an agreement on 21 February 2014 for early elections, despite knowing he faced almost certain defeat at the hands of Ukraine's voters. The Crimean outcome, he insisted, could have been avoided if only Yanukovych's enemies had shown some patience and waited to trounce him at the hustings,[31] But the continuing street violence and anti-Russian extremism in the Supreme Rada left Russia with no choice but armed action.

Almost the entire ruling group in Russia declared strong support. The exception was the Minister of Finances, Siluanov, who acknowledged the economic damage caused by the invasion, especially to most people's savings. 'Nobody can refund that money, because it went to Crimea, to anti-crisis measures.'[32] Kudrin, his predecessor at the Finance Ministry, went further and called the policy in Ukraine a disaster:

For me the defence of Russian national interests lies in the strengthening of economic might. Without this, we shall not have military might nor might of any kind. But now our economic strength is weakening and we cannot achieve the objective we have set in external and in internal policy, and this is why my concerns have strengthened.[33]

Gleb Pavlovski, a 'political technologist' inside the Presidential Administration until 2011, when he crossed into opposition, suggested Russia would continue to suffer until its forces ceased to interfere in the Donbass.[34] Neither Pavlovski nor Kudrin was driven by a moral or legal calculus: each judged that Putin had chosen an option he ought to have shunned, and the country was going to pay a heavy price.

At least Putin could take solace from the steep rise in his personal popularity. The annexation won Russian hearts, and even the American-led sanctions served to confirm his reputation as a fearless patriot. No Western policy-maker had foreseen this. Meanwhile he went on feeding the hunger for national pride, remarking at the Federal Assembly in December 2014 that Prince Vladimir the Great had received his Christian baptism on the Crimean peninsula in 988:

> [This] gives us every reason to say that Crimea, ancient Korsun, the Chersonese and Sevastopol have invaluable civilizational and sacral importance for Russia. Like the Temple Mount in Jerusalem for the followers of Islam and Judaism.[35]

No Russian media commentator chose to expose this designation of the peninsula as the Russian 'ancestral' homeland as conflicting somewhat with the historical record. But those few Russians who wished that Medvedev had contested and won the 2012 presidential election were wrong if they believed he would not have ordered the Crimean operation. It had been Medvedev who had set in train the 2008 invasion of Georgia. The Kremlin was united in its determination to seize Crimea, and Medvedev would have faced trouble had he decided to ignore the consensus.

Six years later Putin was the president in office, and revelling in his ability to rewrite history as he chose. He denied that it had been Ukrainians who started the Maidan protest movement of 2013–14. He charged the CIA with having conducted a thoroughgoing campaign of interference in Ukraine's politics. The trouble had supposedly started not in Moscow or even Kyiv but in Washington.[36] As usual, it was Patrushev who drew the starkest picture:

> For the last quarter of a century this activity [of the USA and its closest allies] has been directed towards the complete break between Ukraine and the other republics of the USSR and Russia and towards the total reformatting of the post-Soviet space in favour of American interests. The conditions and pretexts were created for the colour revolutions, which were ensured by generous state financing.[37]

'We cannot allow,' fulminated Patrushev, 'the genocide of the Russian-speaking population of the Donbass.' He charged the European Union with permitting the growth of neo-Nazi groups, and the West as a whole with planning to instigate a 'colour revolution' in Russia, as it had done in Georgia and Ukraine, by subsidizing non-governmental media organizations to spread destabilizing ideas among the Russian people.[38]

Though the dominant emotion among Russians in 2014 was joy

about Crimea joining Russia, leaving Putin basking in its sunshine, there were already signs of approaching bad weather. Putin had dreamed of tempting a fraternal Ukraine into the Eurasian Economic Union. Perhaps he might never have achieved this goal, but the annexation of Crimea deprived Russia permanently of the opportunity to use the Crimean Russians to exert permanent peaceful pressure on Kyiv.[39] Cain's hands were bloody after he attacked Abel. But the Ukrainian Abel survived the assault and remained full of resentments. If the Ukrainian people had been divided about Europe before 2014, they were now united in the national cause of defence against a future Russian yoke. The price was paid by both countries: Ukraine losing Crimea and being forced into a bloody defence of eastern Ukraine; Russian troops committed to a war that has no foreseeable end. There will be no rapprochement for generations.

13. TRANSATLANTIC OBSESSION: TROUBLES WITH AMERICA

The Ukraine crisis put on ice the slim chance of entente between Putin and Obama, and the freeze seemed likely to last for decades beyond Obama's time in office. The two leaders had never got on well: they stiffened in each other's presence. Each felt he had tried his best to improve relations, only to come up against a brick wall. Of the two, Putin had always been the more difficult to please. For years before he returned to the presidency in 2012 he had been obsessed with America's handling of Russia, and that preoccupation reached a peak during his 2011–12 electoral campaign.

The American and German leaderships had an obvious preference for Medvedev as president, and would have liked him rather than Putin to have stood again. Chancellor Merkel's demeanour made this unmistakable.[1] In March 2011 Vice-President Joe Biden came close to voicing his desired choice on a visit to Moscow when he met leading figures of the Russian Opposition.[2] He reportedly told people that he had 'looked into Putin's eyes and saw no soul' – a negative echo of George W. Bush's initial approval of Putin in 2001. At a reception in the United States embassy at Spaso House Biden hinted that he hoped for a Medvedev victory.[3] In May the same year, the Obama administration nominated the political scientist Michael McFaul to the Moscow embassy. McFaul, a Russian speaker, was a leading advocate of a 'reset' in American policy on Russia, in the direction of increasing dialogue and resolving matters that had become divisive. But he had also been active in encouraging democratic movements in the Soviet Union and the Russian Federation, and Putin would soon regard his appointment as a hostile measure on Obama's part.[4]

Putin was angrier still when Secretary of State Hillary Clinton let rip about the severity of the police in breaking up Moscow street protests against the cheating by the authorities in the December 2011

Duma elections. 'Putin is a thief!' demonstrators had yelled, and
'Russia without Putin!' Clinton issued her objection while on a visit to
Lithuania, in a speech at the 'Civil Society Meet and Greet' in Vilnius's
Tolerance Centre on the need for governments to be held accountable.
She criticized rulers who looked on civil society and its organizations
'as adversaries instead of partners'. Clinton talked of the 'flawed Duma
election' in Russia, and criticized the official interference with impartial
electoral monitoring. 'So for us,' she declared, without naming Putin,
'it is just an article of faith that democracy is not only about elections;
but in the absence of free, fair, transparent elections, it's hard for
democracy to be sustained.'[5]

On 8 December, two days after her speech, Putin felt stung into
replying. Clinton had given her assessment of the Duma electoral
process, he said, without waiting for reports by valid international
observers. He charged the American with pouring hundreds of
millions of dollars into a hostile propaganda campaign.[6] He was exaggerating America's efforts, and anyway it was Clinton's speech, not
American external finance, that had annoyed him. When she later
tried to understand the source of his anger, she guessed that he
objected to her making trouble for him in Vilnius, whereas he would
never travel to Mexico City to revile Obama. Probably, she thought, he
had asked himself: if the United States wanted a 'reset', why was Obama
permitting his secretary of state to shoot her mouth off?[7]

Putin had his own presidential campaign on his mind. The
Moscow demonstrations were the biggest since the early 1990s, and
the anti-Putin surge in Russia continued after Putin's election in
March 2012, culminating in a huge demonstration a week before he
was inaugurated for his third presidential term in May. Police arrested
Opposition leaders Nemtsov and Navalny, who had headed the
protests. This was six months before Obama secured his second and
last term of office.

Russian leaders never forgave the political interventions by
Obama's team in what they saw as their privileged zone of influence. A
tape of Assistant Secretary of State Victoria Nuland in conversation
with Ambassador Geoffrey Pyatt soon came to light in which she
discussed the composition of a future Ukrainian government. Nuland
briskly rejected talk of ex-boxer Vitali Klichko holding a cabinet post:
'I don't think it's necessary. I don't think it's a good idea.' To the Kremlin
leadership this was definitive proof of American meddling.[8] It was this
kind of thinking that in February 2014 nudged Putin over the brink

into armed action. By conventional standards of international diplomacy, Nuland's presence and activity in central Kyiv was a grandstanding performance that encouraged the protesters at a critical moment when Yanukovych was struggling for his survival. It is not known whether Obama had authorized the State Department's initiative. But Putin judged things by what was happening on the streets of Ukraine. He was angry that American officials felt free to incite trouble for Yanukovych which could redound to the Kremlin's discomfort.

Resentment of Washington has come to guide all Putin's thinking. He repeatedly put on record his contention that there is a single power in the world menacing Russian interests. Though he has castigated the United Kingdom for its action against Russian leaders and intelligence agencies, it is the Americans who are his supreme fixation: he has yet to object publicly to the behaviour of China, Saudi Arabia or even Germany – all are countries that have directly thwarted Russia economically or diplomatically. He handles his problems with them in private and judges every step in Russian foreign policy by what he may gain or lose in regard to the American administration.

Putin has emphasized how hard it is to effect change in American public life. Having observed several American national elections, he concluded that there is always pressure for candidates to adopt a militant anti-Russian stance: politicians who seek endorsement from their political parties find it advantageous to condemn the Kremlin leadership.[9] Take Obama, he explained in an interview for France's *Figaro* magazine:

> a forward-thinking man, a liberal, a democrat. Did he not pledge to shut down Guantanamo before his election? But did he do it? No, he did not. And may I ask why not? Did he not want to do it? He wanted to, I am sure he did, but it did not work out. He sincerely wanted to do it, but did not succeed, since it turned out to be very complicated.[10]

When Obama left the White House, scores of alleged jihadis remained behind bars at the Cuban military base without trial. Putin saw this as an object lesson in the limits of presidential power in the American political system.[11]

In March 2012 Obama had tried to dispel mutual distrust by confiding in Medvedev – still Russian president at the time – at their encounter in Seoul. Neither was aware before the start of their press conference that nearby microphones could pick up their conversation.

It was a mistake that provided insight into the manoeuvres that take place out of public hearing:

> **Obama:** On all these issues, but particularly missile defence, this can be solved, but it's important for him to give me space.
>
> **Medvedev:** Yes, I understand. I understand your message about space. Space for you . . .
>
> **Obama:** This is my last election. After my election I [shall] have more flexibility.
>
> **Medvedev:** I understand. I will transmit this information to Vladimir.[12]

Obama wanted Putin to understand that, regardless of what he had to say as a presidential contender, he remained desirous of a deal with Russia on the matters causing tension. The 2009 reset had run into difficulties, but should be saved and reactivated. Obama had achieved progress with Medvedev. He wanted to avoid warmth turning to frost when Putin re-entered the Kremlin as president.

Putin felt the need to keep up his guard. Mitt Romney, who won the Republican Party's nomination to fight Obama, called Russia the 'number one geopolitical foe'.[13] But Romney's defeated rival, John McCain, was no less severe about Putin, charging Obama with showing dangerous weakness – and was later to argue that Obama's foreign policy had the effect of tempting Putin to engage in his armed adventures in Ukraine.[14] Though Putin expected to be a butt of criticism during the United States hustings, he was disconcerted by the way American policy continued to develop. On the one hand, the Jackson–Vanik Amendment, which the US Congress had passed in 1974 to restrict trade with countries such as the USSR with a bad record on human rights, was repealed in December 2012 and Obama endorsed Russia's entry into the World Trade Organization. But with many Congressmen and Senators remaining uneasy about Russia, they passed the Magnitsky Act, which levelled sanctions against those responsible for the death of Bill Browder's Russian lawyer, as part of the legislation to repeal the Jackson–Vanik Amendment. The immediate response from Russia was a Duma decree prohibiting Americans from adopting Russian children. A list was compiled of American officials to be banned from travelling to Russia.

The Americans also became aware that the Russians had begun to infringe the 1987 Intermediate Nuclear Forces Treaty. In 2007 Putin had announced his dissatisfaction with the obligations it imposed. By

2014, as the international crisis deepened over Crimea and eastern Ukraine, Washington issued formal notification of Russian breaches, including the development and deployment of cruise missiles with the geographical range that was banned by the treaty. For Moscow, the criticism was unfair, because it took no account of the countries in Asia that were acquiring weaponry Russia's defences had to match. Meanwhile, Russian spokesmen indicated, American arrangements for the installation of the controversial missile defence system were still going ahead in Poland, the Czech Republic and Romania. The Russians also asserted that American military drones, which had not existed in the 1980s, constituted a violation of the Intermediate Nuclear Forces Treaty.

Obama, in Putin's eyes, had always been part of the problem. Though he had signed the New Strategic Arms Reduction Treaty and reduced expenditure on American armed forces, he followed Reagan in approving a massive modernization programme for all types of weaponry, and planning new missile and delivery systems. Since the last years of the twentieth century American armaments had aged; Obama resolved to change all that. A stupendous outlay of $1 trillion was guaranteed for the period through to the year 2040.[15] Attention was also given to cyber-warfare preparations. Presidential orders were issued for a newly established Cybercommand to start work in 2010.[16] The Pentagon's budget swelled. Whereas its research and experimental contract operations in 2014 were a mere half of what Microsoft spent that year, there could be no doubt about America's commitment to remaining ahead of its potential enemies.[17] When Obama left the White House in January 2017, he had cut America's defence finances in absolute terms, but the United States continued to account for two-fifths of the entire world's military expenditure. In truth there was only a single superpower.[18]

Experience has inoculated Putin against disappointment in American leaders. He is insouciant, at least in public: 'Presidents come and go, and even parties arrive in and then leave power. But the main policy track does not change. So by and large we don't care who will be at the helm in the United States. We have a rough idea of what is going to happen.'[19]

Putin's phlegmatic recommendation is that Russian leaders act on the assumption of no great improvement in relations with the United States, regardless of who occupies the White House. He describes it as 'a curious thing' to which he has simply had to adapt.[20]

It has been his habit, when talking to American politicians and diplomats, to single out the CIA and the Defense Department as the main perpetrators of hostile actions against Russia as it goes about pursuing what he sees as its national interests.[21] He avoids giving the impression of personal rancour and on occasion still refers to America as Russia's 'partner'. Such are his contradictions that he warns against those who seek to 'demonize' George W. Bush.[22] He called Obama 'my colleague' and described him as a thinking person.[23] His desire is to come across as a courteous, thoughtful leader who gives others the benefit of the doubt. When he wants, he can appear as the voice of reason.

In 2008 Putin had been irritated when the newly elected Obama assured him it was no longer American policy to rampage around the world seeking 'regime change'. Obama found it difficult to persuade him of his sincerity, and after the United States intervened in the Libyan turmoil in 2011, Putin told Obama his own doubts about a transformed American foreign policy were vindicated.[24] The press in Russia and America could not fail to notice how grim they both looked in June 2013 sitting together at the G8 summit in Northern Ireland. By autumn the same year Obama decided to cancel a scheduled meeting after Putin granted political asylum to the American IT consultant Edward Snowden, who had published thousands of classified documents before fleeing the United States.[25] After Crimea, they talked by phone but seldom met. An exception was their encounter in September 2015 at the United Nations headquarters in New York, where they discussed difficult matters including Ukraine and Syria. But the icy relations between Washington and Moscow never thawed, even at the edges. Neither president invited the other to his capital. There was no summit meeting. Obama regarded Putin as a lost cause, and Putin reciprocated.

When the dangers of military escalation were all too obvious, however, neither of them could afford to let relations unravel completely. John Kerry, Hillary Clinton's successor as US Secretary of State from 2012, made several trips to Russia, his mission to convince the Kremlin that America was seriously interested in improving the international atmosphere. Putin received him grudgingly, and the exchanges were formal and lacking earlier pleasantries. As was Putin's habit with American secretaries of state, he kept Kerry waiting for scheduled meetings – on one occasion the delay stretched to four hours. This habitual discourtesy was a deliberate attempt to let the

Americans know that Russia was a power to be reckoned with.[26] But it was also a pathetic gesture. If this was Putin's only way of inflicting pain on Washington, Russian power was evidently weaker than he wanted others to believe. At any rate, Kerry reacted with consummate self-control, showing that Putin's ploys were too blatant to deserve a response. Although Kerry had his problems with Putin, direct communication between Washington and Moscow never ceased. In the first five months of 2016 Lavrov spoke to Kerry more than thirty times and met him for talks on four occasions.[27]

Only one eminent American was treated with good manners. This was President Nixon's Secretary of State Henry Kissinger, who defied age and the conventional wisdom of American foreign policy after Crimea by urging policy-makers in Washington to show an understanding of Russia's legitimate regional interests. Kissinger was accustomed to a warm welcome on his Moscow visits. As the co-architect of President Nixon's policy of détente with the USSR in the 1970s, he continued to urge Americans to show some 'realism' about Russia in the world of the twenty-first century: music to Russian ears. Lavrov purred his name in a reverent tone.[28] Kissinger argued that, to Russia, Ukraine can never be just a foreign country, but he balanced this with the statement that Russia should not 'force Ukraine into a satellite status', and added that Putin should beware of bringing back a situation like the Cold War. In Kissinger's opinion, Ukraine had the right to makes its own choice of an economic and political association with the European Union and Russia should accept this. He advised, however, against admitting Ukraine into NATO membership, arguing that the Ukrainians should aim to achieve the kind of relationship with Russia that Finland possessed. And even Kissinger was adamant that Crimea should be handed back to Ukraine.[29]

In 2013 he was awarded an honorary professorship from Russia's Diplomatic Academy – he ruefully told Putin that kind words from him did him no favours in America.[30] Kissinger continued his quest for conciliation between the two countries. Though his *Washington Post* article on 5 March 2014 required concessions from Moscow, his desire for rapprochement meant that Putin was enthusiastic about meeting him – and Putin refrained from his usual trick of keeping a visitor waiting.[31] In June 2017 Kissinger talked to Putin in Moscow for two whole hours. It was the twenty-eighth time that he and Putin had held a discussion.[32]

The Crimean annexation hardened Obama's Russian policy. Without issuing threats, he wanted Putin to know that Russia was going to pay a price for its gross infringement of Ukrainian sovereignty.[33] But Obama was more cautious in public, and applied economic sanctions without flights of rhetoric. Yet he used turns of phrase that he knew would give offence to Putin. At the international nuclear security summit in The Hague in March 2014, he casually referred to Russia as 'a regional power'. As former Secretary of State Zbigniew Brzezinski remarked, nothing was more likely to cause annoyance in Moscow. Not that this discouraged Brzezinski from scoffing that the Russians had to have Ukraine if they were to become even a regional power again. Foreign Affairs Minister Lavrov managed to affect a verbal shrug when recalling this in January 2017.[34] But Putin took it as an affront. In an interview with Germany's *Bild* magazine two years later he was still indignant:

> If there's talk of Russia as a regional power, it's necessary to start by defining what region is being spoken of. We need to look at the map and say, 'What's this, the European part? Or is it the eastern part where we have as our neighbours Japan and the United States, if we keep Alaska in mind, and China? Is it the Asian part? Or perhaps the southern part? Or should we look north? Essentially, in the north we border on Canada over the Arctic Ocean. Or in the south? Where, then? What region are we speaking about?[35]

Putin's conclusion laid bare his sore feelings:

> I think that arguments about other countries – the attempt to talk of other countries in a demeaning manner – is the reverse side of the coin from trying to demonstrate one's exceptionalism. This seems to me a mistaken position.[36]

He was never one to take an insult lying down.

Mostly, however, Putin preferred to use non-inflammatory language – it was his way of dealing with the Americans that he tried to mask it when the blows hurt. But he could not resist occasional jibes. In December 2014, fed up with criticism about the seizure of Crimea, he noted the widespread conviction in the US that it had been 'fair to snatch Texas from Mexico'.[37] Interestingly, he avoided naming the United States as the snatcher: he had made his point clearly enough. Equally significant was that an event in the mid-nineteenth century was being adduced to validate current practice. Putin was trying to show that he could continue to punch for as long as opponents were confronting him, while at the same trying to avoid making a bad situation worse. This was the style of the entire Kremlin elite: leave it to others lower down the hierarchy of public life to issue the direst warnings. At a conference of retired Russian and American commanders in March 2015, the Russians said if NATO should ever attempt to recover Crimea there would be a Third World War.[38]

Putin likes people to think he feels calm when handling relations with the United States, saying of the Obama presidency:

> I do not think that the United States is a threat to us. I think that, to use a hackneyed term, the ruling establishment's policies are misguided. I believe that these policies are not in our interests and undermine trust in the United States, and in this sense they damage the United States' own interests by eroding confidence in the country as a global economic and political leader.[39]

and poking fun at the overreaching nature of American ambition:

> Essentially, the unipolar world is simply a means of justifying dictatorship over people and countries. The unipolar world turned out too uncomfortable, heavy and unmanageable a burden even for the self-proclaimed leader.[40]

Putin's insouciance is a pretence. To both himself and Security Council Secretary Patrushev it was manifest that America and its allies thought the Cold War was far from over.[41] As usual Patrushev could be relied upon to gloss Putin's thinking in the sharpest terms:

> The leadership of the USA has set itself the objective of world domination. In this connection, they have no need for a strong Russia. On the contrary they need to weaken our country to the maximum extent. They don't rule out the achievement of this aim even through the break-up of the Russian Federation. This will open access to the United States to the richest resources which Russia in their opinion undeservedly has at its disposal . . . Washington thinks that it can, whenever it wants, fulfil the role of catalyst in this process.[42]

America, in this analysis, was bent on finding any pretext to do Russia harm. Russia, the Russian leadership seemed to believe, would have suffered punishment, in the form of economic sanctions or geopolitical encroachment, regardless of what it decided to do in Crimea.

While Obama was in office, Putin maintained his resentment and suspicion and focused on how to give grief to the American administration. Moscow and Washington screamed at each other like vengeful hawks, and the prospects of reconciliation appeared negligible. But everything changed when the unexpected happened in the course of the 2016 American presidential campaign and one unfancied Republican candidate swam against the stream of conventional wisdom by heaping praise on Putin and saying, 'I think I'll be able to get along with him.'[43]

14. CONTINENTAL DISRUPTIONS: RUSSIA'S PENETRATION OF EUROPE

Russia's purpose under Putin has been to prise Europe – whether individual leaders, particular political parties, economic groupings or even whole countries – from the American embrace. Moscow has a lengthy tradition of using subversive activity to interfere in European politics. The Soviet communist leadership provided millions of rubles to organizations that might be used to further its interests: not only communist parties but also the 'peace movement' and the campaigns for unilateral nuclear disarmament.

At the start of his third presidential term in 2012 Vladimir Putin set the tone by feigning surprise at how the Americans were allowed to bully banks in Frankfurt, Berlin and Paris by fining them billions of dollars for alleged misdemeanours on world markets, contrasting this with how the Eurasian Economic Union was designed to act towards its member countries[1] – all the while maintaining that Russia wanted harmonious links with European countries. Whereas he is often touted in the Western media as an unreconstructed Stalinist, Putin has been scathing about the Soviet policy of using massive force to impose communist states in the lands conquered by the Red Army. The result, he has acknowledged, was that the USSR acquired only involuntary allies, which was no prescription for effective joint action.[2]

The United States, meanwhile, was growing alarmed at the reliance of several European countries, including Germany and Italy, on Russian natural gas supplies, raising the question of whether the USSR would become able to threaten America's NATO allies by a sudden suspension of delivery via the pipelines constructed in the 1970s if they were to follow policies damaging to the Kremlin's interests. Such qualms did not disappear after the fall of communism in Moscow in 1991. In the rest of the decade, observers noted, Russia used fuel exports as a weapon in its early conflicts with Ukraine, even cutting off supplies to bring Kyiv into line. If this was done to Kyiv, it could be done to Berlin and Rome.

Two women, one in the US and one in Europe, had spectacular qualifications for dealing with Putin. The first was Condoleezza Rice, US Secretary of State from 2005, who began her academic career researching the US–Soviet arms race in the 1980s. Her grounding in the politics and military technology of the USSR, as well as her command of the Russian language, gave her an advantage in talks with a man like Putin. The two of them had discussions that sometimes turned fiery. In 2006 he lost his temper over Russia's Georgian policy and stood up to peer down on her. Rice was ready for menacing tricks like this. Rising on her high heels, she returned his stare from a superior height.[3] Putin never managed to intimidate her. On another occasion he showed his appreciation of her firmness and expertise: 'You know us!'[4] Rice left office at the end of the Bush administration in January 2009, having led the State Department during the difficult years when Putin turned Russian policy towards confrontation with America. The difficulties were about to intensify.

The second woman was Chancellor Angela Merkel – in 2015 alone she met Putin seven times and had twenty conversations by phone.[5] Born in Hamburg but raised in the German Democratic Republic, she had had direct experience of East German and Soviet communist officialdom as she was growing up, and had never known a time when Russia was far from her mind. Merkel's father, a Lutheran pastor, passed on to his daughter a commitment to remove the yoke of communism. A brilliant linguist at high school, she won her year's Russian-speaking national Olympiad, but although she has no need for an interpreter, she keeps one by her side when talking to Russians – she once confessed to a phobia about speaking in Russian after having her bicycle stolen as a young girl by a Soviet soldier.[6] Putin for his part gained fluency in German during his five years on active secret service in Dresden. The two have had frequent lively discussions. Merkel knows her own mind, and has regularly shared its contents with him. At the same time she is renowned for her readiness to listen to others, and Putin has discovered that patches of silence are not a sign of weakness. She has an acute sensitivity to the dangers of Russian expansionism, and in 2014 rebuked him for invading Crimea and making war in eastern Ukraine. As German chancellor she backed the sanctions regime initiated by the Americans.

Putin was willing to await events. Not only the FSB but the German daily press too revealed that industrial and financial lobbying was growing for Germany to accept the new geopolitical reality of Crimea as a Russian province. Merkel ignored her German critics, warning Putin again that he would pay dearly if he were to repeat his expansionist moves. Neither Russia's nuclear weapons and tank regiments nor its importance as a fuel supplier gave her pause for thought. She refused to be bullied. Her constant refrain to Putin was that he should show greater respect for democratic procedures and the rule of law. In rejecting her advice he apparently remembered that Catherine the Great, who was born as a princess of Anhalt-Zerbst, is a heroine of Merkel's – she has a portrait of the empress hanging on the wall in her Chancellery. Putin is said to have told her:

> Imagine yourself sitting in the Kremlin and you have electors who live in Kaliningrad while there are also those who live in Petropavlovsk-Kamchatski. And you have to somehow bring unity across this entire territory which is so diverse in languages, views and life-styles. You've got to say something to bring these people together. One of your compatriots, a truly great compatriot, was our empress. That was Catherine II. She started by wanting to bring about a rapid abolition of the feudal system (*krepostnoe pravo*). But then she learned about how Russia was constructed, and do you know what she did? She reinforced the rights of the landed gentry and destroyed the rights of the peasantry. There's no other way in our country: you only need to take a step to the right or to the left, and you lose power.[7]

If this transcript is authentic, Putin was asking Merkel to accept that Russia required its own peculiar mode of governance.

Gerhard Schröder, Merkel's predecessor as German chancellor, was more to Putin's liking. Schröder had always defended Putin against charges of authoritarian rule and worked for an improvement in relations with Russia. His Russian friend's gratitude was confirmed with the remarkable invitation from the Gazprom board in December 2005, just weeks after he left office, for him to join its Nord Stream consortium which was planning a gas pipeline to Germany – a scheme that would use a North Sea route and bypass Ukrainian and Polish territory. A barrage of criticism greeted his acceptance. Schröder was no doubt pleased about the size of his Russian salary. Putin was even happier: for the price of the German's contract he had driven a wedge into German public opinion. Russia was recruiting a foreign statesman willing to validate Putin's credentials as a 'flawless democrat', a description that Russian public figures continued to quote for years afterwards.[8] But Schröder was no longer chancellor, and Putin had to deal with an annoyed Merkel, who refused to tailor her policies to Moscow's requirements.

France seemed more promising. Though President François Hollande and his Socialist Party denounced the Crimean annexation and joined those countries applying economic sanctions, there was a degree of vacillation. The French authorities were notably lax about enforcing the travel ban on named individuals. When the then Duma Speaker Sergei Naryshkin arrived in Paris to address a UNESCO conference he was not stopped at Charles de Gaulle airport despite being banned from setting foot in France.[9] In his address Naryshkin voiced ecstatic approval of Putin's military action in Crimea, and hailed those few European politicians such as the French Republican parliamentarian Nadine Morano who called for a partnership with Russia. He saluted Italian political figures demanding a cancellation of economic sanctions: to Naryshkin it seemed clear the European Union had made 'strategic mistakes', especially in the matter of what he dismissed as 'illegal sanctions'. Europeans, he went on, had to learn that it was pointless to try to '"correct" Russia's cultural code'. No amount of 'economic pressure and blackmail' would ever achieve anything: the West had to cease its centuries-long attempt to 'educate' the East. What he understood by 'the West' was America and its European allies, and he accused the Americans of inheriting from Europe an assumption that they had the right to interfere at will in the Middle East. All this had to change. Rival powers, Naryshkin declared, had to appreciate the benefit of collaboration with Russia.[10]

Hollande, however, remained firm and cancelled France's contract to build two Mistral-class helicopter carriers for the Russian navy, despite huge commercial and industrial pressure to complete a contract worth $1.6 billion. Tens of thousands of French jobs were at stake, he knew, and many of his own party's supporters were likely to suffer. Nevertheless, he decided it would give the wrong signal to Moscow if it received advanced military equipment after using its armed forces to invade and annex a foreign country in breach of international law. A settlement was reached in which the French government agreed to pay financial compensation to Russia for its expenses while seeking an alternative buyer for the helicopter carriers.[11]

The Kremlin, meanwhile, noted the hostility of Marine Le Pen and her Front National towards the European Union. Le Pen regularly denounced what she saw as Brussels' mishandling of France's legitimate interests, and intimated that if elected president she might decide to withdraw her country entirely from the European Union. She also objected to the Western economic sanctions against Russia and, like Putin, blamed the West for starting a new Cold War. As the Kremlin was aware, she was in dire financial straits as she prepared to stand again for the presidency, the French banks having refused to lend to the Front National, which the political establishment had hoped would strangle the political far right. As Le Pen looked for money abroad, she found a ready listener in the First Czech-Russian Bank. Though the institution was based in the Czech Republic, its principal owners were Russian. Le Pen obtained a loan of €9 million, which would come to light when the bank subsequently ran into trouble and called in its debts. The French media was immediately interested, and in some newspapers Le Pen was denounced as a puppet of the nefarious Putin.[12]

This was, however, far from proof that Putin had 'bought' her. The European Union has a growing number of groups and organizations on the political far right who are both seeking to throw off the trammels of Brussels and genuinely respect much that Putin stands for: national sovereignty, conservative social values, the Christian faith, hostility to interference by unaccountable international bodies. There is also admiration for Putin's style of strong leadership.

Russia's leaders shared the commitment to conservative social values, warmed to parties that advocated the sovereign rights of nation states, and relished the chance to weaken the mortar that held the European Union together. But when they actively helped the European political far right, it was for their own reasons. A diminished European Union would increase the opportunity for a resurgent Russia to exert continental influence. The recipients of the Kremlin's assistance are not paid stooges, but Europeans who have an alternative vision for Europe: not all of them call for withdrawal from the European Union, but any disruption they achieve is regarded with satisfaction in Moscow. Putin sees his policy as tit for tat. The European Union saw fit to try to lure Ukraine into its orbit in 2013, so Russian leaders feel free to interfere in the affairs of nations throughout the continent.

Visiting Moscow in April 2014, when Russia was under criticism for annexing Crimea, Le Pen confirmed her support for Putin, and the Kremlin quietly assisted her bid to become president in the forthcoming French election.[13] In March 2017 Putin welcomed her to

Moscow. While stressing that Russia would never want to interfere in the French electoral process, he had made no effort to invite any other presidential candidate, and he accorded Le Pen a magnificent reception.[14] Before meeting Putin, she talked to Duma Speaker Vyacheslav Volodin and agreed to campaign for the removal of the ban on Russia's participation in the Parliamentary Assembly of the Council of Europe.[15] According to the official Russian transcript, it was she who raised political matters with Putin by calling for strategic as well as cultural and economic ties between the two countries. She also wanted a greater exchange of intelligence data to counteract Islamist terrorism, and trumpeted her desire to end the prohibition of visits to the European Union by Russian parliamentarians singled out by America and its allies for travel bans.[16] Despite Putin's denial that Russia was interfering in the French electoral process, he had not bargained for an Interfax news agency report in Moscow that Le Pen's campaign was receiving finance from Russian banks. The report was quickly retracted: 'Correction, Kremlin announces it has no information about the financing of Marine Le Pen's election campaign by Russian banks.'[17] Evidently the Kremlin was happy to pass on finance but drew the line at being seen to do so.

It was just as embarrassing for the Front National in France, and Florian Philippot, its deputy president, had to deny that Le Pen's true purpose in going to Moscow was to seek financial help from Russian banks.[18] Le Pen survived the criticisms in the press and flew back to Paris to take on Emmanuel Macron in the presidential election. She went down to a crushing defeat in the second round in May, and Putin had to revise his plan for partnership with France. Overtures were therefore made to Macron, who in May 2018 was guest of honour at the St Petersburg Economic Forum.

Where possible, Russian leaders sought actually to improve ties with European governments. The most remarkable attempt was on 8 April 2010, when Putin, prime minister at the time, attended a solemn ceremony at Katyn in western Russia to commemorate the Soviet NKVD's murder in 1940 of four thousand captured Polish army officers, standing next to Poland's prime minister Donald Tusk as they both bowed their heads in prayer. They laid wreaths at the cemetery's monument. An Orthodox priest conducted a requiem. In a dignified speech, Putin denounced the crimes of the Stalin period and called for improved relations with Poland, where the Katyn massacre was still a painful memory. But though he offered condolences in respect of the

Polish victims, he stressed that Stalin and his associates had also carried out mass murder on Russians, and that the Russian people could not be held responsible for the slaughter at Katyn. No particular nation, he emphasized, could be blamed for the crimes of a totalitarian regime, and he expressed hopes for a rapprochement between Russians and Poles.[19]

Though opinion in Poland was impressed by his respectful display, its effect was marred two days later by a catastrophic accident when the plane carrying President Lech Kaczyński and dozens of Poland's leading public figures to Russia to continue the commemorative ceremonies crashed as its pilot tried to land at Smolensk airport. There were no survivors. Many Poles speculated that the disaster was the work of Russian secret services. Russia's spokesmen expressed sympathy for the Polish fatalities while brushing aside any conspiracy theory. Russia's case was not helped by the refusal to release any of the remains of the plane to Polish investigators. In Poland, it was widely surmised that President Kaczyński had intended to designate the Katyn massacre an act of genocide. If so, it was speculated, Russian leaders would have taken offence at Poles stirring up a controversy when the Kremlin was trying to do the right thing. Spokesmen in Moscow argued that the debris from the crash was in any case best handled at a single site. It was also commented that Kaczyński had had a habit of harassing flight crews into taking risks in landing, and that the Smolensk weather that fateful day was undeniably hazardous.

Relations between Moscow and Warsaw worsened in the years that followed, and Russia's official historical line lost its tone of remorse for the Poles slain at Katyn in 1940. By April 2017 Minister of Culture Vladimir Medinski felt it worth pointing out that far more Russians died at Katyn than Poles.[20]

While Poland relapsed from its moves toward reconciliation, Hungary surprised the rest of the world by encouraging cooperation with Russia. The USSR had imposed communism on the country after 1945 and invaded it again in 1956 when the Hungarian communist leadership pursued a campaign for a gentler form of communism than the Kremlin would accept. The bloody repression of Hungary's revolt against Soviet oppression only deepened the hatred of Russians and things Russian. Nevertheless, prime minister Victor Orbán was open to Moscow's approaches. He shared many of the conservative principles Putin espoused, and also resented Germany's growing dominance in the European Union. In January 2014 he leapt at Russia's offer of a thirty-year $14 billion loan to expand a Hungarian nuclear plant,[21] the work to be done by the Rosatom company. Hungary was splitting off from the European political mainstream, even though Russian civilian technology was starting to be admired in Europe. The Kremlin did not mind the cost, even though the Russian budget was creaking, and in following years the terms were eased still further in Hungary's interest.[22]

Orbán had to avoid any suspicion of rendering the country subservient to Russia. The slightest hint of secret bribes being paid would mean the political end for him. But Orbán could and did call for an end to Western economic sanctions against Russian politicians, businessmen and companies.[23] At the same time Russia's leaders understood that they had to avoid too much crowing about their success. They contented themselves with the thought that the European Union was showing growing signs of internal tensions.

When in 2015 the Hungarian government refused to admit refugees fleeing the Syrian civil war, the rift between Berlin and Budapest widened sharply. Orbán and Putin were agreed that Angela Merkel, by encouraging the influx of refugees and migrants into the European Union, had acted unwisely and peremptorily. Putin put this into a broad frame of criticism. The refugee emergency in Europe, he stated, flowed from Western policy over several years:

> We actively objected to what was happening, for instance, in Iraq, Libya and several other countries. We said: you shouldn't do that, you shouldn't pile in there and you shouldn't make the mistakes. Nobody listened to us! On the contrary, they thought we were taking an anti-Western position, one that was hostile to the West. And now, when you have hundreds of thousands of refugees – there are now already a million of them – how can you think that our position was either anti-Western or pro-Western?[24]

He was pleased to find European leaders like Orbán who declined to be browbeaten by Brussels or Berlin, but it was the United Kingdom, rather than Hungary, that voted to leave the European Union. British involvement with Brussels had had a lengthy and tormented history that prime minister David Cameron tried to resolve in June 2016 by holding a referendum. The question before the electorate was simply whether to remain or leave. After his own lacklustre campaign for 'remaining', but to his astonishment none the less, 52 per cent of voters chose to pull the country out. Cameron stepped down from power, being succeeded as prime minister by Theresa May, who had voted to remain in the European Union but committed her cabinet to respecting the referendum result by negotiating the country's departure. The ensuing political crisis in both London and Brussels dwarfed every trouble emanating from Budapest. The European Union was breaking up, or at least one of its leading states was choosing to split away. Russian leaders had tried for years to produce divisions inside the EU, but never in their wildest dreams had they imagined such a result. Since 1989, with the fall of communism in eastern Europe, the continent had undergone a process of unification. The trend was suddenly in the opposite direction.

The United Kingdom had been the cause of much trouble for Russia in recent years. It had regularly backed the cause of economic sanctions against Russia and was a vehement critic of the Crimean annexation. Now Putin enjoyed his moment of schadenfreude:

> The Prime Minister is only just beginning her work and there are internal questions for her to grapple with. But there was a time when Great Britain and Russia had firm, comprehensive relations, and we are ready to return to that. It is up to the British side, not to us. We've noted that measures have been put in motion connected with the jubilee year of the [wartime British] northern convoys [to Archangel] and that Princess Anne paid a visit.
>
> We've had a lot of problems in historical periods but there were also moments which undoubtedly bound us together. We remember and know about this, and we're ready to restore relations with Great Britain and go with them as far as they desire, but, of course, we're not going to impose anything, and indeed we can't. We cannot decide for them the scale of relations to be restored. Nevertheless, you see, there is something of the order of 600 companies from Great Britain in our economy and they don't intend to leave it.[25]

Without laughing out loud, Putin could not have shown greater delight. An isolated European country was one Russian leaders looked forward to dealing with from a position of strength.

As British remainer politicians sought to explain their defeat, evidence emerged that Russian internet companies had disseminated propaganda to voters in favour of the leave cause. There was well-grounded speculation that the Kremlin had sponsored these efforts, and as to whether Russians had also supplied financial support for British pro-leave organizations. Russian meddling became a continuous topic of media interest. Though nobody could fairly conclude that the referendum result was entirely the product of Russia's machinations, a degree of interference from Moscow was hard to deny.

In Montenegro Russian intervention went much further. As one of the smallest successor states to former Yugoslavia, Montenegro was notorious for corruption in public life and for organized crime. The cabinet in Podgorica was committed to seeking admission to the European Union, which led to chronic dispute and outbreaks of violence. The imbroglio reached its peak in October 2016, when the authorities accused fourteen individuals of plotting to assassinate prime minister Milo Đukanović and organize a coup d'état. Most of those charged belonged to the Montenegrin political opposition, including the pro-Russian Democratic Front, but two, accused of terrorism, were Russian citizens. All had campaigned for Montenegro to steer a course away from Brussels and towards Moscow. Allegations were made that the Russian secret services had been subsidizing the Democratic Front, and Đukanović was in no doubt that Moscow's hand had directed the alleged conspiracy. He could not arrest the Russians, who were based in nearby Serbia and could therefore return to Russia without fear of extradition. Russian ministers in Moscow spoke with distaste of Đukanović's desire for accession to the European Union and NATO, and accused Đukanović himself of gross financial corruption.

Đukanović got his way even after resigning as prime minister. Negotiations continued for Montenegro to join the European Union, and in April 2017 the Montenegrin parliament voted to enter NATO. Aware of the pressure that Russia was exerting, Western leaders held firm by welcoming Montenegro into the military alliance in June. In Moscow the news was met with disquiet. Not only had Russia's political pretensions been thwarted, but Russian organized crime groups were uneasy about a future where Montenegro might soon cease to offer a haven for their activities. The Russian Foreign Affairs Ministry issued a statement interpreting Đukanović's success as a dangerous increase in instability in the Balkans, and Foreign Affairs Minister Sergei Lavrov and his fellow Russian diplomats tried to divert attention from Putin's objective of increasing instability in Europe.

Putin had set his face against the prospect of a unified and expanded European Union and a strengthened and extended NATO. Though he had suffered a setback in Montenegro, he could point to achievements in France and Hungary, where unease with the European Union was on the rise. The United Kingdom was on the brink of ending its membership. Even in Italy, where Russian secret services were seemingly less active, a surge of displeasure with Brussels culminated in an election in March 2018 that brought to power a coalition consisting of the right-wing League and the left-of-centre Five Star Movement, both of which campaigned for greater national freedom from the European Union's control. Moscow was delighted.[26] The League endorsed the Crimean annexation, apparently without recourse to covert Russian subsidy, and promoted the cause of Italian business investment in Crimea.[27]

Russian leaders in the 1990s had grown accustomed to failure and humiliation, but times had changed, and the sequence of successes and semi-successes could be celebrated. As Lavrov and Putin saw it, if history was not on their side, at least it appeared not to be against them.

MANAGEMENT

15. POLITICAL ORDER: PARTIES, ELECTIONS, PARLIAMENTS

Putin has made the presidency so dominant in Russian politics that it is tempting to assume other institutions count for little. The very idea must give Putin some rueful amusement. Though members of the ruling group set most of the public agenda, they have not always been able to count on compliance, the Federal Assembly in particular sometimes showing an inclination towards obstruction.

When Putin first became president, the members of both the Federal Assembly's upper and lower houses were elected. The upper house, the Federation Council, consisted of two representatives from each of the eighty-five regional units of the second tier of governance, and many of them had grown accustomed to running their republics or provinces with scant regard for Yeltsin's decrees or the cabinet's policies. In 2004 Putin, believing Russia had become ungovernable, persuaded the State Duma to agree to dispense with elections to the Federation Council and let him appoint the regional governors, apparently convinced that 'the power vertical' would immediately work for the general good. The reality turned out differently, and when local problems arose the governors Putin had appointed incurred the blame.[1]

The Duma remained elective, and Putin's first prime minister, Mikhail Kasyanov, had to handle its debates with some delicacy when pursuing his course of economic reforms. It wasn't just the Communist Party and Liberal-Democratic Party that contained critics of governmental policy: even Putin's own Unity Party did. Unity had been formed in 1999 to contest the Duma elections, but obtained fewer than a quarter of the seats, and when Putin won the presidency he and Kasyanov had to confront the problem that the communists were the biggest party in the Duma. They manoeuvred their way round this by negotiating Unity's merger with the All-Russia-Fatherland party that had been led by Luzhkov and Primakov, both of whom he had pushed out of the 2000 presidential electoral contest by means of black propaganda. The newly amalgamated party, United Russia, was proclaimed in April 2001. Although it lacked a majority in the Duma, Kasyanov succeeded in winning enough additional assistance to pass his reforms into law.[2]

Kasyanov's rhetoric, he knew, would not win over the Duma by itself, so he bought the support of individual Duma deputies or their constituencies by dispensing local grants – a practice the Americans call pork-barrel politics. It was a process strewn with obstacles. In the Duma elections in December 2003 Putin and Kasyanov were determined to secure an absolute majority. They were disappointed: true, United Russia had emerged as the biggest party, which was an improvement on 1999, but it still lacked a majority. This would require agile management by the next prime minister, Mikhail Fradkov. Financial and political blandishments were offered to obtain defections from other parties so the cabinet could secure the passage of its bills, an uncomfortable mode of politics for Putin, who required a reliable parliamentary base. In December 2007 the administration threw abundant resources into the Duma elections: promises about welfare; more grants for many Russian constituencies to mollify local grievances. Buoyed by a resurgent economy, the current leaders asked the electorate to stick with them as the best way to achieve progress, using campaign buzzwords such as 'leadership', 'order', 'stability' and 'patriotism'.

Since his party controlled the national TV channels, Putin was assured of getting his message across. United Russia secured 295 out of 450 seats, an absolute majority, comfortably obviating the need for talks with would-be defectors.

This had not come about without the deployment of 'political technology'. While aiming at victory for his party, Putin maintained the appearance of multiparty competition and procedural fairness, licensing his Deputy Chief of Staff Vladislav Surkov to devise electoral rules that would enable a number of opposition parties to gain a minority of seats. As ever, the Kremlin was indulgent towards Zyuganov's communists and Zhirinovski's liberal-democrats, since they no longer stood any chance of defeating United Russia and in any case shared Putin's priority for central state power and an assertive foreign policy. Putin and Surkov were delighted that Yabloko, the liberal party, won only four Duma seats in 2003 and none at all in subsequent elections. Surkov was a wily operator: whenever a new party emerged on the political spectrum to offer a serious threat – or even a half-serious one – to United Russia, he enabled the creation of rival parties that would take votes away from the newcomer. He took the same precautions against the old Communist Party by surreptitiously helping to found Rodina (Motherland), a patriotic party led by Dmitri Rogozin seeking support from working people.[3]

Until Surkov's arrival, politics in Russia were officially a 'managed democracy', its procedures different from those in liberal democracies. Such management from on high, it was suggested, was necessary to achieve the full benefit from elections and public debate. Surkov disliked the term for its authoritarian ring:[4] he wanted control from above to be exercised but not flaunted. In 2006, with Putin's permission, he replaced 'managed democracy' with 'sovereign democracy'. Medvedev regarded both slogans with distaste and argued the case for simply 'real democracy', which was Kasyanov's preference too. But unlike Kasyanov, Medvedev reserved his opinion for behind closed doors until such time as he became president.[5] Not that Medvedev made conditions easier for United Russia's rival parties. Like his patron Putin, he permitted or encouraged the emasculation of democratic procedures. For the ruling group this was the qualification for membership.

While rejecting the charge of Machiavellian manipulation, Surkov was astonishingly frank about his ambitions on behalf of the leadership. Appearing before a United Russia gathering in February 2006, he opined that the objective should be not just to win the Duma the following year but to hold on to it for a minimum of 'ten to fifteen years'.[6] He saw the issue in almost apocalyptic terms. A year later he recounted that the Presidential Administration 'was engaged in preventing revolution in the country' on a daily basis.[7] He saw Putin and his United Russia as crucial for the maintenance of stability and progress. If this necessitated devious practices, even deception, Surkov was the man for the job – and Putin endorsed him.

But Putin saw 'sovereign democracy' as a useful euphemism for what he was trying to achieve for his country, and Surkov's term was officially adopted, signifying Russia's determination to behave as it liked anywhere in the world: most of the world's democracies, Putin was fond of declaring, were subservient to America's geopolitical interests and demands,[8] whereas he, as Russian leader, refused to be cast as the US president's little brother. Like Putin, Surkov saw Washington's connivances as the greatest threat to national independence, and this was the rationale for the restriction of internal freedoms in Russia. No foreign power was going to be permitted to interfere in Russian public affairs. The country's rulers were determined to thwart America's potential interference in its electoral process: as a result they distrusted all international media organizations, IT corporations and charitable non-governmental bodies. The Kremlin leaders themselves, of course, were adept at manipulating Russian elections, but feared that foreigners would seize every chance to deploy the same skills.

Other Kremlin officials had their doubts, and argued for a looser form of politics that could accommodate greater debate and dissent. Putin increasingly disappointed them. In hindsight, Gleb Pavlovski, Putin's one-time adviser, believed on the basis of his experience in the Presidential Administration that Putin had originally hoped to construct a two-party system, striking a balance between United Russia and the Communist Party, on the premise that the communists would turn themselves into a social-democratic party.[9] If Putin truly had such an ambition in mind, he soon discarded it – and the communist leader Zyuganov relapsed into a blinkered chauvinism rather than social-democracy. Putin, it would seem, continued to believe in the need for a more flexible political order, but thought this might best come about through the growth of active factions inside his own United Russia. Pavlovski has also written that Putin is aware Russia faces 'stagnation' unless it changes its system of governance and transforms its economy so that the 'generals' no longer hold the whip hand.[10] It was political self-interest, according to Pavlovski, that dissuaded Putin from taking the plunge, apparently having realized that political reform would threaten his own supporters' interests.[11] But Putin had once told Secretary of State Rice that the Liberal Party had succeeded in governing Japan for nearly all the years since the Second World War, and he saw no reason for Russia not to take the same route.[12]

There was little fuss in the way the State Duma and Federation Council processed bills. Legislative activity, which while Kasyanov was premier had been large scale and frenetic, dwindled to reforms of secondary importance. The two houses tended to work in harmony with the government, the president and each other. It became rare for either the Federation Council or the president to veto legislation. In turn, the Duma took its revising work seriously, especially when the ruling elite was divided – and United Russia became the locus of heavy internal lobbying.[13] Bills initiated by the Presidential Administration were consistently successful: between 2007 and 2011 not one met with failure, even though debates were often fiery. The liberal-democrat leader Zhirinovski was not alone in his combustible behaviour, and he and successive Duma Speakers had to work hard to keep order. But United Russia had both an absolute majority and internal discipline. It could trounce all polemics from the podium or from the seated tiers of the debating hall.[14]

With his reputation for political adroitness, Surkov was assigned the task of repeating his magic at the next Duma election in December 2011. Medvedev was still president, but had already announced that he would stand aside for Putin, and Putin indicated his wish for Medvedev to resume the premiership if he himself were to return as president, a project that became known as 'the tandem'. Putin and Medvedev were treating the country as their patrimony. The announcement of their intentions prompted a wave of public protest, and demonstrations filled the central squares in Moscow.

Surkov performed his tried-and-tested trick of promoting parties that would help United Russia by taking votes away from others. To this end he approached the Just Cause party that spoke for business interests and enabled the billionaire financier Mikhail Prokhorov to assume its leadership. Prokhorov's vision for Russia was more liberal than Putin's, and for a while support for Just Cause rose in the opinion polls – high enough to have an impact on the outcome of the election but not enough to threaten Putin. Unfortunately for Surkov, Prokhorov unexpectedly outlived his usefulness for the Kremlin by starting to think of himself as a true contender and to fulminate against Putin's record. This was not in the script. A political ingénu as well a man of considerable vanity, Prokhorov was surprised when the Just Cause party disowned him. He quickly discovered that Surkov had engineered this.[15] An affronted Prokhorov announced his intention to stand as an independent in the 2012 presidential poll. His campaign predictably ended in defeat, with barely 8 per cent of the vote.

Surkov's confidence, however, proved equally misplaced. His reputation as a wonder worker evaporated when at the December 2011 polls United Russia obtained only 49 per cent of the vote. Luckily for him, victory in the constituencies meant the party obtained 238 out of 450 seats in the Duma, a decline from the previous election but still a small absolute majority.

Voices were raised about widespread fraud in the counting of votes. At some polling stations ballot boxes were filmed being stuffed with false voting slips. Alexei Navalny and others in opposition organized protests on central Moscow's Bolotnaya Square. Not only Prokhorov but even Putin's friend and ex-Finance Minister Kudrin made an appearance. Although police and their batons contained the trouble, Medvedev and Putin took no chances. The election result was officially confirmed. Meanwhile they promoted a bill to limit public demonstrations. For the Duma's anti-government minority, this was a signal that the Putin team aspired to govern forever. United Russia's critics staged an 'Italian strike' by proposing a stream of amendments. Leading oppositionist Gennadi Gudkov, an ex-KGB colonel who had taken the unusual step of joining the Opposition, was charged with business fraud and suspended from the Duma.[16] Trouble in parliament sparked trouble on the streets. Bolotnaya Square was again filled with protesters. Violent policing destroyed the Opposition's hope that other cities would follow the Moscow precedent, and the Kremlin survived the trial of strength. But not without concluding that complacency was unsustainable.

Everyone could see that the Duma, however neutered by pre-election legal manipulation and outright electoral swindle, retained an importance in the public imagination – even though opinion polls yielded far from complimentary verdicts on the performance of the elected politicians themselves. Bolotnaya Square had erupted once and could again, regardless of whether Navalny was in custody. The protesters had shown historical insight in their choice of venue: no ordinary metropolitan spot, but the place where the great rebel leaders in earlier centuries, Stenka Razin and Yemelyan Pugachëv, had been executed. The police in 2011–12 did not carry out the excruciating punishments that Tsar Alexei and Catherine the Great had dispensed, but many in the crowd endured severe beatings, and judicial proceedings were initiated against the organizers. When Nemtsov and Navalny led protests against Putin's presidential inauguration, they were taken into custody.

Though Putin had won the contest with ease in the first round and was easily the country's favourite politician, his team had behaved in character by engaging in some precautionary ballot rigging. There was also a strong suspicion that a cyber-attack on the opposition newspaper *Novaya gazeta* had been carried out on the Kremlin's orders. Putin has never been content simply to win: he feels a compulsion to annihilate by whatever dirty methods are required.

The Duma settled down into the routine of enabling the Kremlin's purposes. In the parliamentary election of December 2016, United

Russia consolidated its dominance by gaining 54 per cent of the popular vote and 343 seats, easily sufficient to take control of the legislative process. Medvedev, party chairman since leaving the presidency in 2012, kept watch over the discipline necessary to pass the laws he and Putin desired. The other parties were as noisy as they always had been, but the Duma failed to discomfit the Kremlin leaders and their clique. Neither the Duma nor the Federation Council exploited the chance to follow up the corruption scandals in the press and on the internet. In many other countries – and not just North America and the rest of Europe – parliamentarians would have raised a fuss about the sumptuous palaces allegedly being built for Putin, Medvedev, Patrushev and others, but those who set the agenda of Duma and Council saw to it that no such discussions took place. Malfeasance could be scrutinized only if United Russia's leaders gave permission – and they were unlikely to facilitate the shaming of their patrons.

Even though United Russia has faced no serious electoral challenge since 2003, Russia's is not a one-party system. This is in marked contrast to the way in which the USSR was governed. Nowadays there is no Communist Party to oversee and coordinate policies and impose obedience. Indeed, United Russia, lacking the machinery to perform even quite simple administrative tasks, has never been asked to fulfil such a function. Its conferences have little impact on government programmes, and its central board has only titular status.

When Medvedev came before the Duma on 11 April 2018 to give his prime ministerial report on the government's performance over the previous six years, he boasted of fifteen hundred initiatives passed into law. He could hardly pretend they amounted to much, but he made the most of legislative reforms that introduced the obligation to use up-to-date technology in public institutions, to achieve transparency in the national budget and to extend the territory available for agriculture.[17] Other laws tended to relate to foreign policy. In December 2012 the so-called Dima Yakovlev law prohibited Americans from adopting Russian orphans. In March 2014 the Duma approved the legislative instrument for Crimea to 'join' Russia. In July 2016 the law on extremism and terrorism was updated so as to compel internet servers in Russia to store the records of their users and make state surveillance easier. The same month saw the passing of a bill to prevent missionary work by non-registered religious organizations. In January 2017 a Duma majority legislated to decriminalize physical beatings inside the family home.

The Duma rarely attracted much attention in the media after the disturbances of 2011–12 died away. Rumbustious debates, especially when deputies pushed each other about, were more likely to gain TV viewers than measured legislative proceedings. Just once was there a touch of levity. On 1 April 2013 a deputy from the Liberal-Democratic Party presented a bill restricting the sale and consumption of garlic. Public buildings and even private residences would be affected, and sales were prohibited except in adequately ventilated premises. To protect the health of pregnant women, teachers and children this mal-odorous vegetable was to disappear from public spaces altogether. The joke was lost on many observers until the bill's promoter explained that it was April Fools' Day.[18]

Most people, however, took little notice of the Duma's proceedings, be they solemn or light-hearted. United Russia offered no prospect of lively public engagement because people joined it mainly to improve their careers or increase their bank balances – Putin had long tried to keep himself separate from its management, leaving the chairmanship to Medvedev. But Putin now saw the need for a broader kind of politics, something more imaginative than a political party to reinvig-orate the system.

He turned away from Surkov towards Deputy Prime Minister Vyacheslav Volodin, who persuaded Putin that the way to enhance his appeal was to hold conferences and large meetings and bask in the warmth of a patriotic audience. In spring 2011 Volodin proposed a movement to be called the All-Russia Popular Front: there had been a front of that name, alongside fronts of the USSR's other nations, in the years of Gorbachëv's perestroika. Now it was revived and remodelled to the Kremlin's satisfaction, as a more effective sounding board than United Russia, which was stuffed full of careerists, for the Kremlin leadership to learn about the grievances arising in society. People of other parties were encouraged to join the Front, and funds and organ-ization were put at its disposal for a series of events around the country. Putin, who was elected its chairman in June 2013, attended some of them and was feted as the hero of his time. Apparently Volodin also recommended the Front as a way for Putin to outflank Medvedev, who was then contemplating a run for a second presidential turn.[19] Surkov, a Medvedev supporter, was annoyed to learn about the plan only from news agency reports.[20]

Volodin was rewarded with appointment as First Deputy Chief of Staff in the Presidential Administration, and the Front set up working parties to discuss ways of monitoring and publicizing the fulfilment of presidential decrees – with Putin happily acknowledging the help these working parties had given.[21] But the net effect on public affairs was minimal, and the Popular Front organizers contented themselves with their assemblies and galas. Once again a flashy political innovation came to naught.

Still seeing his difficulties in apocalyptic terms, however, instinctively distrusting any club, enterprise or association that operated beyond the reach of state control, Putin sometimes spoke as though the entire country was warrened with conspiracies:

> Indirect ways are always being found to get hold of funds and spend them on the purposes intended by the donors. Of course, the recent decisions [on foreign agents] restrict the use of foreign sources for internal political struggle in Russia. These decisions established definite obstacles, but they are being bypassed and it's essential that this doesn't happen.[22]

Though Putin accepted that most Russian non-governmental organizations (NGOs) did not constitute a genuine 'fifth column', he added: 'This doesn't mean, however, that there aren't any people who serve foreign interests in Russia. Such people do exist. Who are these people? They use money in the struggle of internal politics that they have received from foreign states and they had no scruples in taking it from them.'[23]

All Russian NGOs were therefore put under pressure to conform. In November 2012 the law was amended to require those carrying out 'political activities' to register with the Ministry of Justice as 'foreign agents',[24] compelling several outstanding bodies to seek official sanction to continue. Among them is Memorial, which courageously campaigns for human rights and maintains an archive on the abuses of the Soviet past. Another is the Levada Centre, an independent polling body of global renown. Many organizations with international funding have had to withdraw from Russia altogether, and the Kremlin has severely curtailed the space available for uncongenial public critiques of its actions.

Politics steadily became more authoritarian. Previously many had thought this an unfair epithet, since Russia had regular elections, oppositionist parties and critical media outlets, but a consensus developed on the harsh and corrupt practices in public affairs. Putin has sometimes been characterized as a dictator, but this is too strong a word as his control of the ruling group has never been absolute. But rulers throughout the world with his reputation have still stopped at nothing, including assassinations, to tighten their grip on power, their methods frequently reminiscent of organized crime, to the extent that Russia has sometimes been called a mafia state and a kleptocracy.[25] The evidence is compelling that high-ranking politicians from the 1990s onwards have had links to big criminal groups. But it's doubtful that the bosses of organized crime can issue orders to Putin and his ministers: more likely, the mafias carry out profitable errands for the Kremlin. The FSB has found that criminals are able to get their dirty business done more expeditiously than the intelligence operatives.[26]

This symbiosis of state and organized crime makes Russia a dangerous place for the administration's enemies at home and abroad. But Putin refuses to see much wrong with Russian politics. He asks people to imagine the alternatives:

> Do you want dozens of people like [ex-Georgian President] Saakashvili running around our public places here? The person you named is a Russian version of Saakashvili. And do you want such Saakashvilis to destabilize the situation in the country? Do you want us to live from one [Kyiv-style] Maidan to the next? To have attempted coups? We have already been through all this. Do you want to bring all this back again? I am sure that the absolute, overwhelming majority of Russian citizens do not want this and will not allow this.[27]

He is a ruler who believes his people are lucky to have him as their president.

16. MEDIA PRESSURES: TV, PRESS AND THE INTERNET

Political order in Russia depends on methods of control. Though parliamentary manipulation is crucial, the shaping of public opinion is equally important. It is sometimes said that Russia has again become a totalitarian state and society, but authoritarianism is a better word, as there remains much free air to breathe in Russia. Although Putin has nullified many of the liberties enjoyed under Gorbachëv and Yeltsin, he has stopped a long way short of re-enslavement. The press can still publish damaging revelations about the Kremlin. The new 'social media' can offer critical commentary and organize public protest. Russians have access to the world's websites. Russia is not in informational quarantine.

Putin and his comrades make no pretence to be liberals: it is for practical reasons that they permit the freedoms they do. They understand that if Russia is to grow as an international power, it requires a dynamic society. Soviet-style economic and cultural restrictions have been demonstrated as having had a petrifying effect. The Russian leaders accept, at least for the time being, that the people need to speak and communicate unhampered by the old excesses of state interference. Russia's ability to compete with the rest of the world depends on it. The leadership is also aware that it must have a reliable gauge of the popular mood. The FSB, though its stock has risen since the millennium, cannot be relied upon as the exclusive provider of data and analysis: indeed, Putin actually broadcasts his scepticism about its reports on the public mood.[1] An animated environment for the media is a way of admitting alternative points of view that could be vital for the Kremlin to anticipate trouble, and help to release the pressure of discontent where excessive policing would be counterproductive.

That doesn't mean Russian leaders have passively licensed the press and broadcast media to act simply at the behest of their owners and editors. It was Mikhail Lesin, Minister for Affairs of the Press, Broadcasting and the Means of Mass Communication, who oversaw Vladimir Gusinski being stripped of his ownership of the NTV television channel after it showed disrespect towards Putin, and upgraded the Kremlin's media facilities the better to disseminate its own version of the news. At a press conference in 2001 he boasted, 'I long ago stopped being ashamed of the word "propaganda".'[2]

Putin understands his ambitions are best attained if he can win over the media. As a way of generating sympathetic treatment of the administration by television, radio and newspapers, it has therefore been his habit to invite the Kremlin reporters' pool to sample canapés and drinks at his official residence at Novo-Ogarëvo outside Moscow, where he offers to answer any question they might have before presenting a diploma to each of his guests. At one of these get-togethers a reporter showed a reluctance to accept the award for fear of being criticized for collusion with the authorities. Putin assured him he was not trying to undermine his professional integrity: the diploma, he explained, was strictly for reporters contributing to the furthering of a civil society. Nobody was fooled: Putin was transparently pursuing his own agenda, and individuals who voice objection to his policies don't usually receive a second invitation.[3]

Putin's charm offensive has never worked with Alexei Venediktov, Ekho Moskvy radio's editor, who often meets him for chats about Russian history.[4] Venediktov has run the station since the last years of the Soviet perestroika, and opponents of the Putin administration admire his independent spirit and ability to survive in post. In 2009 an axe and a chopping block were deposited outside his apartment. Unsurprisingly, he now employs a bodyguard. Though Putin has stopped short of issuing threats, he does not like what he hears on Ekho Moskvy:

> Listen, I've never known such raving madness . . . Listen, I was lying there in bed before going to sleep or after waking up – I don't remember which – and was thinking: this just isn't information, what they're putting out isn't information but a service for the foreign policy interests of one state with regard to another, specifically with regard to Russia.[5]

Truly Putin and Venediktov are Russia's political odd couple, but there was menace in Putin's tone even when he was in jocular mood:

Putin: And by the way, who are you going to vote for in the elections?

Venediktov: Vladimir Vladimirovich, I haven't voted since 1996.

Putin: Why not?

Venediktov: Well, I'll explain why.

Putin: And you have taken offence at what I said. I can feel it, I can see it on your face. There's no point.

Venediktov: Yes, I took offence, I took offence. I will tell you [about it] later.

Putin: And here am I not taking offence at you when you pour excrement on me morning, noon and night, whereas you have taken offence. I only have to say a couple of words and you are already offended.

Venediktov: I was joking, I'm not offended . . .

Putin: Well, I'm not joking.[6]

Ekho Moskvy's survival has come to depend on official indulgence. Two-thirds of its shares belong to Gazprom Media, which is firmly under state control, which means the Kremlin can pull the financial plug on it at any time. Venediktov protects himself by recruiting a number of anti-liberal nationalist commentators such as Alexander Prokhanov to counterbalance the criticisms of government that are the station's staple fare. Prokhanov, criticizing Putin for insufficient patriotic zeal, enables Ekho to present itself as a sounding board for the entire nation rather than an exclusively opposition organ. According to Venediktov, moreover, Putin knows that by allowing Ekho to continue in existence, he can give the impression that Russia is freer than it really is. Venediktov is a man without illusions, dolefully describing Ekho as a mausoleum like the one on Red Square housing the physical remains of Lenin – but in this case radio as a battered last bastion of pluralism.[7]

Whereas Putin enjoys his joshing encounters with 'Alexei' from Ekho Moskvy, he gives no leeway to the campaigning newspaper *Novaya gazeta*. *Novaya gazeta* challenged Putin's account of the apartment-block bomb plots that were used as the pretext for war in Chechnya. It accused him of financial corruption in connection with the 'palace' being constructed by the Black Sea. It published the charges levelled by ex-FSB officer Alexander Litvinenko that there was an FSB plan to liquidate Boris Berezovski, and the editors continued to publish pieces by Litvinenko after he fled abroad in 2000. One of Litvinenko's last sallies before his murder in 2006 attacked Putin as a paedophile, though no evidence was produced, and although this particular allegation made no appearance in *Novaya gazeta*, Putin was unlikely to overlook the part the newspaper had played in accrediting Litvinenko as a crusader for truth.

Novaya gazeta's financial backers include Mikhail Gorbachëv, who has called consistently for a government based on principles of democracy, justice and open discussion. Gorbachëv's stake was originally managed by the businessman – and former KGB officer – Alexander Lebedev, who fell out with the Putin team and moved several of his operations and bank accounts from Moscow to London. Between them Gorbachëv and Lebedev own 49 per cent of the shares, the rest belonging to the staff, and nearly all the shareholders are committed to a campaigning brief for the paper that sees *Novaya gazeta* regularly challenge the Kremlin. Whereas in Russia its journalists are the object of official distrust, abroad it is a different matter, with awards cascading upon editor-in-chief Dmitri Muratov, including the Four Freedoms Award for Freedom of Speech in the Netherlands and the Légion d'Honneur in France. This can hardly endear the newspaper to Putin with his paranoia about foreign interests impinging on the scene, and the international acclaim for Muratov saw him categorized as suspect. In 2017 he resigned.

Novaya gazeta encourages robust investigations from its reporters, and several have paid the ultimate price. In July 2003 Yuri Shchekochikhin, Muratov's deputy, perished in mysterious circumstances, probably poisoning, after denouncing a group of FSB officers for money laundering. In October 2006 Anna Politkovskaya was killed outside the entrance of her apartment in Moscow. Politkovskaya had achieved several scoops, including her shocking revelations about the torture conducted by Russian armed forces in Chechnya, and she had a growing following abroad. Her death was followed by the shooting of Anastasia Baburova, who had taken over the cause of exposing wrongdoing in Chechnya. There has never been a satisfactory police inquiry into any of these cases, and it is highly probable the assassins were not acting alone, but on behalf of persons linked to the highest authorities. Suspicion has been directed at current Chechen president Ramzan Kadyrov, whom Politkovskaya roasted in several newspaper dispatches when he was the republic's prime minister. Putin has sometimes been accused of having given the ultimate approval for the killings himself, but conclusive evidence has not come to light. What is certain is that courageous investigative journalism carries a mortal risk when it exposes the wrongdoings of the Kremlin elite and its supporters.

Though most other media outlets have been handled less brutally, Putin is single minded in limiting adverse public criticism. Top of his agenda come the national TV channels, where he has elbowed aside owners who fail to rein in their editors. Vladimir Gusinski and Boris Berezovski were early victims, and it did not pass unnoticed that both of them had to sell up their assets for a lot less than they were worth. Putin concentrated his fire upon the television sector rather than the press because newspaper readership was already in steep decline, but the authorities remained on the alert for any trouble and discreetly compelled newspaper proprietors to sack obstreperous editorial teams. If this didn't work, the authorities forced the owners to sell up. As Venediktov noted, the policy was extended to the online media.[8] The most striking example of the Kremlin's imperiousness was the way Alexander Mamut, owner of the lenta.ru news website, fired its chief editor in 2014. Observers drew the reasonable conclusion that Mamut was fretting that the authorities were displeased by the line it was taking on the Crimean crisis.[9]

Cautious editors recruited obedient reporters, commentators and presenters, and as the political wind changed direction, most in the media learned to keep their heads down. Many supporters of Gorbachëv or Yeltsin have even switched their allegiance to Putin. This was how Dmitri Kiselëv came to obtain appointment at the Russia Today international TV channel. He had come to fame as a TV reporter in 1991 when he pluckily refused to broadcast a news item containing lies about the violent closure of the Vilnius TV station. After the fall of the USSR, he continued to speak out in favour of high professional standards.[10] But when Putin became president, Kiselëv changed his approach and began advocating a nationalism and trad-itionalism that went even further than the official line. In August 2013 on the *Vesti nedeli* (News Weekly) programme for the Rossiya-1 tele-vision channel, he ranted:

> I think that fining gays for conducting propaganda among minors
> is not enough. It is necessary to ban them from becoming donors
> of blood and sperm and, in the case of a car accident, to bury their
> hearts in the ground or burn them as being unsuitable for the
> continuation of any kind of life.[11]

Kiselëv was not alone. Tatyana Mitkova, his collaborator in standing up against the misrepresentations in the Vilnius story, returned the medal she had received from Lithuania.[12] She too adapted to changing times. Or perhaps she and Kiselëv were just swept up in the general climate of opinion.

Russian rulers latch on to any ideas that serve their purpose. Mindful of the boredom felt in the Soviet era about Marxism-Leninism, they ration the use of political bromides, and have increasingly fastened on religion to enhance national stability. Putin and his old friend Yakunin join the congregations at Orthodox Church festivals. In 2005 Yakunin went to Jerusalem and brought back a bowl of consecrated fire for Putin to carry into an Easter service in Moscow's Cathedral of Christ the Redeemer.[13] At Lake Seliger, 250 miles north of Moscow, in 2018, Putin climbed shirtless into an ice hole as part of the Epiphany celebrations.[14]

Together with most Kremlin leaders Putin has favoured the Russian Orthodox Church, which has abided rigidly by its centuries-old liturgy and doctrines. The old Church Slavonic language is still used in its services despite being barely comprehensible to most Russians. To a greater degree than even the Roman Catholic Church, Orthodox leaders see no point in 'modernizing'. As a result its patriarch and hierarchy strongly support the Kremlin's conservative social policies and, to regain the importance the Orthodox Church enjoyed under the tsars, have called for official designation as 'the church of the majority'. Like Yeltsin before him, however, Putin is reluctant to formalize its status in this way, and has also withheld the automatic right for Orthodox Christianity to be taught in all state schools. But the Church's high standing in Russia nowadays was demonstrated in May 2018 at the inauguration ceremony for Putin's fourth presidential term. As he stepped down from the platform, Patriarch Kirill was the first dignitary he greeted. Only then did he turn to the ex-German chancellor Gerhard Schröder and his own prime minister Dmitri Medvedev.

Putin generally stretches out a respectful hand to faith communities. Belief in God is officially endorsed for its help in cementing Russian statehood, and offending religious feelings can be punished by a 1,000-ruble fine. The exception to the policy of toleration of religious denominations and faiths are the Jehovah's Witnesses, who were banned in 2017, their Western origins and door-to-door evangelism deemed inimical to Russia's interests.

On Unity Day, 4 November 2016, he laid flowers at the monument on Red Square to Kuzma Minin and Dmitri Pozharski, the patriots who raised a volunteer army to expel an invasion by the Polish-Lithuanian Commonwealth in 1612. His speech was followed by others by Patriarch Kirill of the Russian Orthodox Church and by Natalya Solzhenitsyna, widow of the great Russian writer. Also prominent at the ceremony were the heads of approved religious bodies: the Chairman of the Council of Muftis of Russia, Ravil Gainutdin; the Chief Mufti and Head of the Central Spiritual Directorate of Muslims of Russia, Talgat Tadzhuddin; the Chief Rabbi of Russia, Berel Lazar; Metropolitan Kornili of the Russian Orthodox Old-Rite Church; Archbishop Paolo Pezzi of the Roman Catholic Archdiocese of Moscow; and the leader of Buddhist Traditional Sangha of Russia, Damba Ayusheev. Youth organizations were also in attendance.[15] Always the official emphasis is on persuading Russians to be faithful to their God, on the assumption that the faithful are likely to remain loyal patriots and obedient citizens.

Direct state censorship no longer exists – the notorious Glavlit institution that used to supervise public access to novels, poems, operas, paintings and even ballets was closed down in autumn 1991. But there are many other methods of restricting freedom of expression. Rather than having to submit a piece of prose to Glavlit, nowadays people have to judge for themselves what the Kremlin might make of their opinions. The result can be a greater degree of self-censorship.[16] The authorities have left little to chance: a January 2016 law limited foreign ownership in Russian media enterprises to 20 per cent.[17] Russian public life was to be a matter for Russia alone.

This had been the hallmark of Putin's time in high political office. As early as September 2000 the authorities had announced an Information Security Doctrine, drafted by Security Council Secretary Sergei Ivanov and endorsed by Putin.[18] Russia, it was suggested, would remain insecure until it strengthened its cyber defences and, it was forcefully implied, those Russians who obstructed the path of political, economic and spiritual development approved by the Kremlin should be pushed aside: the classic mindset of Fortress Russia, whose walls would give the Russian people their sole hope of safety – under the leadership already in power.

On 5 December 2016 Putin signed off an updated version of the doctrine, emphasizing the importance of protecting and expanding Russian's 'information infrastructure'. The main threats were said to come from terrorist groups based abroad and, less obviously, from prejudices underpinning the foreign online media. Russian agencies, the doctrine noted, had to take on the challenge of foreign 'technological superiority' and secure Russia's genuine independence in 'the informational space'. Annoyance was expressed at the absence of adequate global legal standards in IT. The immediate solution was for Russian companies to become truly competitive in the development of advanced technology. Characteristic of an official doctrine was the stress given to strengthening the 'vertical' system of control, indicating that the authorities would maintain surveillance over online communications.[19]

In 2013, as concern grew about the discrediting of the Kremlin on the internet, Andrei Lugovoi drafted a blacklist to ban the websites that were promoting street demonstrations. Lugovoi, notorious in the West for his alleged part in the London murder of Alexander Litvinenko, was now safely ensconced in Moscow, elected to the State Duma for the Liberal-Democratic Party and assigned to its Security and Anti-Corruption Committee. His proposal secured Putin's approval and came into effect in the following year.[20] In April 2014 Putin castigated the internet as having originated as merely a 'CIA special project', with the implication that Russians should beware its influence.[21] Google and YouTube were prevailed upon to pull down a BuzzFeed piece on violence in Chechnya that was alleged to have 'extremist' content.[22] Facebook similarly yielded to official demands.[23] Twitter agreed to block access for Russian users to Ukrainian political far-right websites. In all this the Kremlin was seeking to ensure that the Russian people was guarded from influence by unapproved foreign political groups.[24]

That America's intelligence services and IT companies penetrated foreign walls of secrecy only invigorated Russia's campaign to enable governments to exercise 'digital sovereignty'. In December 2012, at an International Telecommunications Union conference, Russian delegates had called for a change in the existing rules of the internet to permit governments to censor the websites available in their territories, as was already the case in China, North Korea and Saudi Arabia. But Russia's initiative was voted down, and indeed the Russian authorities themselves refrained from overtly reintroducing censorship.[25]

In the Duma, even so, calls were made for Russia to prevent information technology infringing its sovereignty.[26] As things stood, it was suggested, the American secret services could hack into the data of Russian citizens through internet servers based in the United States. Russian politicians were howling about American hackers long before America's political establishment became alarmed about the FSB's hacking activities. Russian companies were given incentives to lessen the country's reliance on international corporations. The campaign culminated in a regulation introduced in October 2013 for all IT firms operating in Russia to store their telephone and search-engine data for twelve hours and make them readily available to the authorities.[27] From May 2014 bloggers with more than 3,000 followers had to apply for official registration.[28]

The freedom to criticize, expose and ridicule the ruling group is shrinking but there remains particular concern in the Kremlin about the capacity of the 'social media' to circumvent conventional means of communication. The content of foreign websites also bothers Russian rulers, and in February 2019 the Duma passed the first reading of a bill to allow ministers to suspend internet access to Russia if they felt the need for emergency controls.[29] The government and FSB employed trolls to challenge and disrupt the output of critical websites,[30] and even considered blocking websites that inflamed public opinion altogether.[31] The Kremlin does not intend to let people think for themselves if their thoughts are likely to harm the administration's interests. The leaders talk a lot about the nation's needs, but have ceased to distinguish between the national need and their own requirements for power, privilege and comfort. For a country that aspires to become a dynamic world power many Russians see this as an unhealthy development.

17. RUSSIAN SOFT POWER: GLOBAL CHARM OFFENSIVE

The ambition to achieve impact for Russia on public opinion abroad has never left Vladimir Putin. He understands that international influence these days is secured indirectly through the media and commerce, so-called soft power, as well as the hard and direct power of the armed forces. He also recognizes that his administration is more attuned to Russian society than to attitudes around the world.

In 2006 he enlisted the assistance of Ketchum, a New York public relations company, to bring a fresh approach to its requirements. That Ketchum and its Brussels-based partner GPlus lacked staff with expertise on Russia did not discourage the Kremlin, which wanted a firm of proven international standing on board. One of Ketchum's first steps was to recruit the former *Sunday Times* Moscow reporter Angus Roxburgh – who ironically had been deported from the USSR in 1989 in retaliation for Margaret Thatcher's expulsion of a group of Soviet spies. At Ketchum, he joined the unit working alongside Putin's press spokesman Dmitri Peskov.[1] The company reportedly received a total of $30 million for its services in improving official Russia's image abroad and generating foreign direct investment. Two years into its assignment, the worldwide criticism of the Russian war in Georgia had a convulsive impact on its work. The further annexation of Crimea, the downing of a Malaysian passenger plane by Russian rebels and the deployment of Russia's troops in eastern Ukraine made Ketchum's task impossible.

But Ketchum had achieved an impressive success on 12 September 2013 when they placed a piece by Putin in the *New York Times* headlined 'A Plea for Caution from Russia'.[2] Albeit ghost-written, it was a plea for the United States to analyse Russian foreign policy more sympathetically. Putin welcomed the 'growing trust' between himself and Obama, even though he criticized what he saw as Obama's presumption of 'American exceptionalism'. The article's thrust was towards finding a way for Russia and America to work together for an end to the Syrian civil war, and won approval from those in the United States calling for a less frosty approach to the Kremlin after the icy exchanges about American allegations of fraud in the 2012 Russian presidential election. The final words borrowed from American religious and political culture: 'There are big countries and small countries, rich and poor, those with long democratic traditions and those still finding their way to democracy. Their policies differ, too. We are all different, but when we ask for the Lord's blessings, we must not forget that God created us equal.'[3]

Roxburgh's unvarying advice to the Kremlin had been to 'open up to the press'. The idea, conventional enough in the West, was that the more politicians gave interviews, the more people would listen to them. Laws, decrees and printed announcements had less impact than leaders willing to discuss policies with reporters. The snag was that few ministers liked the prospect of scrutiny by the media. Western reaction to the murders of Anna Politkovskaya and Alexander Litvinenko in 2006, Roxburgh noted, had the effect of making the political elite even edgier about explaining their case.[4] Another problem was that Peskov and his team assumed that the way to obtain improved coverage in the *Wall Street Journal* or *The Economist* was simply to pay for it. It was further assumed that the best way to deal with reporters who carped about Kremlin policies was to ban them from press conferences. Russian officials failed to comprehend the harm this would do to public relations.[5]

As the Ketchum unit saw it, Kremlin leaders had to abandon the idea that what worked in Russia would be effective everywhere. Ketchum's team wrote draft speeches for ministers, only for the ministers to get them rewritten by their intimates. Sergei Lavrov in the Foreign Affairs Ministry refused to allow the team even to send him a draft.[6]

Ketchum complained that the Russian official attitude frustrated their capacity to achieve the impact on international opinion their contract demanded. But were the Russians so ineffective in changing the attitudes of millions of Westerners? Putin, Medvedev and Lavrov received a share of favourable media coverage even after the Georgian war and through to 2014. Though they never ceased to be controversial, they could usually count on a respectful hearing. Whereas Ketchum focused on the world, Russia's rulers had to remember about Russia.

Putin's Deputy Chief of Staff Alexei Gromov told Roxburgh that 'we have to think about domestic public opinion, which is generally positive about the Soviet Union. We have to think about political stability inside the country first and foremost.'[7] Work in public relations was always going to be a strain for any Western company, something the company's directors can hardly have failed to expect. The only consolation for Ketchum was that the Russians honoured the financial terms of the contract. Money rolled in at the rate of nearly $1 million a month.[8]

But events in Crimea delivered a hammer blow to the collaboration. Ketchum attracted such opprobrium in America that in 2015 it withdrew from its lucrative contract – Peskov saw this made sense for both the company and the Kremlin in the light of the international atmosphere. Just then no amount of public relations cleverness was going to rescue Putin's reputation in Western countries.[9]

Putin also had a technique of his own to spread Russian influence, which was to invite foreigners – former leading politicians as well as foremost journalists and academics with a professional interest in Russia – to an annual event known as the Valdai International Discussion Club. Meeting annually near the little town of Valdai to the south-east of Novgorod, the conferees discuss global affairs around a theme Putin chooses for them. Visitors over the years have included many ex-national political leaders from abroad: Thabo Mbeki, Dominique de Villepin and Hamid Karzai have been enthusiastic participants. Invitations have even gone out to a few reporters known for their antipathy to Putin. The main contributions are screened online to show the Russian president in the company of foreigners who treat him with respect, and transcripts of admiring comments are posted on the presidential website. At the end of the event, Putin rounds things off with a speech and a Q&A session. Though he can be quizzed about sensitive matters, the tacit rule is that questions are put in a temperate fashion: direct criticism is considered bad form. The idea is for everyone to come away intoxicated by a president who goes out of his way to show off the affable, thoughtful side of his nature. He offers this rationale for the Valdai proceedings:

> I have two purposes. The first is to listen to what clever people – experts – have to say. I am really interested in your opinion; this is useful both for me and for my colleagues. And the second is to relay our opinion in person to you and through you. That's the whole thing. I think this is important.[10]

Whether he takes account of what the audience says is open to doubt, and at any rate nobody to date has put a very aggressive question or objection to him. Valdai permits Putin to polish his self-image as a straight-speaking leader trying to do the right thing in the world despite all the mud that is thrown at him:

> I want to say in this respect that I will also not let you down and will speak directly and frankly. Some things might seem unduly harsh. But if we don't speak directly and speak honestly about what we genuinely and really think, then there's little point in meeting in this format. It would be better in that case to keep to diplomatic get-togethers, where no one says anything sensible and, recalling the words of a famous diplomat, you realize that diplomats have tongues so as not to speak the truth.[11]

Some Russians suspect that foreigners are gulled by the cosseting experience they have at Valdai. Surely, they ask, guests from abroad ought to be able to see that chauffeur-driven limos, plush hotels, cordon bleu meals and visits to beauty spots are provided with a political purpose?[12] Putin is a busy man and Russia's economy is in a troubled state, so the Kremlin's calculation must be that the foreign guests will return home with a good impression of Russian politics – and, the hope is, an influence on public opinion outside Russia.[13]

But Putin has reason for satisfaction that some Western reporters have conveniently dropped the approach they usually apply to examining their own leaders. In October 2014 Seumas Milne, a trenchant critic of mainstream politicians in the United Kingdom, turned pussycat in Putin's presence:

> I would like to ask a two-in-one question. First, Mr President, do you believe that the actions of Russia in Ukraine and Crimea over the past months were a reaction to rules being broken and are an example of state management without rules? And the other question is, does Russia see these global violations of rules as a signal for changing its position? It has been said here lately that Russia cannot lead in the existing global situation; however, it is demonstrating the qualities of a leader. How would you respond to this?[14]

The prize for the most fawning performance, however, had to go to Peter Lavelle, an American reporter who worked for the RT television channel. Lavelle offered a prepared encomium:

I am very happy to see you, Mr President. I would like to ask a question on behalf of the media, because all the questions were very interesting. For several days, we discussed many of the issues that were mentioned here today. However, I would like to talk about your image in the world. I am an American, as you can tell by my accent. There are quite a few Americans here.

The air filled with the intense scent of obeisance:

You are possibly the most demonized politician in the world today. We now see a demonstration of various levels of ignorance, of inability to speak out and to establish necessary contacts. On the other hand, if we take a global view, you may be one of the most popular people in modern history. I would even say that from a distance – from the Eurozone and from America – you are seen as a saviour, a man who is saving the situation. What do you think about this?[15]

Putin's press spokesman Dmitri Peskov told the Ketchum team, however, that Putin sometimes despairs at the limpness of the questions that are put to him. A natural warrior, he would evidently like the sparks to fly a lot more.[16] Presumably he liked it, then, when Neil Buckley, eastern Europe editor of the *Financial Times*, broke the obsequious pattern:

Mr President, as I heard, one of your international colleagues said that you do not consider Ukraine a real country. You see Ukraine as a country formed out of what were pieces of other countries. Could you confirm this view? Is this your view? Do you think that Ukraine has the right to exist as a sovereign and independent state, and is it indeed a real country?[17]

Putin shimmied round the question by concentrating on the number of times the borders of Ukraine were redrawn in the twentieth century. He omitted to say whether he regarded it as a real country, and Buckley had no right to a follow-up question. These are the rules at Valdai: guests are there at the president's pleasure and on his terms.

Another instrument designed to enhance Russia's image was a network known as *Russkii Mir* (Russian World). Founded by presidential decree in 2007, it took Germany's Goethe Institutes and China's Confucius Institutes as its model in an effort to popularize the Russian language and culture. To begin with, funding was promised for centres in a couple of British universities, with the idea of providing a mixture of evening talks, a daytime library and a general ambience for learning and discussion without an overt political or economic agenda. Vyacheslav Nikonov, a well-known nationalist politician, was chosen to head the operation.

A thick sheaf of administrative and financial affidavits had to be completed by the foreign recipients of Russian World's benefactions – Moscow's way of preventing it from becoming a slush fund for Nikonov's staff or the host institutions abroad – and under its bureaucratic weight the project only limped along. Another lame initiative of Putin's second term involved the creation of the Institute for Democracy and Cooperation in New York and Paris. The overtly political purpose was to promote Russian policy and argue that democracy and civil rights were better protected in Russia than anywhere in the West.[18] In 2015 the New York Institute, blighted by the indifference of most Americans, announced it was closing. The Russian authorities pretended its work was fulfilled because official respect for civil rights in America had improved. A more credible conclusion would be that the Kremlin had pulled the plug on an utter waste of money.[19]

The Russian leadership had greater success with the global television news station Russia Today, founded in 2005 and quickly known just by its initials RT. This was a free-to-air channel for news and discussion that was friendly to the official Russian line. Western media were no longer to enjoy an unchallenged run as the RT network set about changing things in the Kremlin's favour. Editor-in-chief Margarita Simonyan noted with displeasure how few people outside Russia gave credit to the USSR for the victory over the Third Reich, remarking that 50 per cent of Americans thought the United States alone achieved the victory whereas only 14 per cent saw the Soviet contribution as having been decisive. Twitter and Facebook campaigns were projected to correct attitudes about Russia past and present. Videos were prepared. It was going to be an uphill task, but Simonyan dedicated herself to reaching the summit.[20]

The RT channel achieved an impact that many in the West have both envied and deplored. In the Kremlin there was manifest delight that official Russia was finally getting its message across to foreign viewers. Putin gave the credit to Simonyan while maintaining to an audience of visitors from abroad that the whole project drew on only modest resources. 'I'll tell you now, friends and colleagues [sic],' he told the Valdai conference in 2016, 'I would really like to have such a [Western-style] propaganda machine in Russia, but unfortunately this is not the case. We have not even global media outlets of mass information such as CNN, the BBC and certain others. We simply do not have this kind of capacity yet.'[21]

In fact RT broadcasts on its TV cable channels and supplies online content in English, Spanish and Arabic; and with a growing number of Russians living abroad, the station also broadcasts in Russian. A French station has recently been added. These ventures, which are supervised by the old news media giant RIA-Novosti, have a strategic importance for the Russian authorities. To anyone interviewed on an RT station the hand of Moscow is immediately discernible (as I experienced in person during the first year of the London station, when the presenter blatantly favoured a fellow guest who toed the Kremlin line).

Despite this, Jeremy Corbyn MP, before becoming leader of the British Labour Party in 2015, cheerfully accepted RT's invitations for a considerable period, and the ex-leader of the Scottish National Party Alex Salmond hosted a regular news show, something viewed askance by his successor Nicola Sturgeon. In the United Kingdom, the football manager José Mourinho was an RT pundit during the 2018 World Cup, and the former England centre forward Stan Collymore was given his own show. During programmes the channel screened banner sublines with a political cast. In the United States RT producers found notable figures harder to recruit: no leading politician or sportsperson there has so far accepted an offer of employment.

This has not stopped Simonyan and the rest of RT from poking a sharp stick at the Western political establishment, tirelessly pointing out breaches of democratic and judicial procedure and highlighting police abuses, drug addiction and widespread poverty. Decadence and hypocrisy, runs its refrain, start west of Russia. The US Department of Justice reacted by instructing RT to register as a 'foreign agent', in line with the Foreign Agents Registration Act (FARA) introduced in 1938 to counteract the propaganda distributed by organizations operating on behalf of the Third Reich. The reality was that, since the Second World War, registration was only rarely ordered. Now RT was being required, as a condition of continuing to operate in the United States, to label the contents of its output, making clear that it was working for the Russian state.[22] In return, Vyacheslav Volodin, the Duma Speaker, indicated an intention to bring forward legislation to make it difficult for the American media to operate in Russia.[23]

Behind closed doors in Moscow, Russian leaders applauded RT for prodding an arm of the American government into a clampdown, however slight, on the station's freedom of expression. Simonyan had always said America's liberties were a mirage, and now the Justice Department was making her case for her. With growing confidence, the Kremlin's spokesmen began to show a sense of humour. In 2017 jokey posters were displayed in the London Underground which read: 'Missed the train? Lost a vote? Blame it on us!' Another one went: 'Watch RT and find out who we are planning to hack.'[24] The following year the jesting continued when video screens at Moscow's international airports carried messages like 'The longer you watch, the more upset Hillary Clinton becomes' and 'The CIA calls us a propaganda machine – find out what we say about the CIA.'[25]

The series of interviews Putin granted to Oliver Stone between July 2015 and February 2017 saw him in relaxed mood. Stone, a Democratic Party supporter and an advocate of rapprochement with Moscow, asked pat-a-cake questions and seldom followed up when Putin became evasive. It was easy for Putin to present himself as a decent, thoughtful leader whose purpose was to make Russia great without disturbing peace on earth. At their parting, Putin advised Stone to prepare himself to take a public beating in the United States for his efforts. Stone agreed: he knew he faced criticism at home.[26] The interviews, cut and edited into four shows, were broadcast in America in summer 2017. Most reviewers saw that Stone had let off Putin lightly. Even so, by achieving an atmosphere of unprecedented informality, Stone pulled off something none of Russia's TV interviewers had managed for more than a few seconds: he got Putin to smile and keep smiling.[27]

By 'humanizing' Putin, Stone did his international reputation a favour that most of Ketchum's efforts had failed to achieve. But the problem remained that Putin the politician had undertaken a land grab in Ukraine, something no amount of soft-focus conversation with Stone would remove from the minds of most in the West.

18. PUBLIC OPINION: THE POTENTIAL FOR UNREST

Kremlin leaders have trampled the rule of law in Russia, protecting their dominance with a regime of fear. But they are not the sole culprits. Lower down the ladder of power stand elected officials and businessmen who have fought to ensure the retention of ill-gotten gains. It was a state of affairs predating Putin's first presidential term, but by introducing greater order to the national patchwork of malpractice he has made a bad situation worse.

The national and regional rulers would not so easily have imposed their kleptocracy had popular attitudes offered a stronger defence. For centuries there was widespread distrust of those in authority among Russian people: from tsarism through to the communist period it was the norm for families to assume that the government in the capital was a parasite on society, and that the courts were skewed in favour of the powerful and well-off. The response was for Russians to put their confidence mainly in relatives and proven friends. When officials of the tsars came looking for taxes and conscripts, it was understandable for peasants to conceal everything they could – and when the landed gentry demanded excessive payment from their peasantry, misrepresentation of the size of the harvest was widespread. Such evasion and downright illegality were only reinforced during the communist dictatorship. When communism collapsed and a wild capitalist economy was introduced to Russia in the 1990s, the natural reaction was for citizens to concentrate trust once more in families and friends rather than a government that had spawned the growth of the so-called oligarchs. Discontent and despair grew as people struggled to cope with the financial depression that subsequently afflicted the economy.[1]

Little about all this was inevitable and less still intentional. Rulers in the last decade of the twentieth century were plotting a route out of darkness and carrying few reliable searchlights. But they quickly took

1. Putin at his inauguration ceremony in May 2012.

2. Prime Minister Dmitri Medvedev.

3. Nikolai Patrushev, Security Council secretary and foreign-policy hawk. Not a man to smile if he can glower instead.

4. Igor Sechin, Rosneft's boss and Putin's multipurpose hard man over many years.

5. Sergei Lavrov, Foreign Affairs Minister, who puts the gloss on Putin's external initiatives.

6. Alexei Kudrin, long-term Finance Minister, friend of Putin and subsequently a permitted critic of official economic policy.

7. Vladislav Surkov, one-time manipulator of multiparty politics on Putin's behalf. Now his emissary in eastern Ukraine.

8. Viktor Yanukovych, Ukrainian president until 2014 and a flagrant accumulator of personal wealth through office.

9. Yevgeni Primakov, failed contender for the Russian presidency in 2000 and an early promoter of 'multipolarity' in world affairs.

10. Mikhail Kasyanov, Putin's earliest prime minister and subsequently one of his fiercest critics.

11. Boris Nemtsov, unrelenting political enemy of Putin until he was assassinated in 2015.

12. Alexei Navalny, leading current critic of the Putin administration.

13. 'March of Millions' protest poster, Moscow, June 2012: 'We're fed up with the scoundrels and thieves'.

14. Opposition giant puppet model of Putin as footballer for the Party of Scoundrels and Thieves – Nemtsov's name for Putin and his entourage.

15. Navalny on stage at an evening rally during his
Moscow mayoral campaign, August 2012.

16. Pussy Riot release-demand poster, 2012. They were released
the following year, shortly before the Sochi Olympics.

advantage of a situation that enabled them to pursue policies in their own self-interest, which surprised only those who had overestimated the chances of installing a healthy democracy and the rule of law. Russia in the last decade of the twentieth century had been a society fed up with political rhetoric, distrustful of politicians and sunk in the tasks of putting food on the table and staying employed. Demonstrations grew fewer. Riots were a rarity.

The rulers knew how important it was to monitor both the public mood and developments in high political and business circles. They understood what could happen when public opinion turned sour. Through the late 1980s Gorbachëv was without rival, but in 1990 pollsters reported a sudden dip in his popularity: it turned out to be irreversible. Yeltsin crested a wave of admiration in 1990–91, only to experience a deepening loss of esteem throughout the rest of the decade. Gorbachëv and Yeltsin had drunk from the chalice of acclaim, and choked on its unpalatable dregs. Both oversaw a crisis that unexpectedly became insurmountable, and both had to step down from power. Those on whom Putin and his team have bestowed favours in the form of ministries, corporations or national projects are quite capable of turning against their benefactors. The media that currently adulates can in a trice switch to attack mode.

When both elite disgruntlement and popular discontent arise simultaneously, as they did for Gorbachëv and Yeltsin (and for Nicholas II in 1917), then the ruler is under severe pressure to depart. No effort is spared in the Kremlin to track the movement of potentially dangerous opinion. In the Soviet era this was done by the KGB and the intelligence services that preceded it. But since the secret police had an interest in exaggerating the dangers to political stability, the communist leadership could never feel entirely confident in the reliability of its reports.

Open polling of citizens was fitful until 1987, when Gorbachëv permitted the establishment of the All-Union Centre for the Study of Public Opinion by the noted sociologists Tatyana Zaslavskaya and Boris Grushin. Rebranded the Russian Public Opinion Research Center in 1992, and known by its Russian-language acronym VTsIOM, day-to-day activity was directed by Yuri Levada, who set high standards in incorporating techniques of investigation and analysis from the rest of the world, with the result that politicians sometimes had to read uncongenial news of what people thought about them. VTsIOM was left undisturbed until 2003, when the government changed its funding basis. A frustrated Levada, believing ministers had objected to unsettling reports on attitudes to the fighting in Chechnya, walked out and formed his own Levada Centre. He died in 2006. The Levada Centre maintained its independence, but got into trouble because a small portion of its funding was from outside Russia, making it liable to be put on the list of 'foreign agents'. Opting to do without finance from abroad still failed to protect it from the ill-will of the Justice Ministry: in 2016, shortly before the Duma election, it was categorized as performing 'the functions of a foreign agent', testimony to the Kremlin's continuing sensitivity of opinion polls.

Putin has described his annual 'Direct Line' TV phone-in as a barometer of public opinion, grandly dubbing it 'the most powerful sociological poll',[2] and he and his team arrange for his public appearances to pass off with the minimum of unpleasantness. And much as they sometimes object to the Levada Centre's investigations, they depend on the information competent pollsters provide. This does not mean that such surveys produce entirely satisfactory findings: Russia is no longer a country where everyone feels free to express a critical opinion about the leadership. Individuals who receive a call from a polling organization have to think carefully when asked whether they can depend on Putin. Memories are long enough to stretch back to the time when any Soviet citizen who voiced disapproval of the authorities got into deep trouble. Though current conditions are not so dire, many could still be chary about saying things that could result in damaging consequences in employment or housing. Even so, it is hard to believe that survey results are more than marginally inaccurate.[3]

The Levada Centre, despite the rough handling it has received from the authorities, continues to provide a useful insight into the way Russian opinion has been developing. In January 2018 it asked what issues most agitated people. The answers were evidence of a steady concern with basic material conditions. The greatest worry, registered by 68 per cent of respondents, were price increases. Next were the widespread poverty (47 per cent) and the rise in unemployment (40 per cent). Such results, if an accurate reflection of reality, tend to show people complaining about the conditions that most directly affect them and their families. The factors they might regard as having caused the situation come lower down: bribery and corruption, for example, were raised by only 38 per cent of respondents. The narrowing access to health care and education came lower still.[4]

Putin's own culpability is a moot point. Two-thirds of people hold him personally responsible for the persistence of corruption, and there is widespread scepticism about the likelihood of eradicating it. But only 6 per cent accuse him of dishonesty. Overall he emerges with his reputation intact: others supposedly are corrupt, but not him. Why? Over half of respondents believed he was simply unaware of it, and that his advisers were keeping him in the dark.[5]

Putin's poll ratings and personal electoral successes over the years have never shielded him from the danger of a severe backlash. His popularity tumbled severely in 2011 after he announced his intention of standing again for presidential office and handing the premiership back to Medvedev. Returning to the presidency in 2012, Putin found his popularity flatlining, and it dipped to 62 per cent in January 2013, as he paid the price for his wheeling and dealing over the presidency as well as the troubled state of the Russian economy after the global recession of 2007–8. As employment conditions worsened, the leadership incurred disapproval, but even the extreme gap in Russia between the super-rich and the very poor attracted criticism from only a third of respondents.[6]

This had been why in 2012 he issued his May Decrees, all eleven of them, on the very day he returned for his third presidential term. He had stormed to victory even though the Opposition had been effective in organizing protests in Moscow and many large cities, leading to a widespread assumption that his position was now impregnable, but that was not how Putin saw it. His decrees were aimed at showing that his administration would look after people's interests while it was creating a modern economy and society. It was noticeable that he promised to raise the salaries of teachers and doctors – he knew professional employees were prominent among the protesters. He also committed himself to increasing grants for students. Although he repeated his dedication to improving the combat readiness of the armed forces, the main thrust of his announcements fell on health, housing, administrative fairness and schooling.[7] To forestall greater unrest, Putin had been scared into issuing a more compassionate agenda for his presidency.

But he knew few would read beyond the headlines. If implemented, these decrees would utterly transform the living conditions for all Russians, yet no one who examined the detail could fail to see them as unrealistic, even utopian. A year later there was already disquiet in ruling circles. Finance Minister Anton Siluanov reminded the cabinet that revenues from oil and gas imports were failing to keep up with official promises to increase expenditure. Minister of Economic Development Alexei Ulyukaev concurred by reporting on the difficulties bedevilling the government's welfare programmes.[8]

It was not the May Decrees but the Crimean annexation that did most to restore Putin's popularity, which in June 2015 reached a peak of 89 per cent.[9] Shortly before the 2018 presidential election it was still at a comfortable 71 per cent.[10] There had been much greater dips in his ratings in the past: in August 2000 it tumbled to 65 per cent, after the *Kursk* submarine disaster, and at a time of growing public unease about the war in Chechnya, when many Russians remembered the earlier war in 1994 and feared the Russian army would run into trouble again and thousands of soldiers would lose their lives. Other falls occurred in later years, notably at the time of the Beslan school siege in 2004.

But the personal firmness he showed in dealing with terrorism was widely recognized, and his rating before the end of his second term climbed back to over 80 per cent. These figures were remarkable, but Putin still made sure that no crowd protests could be staged at any of his public appearances. Whenever possible, he wanted the guarantee of a friendly reception.

The government never matched the president's appeal. During Putin's first two terms it usually scored 20 per cent lower and the gap remained when Medvedev took over the presidency and Putin became prime minister – not even Putin proved capable of raising the ratings for the cabinet. Even though he was easily the country's most favoured politician, there were limits to his popularity.

Most Russians were also convinced that economic sanctions were part of the West's ceaseless project to weaken and humiliate Russia. In autumn 2014, seven out of ten Russians were of this opinion and the ratio was constant in subsequent years. Western complaints about Russian military activity were dismissed as unjustified by six out of ten of those who were surveyed.[11]

By the beginning of 2015, according to a VTsIOM survey, the fear of a possible nuclear war had risen since the Crimean annexation, but the mood was hardly pervasive: only 17 per cent reckoned such a war was likely.[12] The Levada Centre confirmed this finding: its poll in June 2017 indicated two-thirds of Russians wanted to see Putin stay as president and three-quarters desired the same tough line, or an even tougher one, to continue in both Russia's foreign and domestic politics. Less than 13 per cent of respondents asked for a more liberal framework in internal politics and for a movement away from confrontation with the West. Putin's foreign policy had acquired the imprimatur of popular endorsement. As he advanced towards the finale of the presidential contest, his ratings held steadily at over 80 per cent. It appeared that none of the disquiet about the general conditions in society could lessen his appeal. After the election, the smooth running of the FIFA World Cup and the boost to Russia's standing abroad appeared to put him in an impregnable position.

That this was an illusion was exposed in June 2018, when a policy announcement was made about state pensions by Prime Minister Medvedev. It was done on the first day of the FIFA World Cup – quite deliberately: the leadership wanted to bury bad news.

The plan, Medvedev explained, was to fill the hole in the pension fund by requiring people to stay longer at work, something ex-Finance Minister Kudrin had been recommending for years.[13] The current system was for men to retire at sixty and women at fifty-five: Medvedev wished to raise the age to sixty-five for males and sixty-three for females. Putin kept out of it, wanting Medvedev to suffer any opprobrium that arose. Public disapproval grew fiercer, and no amount of success for the Russian footballers was enough to deflect it: pensions, low though they are, can make the difference between poverty and starvation. People living below the official subsistence level had fallen to one in nine in 2012, but the number has risen in each successive year. Poverty has become a growing plague.[14] Getting and keeping a job, or perhaps two, was essential: unemployment relief is miserable at only 15 per cent of the average national wage.[15] With male mortality averaging at sixty-seven in Russia, the government's proposal would have meant that most men would hardly live long enough to benefit at all from the financial contributions they had made. Women on average lived to seventy-seven, but the peremptory addition of an extra eight years to their working lives did not amuse them. And the devious way that Medvedev sneaked out the announcement on a day of sporting celebration made it doubly annoying. Streets filled with protesters in Moscow and other cities. The impact on public opinion was deep and dramatic.

Labour Minister Maxim Topilin gave interviews repeating the government's case that there were too few people in employment to pay for the rising number of pensioners, and stressed that men in their sixties were easily able to keep on working,[16] but every statement by him or Medvedev only added fuel to the flames. According to the Levada Centre, in the days immediately after the announcement trust in Putin fell to 48 per cent: the first time it had fallen below the midpoint since the Crimean annexation.[17] By late August 2018, Putin's trustworthiness rating had plummeted to 36 per cent in a VTsIOM poll. Medvedev's was even lower at barely 7 per cent.[18] But questions about public trust and public approval produced different results: three-fifths of Russians continued to approve of Putin. Were a presidential election to be called he remained easily the most favoured candidate.[19]

Despite this bizarre contradiction, however, there was an unmistakable growth in negative sentiment. Over a quarter of the Russian people said they disapproved of Putin. Moreover, 33 per cent objected to the State Duma and 55 per cent to Medvedev.[20] Only a third said they would vote for United Russia in an election.[21] By October 2018 the Levada Centre found that 61 per cent held Putin responsible for the country's problems.[22] Signs mounted of discontent with his pension reform at home and with a foreign policy that added to international tensions.[23] The media had built up his cult as a dominant leader, and now he was held to account both in people's homes and on the streets.

Unnerved by the surging hostility, Putin went on television to explain why pensions had to undergo change. He blamed it on the demographic lulls in the Russian birth rate in the Second World War and the 1990s – omitting any reference to the effects on the budget of his assertive foreign policy. In a measured performance, he stressed that the government simply lacked the money to maintain the pension fund on its existing basis. But to demonstrate a willingness to listen and to compromise he trimmed the details of the reform. Women, he announced, would be allowed to retire at sixty; those who had three or more children, even earlier. He also planned to make it illegal for companies to fire employees over the age of fifty, who could find it difficult to obtain another job. Unemployment relief would be doubled. Putin ended with an appeal: 'I ask you to approach this with understanding.'[24]

Those who thought authoritarian rule meant the Russian leadership could always flout public opinion were taken by surprise. The poll data that showed consistent support from most Russians for a 'strong hand' in government meant they wanted a firm, decisive ruler who could secure for them the improvements they sought in living conditions, not a dictator. Any ruler, however strong, who fails them in such matters, is likely to breed discontent.[25] In this respect nothing had changed in Russia. It was only the latest clash between public expectations and official policy. Putin and Medvedev would have to tread more carefully in future. And there was another paradox. Whereas trust in

Putin had collapsed, active distrust – which in early August 2018 fell to 5 per cent – remained low.[26]

Even so, there were signs that millions of Russians had lost much of their innocence about Putin, if indeed they ever had it. In July 2018 the approval rating for certain institutions was much higher than Putin's: 85 per cent of a large sample poll for the Russian army, 66 per cent for the Russian Orthodox Church.[27] Once upon a time Putin had been able to match these figures. He was paying the price for taking his people for granted – or, more likely, he had known he would meet with trouble but had hoped the political costs would be bearable.

The authorities tried to restore his standing by means of media manipulation. The Rossiya-1 channel broadcast an unscheduled series titled *Moscow. Kremlin. Putin.* The first show set the pattern, the commentary justifying pension reform. Putin was filmed on his summer 2018 vacation. It was already the standard procedure to broadcast videos of him taking breaks around the Russian Federation: Putin picking and eating wild berries; Putin watching mountain goats through binoculars; Putin taking a strenuous hike. The accompanying interviewees included his spokesperson Dmitri Peskov. 'Putin doesn't only love children,' he stressed: 'he loves people in general. He's a very human person.' Peskov praised Putin for his physical fitness and fearless character: 'You can imagine, bears aren't idiots, if they see Putin, they'll behave properly!' His syrupy words reflected a growing panic in the Kremlin to try to persuade the Russian people to value the caring, all-action president they had elected. And to appreciate the conscientious approach he took to his decision making. It was unclear whether they would be enough.

POWER

19. KNOCKING DOWN SKITTLES: THE FLOORING OF THE POLITICAL OPPOSITION

Kremlin leaders cannot afford to overlook the inherent dangers of the semi-freedom permitted to the country's citizens. The administration has, therefore, maintained a preventive strategy of pulverizing the serious organized opposition. Zyuganov's Communist Party and Zhirinovski's Liberal-Democratic Party are allowed to survive as minorities in the Duma because they lend the appearance of pluralism while no longer offering a serious threat. But Putin has always treated political liberals with severity precisely because he is nervous about the potential menace they pose. Since they had already lost their appeal in the 1990s, when they came to be regarded as advocates of a capitalist economy that pitched millions of Russians into destitution, this was something of an overreaction. In the Duma of 1999–2003, the liberals were poorly represented, with only twenty-nine seats for Union of Right Forces and twenty for Yabloko, and in subsequent parliamentary elections they secured none at all. Even if the administration had employed no dirty tricks against them, they were never popular enough to challenge seriously for the presidency.

In the early 2000s political liberalism underwent many organizational splits and mergers, while the same leaders of the movement remained in place, notably Grigori Yavlinski, Mikhail Kasyanov, Boris Nemtsov and Irina Khakamada. But Yavlinski was no longer as vigorous as when he had pushed for Gorbachëv and then Yeltsin to choose a liberal path in politics and economics. Kasyanov and Nemtsov had their disagreements but tended to concur on the basic questions. They criticized the constitutional and legal manipulations that secured power for the Putin group. They denounced the control exerted by the FSB. They castigated fraud, corruption and cronyism. While approving the official measures to tame the 'oligarchs', they lamented that Putin's favourites in big business continued to receive privileged contracts from ministers.[1] Liberal politicians called for an end to the system of cosy deals between super-wealthy entrepreneurs and the government. They consistently lamented the absence of the rule of law in Russia. They drew attention to the flight of capital and bright young people from Russia and the inadequate level of industrial investment.[2]

These problems, they argued, were why the Russian experience of the global recession of 2007–8 was worse than elsewhere. The costs of the 2008 Georgian military invasion – both financial and in terms of relations with the West – were also underlined. In the eyes of liberals, it was disastrous for the Kremlin leadership to turn away from the opportunities for conciliation with the West. The 2014 Crimean annexation compounded their disappointment about the road not taken. They saw themselves as the true patriots who had the country's best interests at heart and offered a realistic alternative to the impasse that Putin created.[3]

Nemtsov had trained in theoretical physics and entered political activity in the perestroika years in his native Gorki (now Nizhni Novgorod as in the tsarist era). Like Kasyanov, he was good looking and dynamic. Unlike him, he quickly decided that Yeltsin had made an awful blunder in choosing Putin as his presidential successor.[4] Yeltsin had brought Nemtsov to Moscow after being impressed by his five years as elected governor of Nizhni Novgorod province, and Nemtsov became first deputy prime minister despite having a record of opposing Yeltsin's war in Chechnya in 1994 and blaming it for the rise in terrorist incidents.[5] Yeltsin liked his practical efficiency and independence of judgement. But for the political difficulties that beset Yeltsin in 1998–9, he might easily have chosen him as his successor. From 2000, after Yeltsin stepped down from office, Nemtsov ran the Union of Right Forces, a coalition of parties and groups that promoted the values of political and economic liberalism. In the periods between parliamentary elections he produced pamphlets and websites denouncing the trends in ruling policy.

Nemtsov travelled abroad to make his case against Putin. In June 2013 he returned to Washington and pressed the Senate Foreign Relations Committee to broaden the punitive range of the Magnitsky Act that had passed into American law the previous year.[6] This was bound to infuriate the Russian government. Nemtsov had already complained of a DDoS (distributed denial of service) attack in April 2011, when his organization's email system was overwhelmed by a deluge of malicious traffic.[7] As the book trade grew nervous of appearing to be friendly towards him as an enemy of the Kremlin, Nemtsov and his associates were compelled to publish his writings themselves.

Nemtsov and his friends knew the risks he was taking when denouncing the military operations in Crimea and eastern Ukraine. In April 2014 he travelled to Kyiv for a forum called Ukraine–Russia Dialogue and allowed a young person to video him laughing and saying, 'Vladimir Putin would have voted for Yanukovych. He's a fucked-up person, Vladimir Putin, that's what you have to understand.'[8] It was one thing to oppose a policy, but another to use the language of the street against one's elected president in front of a camera, and Putin was unlikely to forgive him. In May the same year, in his capacity as a Yaroslavl regional assembly deputy, Nemtsov filed a question for FSB Director Alexander Bortnikov about reports that Kadyrov's Chechen troops were fighting in eastern Ukraine. Receiving no answer, he became intent on making trouble in all matters Ukrainian, his blogs calling out Kadyrov for the wild rallies he addressed in which he invoked Allah and praised Putin.[9] Nemtsov was no longer the cautious challenger he had once been.

At a time when emotions ran high among all Russians, Nemtsov divided national opinion. Many regarded his ideas as unpatriotic, even traitorous. As a politician, he did poorly in opinion polls on public trust, whereas after the Crimean annexation Putin's ratings flew sky high. But Nemtsov remained a critic who got himself heard in Russia, and made trouble for the Kremlin's management of international relations. On a few occasions he alluded in private to the possibility of assassination, but nothing daunted him. He had witnessed how Yeltsin had confronted the communist leadership in the USSR and won his struggle against terrible odds.

Some of his enemies, however, were out to get him. On 27 February 2015 he and his friend Anna Duritskaya were walking across the Bolshoi Moskvoretski bridge near the Kremlin – on the spur of the moment they had changed their plan to drive home. They were not to know that a gang had intended to shoot him in a nearby underpass not long before, and had failed only because they could not get a clear enough sight of him.[10] As Nemtsov and Duritskaya approached the middle of the bridge, an armed man sprang from behind them and shot Nemtsov before speeding off in a getaway car. When the police arrived, Nemtsov was already dead. Around the world there was an outpouring of sadness that a figure of such courage and outspokenness had been struck down. In Moscow, there were angry demonstrations on the bridge against what many regarded as a state-sponsored murder. It was remarked that the area round the Kremlin was under the heaviest surveillance anywhere in the entire country, and that the gang of assassins would have needed inside information and assistance to carry out the deed.[11]

Alexei Navalny, who was under house arrest at the time of the murder, accused Putin and unnamed security force leaders. Though he had no proof, he speculated that Putin had expressed a general desire for Nemtsov to be eliminated and that the FSB – or possibly Chechen president Kadyrov – had interpreted this as encouragement to kill him.[12]

The widespread sorrow and anger at Nemtsov's liquidation persuaded Putin to avoid the indifference he had flaunted in 2006 when Anna Politkovskaya and Alexander Litvinenko were murdered. That year his ploy had been to say that he wanted the police investigations and judicial proceedings to take place independently of political pressures, including his own. This would not have gone down well after Nemtsov was killed, and so Putin, talking to liberal veteran Irina Khakamada, commented:

> You were friends with him, maintained contact. He was a harsh critic of the government in general and me personally. That said, our relations were quite good at the time when we talked to each other. I have already made a statement regarding this issue. I believe a killing of this kind is a shame and a tragedy.[13]

That he was willing to engage with Khakamada on live television showed the gravity of the situation. But he refrained from saying anything positive about Nemtsov's important contribution to Russian public life.

Gleb Pavlovski, Putin's former political consultant, gave his personal complicity the benefit of the doubt. Much likelier, in Pavlovski's view, was a complex scenario:

> Last year's assassination of the opposition politician Boris Nemtsov, however, clearly went beyond Putin's limits. Could Putin have said something about Nemtsov that someone could have taken as a go-ahead to kill him? That seems impossible to me. I have never heard anything like that from Putin, even with

regard to people he hates. Putin sometimes mocked Nemtsov a bit, but he tolerated him. After the assassination, Putin disappeared for a few days – apparently, what had happened was too unexpected. It soon emerged that the alleged perpetrators were linked to Kadyrov, the Chechen leader who is zealously loyal to Putin (and whom Putin, in return, has allowed to build a private fiefdom in Chechnya).[14]

Responsibility for the killing was eventually attributed to a gang of Chechens, who were tried and sentenced at the Moscow District Military Court. The five defendants belonged to the Russian Guard. They included the gunman who allegedly fired the fatal shots, Zaur Dadaev. The proceedings frustrated the efforts of Nemtsov's lawyers to compel testimony from their commanding officer. No attempt was made to ascertain who gave the order for the murder, even though it was widely assumed to have been a contract killing. The court case started and finished with the five Chechens accused of the crime.[15]

The convicted men went to prison without revealing any wider details. No doubt they worried about retaliation against their families in Chechnya if they said anything to compromise the reputation of public figures. In the vacuum this left, rumours spread like wildfire. The Chechen president Kadyrov added to them by declaring that he laughed off the murder, calling Dadaev 'a true patriot of Russia'. Even before his tasteless comments there were suspicions that he had masterminded the killing. Navalny put forward the hypothesis that Kadyrov might have thought Putin, by criticizing the trouble that Nemtsov was causing, had given the green light for a hit. Navalny also suggested that individual members of Putin's Moscow entourage wanted to darken the political weather, and saw the murder as a way of tugging Putin along with them.[16]

Flowers were placed daily at the spot on the bridge where Nemtsov was slain. The authorities ensured that cleaners removed them every night, only to find more flowers appearing the next day.[17] Official sensitivities are never openly admitted, but the project to name a Moscow street in Nemtsov's memory was quietly shelved while no problem was found with adding a Hugo Chavez Street and even an Akhmat Kadyrov Street to the map.[18] Presidential spokesman Peskov stated baldly that Nemtsov was 'little more than a statistically average citizen' who 'at the political level had not constituted any threat' to Putin.[19]

The Nemtsov family pressed for a proper investigation, and Nemtsov's lawyer Vadim Prokhorov tirelessly gathered information from interviews and written records. His findings were shocking.

The convicted killers had been living in Moscow's Veernaya Ulitsa at the time of the crime – the mother of Kadyrov had an apartment on the same street – and served in the Sever ('North') Regiment of Kadyrov's militia, which was merged into the new National Guard in 2016. They were under the command of Ruslan Geremeev and were said to live in fear of him. Prokhorov wondered whether the killing squad would have dared to go after Nemtsov unless Geremeev was at least aware of the order. When the official investigation of the assassination started Geremeev found sanctuary in Chechnya. Geremeev did not respond to the accusations, nor was he treated as a suspect in the investigation. Acknowledging that there are gaps in the evidence, Prokhorov speculated that a trail of suspicion led back towards the Chechen president, but he added that only a full and open inquiry could ever establish the truth. He had nevertheless discovered enough to convince him that the gang had received orders through a chain of command that was headed by one or more individuals in political authority.[20]

The ruling group resolved to see off the menace posed by other liberal leaders. Nemtsov's colleague Kasyanov was next. In April 2016 a video was circulated among the media showing Kasyanov in a compromising sexual liaison with his assistant, British-based Natalya Pelevina. Kasyanov had recently been less industrious than Nemtsov in pursuing his political cause, but those in authority evidently felt the urge to remove any chance for him to raise his profile.

This left Navalny as the Opposition's leading public figure. For some years Navalny had thought that the Yavlinskis, Kasyanovs and Nemtsovs had made the mistake of trying to beat Putin mainly through old-fashioned methods of party organization, pamphlets and the occasional public meeting. The Opposition had rethought how to organize street demonstrations, and put an emphasis on forming mobile activist groups and publicizing local abuses of power.[21] But Putin was still able to counter them with a traditional use of police and courts. He also denied them fair electoral contests and television appearances. Navalny therefore chose a different path, using social media and his own online videos to get his message across. With his clear blue eyes and direct manner, he is a natural performer, introducing the videos with the words: 'Greetings. This is Navalny!' His exposures of corruption attract a vast number of viewers – for example, his attack on Deputy Prime Minister Prikhodko as an alleged serial taker of bribes earned over seven million YouTube hits in the first couple of months after its appearance.[22]

Navalny, born in 1976, is from a family that experienced many of the twentieth century's horrors. His grandmother had been on the Western Front at the end of the Second World War – she recalled scrawling her name on the Reichstag after the fall of Berlin – but her sister was sentenced to the notorious labour camp at Vorkuta in eastern Siberia.[23] Navalny was brought up in Moscow province, and as a young man in the early 1990s was a passionate supporter of Yeltsin, believing that Gorbachëv had failed for want of audacity, whereas Yeltsin had hastened to introduce a market economy and remove the constitutional obstacles left behind by the USSR. Only gradually did Navalny grow alarmed about the rampant corruption under Yeltsin, as well as about the violence he used to crush the Supreme Soviet in 1993.[24]

He had to build a life for himself. Calling himself a fundamentalist on the need for a new Russian capitalism, he went into business. At the same time he tried to fill the gaps in his education. Having failed to obtain a place in the law faculty at Moscow State University, he settled for a degree at the Patrice Lumumba Friendship of Peoples University. After receiving his diploma, he got a job as a lawyer at the State Property Committee, where he daily witnessed a stinking swamp of malfeasance.[25]

He joined Yabloko because the party reflected the liberal kind of politics he espoused. After leaving the State Property Committee, he resumed his business activity and experienced the difficulties that start-up entrepreneurs faced in Russia. The timber industry in Kirov province offered tempting opportunities, and in 2008 he and his brother Oleg founded their Alortag company, which, like many other Russian start-ups, they based in Cyprus – presumably for the fiscal benefits. But it was politics that consumed his imagination. From 2007 onwards he energetically wrote critical blogs about the Kremlin,[26] and quickly turned into a national sensation, especially among students and intellectuals, even beginning to acquire an international profile. In 2010 he received a grant to spend six months in America as a Yale World Fellow.[27] By 2011 such were his fame and impact that Nemtsov announced that he would challenge Putin in the forthcoming presidential election on behalf of the entire liberal opposition.[28]

Though this failed to happen, Navalny's public prominence continued to increase. In September 2013 he stood against Sergei

Sobyanin, Putin's favoured candidate in the Moscow mayoralty election, and shocked the Kremlin by winning 27 per cent of the vote.
Navalny and his supporters had put up posters that said, 'We're fed up
with scoundrels and thieves.' They organized a 'march of the millions
for honest government [*vlast*]'.[29] Sobyanin easily won, albeit through
methods oppositionist groups denounced as fraudulent, but Navalny
had given an account of himself that riled the authorities.[30] In April
they had tried to destabilize his campaign by trying him and Oleg for
embezzlement. The outcome in July was inevitable since the judge,
Sergei Blinov, had tried 130 cases in his career, and found 130 defendants guilty. The only question was how severe the punishment would
be. No doubt on orders from the Kremlin, Blinov sentenced Navalny
to five years' imprisonment. Public protests led to the verdict being
changed to a suspended sentence. Before his appeal was heard, he was
allowed to fight the mayoral election even while his new Party of
Progress was refused official registration.[31]

In December 2014 Navalny's suspended sentence was confirmed
whereas his brother Oleg was sent to prison for three and a half years,
not least as a way of exerting psychological pressure on Navalny to
withdraw from public affairs. In any case, the fact that Navalny had a
criminal record secured the Kremlin's main aim of disrupting his political progress, because as a convicted criminal he was now permanently
barred from standing.[32]

Thereafter, apart from brief detentions after street protests, Navalny
stayed out of prison. Though the police handled him roughly, he
survived unharmed till May 2017, when an unidentified thug tossed a
green antiseptic dye in his face.[33] Navalny called for a boycott of the
forthcoming presidential election if his own name was banned from
the ballot papers. The electoral commission cited his embezzlement
conviction in turning down his right to stand as a candidate. Navalny
argued that the case had been brought against him on spurious
grounds, and the European Court of Human Rights supported his
claim, but the Russian judicial system ignored the verdict.

While saying little about his general lines of policy, Navalny
marked himself out as a thoughtful politician. In March 2014 he wrote
in the *New York Times* condemning the Crimean annexation,
describing it as an imperialist blunder or worse, and blaming Putin for
having 'artificially' created an anxiety about the peninsula.[34] Putin,
Navalny suggested, had ordered it for purely domestic political reasons,
and with the Crimean referendum had unwittingly set a precedent that

might come back to trouble him: there were ethnic republics elsewhere in the Russian Federation that were restless under Russian rule. Navalny endorsed America's economic sanctions, pleading only that the measures should not harm the Russian people. He urged the targeting of Putin's entourage, especially his rich friends in business – he named Timchenko, the Rotenberg brothers and Abramovich as among about a thousand individuals he characterized as forming 'the war party' and promoting the 'hysteria' that underpinned Putin's militarism.[35] This was also Navalny's way of trying to get at the media pundits and presenters who followed the Kremlin line.[36]

But by October 2014 Navalny spoke against handing back the peninsula: 'I think that despite the fact that Crimea was seized by a dreadful breach of international norms, nevertheless the reality is that Crimea is now a part of the Russian Federation. And let's not deceive ourselves. And I strongly recommend the Ukrainians also not to deceive themselves.'[37]

These sentiments, voiced in an Ekho Moskvy radio interview, annoyed many liberals. Since then he has more cautiously endorsed the idea of a referendum under 'international control' among Crimean residents,[38] and argued for the right of every country to determine its own future, including the freedom for east Europeans to join NATO.[39] For Navalny it was no business of Russia's to complain, far less to intervene in any direct fashion, if the Baltic States chose this way to ensure their security. But he does think it was a mistake for the Americans to install an anti-missile defence system in Poland. On that point at least, he agrees with Putin. Liberals will never win power in Russia, Navalny declares, unless they accept this.[40]

But he aims for a change in foreign policy that will mean Russia no longer fears NATO, and wants to ensure civic protection for the individual in Russian society by adherence to the jurisdiction of the European Court of Human Rights.[41] Russia, he insists, belongs in Europe, and should choose a 'European path' for its destination.[42] He laments Putin's success in turning the Russian people away from this objective by identifying Europe with phenomena such as gay parades and same-sex marriage.[43]

Navalny's own ideas – he dislikes being linked to any 'ideology' – are hard to categorize. While obviously not being a socialist, he has shunned most of the other available labels. His statement marks him out as both an anti-liberal liberal and an anti-conservative conservative. Ultimately, his thinking is a jumble, and all attempts to make coherent sense of it have failed. This does not bother him. Quite the contrary: he revels in his reputation as a maverick in Russian public life, and takes pleasure in the fact that the liberals call him a nationalist while the nationalists reject him as a liberal.[44] Even his sympathizers find this a baffling state of affairs, and have asked him to clarify his position, but Navalny defends his right to be elusive. The nearest he came to defining his philosophy was when he spoke up for 'civic nationalism'.[45]

This conception of national belonging excludes any racial or ethnic qualification, but in the light of Navalny's frequent disparagement of Muslims and others of Islamic heritage he can hardly be said to include them in his idea of nationhood. In 2011 he controversially exclaimed: 'Stop feeding the Caucasus.'[46] He censured the vast subsidies central government poured into Chechnya and Dagestan.[47] He later scoffed at Putin for effectively permitting sharia law in practice in some of Russia's regions while ranting about the danger of a spread of Islamism and cosying up to anti-Islamist foreign politicians like Marine Le Pen, which Navalny has joked is 'the apex of post-modernism'.[48] In contrast with Putin, he calls for a new visa regime to control the influx of migrant workers from central Asia.[49] Every November, Navalny has attended the annual Russian March of nationalist organizations, and defended the gathering as a positive venture.[50] Many oppositionists have indeed wondered aloud whether he was an appropriate choice to lead them at all.

Only occasionally does Navalny focus on specific policies for the Russian people. He seeks a separation of the Orthodox Church from the state, declaring himself a believer, and admitting that some of his followers criticize him for failing to censure the ecclesiastical hierarchy.[51] He aims the thrust of his appeals at Russians, and undoubtedly worried the authorities with his capacity to reach out to young educated voters, even though they are prevented from voting for him. Navalny is an optimist: when people cautioned that Russians are naturally conservative, he replied why, if that were so, does Russia lead the world in the number of abortions per head of the population, adding that independent ways of thinking are limited to 'the modernized part of a traditional society'.[52] Navalny endorses progressive social policies, accusing Putin of deliberately exploiting topics such as gay parades and same-sex marriage as a way of increasing prejudice and deflecting people's attention from his oppressive methods.[53]

The Party of Progress has only the rudiments of an economic

programme. Navalny has had help in policy-making from the dissenting economist Sergei Guriev, and the main idea is to reduce the role of the state in the Russian economy through a further schedule of privatizations, and use the proceeds to boost people's pensions. Navalny also calls for free health care and free education.[54] But since Guriev's emigration, economics have tended to feature less in the party's official statements.

At any rate, Navalny sees his objectives in different terms. For him, the priority has always been to institute the rule of law. He wants Russia to follow a 'European path' of development, and rejects all talk of copying the Chinese example. His ambition is to foster the kind of politics in which the president and cabinet can be replaced through a fair electoral contest: to him Putin's extended supremacy is anti-democratic. He has revised his belief that it would have been a national disaster if Yeltsin had lost the 1996 presidential election to Zyuganov: so long as an open political system had been preserved, Navalny maintains, things would have been righted in the longer term – and if Zyuganov had behaved properly, Russian democracy would have survived and improved.[55] His main slogans and those of his party are to do with legality, justice and fairness in public life. Navalny calls for an independent judiciary and an end to lucrative business contracts for cronies, demands a clean electoral process, and calls for officials who have broken the law by corruptly awarding contracts or throwing innocent people into prison to go on trial.[56]

Of the surviving oppositionists Navalny is unquestionably the principal: Nemtsov is dead and Kasyanov a spent force. Putin, Navalny believes, is actually frightened of him, as the potential leader of an anarchic 'Russian revolt [bunt]',[57] as a result of his willingness to challenge and confront, even at the risk of being manhandled by police at prohibited demonstrations. He is a rebel with an abundance of physical and moral courage.

But Navalny's prospects are not promising. He has never headed a cabinet as Kasyanov did or been a first deputy premier like Nemtsov. Kasyanov and Nemtsov also led substantial political parties, and acquired deep experience of the workings of the state order across the entire range of policy. They were once on friendly terms with ministers. Both men had been cherished by Yeltsin, about whom they retained fond memories: Yeltsin at various times had evidently marked them out for further promotion. Though the economy had been the focus while in government, they knew every sector of public life intimately.

They were privy to how governmental contracts were awarded. Nemtsov under Yeltsin and Kasyanov under Putin were witness to the pressures that ministers, officials and businessmen were able to exert on a president. They understood those sectors in public life that could cause trouble if they failed to receive privileged treatment. As a gifted but inexperienced outsider Navalny could only guess at all this. Not without justification, some thought Nemtsov's murder had beheaded the Opposition.

As the most famous living oppositionist Navalny draws the Western media's attention. He talks well, organizes as proficiently and flexibly as conditions allow, and is brave, determined and agile. But his rating in the opinion polls in spring 2017 was scarcely encouraging: according to the Levada Centre, only 2 per cent of potential voters responded that they would definitely support him. A further 7 per cent answered 'perhaps'.[58] In a further survey in August 2018, less than 1 per cent expressed trust in Navalny.[59] Navalny has tried to spread the Opposition's message to the regions, campaigning for a devolution of power not just to each province but right down to city level.[60] Government, he declares, is overcentralized. But his own party's organizational network grows weaker in proportion to the distance from the capital. Navalny remains predominantly a Moscow politician, and Russia is a huge country.[61]

Putin contains him with the help of obedient police, judges and media – and until recently by a dosage of pensions and welfare policies as well as an assertive foreign policy. Stooped double by persecution, the Opposition refuses to give up, and in Navalny it has a leader of spirit. If and when public opinion becomes inflamed, he could emerge as a champion of a new, different Russia. The persecution he has endured might increase his appeal as a victim with whom many Russians would identify. He is a complicated political figure, rightly praised for his courage and dynamism but handicapped by a way of thinking that would restrict the scope of liberal politics if he ever came to power. It is also unclear how he would cope with a powerful business lobby and the security forces, whose interests lie in maintaining the status quo.

20. ETERNAL VIGILANCE: THE UNBROKEN RISE OF THE SECURITY STATE

The Russian secret services have a prominence and influence unparalleled in democratic countries. They have acquired such importance because they remained upright when the rest of the communist edifice crumbled. Before 1991 the KGB had itself suffered a collapse in its morale and organizational effectiveness, many of its ablest officers leaving when the USSR disintegrated. But the new FSB showed remarkable resilience, and the Kremlin's leaders have come to rely on it to enforce their will in Russia and, for as long as the country fails to command international respect and achieve economic dynamism, to make the world tremble. Internal repression and external espionage and subversion mirror one another. The West has to be exposed as a plague on the house of Russia. 'Colour revolutions' in nearby countries must be cauterized so that no such revolution might spread to Moscow. American influence must be eradicated in Moscow and America's own political system attacked.

The FSB is integral to the anatomy of governance, penetrating every important institution and exercising authority with few restraints except those the president himself imposes. Legislation has been passed to permit the security organizations to pursue the national interest without parliamentary interference. Vladimir Putin's vision of them as a bastion of defence against internal subversion and external assault had always been the FSB's own attitude: its house journal *Sluzhba bezopasnosti* (Security Service) even called for monuments to be built in honour of Felix Dzerzhinski, the founder of the communist secret police in 1917. Taking it for granted that 'democracy' had discredited itself in Russia, it urged the necessity of continuing to operate elsewhere in the former USSR. It was encouraging its officers to take pride in the heritage of the Soviet secret services even before

Putin's year as FSB director.[1] The books page in the journal was coyly named 'The Andropov Library', in honour of the man who headed the KGB for fifteen years from 1967.[2] As prime minister in 1999, Putin restored Andropov's plaque on the Lubyanka building. He was going with the flow.[3]

On becoming president, nevertheless, Putin needed to give a public expression of regret for the wrongs committed in the Soviet past. In 2017 he designated 30 October as the annual Day of Remembrance of Victims of Political Repressions. He unveiled a monument, the Wall of Sorrow, at the end of Sakharov Prospekt in central Moscow, made from stones taken from the camps of the Stalinist Gulag. Standing with Patriarch Alexei II, he asked permission from Natalya Solzhenitsyna, widow of the distinguished ex-prisoner and writer of *The Gulag Archipelago*, to quote her words: 'To know, to remember and to judge. And only after that to forgive.' In the darkening hours of the day he placed a wreath at the base of the monument after making a speech about the tragedy suffered by the whole people. Not a word about Stalin, communism or the NKVD and other forces that organized wave after wave of terror. No use of the word 'terror'. Instead, the emphasis fell on maintaining solemn decorum. On the platform, as in the crowd on Sakharov Prospekt, all heads were bowed.[4]

Opposition activist Vladimir Kara-Murza, who had recently been the victim of a suspicious attempt at poisoning, wrote of the hypocrisy of a president who commemorated the foul brutalities of the 1930s while continuing to detain 117 political prisoners in the gaols and camps of the Russian Federation. Mikhail Khodorkovski's former security leader Alexei Pichugin, added Kara-Murza, was still languishing in confinement.[5]

Putin revealed his true interest by publicizing his annual attendance at FSB board meetings.[6] The FSB's virtues were a standard theme in his public statements, the presidential website reporting on the regularity with which he chaired the Security Council, and the still more frequent occasions when he called in its leading members for consultation. He treats such leaders as crucial for the development of policy outside the parameters of normal security questions. In November 2017, for example, Putin gathered this informal group round him to plan how to handle proceedings at the Asia-Pacific Economic Cooperation summit he was about to attend in Vietnam.[7] No minister with economic responsibility was present, even though Russia's trading opportunities and difficulties were the item for discussion.

Early in his first term as president Putin had given a passionate speech to an audience of FSB generals in celebration of Chekist Day (Den chekista). His then prime minister, Kasyanov, had tried to pass off Putin's fulsome praise of the security agencies as a joke, even when Putin stated that the FSB had, through him, at last achieved the objective of taking absolute power. There were shouts of hurrah in the hall. It was some hours later that Kasyanov fell to worrying about the kind of president Putin was likely to become.[8]

Putin gave orders for FSB officers to receive improvements in salary, pensions and social entitlements; more housing was made available for them. Welfare provision was improved for the families of security personnel who died on active service.[9] None of this was a secret. The secret services enjoyed increased official acclaim. In 1991 Felix Dzerzhinski's statue on the square outside the Lubyanka building had been pulled down, to public acclaim, but in September 2017 the Kirov City Council unveiled a new bronze monument to his memory.[10] This and other provincial initiatives have yet to be copied in Moscow, and Putin has so far held back from a formal political rehabilitation, probably seeking to avoid the likely mass demonstrations any such measure would prompt. His way of dealing with the question is to say that it is up to the Moscow city authorities to decide whether to restore the statue to the Lubyanka square. But nobody can be in doubt about his respect for the feared Dzerzhinski.[11]

Elected political institutions carry out little scrutiny of the Russian secret services. Neither the Federation Council nor the State Duma imposes accountability through its internal committees. Whereas the Duma Foreign Affairs Committee scrutinizes the entire range of Russia's diplomatic activity, albeit rarely with critical intent, there is no parliamentary body to supervise the FSB and the other intelligence bodies. Control is left in the hands of the president and the Security Council: the foxes have charge of the hen house. Putin himself had a long career in the KGB and spent a year as the FSB's director, and the Security Council is composed almost entirely of officials from the secret services. Some idea of the Security Council's objectives comes from its orders to its own 'scientific council' of prominent scholars, who are ordered to conduct 'the scientific-methodological evaluation and prognostication of internal and external threats bearing on the socio-economic development of the Russian Federation'. Preventing the kind of revolution that took place in Georgia and Ukraine is a cherished objective.[12] Few of the scholars were likely to say anything

Putin would find objectionable. Their function is to legitimize the Kremlin's official line.

Such accountability as is demanded from the intelligence agencies is exercised by the president. While this bestows huge authority, it also lays an immense burden of responsibility upon Putin in a working routine involving countless other demands on his time. Even though he presumably requires to be consulted about plans for the biggest covert operations, he necessarily leaves the details up to the leaders of the secret services. In 2000 he told Kasyanov he would not tolerate prime-ministerial interference in security affairs: the president alone has overarching control. This is far from meaning he has simply left the secret services to their own devices. In his first presidential term he ordered some drastic reforms, among them a purge of FSB personnel deemed inadequate, and entrusted the task to friends and associates from his time in the KGB or in the St Petersburg mayor's office. He is aware that the men – they are all men – who head the secret services have the logistical capacity to do him harm. By strengthening the licence for the secret services to act as the ultimate instrument of state power, he had provided them with a chance to act on and even beyond his orders.

This accentuates his requirement for personal reliability. Recently he has taken the precaution of reshuffling the leading personnel, leaving him the solitary element of state power not to have been replaced. He also finds it convenient for the many security services to compete with each other, something assured by the overlapping boundaries of their operations. Rivalry below presidential level makes the president rest easy.

In 2006 a flurry of legal enactments authorized the security forces to take more action against subversion. The legislation was cast in characteristically vague or opaque language, but the intention was obvious. On 6 March Putin signed a law 'on counteracting terrorism' that came to him from both houses of the Federal Assembly, which defined the 'basic concepts' of terrorism very broadly, and empowered action against all who carried out, organized or ordered acts of terror as well as those who propagated ideas calling for or justifying such activity. Enforcement would not be confined to Russian territory: the lawmakers required the armed forces, including the secret services, to carry out 'the suppression of international terrorist activity beyond the frontiers of the territory of the Russian Federation'. The president was given explicit authority to order anti-terrorist operations, Article 15 laying down that the forces used for such operations could include those of the security agencies.[13] Although the FSB was not expressly mentioned, its expanded role was an essential element of the new law.

Parallel legislative work was done to amend legislation on 'extremism'. The impetus came from events abroad. On 3 June 2006 Russian diplomat Valeri Titov was fatally wounded in a terrorist attack in Baghdad. Four of his colleagues were abducted. The terrorist group responsible issued an ultimatum that unless Russia's government withdrew from Chechnya and released all Muslim prisoners, the kidnapped diplomats would be killed. A videotape was released showing one of them being beheaded. The other three were soon also confirmed as having perished.

On 28 June Putin issued a public order to Russian 'special services' to hunt down and 'annihilate' the killers.[14] Patrushev, head of the FSB at the time, pledged that no terrorist would be able to 'evade responsibility' for crimes committed.[15] TV and radio stations endorsed his declaration. The FSB, meanwhile, achieved a notable success in its anti-terrorism campaign. On 10 July 2006 Shamil Basaev, one of the leading Chechen terrorists operating on the territory of the Russian Federation, was killed in an explosion in Ingushetia, close to the North Ossetian border. There is still no conclusive evidence that Russian special services were responsible for Basaev's death, and it is quite possible that the explosion was an accident while he was inspecting a land mine,[16] but the fact remains that Basaev had long been the FSB's quarry and that the Russian authorities celebrated his elimination, or – in Putin's terminology – annihilation.[17]

This created a propitious atmosphere in July for the Federal Assembly to pass by an overwhelming majority an amendment of the legislation on extremism and for Putin to sign it into law. Extremism was defined as anything from violent attempts to change Russia's constitutional order and territorial integrity to the stirring up of racist, national or religious strife. Even 'obstructing the legal activity of organs of state power' and slandering holders of state power were classified as extremist acts.[18] The amendment was a mere listing of categories rather than a careful legislative definition – again a deliberate vagueness, giving the authorities a field day for unfettered repressive activity and unlocking the door for a large swathe of opponents to be branded as extremists who had to be eliminated. Putin was reserving the right to move heavily against anyone who made strident criticism of his rule.

Russia was delivering a warning that fire would be met with fire but, as United Russia spokesmen indicated, the new laws only ratified what was already happening. In its repressive activities the FSB had never stopped at Russian frontiers,[19] but this was the first time that Russians were told what they could expect from the foreign operations of their secret services.

The precise motives for Alexander Litvinenko's murder remain unclear, and there are many possibilities: Litvinenko had besmirched Putin's personal reputation; he had acted as Boris Berezovski's helpmate; he had revealed Russian state secrets and become employed by a foreign intelligence service, MI6; he had divulged details of money laundering by Russia's richest entrepreneurs. Any of these was likely to provoke a violent reaction from Moscow.[20] In November 2006, after a sequence of unsuccessful attempts on his life, he was rushed to University College Hospital in London where he died a lingering death after drinking tea laced with the radioactive poison polonium-210. The British authorities quickly blamed the Russian state and expelled four diplomats from the London embassy. Relations remained frozen for some months, but the Labour government decided to avoid further trouble for fear of damaging British economic interests. The Conservative–LibDem coalition government took the same line until after the Crimean annexation. In 2015 a judicial inquiry was at last approved.[21]

The Russian political establishment took little notice. In July that year the Constitutional Court ruled that Russia's courts could ignore international judicial bodies when their rulings contradicted the Russian constitution. Judges in Russia became free to conduct proceedings without fear of verdicts in courts anywhere abroad.[22]

The judge in charge of the inquiry, Sir Robert Owen, had been calling for such an investigation in the long intervening years when prime ministers Blair, Brown and Cameron had preferred a policy of encouraging trade and not annoying the Kremlin, but it would have no immediate consequences for Russian individuals or agencies, because it was an inquiry into events rather than a trial with defendants. In London months of testimony now followed, both openly and in camera. At the end, in January 2016, Owen issued his verdict. He had no doubt that FSB agents Andrei Lugovoi and Dmitri Kovtun had administered the poison, noting their carelessness or lack of training in leaving traces in other parts of London and on the airliner they had flown on. On the political side, Owen concluded that Putin had 'probably' been responsible for ordering the murder. His verbal caution left unexplained the nature of the information suggestive of

Putin's culpability. He did not even say whether it was the evidence of a spy or an electronic intercept. Presumably this was on advice from the UK authorities.

Russian TV channels and newspapers laid stress on Owen's less than definite conclusion about Putin, ignoring the compelling evidence of Lugovoi and Kovtun's guilt and their FSB connection. Foreign Affairs Minister Lavrov commented on the high number of deaths among Russians residents in London in the previous ten years, and complained that the British authorities declined to seek Moscow's assistance in their investigations.[23] Lavrov's tasteless levity became the pattern for Kremlin spokespersons and newscasters.

It was repeated in March 2018 after the attempted assassination of Sergei Skripal in Salisbury. Skripal was a former double agent working for the United Kingdom while serving as a colonel in the GRU (in 2010 Russia's military intelligence organization was renamed as the GU but was still known by its old acronym). Arrested by the Russian authorities, Skripal had been freed in a spy swap involving the FSB sleeper 'Anna Chapman', who was in prison in America. Skripal and his daughter Yulia were found slumped on a park bench in Salisbury, where he had made his home. They were victims of a nerve agent poison called Novichok, a compound toxin developed in Russia that attacks the nervous system. A policeman who went to their rescue became gravely ill. Weeks passed before all three of them could be discharged from hospital.

During that time two further people became victims. These were civilians living in or near Salisbury who came into contact with the discarded container of the Novichok. One of them, Dawn Sturgess, failed to respond to intensive medical care and died. Her partner, Charlie Rowley, was reported as suffering heart attacks after being discharged from hospital.

The British authorities blamed the Kremlin as soon as the toxin was detected. Foreign Secretary Boris Johnson named Putin directly as having given the order for the attempted murder. Details of what London discovered about the outrage were confidentially passed to the NATO allies, who found them convincing. In Moscow there was an official fit of anger at the UK's government's speed in attributing blame. This gave way to sarcasm as the Rossiya-1 TV channel advised émigré Russians to reconsider whether 'Albion' was a secure place of refuge. A bout of mutual diplomatic expulsions followed. In September 2018 the UK's Crown Prosecution Service announced that the police investigation had identified two Russian suspects, Alexander Petrov and Ruslan Boshirov, who were GRU officers. As had happened after the Litvinenko murder, there was no chance of dragging them back to face justice in a British court. The real identities of Petrov and Boshirov were quickly revealed, and their preposterous story about going to Salisbury not once but twice to satisfy their passion for the architectural magnificence of its cathedral fell apart. Even Moscow newspapers mocked the GRU's ineptitude.

Putin brushed the adverse publicity aside, speaking at a press conference in June 2018 of the 'shaky ground' of the British allegations, which he dismissed as '"creative" chatter'.[24] In October he exclaimed that Skripal was nothing but a spy and a traitor: 'He's simply scum. That's all there is to it. And a whole information campaign has been blown up around this. I sometimes look at what's happening around this affair, and I'm simply astonished. Some fellows made a trip and started to poison homeless persons in your country, in Great Britain. What sort of madness is this?'[25]

It had always been Putin's habit to commend the work of Russian security organs, and on 26 March 2015 he congratulated his 'respected comrades' on achieving a drastic decrease in 'crimes of a terrorist orientation'. In 2013 there had been 2.6 times more cases than in 2014, and nine times more in the 2009–14 period. Putin took this as proof that the situation had been brought 'almost to order'.[26] But there was no room for complacency. He expressed concern about the possibility that jihadists who had left the Russian Federation to fight in the ranks of Islamic State 'could be used against Russia and our neighbours', and called for them to be prevented from returning, especially to Crimea.[27] Security Council Secretary Patrushev divulged that the Russian authorities were hunting down the returnees from active combat for Islamic State in the Middle East, and by mid-2017 had put 151 of them on trial and apprehended a further 29.[28] At an FSB Board meeting on 26 February 2016 Putin thanked its officers for breaking up many terrorist groups before they could become active.[29]

Further counter-intelligence work was now required, he said, to prevent foreign security forces from gaining a toehold in Russia, expressing thanks for the interception of 400 such agents – 23 had been handed over to the judicial authorities.[30] In 2016, he announced, the FSB had put a halt to the work of 53 foreign intelligence officers and 386 agents.[31]

Before the Sochi Winter Olympics there were rumours that the

FSB took some unusual steps to prevent a terrorist outrage. Apparently intelligence agents travelled to villages in the North Caucasus and let it be known that armed militants would be allowed to go to the Middle East and join Islamic State. An investigation by the opposition newspaper *Novaya gazeta* concluded that a 'green corridor' was established for them to fly to Turkey and then make their way into Syrian territory. Though the Russian leadership valued the alliance with Syria's President Assad, its priority was security in the Russian Federation. There was little concern about where the jihadis operated, so long as it was not on Russia's territory. In the village of Novosasitli in Dagestan's Khasavurt district, according to the newspaper, 1 per cent of the population left for Syria from 2011 onward. The departure of militants was endorsed by Akhyad Abdullaev, who headed the Novosasitli administration:

> I know someone who has been at war for fifteen years. He fought in Chechnya, in Palestine, in Afghanistan, in Iraq, and now in Syria. He is surely incapable of living peacefully. If such people go off to war, it's no loss. In our village there is an individual, a negotiator. He, together with the FSB, drew several leaders out of the underground and redirected them abroad on jihad. The underground has been weakened here, and this is good for us. If they want to fight, let them fight, only not here.[32]

The FSB chief Alexander Bortnikov, usually one of the more reticent of the Kremlin rulers, disclosed that 2,900 citizens had left to join Middle Eastern jihadi organizations by December 2015. But not once has he responded to requests for details from the media: the government and the secret services have acted on the principle that if they stay quiet, perhaps the story will fade from view; and indeed the story has since struggled to attract public attention either in Russia or abroad.

In 2016 Reuters news agency did track down a Dagestani jihadi, Saadu Sharapudinov, however, and several others who confirmed the *Novaya gazeta* allegations personally. By his own account Sharapudinov took up the FSB's offer as a way of joining jihadis across the Turkish frontier in Syria.[33] In February 2017 Putin announced that about four thousand citizens of the Russian Federation (and another five thousand from the rest of the former USSR) were fighting for ISIS in Syria, and thanked Russia's armed forces for their efforts to kill all of them. Not for him the kind of euphemisms that Western leaders employ on such occasions: he wanted those ISIS fighters slaughtered. The Syrian civil war, he noted, could become a breeding ground for terrorists who might leave Syria and take advantage of the absence of visa requirements between Russia and ex-Soviet republics to cause havoc on Russian soil.[34]

The priority the Kremlin gave to Russia's internal security was manifest too in the pressure laid upon Western IT companies working inside the country, as the FSB began to insist on their complying with 'source code' checks as a condition for continuing their operations. This affected several large American firms, including Cisco, Hewlett Packard, IBM, McAfee, SAP and Symantec. The official rationale was to prevent firewalls, anti-virus programmes and general software from being exploited by the West's secret services in order to penetrate Russian defences. Symantec decided the demands were excessively intrusive and would compromise its independence from governments, while US officials expressed anxiety that any companies acceding to Moscow's requirements might inadvertently supply the FSB with the technical knowledge to pierce America's defences.[35]

Meanwhile, in January 2017 there was upheaval at the top of the Russian intelligence agencies. Sergei Mikhailov, deputy chief of the FSB's Centre for Information Security, was taken into custody, and arrested along with him were one of his leading officials, Dmitri Dokuchaev, and Ruslan Stoyanov, who headed the Kaspersky Lab, a multinational private firm that collaborates with the FSB in matters of internet security.

All were charged with treason. It was said that Mikhailov was apprehended in the middle of a meeting of FSB leaders and hooded with a black bag before being hauled off to the infamous Lefortovo prison. The story was leaked to the opposition press that the detainees were suspected of passing information to Western sources about Russian cyber-attacks in the West. Mikhailov was charged with treason on the grounds that he had cooperated with the CIA against Russia's security interests.[36] Exactly what caused the arrests is obscure. One possibility is that Mikhailov was indeed in league with American intelligence operatives, another that he was being punished for failing to keep Russian secret activities properly secret. Or perhaps this was just one dastardly stage in the tug-of-war between Russia's several 'special services'. Whatever the truth, there has never been a time in East–West relations when Russian and American secret services have been so enmeshed in each other's business.

The affair became stranger still in April 2017 when the US Senate Intelligence Committee began to query the US Defense Department's contract with Kaspersky Lab for the supply of protection for its electronic communications. It was pointed out that the company had its origins in Moscow, and unease was expressed that some of its early employees had worked for the Soviet and Russian secret services.[37] Senator Joe Manchin, one of many leading Democrats calling on the Trump administration to take a harder policy line on Russia, raised the alarm. The Intelligence Committee sent its grim warning to National Intelligence Director Dan Coats and Attorney General Jeff Sessions.[38] On 27 June the Senate Armed Services Committee belatedly entered the game when Democrat Senator Jeanne Shaheen amended a defence spending bill by demanding a suspension of the Pentagon's contract with Kaspersky.

The competition between the Russian and American intelligence agencies only occasionally broke surface to public notice. As in the Cold War, it was a murky, brutal struggle. Much less secret was a success that Russia's authorities had achieved in July 2013 without lifting a finger. Sensationally, Edward Snowden, an IT consultant who had worked on a contract basis for the US State Department, fetched up at Moscow's Sheremetevo airport, having become a fugitive after leaking hundreds of thousands of classified documents, including diplomatic cables, out of a zeal to expose what he saw as the deceitfulness of successive American administrations. Snowden also had piles of evidence to show how America's authorities snooped on enemies and allies abroad as well as on its own citizens. With his libertarian passion for transparency of governance, he had contacted the *Guardian* and *Washington Post* newspapers, which released the data to the worldwide web, causing real damage to the Obama administration's reputation. When a warrant was issued for Snowden's arrest, and having failed to obtain political asylum elsewhere in the world, Snowden put himself at the mercy of the Russian authorities.

A delighted Kremlin ignored American requests to hand him over. After forty tiring days and nights at Sheremetevo airport, he was granted political asylum in Moscow. Russian spokesmen boasted that it was Russia, not America, that gave succour to those who shone light on evil practices. Putin himself enjoyed Obama's embarrassment: for once, in discussions of human rights, the boot seemed to be on the other foot. The terms of Snowden's asylum were not publicized, particularly as to whether he had to share his cache of data as the price. He and the Kremlin authorities kept his public appearances to a minimum and he wrote only rarely for the media. Meanwhile Obama had to apologize to Angela Merkel after the revelation that the Americans had bugged her private mobile phone. WikiLeaks also published material about debates inside the State Department that contained devastating critiques of the policies and practices of America's leading allies. Stories that might have sounded like propaganda if issued by the Russian intelligence agencies acquired credibility, and Kremlin leaders made the most of their opportunity.

In April 2014, in his annual 'Direct Line' TV phone-in, Putin affected surprise when told that Snowden was calling in with a query. Snowden was introduced as a 'former agent of the American special services'. In an obvious set-up, he asked Putin whether Russia stored, intercepted or analysed the communications of millions of members of society. Putin answered in tones of unctuous courtesy:

> Respected Mr Snowden! You are a former agent. I used to have a relationship with intelligence work, so we'll both talk a professional language. To start with, we have strict legislative regulation of the use of special methods by the security services, including both the tapping of private conversations and the surveillance of online communications and so on. This regulation is linked to the need for a court's warrant in relation to a concrete individual citizen. And so we have no indiscriminate mass [operations] and can have none according to the law.[39]

Snowden, living under the constraints of Russian keepership, obediently played the role assigned to him.[40]

In later comments, Putin defended Snowden against the charge of treason while suggesting that Snowden should have done the right thing by resigning his job with a company working on a State Department contract. In Putin's judgement, Snowden was wrong to leak governmental secrets:[41] taking a high moral stance, he was assuming the role of an ex-Soviet security officer taught to keep a lid on confidential information. This was mere display: he really only wanted silence about Russian secrets, and was delighted by Snowden's breaking of the rules and by Obama's discomfort. On another occasion he teased the American administration by saying it could have avoided its problem over Snowden by agreeing to the Russian proposal for a criminal extradition treaty.[42] So much for any illusion Snowden might have had about the beneficence of his Moscow protectors! – he is a useful pawn who may be traded for other pieces on the chess board of world politics. He went to Moscow as an act of desperation, knowing the Russians would use him if and however they could.

Meanwhile, Moscow's own activities abroad were anything but innocent. In 2007 Russian secret services were identified as having hired hackers to put Estonia's entire internet out of action for days. Though the Kremlin denied involvement, the circumstantial evidence was compelling. It proved to Western powers that Russia's secret services were capable of undertaking a comprehensive attack on Western cyber-defences, and they warned that any repetition could constitute an act of war. Other hacking initiatives were reported in advance of the 2017 French presidential election, when thousands of email messages from Emmanuel Macron's team were leaked on the internet – the Russians preferred other candidates who were friendlier to Russia. And during the United Kingdom's Brexit referendum, it later transpired, Russian companies employed devious methods to use Facebook data to discover the identity of voters hostile to the European Union, and then target them with 'fake news' designed to stiffen their will to vote 'leave'.

Moscow's secret services are proud of their achievements in Russia and abroad: when Patrushev was FSB director, he gave an interview to the *Komsomolskaya Pravda* newspaper and in one purple passage stated:

> I don't want to use high-flown words but our best colleagues, the honour and pride of the FSB, aren't doing their work for the money. When I have to hand over government awards to our people, I look them carefully in the eye. There are high-browed intellectual analysts, broad-shouldered, weather-beaten special forces fighters, taciturn explosives specialists, exacting investigators and reserved counter-espionage operational officers . . . In appearance they are very different, but they have one important quality that unites them: it is that they are people with a commitment to the idea of service. They are, if you like, our 'neo-nobility (*neodvoryane*)'.[43]

Under the tsars the *dvoryanstvo* had originally been a social group awarded landed property and authority over their peasants in return for military service to crown and state, and the nobility or gentry were the essential component of the army, administration, courts and diplomacy. Patrushev, in setting out the case for the FSB's unrivalled capacity to look after the Russian people's security at home and abroad, saw its officials as possessed of the same selflessness in protecting the country as supposedly the *dvoryanstvo* of old.

Though the FSB describes itself as an enforcer of honest economic practice, there are many indications that some of its agents have been involved with the criminal underworld. In 1998 Alexander Litvinenko contacted Putin personally about a gang of Uzbek criminals who he alleged were running a huge illicit drugs trade with the Afghan warlord and politician Abdul Rashid Dostum.[44] He also revealed that FSB officials had colluded in a plot to kill Boris Berezovski. He went even further, accusing Russian political leaders and their secret services of profiting from the very activity that they were meant to prevent,[45] in particular charging Putin specifically with lending protection to Semën Mogilevich and the so-called Tambov gang in St Petersburg, which Litvinenko described as Russia's 'bandit capital'.[46] Litvinenko also suggested that in the 1990s Mogilevich had links with both Al-Qaida and Putin.[47] Independent evidence about Mogilevich and Putin emerged from the leak of a taped conversation in July 2000 between Ukraine's President Leonid Kuchma and Leonid Derkach, head of the Ukrainian security services. Kuchma and Derkach were speaking about the crisis of Russo-Ukrainian relations over the status of the RusUkrEnergo enterprise, which played an important role in the gas exports to Ukraine. Derkach talked of Semën Mogilevich's expected arrival in Kyiv for negotiations to resolve the various disputes: 'He's on good terms with Putin,' Derkach remarked. 'He and Putin have been in contact since Putin was still in Leningrad.'[48]

Other tapes have Kuchma and Derkach discussing whether to acquaint Putin in person with Ukrainian intelligence material from the early 1990s – by which time Putin had left the KGB but was yet to head the FSB – that could be seen as pointing to his part in a St Petersburg deal involving money laundering in Germany.[49]

The testimony against him is patchy at best, and frequently unsubstantiated. The Kremlin has not commented on the allegation. What can be said with confidence is that if Putin really did get involved in illicit business activities, he was not the only one among the former or current intelligence community. 'Security' questions are pervasive in top-level international commercial negotiations for Russia. Entrepreneurs and lawyers working there testify that large commercial deals cannot come to a conclusion unless and until authorized by the FSB,[50] and many intelligence officers have the opportunity to demand bribes as the price of giving contracts the go-ahead. It is an environment that entices one secret agency to denounce another, and Putin has difficulty holding the ring.[51]

21. MILITARY RENEWAL: A GREAT POWER PREPARES

The weeks after the Crimean annexation saw Russian military power on brash display. Soldiers and hardware paraded down the central thoroughfare of Sevastopol. In eastern Ukraine the show was restrained to hold to the fiction that only Russian volunteers had joined the rebel side. Defence Minister Shoigu trumpeted the achievement of Russia's forces in protecting Russian interests: there was nothing the Americans could do, he and Putin declared, to frighten Russia into timidity. Not only were its army, navy and air force capable of defending the country but also, when the situation called for it, they could attack. In global politics, Putin wanted America to learn, power was henceforth going to be shared.

Modernization of the military had begun in earnest after the Georgian war of 2008. Saakashvili had been humbled and Georgia's security and foreign policy lay in tatters, but Putin and his advisers were unimpressed by the success. It had been an ill-coordinated performance by their armed forces. The Russian army had superior equipment and the advantage of surprise, and yet although it won the war in a matter of days, it had still failed to deliver its blows with satisfactory efficiency. Since the late 1980s the country's capacity for military deterrence had largely depended on its strategic nuclear firepower. But its conventional forces had seen a steady decline, and even the intercontinental nuclear warheads and their rockets and submarines required modernization. This was not something Putin would tolerate any longer, especially now the Defence Ministry was boasting that Russia was no longer confining its ambitions to Russia and its 'near abroad'. On 26 February 2014, the very day before Russian troops took over the whole of Sevastopol, Shoigu talked of Russia's intention to station its armed forces in faraway Singapore, the Seychelles, Nicaragua and Venezuela.[1]

Putin refused to listen to those who wanted defence spending to remain at the old level. In the early 2000s there was a steady rise in Russian military expenditure: by 2013 it was 172 per cent higher than in 2000, achieved largely through increased revenue from oil and gas exports. In 2000 3.6 per cent of gross domestic product had been allocated to the military. Thirteen years later it was 4.2 per cent,[2] and by 2016, despite the recession that had taken hold two years earlier, it was raised to 4.5 per cent.[3] Predictably, this would prove hard to sustain, and the projection for 2017 was to pull it down to 3.1 per cent to staunch the haemorrhaging of funds from the Finance Ministry.[4]

All this jarred with the strategic assumptions made by America since the 1990s, when the recent arms reduction treaties had induced the Americans to scale down their presence in Europe. Yeltsin's ardour for a partnership with the Western powers had fostered an assumption among politicians and military planners in the United States and allied countries that it was safe to strip back the dimensions of defensive readiness. The trend continued into the new millennium after the terrorist destruction of the Twin Towers in 2001, with NATO's main activity redirected to Afghanistan. Iraq was added to the West's agenda in 2003, and the United States soon found itself engaged in armed intervention across a vast zone stretching from Libya in north Africa through the Middle East and across to Afghanistan. From autumn 2011 President Obama revealed his intention to break free of this entanglement, and ordered a revision of American global policy to shift priorities towards the Asia-Pacific region and America's increasing rivalry with the People's Republic of China. This became known as a strategic 'pivot' away from Europe and the Middle East, and was confirmed by Obama in an address to the Australian parliament in November. The following year, albeit reluctantly and on a limited scale, Obama intervened in the Libyan revolt against Gaddafi. America, Kremlin analysts concluded, was no longer committed to clasping Europe to its bosom.

The Americans now kept only fifty-three tanks and forty-eight helicopters on European soil, and the number of German tanks fell from 2,815 to 322. NATO's European member states were generally cutting their defence expenditure – by 2013 on average they devoted 1.6 per cent of national gross domestic product to such purposes, down from 2.7 per cent in 1990.[5] In 2014–16 only the United Kingdom and Poland complied with NATO's agreed target of at least 2 per cent budget expenditure on defence, with Estonia committing itself to attaining that level by 2020. Most of the allies showed no sign of getting even near.

Measured by the number and quality of tanks, Russian military preponderance was unmistakable. But the appearance of decline in the American armed forces was illusory. At the same time as America was running down its conventional forces in Europe, it was also over-hauling and extending its anti-missile defence system. By 2007 this annoyed the Russians enough for them to suspend their commitment to the Conventional Forces in Europe Treaty. Signed in 1990, it had been one of the milestones on the road to ending the Cold War. Russia's definitive withdrawal in 2015 was a warning from the Kremlin that it was willing to retaliate against a threat to the Russian national interest – and by then, faced with the West's reaction to the Crimean annexation in the previous year, Putin and his associates felt they had nothing to lose.

In Soviet times the working assumption had been that the larger its armed forces, the greater the USSR's security. Efficiency was lost in the drive for size. The policy had changed under Gorbachëv and then Yeltsin, but now Putin ordered the Defence Ministry to formulate a plan for Russian forces to become a realistic match for any potential enemy.[6] Quantity now gave way to quality, with the overall number of Russian troops reduced. Serving officers and soldiers fell from a million to 845,000; the number of battle tanks tumbled even more drastically, from 12,920 to 2,550. By the end of 2016, all NCOs in the Russian army were professional recruits rather than ex-conscripts.[7]

On 26 December 2014 Putin had signed off some amendments to the 'military doctrine' in place since 2010,[8] to take account of the change in world politics, especially after Russia's armed action against Ukraine. A week earlier Putin had laid out his ideas at the Defence Ministry Board:

> . . . we must develop all the components of our strategic nuclear forces, which constitute the most important factor in maintaining global balance and truly rule out the possibility of large-scale aggression against Russia. In 2015, more than fifty intercontinental ballistic missiles will join the strategic nuclear forces – you can imagine what a powerful force this is. The task is to continue modernizing our strategic aviation and put the two missile-carrying submarines *Vladimir Monomakh* and *Alexander Nevski* on combat alert.

He went on to list a further commitment to modernize Russia's ground-based nuclear forces, developing new strategic bombers and overhauling the Russian missile defence system.[9] The doctrine was unequivocal about Russia reserving the right to deploy its nuclear forces against any external offensive, nuclear or otherwise, that threatened the existence of the state – and it would be the president who would take the ultimate decision.[10]

On 4 June 2014 Putin defended Russia against the charge of militarism, arguing that the defence budget had risen by barely 0.1 per cent of gross domestic product.[11] The following year, in an interview with *Corriere della Sera*, he stressed that America vastly outstripped Russia in its budget for its armed forces:

> The USA's military expenditure is higher than that of all the countries in the world put together. The total military expenditure of the NATO countries is ten times – please note that it's ten times higher than the military expenditure of the Russian Federation.
>
> Russia has practically no bases abroad. We have the remnants of our armed forces which have stayed on since Soviet times in Tajikistan to deal with the dangerous terrorism situation on the border with Afghanistan. The same role is played by our military air base in Kyrgyzia; it too is aimed at dealing with the terrorism threat and was created at the request of the Kyrgyz authorities after an attack on Kyrgyzstan by terrorists from Afghanistan. We have kept a military unit since Soviet times at a military base in Armenia. It plays a certain stabilizing role in the region, but it is not targeted against anyone. We have liquidated our bases in various regions of the world, including Cuba, Vietnam and so on. This means that our policy in this respect doesn't carry a global offensive, aggressive character.

Putin asked the newspaper to publish a map of all the American military bases round the world so that everyone could see the contrast between America and Russia.[12]

There had been hopes in Moscow, at the start of Obama's first presidency in 2009, that the new administration might agree to suspend or even terminate the anti-missile plans his predecessor George W. Bush had introduced. Despite a lack of personal chemistry between Obama and Putin a softening of Russo-American relations did indeed take place, eased by the fact that it was Medvedev, not Putin, who was Russian president from 2008. Obama and Medvedev got on well socially as well as politically from their first meeting. Neither intended to pass up the chance for improved relations. Quiet progress was made in talks about nuclear missiles, and by 8 April 2010 the two presidents were able to sign the New Strategic Arms Reduction Treaty (New START), limiting the United States and the Russian Federation to 1,550 strategic warheads apiece. Scheduled to last for ten years, the treaty was the most impressive achievement in decreasing the risk of thermonuclear war, whether through political confrontation or by accident, since the years of Gorbachëv, Reagan and Bush Sr.[13]

Yet both the Americans and Russians knew that nuclear military power was one of the keys to global influence, and both sides pressed on with the modernization of their warheads.[14] Obama was as enthusiastic about it as Medvedev and Putin. Putin had always understood that Russia's strategic missiles were essential for the maintenance of his country's international authority. They were a high-value chip in negotiations over Ukraine. Russian ground forces were superior to anything the Ukrainians could assemble, but Moscow's strategic and tactical nuclear forces were completely unmatched. Putin might be willing to reduce his arsenal, but he would never bargain it away entirely. In 2015, when it became known that the United States had failed to run down its stock of weaponry in line with the New START schedule, Putin said he would consider withdrawing Russia from the treaty, omitting to acknowledge that the Russians had been equally slow to comply with their obligations.

While disquiet was voiced about international tensions, no countries were picked out by the Kremlin as real or potential enemies: Putin and his inner group had decided to avoid giving needless offence by naming the United States as Russia's likeliest future adversary. Instead, Russia's official military doctrine merely noted the global menace NATO posed by its infringement of the norms of international law and its eastward growth towards Russia's frontiers – a reference to NATO forces in the Baltic States.[15] But to anyone with the slightest acquaintance with world politics it was obvious Putin held America in his sights, and though the doctrine made no direct reference to Ukraine, alarm was expressed about the danger of destabilization in neighbouring states. The doctrine highlighted the menace of the 'political and military pressure' being applied to Russia. Moscow also continued to object to the Americans' anti-missile defence systems in Poland, Romania and the Czech Republic.

Putin likes to appear unperturbed about Western economic sanctions, but on 3 October 2016 he momentarily gave a different impression. A bill he passed for publication by the Federal Assembly ostensibly aimed to suspend the long-standing agreement with the United States on international commerce in plutonium nuclear material – but why would Russia want to end the restrictions on such a dangerous trade? The answer came in what Moscow required of Washington for the agreement to be reinstated. Putin's demands reflected simmering resentments. The Americans had to reduce their forces and 'military infrastructure' in the countries that joined NATO after 2000 to the levels they had been at before. Having complained for years about NATO enlargement, the Russians were at last spelling out their terms for a settlement of security questions in eastern and east-central Europe,[16] and essentially what Putin wanted was a return to the status quo. Russia's actions in Georgia, Ukraine and Syria had given notice of its status and authority as a great power.

If Washington wanted to have better relations with Moscow, American concessions were essential, and maybe at that point in the American presidential election campaign Putin believed there could be only one winner, Hillary Clinton, and only a miracle could save Donald Trump from defeat. The Russian president's aim, then, was apparently to send an intimidating message to the presumed next American president. He was preparing for a bare-knuckle contest when Clinton entered the White House.

Putin could have sharpened his case about Russia's peaceful intentions by calling attention to the cut made in Russian military spending in 2016, but this would have undermined his parallel desire to assure Russian public opinion that he was standing firm in defence of the national interest. The Finance Ministry was strongly in favour of reducing expenditure on the armed forces as the dip in world market prices for oil and gas started to bite, but, according to reports, was hotly resisted by Defence Minister Shoigu, who shouted at Finance Minister Siluanov that he was jeopardizing crucial agreed plans for the modernization of the armed forces.[17] Siluanov replied that there was no longer the money for them: they would cost double what the Finance Ministry thought prudent. Putin listened as the two sides clashed. If Shoigu got his way, Siluanov explained, social welfare expenditure would have to be hacked back.[18] This touched a raw nerve: Putin and Kudrin, Siluanov's predecessor, had quarrelled over Kudrin's call to speed up the reduction of welfare payments, and Putin had accused Kudrin of underestimating the political risks. But Siluanov had chosen his argument carefully, knowing Putin was chary about annoying those parts of the electorate who depended on the government's welfare payouts. Putin chaired working groups to come up with a compromise, and eventually came down in favour of decreasing military expenditure,[19] though the details of the discussion remain secret.

Meanwhile he was continuing to press the West to recognize the aggressive posture it appeared to Russia's eyes to be taking in recent years: 'American submarines are on permanent alert off the Norwegian coast – the flight time of the missiles to Moscow is seventeen minutes. But we long ago dismantled all our bases in Cuba, even those without strategic importance. And you want to say that we behave aggressively?'[20]

Defence Minister Shoigu weighed in by drawing attention to the American anti-missile systems installed in Poland and Romania, and asked why NATO's surveillance activity along Russian borders had intensified. Only 107 flights were recorded in the entire decade of the 1990s, but in 2016 alone 852 entered the register. It was this, contended the Defence Ministry, that had forced Russia to increase the number of fighter flights by 61 per cent to prevent violations of Russian air space in the Baltic, on the Black Sea and in the Arctic. The increase in maritime reconnaissance by Western powers offered the same grounds for reacting. Shoigu announced with horror that the British were holding training exercises on Salisbury Plain with Russian-produced tanks and Russian army uniforms: always Russia the designated enemy.[21]

Shoigu also highlighted the decision by the Warsaw NATO Summit in July 2016 to deploy some of its forces to countries of eastern Europe, an exercise codenamed Enhanced Forward Presence. The next year Estonia acquired a battalion of 800 troops led by British commanders and strengthened by Danish and French units, and Typhoon war planes were sent from Germany. The Canadians led a battalion of 1,200 troops to Latvia that included Albanians, Italians, Poles, Spanish and Slovenians; the German battalion of the same size that went to Lithuania contained units from Belgium, Croatia, France, Luxembourg, Netherlands and Norway. The largest battalion was the American one in Poland that came with 250 tanks. At the same time the governments of Estonia, Latvia and Lithuania announced their intention to bring their military expenditure up to 2 per cent of their gross national product.[22] Russia's forces still vastly outnumbered those of the Baltic countries, but NATO had to show its solidarity, went the thinking, with those members who felt under threat after the Crimean annexation. It was also calculated that Russia would refrain from conducting an operation that might result in deaths of soldiers from the wider NATO alliance.

But Baltic politicians continued to worry about the fragility of their countries' security, especially when the Russians announced their plan to hold a military exercise in Belarus in September 2017 involving 100,000 of its troops. Zapad-2017, as it was called, was a joint exercise with the Belarusian armed forces, and aimed against an imagined enemy known as Vneshegoria. The chosen terrain, commentators noted, bore a distinct resemblance to parts of Estonia, Latvia and Lithuania.[23] In Poland there was concern that the Russian plan envisaged a nuclear attack on Warsaw.[24]

In advance of the exercise, Ukraine's President Poroshenko told his parliament the Kremlin was preparing for 'an offensive war of continental proportions'. There was speculation that the Kremlin was planning, not too discreetly, for a potential international crisis when it might move Russian air and ground forces into the Baltic countries.[25] Nor did the Ukrainians discount the possibility that the Russians might deliberately foment such a crisis. Unsurprisingly, Poroshenko continued to plead for the delivery of advanced lethal weaponry from the West. Putin was accompanied by his Chief of General Staff for the operations, which were held near St Petersburg. Defence Minister Shoigu pronounced the whole exercise a success and spoke out against the 'lies' in the Western media about Russia's aggressive intentions. Proud that their latest equipment and training performed up to expectations and pleased by the agitation caused in the capitals of NATO members, Russia enjoyed the attention from Western politicians and military planners.

In summer 2018 the Russian General Staff held another such exercise in Siberia, this time involving Chinese and Mongolian forces.[26] The obvious purpose was to stress that Russia remained as much an Asian as a European power. Obama's announcements in 2011–12 of his new priority of the so-called Pacific Rim had underscored the strategic importance of the Siberian territories for Russia and now, with this Vostok-2018 exercise, Putin intended to show the Americans he was serious about protecting Russia's interests throughout and even beyond its domains.

Evidence accumulated that the Russians were developing and testing new cruise missiles that could threaten the security of countries in Europe. Two battalions of the missile system were based near Volgograd in southern Russia.[27] Putin ignored American complaints about infringements of the Intermediate Nuclear Forces Treaty signed by Reagan and Gorbachëv, and nothing was done by the American side until October 2018, when President Trump, who had unexpectedly triumphed over Hillary Clinton in the election, announced his intention to retaliate by withdrawing unilaterally from the treaty. This appeared a tit-for-tat exchange between the two signatories, but there was more to it. China had never been included in the provisions of the treaty despite Gorbachëv's complaints about the omission, and by the time of Obama's presidency it was not the Russians but the Americans who spoke of the Chinese as a menace. Trump and his National Security Advisor John Bolton had searched for ways to counter China's growing military strength, and now Putin's cheating gave them some cover for their decision to withdraw from the treaty without naming the Chinese as an enemy. Tensions mounted. The triangular rivalry of America, China and Russia was set to be a cause of global tension throughout the twenty-first century – and the Russians had as much reason for agitation as everyone else.

22. TRANQUILLITY OF THE GRAVEYARD: CHECHNYA UNDER KADYROV

The first time Putin achieved an impact on Russian public opinion was in September 1999 when, as Yeltsin's prime minister, he started the war to subjugate the rebellious republic of Chechnya, flying from Moscow to Grozny to inspect the course of military operations himself. As Russia's armed forces went on the rampage the mountainous republic was pulverized into submission. Grozny became a necropolis. The following year the fighting was yet to reach its end when Putin ascended to the presidency. The Chechen resistance was already doomed to defeat, but Putin understood that military victory by itself could not secure a political settlement. Yeltsin had had to deal with Chechen rulers who demanded to run the republic with the minimum of Russian interference, yet those same rulers had failed to dig out the roots of Islamist rebellion. Putin was not going to yield to what he saw as banditry, and looked for an efficient satrap, a hard man of the Chechen nation who would carry through a programme of pacification. He had learned from history that although Russians could secure Chechnya's temporary submission, it would take a Chechen to govern the Chechens on a durable basis.

He found such an individual in Akhmat Kadyrov. Ostensibly an unlikely choice, in the 1990s Kadyrov had been one of the rebel leaders, and the Chief Mufti of Chechnya. But the Kadyrov family calculated that they could never finally beat the Russians, and in 2000 with Putin's consent Akhmat mounted to the Chechen presidency with the obligation to keep the territory inside the Russian Federation and abide by the Kremlin's policies. When Akhmat Kadyrov was assassinated by a terrorist bomb in 2004, his son Ramzan recommended himself to Putin as the safest choice for president. Putin agreed, waiting only for Ramzan's thirtieth birthday in 2007 to allow him legally to take office.

The younger Kadyrov cultivates a frightening image. He has

himself filmed cuddling wild animals, including a small tiger, which he keeps in the palatial residence he has had built at vast cost in his native village, Tsentaroi. A hundred people are employed to carry out the maintenance and housekeeping. No expense is spared to surround the Chechen president in an ostentatious embrace of luxury, and special quarters are said to be reserved for visits by Putin.[1] In his daily routines Kadyrov is no idler, showing off his commitment to physical exercise and swaggering about in macho style. He shares with Putin a fanatical commitment to improving his physical fitness, promotes the virtues of Mixed Martial Arts, and is at his happiest in his private gym pumping iron. He combines luxury with faith, in 2015 arranging to have a blood transfusion from the UAE-based Sufi scholar Habib Ali al-Jifri, who was said to be a descendant of the Prophet Muhammed.

Ramzan Kadyrov makes little distinction between his personal money and that which belongs to the people of Chechnya. His showiness is extraordinary. In 2005 he invited former heavyweight champion Mike Tyson to a boxing tournament at Gudermes, a town to the east of Grozny, paying him a fee of €2 million. Retired footballer Diego Maradona received €1 million for taking to the field in a match in which Kadyrov also played. In 2011 he enticed actress Hilary Swank to attend his thirty-fifth birthday party. She too was sumptuously rewarded.[2]

The adverse publicity that followed in the United States, however, persuaded Swank to offer to pass her fee to charity and express regret at not having acquainted herself in advance with Kadyrov's oppressive policies. Global celebrities began to ignore the Chechen president's blandishments, until in June 2018 he pounced on Mohamed 'Mo' Salah, the Liverpool and Egypt international footballer, while the Egypt team were based in the Chechen capital Grozny during the FIFA World Cup – Kadyrov had lobbied for Grozny to be used as a group stage centre, but had to content himself with the Egyptians using it as their training base. Kadyrov collected Salah from the team hotel to take him to the stadium,[3] where the two were filmed in informal conversation walking beside the pitch. Salah, a fellow Sunni Muslim, was awarded Chechen honorary citizenship.

Chechnya under rule by the Kadyrovs presented a horrifying picture to the rest of the Russian Federation and the outside world. Its lawlessness was notorious, and visitors from abroad decreased. Even Russians thought twice about setting foot there. But Putin, ignoring Akhmat Kadyrov's past Islamist militancy, still talked of his own role in bringing the territory back under the authority of the Russian Federation. The prospect of peace was for him the important thing, and he proclaimed that solid decent foundations were already being laid for economic regeneration, though he admitted the 'shadow economy' still bulked large in Chechnya. The Chechen transport infrastructure and labour resources, he claimed, had become the best in the Russian Federation. Putin remained unquenchably optimistic about the achievements of Russia's hitherto untameable mountain republic.[4]

Under Ramzan's rule the ruins of Grozny and other Chechen cities were replaced by splendid new buildings in the modern style. The capital acquired skyscrapers as well as a multipurpose sport venue, the Akhmat-Arena, named in memory of Kadyrov's assassinated father. One of the main thoroughfares in the rebuilt city centre was named Putin Prospekt. A ski resort was constructed in Veduchi, in the mountains fifty miles directly south of Grozny, after Kadyrov enlisted the Chechen billionaire Ruslan Baisarov's skills in finance and construction.[5] A new thermal power plant neared completion in Grozny's Zavodskoi district after a contract was signed with Siemens for the supply of gigantic gas turbines. Highways were repaired and modernized. In 2008 the Heart of Chechnya Mosque, informally named after Akhmat Kadyrov and one of Europe's biggest, was finished in a neo-Ottoman style. Nearby is the Russian Islamic University, offering courses that avoid the even more conservative religious teachings common in Saudi Arabia, Pakistan and elsewhere. Kadyrov's latest grandiose scheme is to find finance for the tallest skyscraper on the European continent, inevitably to be called the Akhmat Tower. So far only the foundations have been excavated.

The funds for most projects came from a republican budget supplied by the Finance Ministry in Moscow. Year after year, Chechnya received massive subsidies that from 2007 to 2015 amounted to an average annual transfer of 60 billion rubles (or $1–2 billion as the exchange rate varied).[6] The state-owned Vneshekonombank advanced huge loans for further development, in line with Putin's determination to maintain buoyancy in the Chechen economy. Kadyrov also levies money on a monthly basis from the citizens of Chechnya to support the Akhmat Kadyrov Foundation – even Chechen businessmen operating elsewhere in the Russian Federation are compelled to contribute.[7] Much of the money Chechnya receives is siphoned off by Kadyrov to pay for his extravagant lifestyle, and no serious attempt is made in

Moscow to put a stop to his corruption. When Sergei Stepashin was asked as Russia's Chairman of the Accounts Chamber of the Russian Federation to comment on the flagrant financial abuses, he shrugged: 'Kadyrov owns the entire republic, so don't worry about him.'[8] Evidently the authorities in Moscow know that Putin wants Kadyrov to remain untouched – and Kadyrov's reputation for vengeful violence discourages opposition.

At a time of financial trouble Russia's Finance Minister Siluanov contended that Chechnya's budgetary privileges should not remain immune, and with Putin's support, he held meetings with Kadyrov to smooth the process. Kadyrov objected that 'the republic won't be able to develop' if the government were to decrease its subventions; the high birth rate among Chechen families, he argued, entitled it to its usual generous outlay. But Siluanov held firm, and in September 2017 pushed Kadyrov into accepting a compromise.[9]

Putin receives Kadyrov at least twice a year, occasions of staged deference in which the Chechen president performs the role of loyal executor of Putin's instructions. In March 2016, he told Kadyrov:

> I know that Chechnya has been transformed in recent years, and we can see this with our own eyes. This is a self-evident fact. And Chechnya hasn't just been transformed superficially. Where once there were ruins and destroyed towns and villages, now – without any exaggeration – there are flourishing places of habitation where people live in comfort and convenience. The number of beautiful new buildings is on the increase, of which Chechnya and the entire Caucasus can be proud but which are also to a certain extent a source of pride for Russia.[10]

In April 2017, again protesting his republic's total compliance with Russian policy, Kadyrov boasted that he had taken his positive message about Russia on his tour of Bahrain, Dubai and Abu Dhabi, where, as a Muslim talking to Muslims, he was able to make a persuasive case about the virtue of the Christian Putin.[11]

When Putin talks of Chechnya, he acknowledges the wrongs done to the Chechen people in the 1940s, but adds an undercurrent of Russian nationalism:

> One can endlessly speculate about the Chechen people's tragedy in the period of their deportation from Chechnya by the Stalinist regime. But were the Chechens the only victims of those repressions? Well, the first and greatest victim of those repressions was

the Russian people, who suffered the most from the process. This is our common history.[12]

When Saudi Arabia's King Salman visited Moscow in October 2017, Putin invited Kadyrov to join in the formal ceremonies, tantamount to accepting him as a trusted member of the Kremlin inner core. Kadyrov returns the favour by treating Putin in public with an admiration bordering on worship. On coming to power in Chechnya, he told a reporter:

> I respect Putin not only as president but also as a person. I'm not a man of the FSB or GRU, I'm Putin's man. His policies and his word are law for me. We are travelling his road. Putin saved our people; he's a hero. He not only saved us but also he saved Russia. Why not bow down before him as before a person? I've never liked to express beautiful words in front of anyone, but Putin is a gift from God. He gave us freedom.[13]

In the same interview he called for Putin to be made Russia's president for life.

Putin is not Kadyrov's solitary supporter in Moscow. When Vladislav Surkov, himself half-Chechen by birth, worked in the Presidential Administration,[14] he too promoted the idea of Kadyrov's usefulness to Moscow. The pugnacious Viktor Zolotov, Putin's bodyguard chief till 2013 and head of the National Guard from its creation in 2016, is another supporter: Kadyrov and Zolotov have posted pictures of themselves together on Facebook, and it is suggested that Zolotov speaks up for the Chechen president in Kremlin discussions.[15] But not everyone in the ruling group shares this attitude: the Chechen president's interference in affairs beyond the borders of Chechen territory is resented, and his lawlessness is regarded as a menace not only to the Opposition but also potentially to those who wield power in Moscow. Sechin in particular has not been afraid to challenge Kadyrov, and hilariously this led to them being compelled to show they could settle their differences over Rosneft's investments in Chechnya by posing for a publicized embrace. Crocodile hugged crocodile.[16]

But Kadyrov holds on to the advantage of Putin's protection. A flamboyant user of Facebook, Instagram and Twitter who loves to post pictures of his antics, whether playing football or sitting at home with his zoo animals, Kadyrov was banned by several US social media companies at Christmas 2017 after being named as a target of American economic sanctions. Facebook and Instagram withdrew his access whereas Twitter cited the American constitution's commitment to free speech and declined to ban him. Roskomnadzor, the Russian institution responsible for supervising the internet in Russia, took up his cause, but predictably had no success in changing the decisions, and Kadyrov had to turn to Russian social media outlets. Disappointing as it was to lose his global following, he continued to bombard his supporters in Russia with his personal boasts.

Kadyrov performs the invaluable service to Putin of holding Chechnya as part of the Russian Federation. He does this in a peculiarly autocratic fashion by clearing out all political opposition. For years United Russia has been Chechnya's only political party. 'I have said that the word "Opposition" should be forgotten [in Chechnya],' he brags. His reasoning is that of a contented autocrat: 'We have no Opposition, which serves only to undermine authority. I will not allow [political opponents] to play with the people.' Independent monitoring of elections has become too dangerous for its sponsoring organizations, so Kadyrov and United Russia are assured of victory unobserved by potential critics. Putin can be equally confident: courtesy of Kadyrov, at the 2012 presidential elections he received 99.73 per cent of the vote in Chechnya.[17]

As well as being Chechnya's president, Kadyrov acts as a religious preceptor, in 2010 declaring, 'Sharia law is above Russian laws.'[18] Muslim customs – or rather those of which Kadyrov approves – are imposed on citizens regardless of their religious affiliation. Modest dress is demanded, and women are ordered to wear headscarves in public places, with the police arresting any who appear in public with their hair uncovered. But while promoting Islam, Kadyrov is fiercely opposed to symptoms of jihadi radicalism. There is a ban on the full Islamic robes that are worn compulsorily in Saudi Arabia, and Salafists are strongly discouraged. Females who veil their faces in public are liable to arrest and several days of re-education.[19] 'I tell you that a woman who goes out in black clothes, with a covered chin,' Kadyrov has said, 'her husband should know that we will take this woman away and look her over . . . we will force her to take off her clothes and trousers.' In Kadyrov's mind such apparel is associated with extremism, which he is committed to eliminating. His security men and clerics stop buses and cars to carry out checks, hauling off the offending female passengers and subjecting them to 'guided discussions' without informing families of their whereabouts.[20]

Kadyrov bulldozes the houses of families of active jihadis, and in April 2017 decreed that relatives were to have their pensions withdrawn to prevent financial support for terrorist groups: a doctrine of collective responsibility. Such sanctions were applied both inside and outside Chechnya: if Chechens went outside the republic to organize outrages, including Islamic State in Syria, the family members they left behind should expect to pay a price.[21]

In August 2016 his zeal to impose his own version of Islam got him into trouble when he organized an international Islamic conference in Grozny. Though Kadyrov did not participate in person, it was he who supplied the guiding influence and financial and organizational underpinning. Chechen clerics issued a fatwa that obediently repeated their intolerance of violent jihadism, condemning not only Islamic State in Iraq and Syria but also the Salafist teachings that enjoy official approval in Saudi Arabia. As a result, Muslim leaders from other parts of the Russian Federation, including the Mufti, Ravil Gainutdin, stayed away. The Saudi clergy were infuriated both by the attack on their doctrines and the open attempt to sow internal dissent in global Islam.[22] There were rumours, which Kadyrov's spokespersons denied, that he subsequently flew to Riyadh to make his peace with the Saudis and even apologize. The conference was not his most effective intervention in religious affairs beyond Chechnya's borders.

The moral regime under Kadyrov is defiantly extreme too. Polygamy is practised in Chechnya without interference by state authorities: 'Those who consider us barbarians for this reason,' contends Kadyrov, 'are clearly barbarians themselves, since this is a normal, pure and proper attitude toward women.'[23] He is vehemently hostile to homosexuality. Gays have suffered persecution in Chechnya, and in 2017 there were well-attested reports of a 'prophylactic sweep' of abduction and torture. Men returned barely alive after their brutal experience; some were murdered outright.[24] Kadyrov responded to repeated charges about such atrocities by simply denying their veracity, on the grounds that no gay lived on Chechen territory. Inquiries about human rights abuses are brutally discouraged. The Memorial organization, which publicizes breaches of the law in past and present, has acute difficulty operating in Chechnya. In 2009 the human rights activist and investigative reporter Natalya Estemirova was murdered after exposing the series of abductions carried out by members of Kadyrov's militia. In 2018 Memorial's local director, Oyub Titiev, was arrested on charges of drug dealing that were patently trumped up. A storm of protest brewed among Russian liberals.

But Kadyrov's posture of adoration has recently slackened. In summer 2017 he took a stand against the shocking maltreatment of the Rohingya minority in Myanmar. As fellow Muslims, the Rohingyas attracted his sympathy when their houses were burned down and women were raped. Kadyrov criticized Russian foreign policy for its limp response. At a rally attended by around a million people, he endorsed the idea of sending volunteers to confront the Myanmar armed forces. If he had nuclear weapons, he said, he would consider using them.[25]

Kadyrov had got used to appealing to Chechen sentiment. In August 2018 a certain Yusup Temirkhanov died in a penal colony in Omsk. Temirkhanov was serving a sentence for murdering Colonel Yuri Budanov, who in 2000 had abducted and murdered an eighteen-year-old Chechen girl. Like many Chechens, Kadyrov regarded Temirkhanov as a national hero who had carried out an honour killing. He attended the funeral and gave an impassioned oration in the prisoner's memory,[26] according to reports exclaiming that the affair was 'an insult to all of us' and demanding, 'If we are Russian citizens, then treat us like Russian citizens.'[27]

The terrorism that Kadyrov says he has expunged from Chechnya did not really disappear. Hundreds of Chechen volunteers joined the Islamist militant jihadis who travelled to Turkey in transit to the jihadi organizations of the Middle East. Kadyrov even admitted as much. But he was less forthcoming about terrorists who stayed in the republic and killed members of his security forces and planted bombs in public spaces in 2014 and 2015.[28] In August 2018 there were three separate attacks on Chechen police, for which Islamic State claimed responsibility. Kadyrov countered that Chechnya's youth had been inoculated against Islamist radicalism, but he failed to explain the rationale for the violence. Probably his own rough treatment of fellow religionists who want independence for the Chechen land and a more conservative form of Islam has had the effect of radicalizing youthful rebels. Keeping the lid on has a very high cost.

Kadyrov also remains a lurking threat to order in the rest of the Russian Federation. His tentacles have always stretched out beyond Chechnya's borders, and if he fell out definitively with the Kremlin his links with criminal groups would enable him to cause general mayhem. It is not wholly impossible, indeed, that Kadyrov might seek to put himself at the head of a secessionist movement in his republic; his revered father, of course, was originally an independence fighter, and he has friends abroad, especially in the United Arab Emirates. With thousands of men under arms Ramzan Kadyrov could decide to rise against Russia's military might. Of course, he is aware that the Russians know where he keeps his arms and his money, and that he lacks war planes and long-distance missiles. If the order is given, the Russians could swiftly reduce his palatial home to rubble, and it is doubtful Kadyrov himself would survive for long. He would not win, but that doesn't mean he is prudent enough to restrain himself: he has an autocrat's temperament and is used to doing what he likes in Chechnya.

How long Chechnya can endure his murderous regime is another question. Behind the facade of reconstruction in Chechnya lies a grim reminder of the recent wars across its territories. On Grozny's outskirts the shanty settlements persist, and in village after village there is no sign that Moscow's money has trickled down to the poor. Many of the fine office buildings in the Chechen capital have unoccupied floors. The unemployment rate in Chechnya, with one in seven being out of work, is second only in the Russian Federation to poverty-stricken Ingushetia. Admittedly there are many Chechens who work outside the law and pay no taxes: official statistics have to be taken with a pinch of salt, not only in Chechnya but also throughout Russia. What is hard to deny is that there are plenty of alienated young hotheads whom the jihadi recruiters are able to discover and recruit. What keeps Kadyrov in power are not just his violent practices but Putin's awareness that he relies on the Chechen leader to prevent a reversion to the rebellions of the 1990s. As long as Putin supplies Kadyrov with the freedom and bounty he requires, Kadyrov's loyalty appears dependable.

The republic has often been advertised as a gemstone set in the crown of Russia's economic recovery. In reality Chechnya is an extreme example of the Putin administration's many failures in regional policy. Kadyrov and his armed Kadyrovtsy have terrorized their own nation in a way that would have produced revolt if Russia's armed forces had used the same methods. The North Caucasus, brutally pacified by Alexander II's Imperial Army in the 1860s, is still recent history in the minds of many of its inhabitants. Within living memory, moreover, the entire Chechen people was deported to the wastes of Kazakhstan in the Second World War. Time will tell whether the Russians are wise to hang on to Chechnya and the other territories on the northern slopes of the Caucasus, rather than let them go as they did in 1991 with the Soviet republics of the USSR.

23. IMPERIAL INSTINCT: MOSCOW AND THE 'NEAR ABROAD'

The Kremlin's fears for the territorial integrity of the Russian Federation worked against any systematic planning of economic development. Moscow and St Petersburg may be dynamic metropolises, but many other parts of the country languish in chronic neglect – indeed, Moscow and its surrounding area distort the national statistics by earning 40 per cent of the gross domestic product. Putin may finance big infrastructure projects like the Olympics zone around Sochi, the science city at Skolkovo and the Kerch Bridge but, as his friend and former Finance Minister Kudrin has tirelessly pointed out, this is never going to be enough to create a globally competitive economy. Instead, Kudrin called on the government to nurture ten to fifteen urban 'agglomerations' as a way of raising regional morale and productivity: only then would Russia be able to cope with competition across its borders with China and Europe. The metropolitan fixation had to give way to more equal distribution of government favours.[1]

But Kudrin's pleas have fallen on infertile ground. Putin's attitude to 'the regions' is regulated by the desire to stop their leaders making political trouble, and the ruling group's insistence on maintaining their income and privileges. In 2007, in a parody of a quantitative approach to administration, an assessment system was introduced using forty-three tick-boxes to gauge the performance of leaders in the republics and provinces, with additional grants offered to leaderships judged successful. Predictably, provincial leaders fudged and distorted the figures. But it ignored the essential problem: that the authorities in Moscow feared anarchy and fraud if the localities were freed to have self-governance. Numerical assessments were not going to provide a solution.[2]

Moscow's desire for political and economic control over far-flung regions has its parallel in its treatment of the independent states of the former Soviet Union. Though Ukraine remains the most acute case, there is no part of the ex-USSR which does not disturb Moscow if it ever moves hard against Russian interests or accepts the American embrace. Russia's leaders hold on to some of the same assumptions about security as earlier rulers. Their country has endured centuries of being overrun, by Mongols, Poles, French and Germans, and their ideal is compliant buffer states. The 'near abroad' – the ex-USSR – is a zone where Russia's interests have absolute precedence, as Georgia learned to its cost in 2008.

It was a policy difficult to apply in an absolute fashion. In the successor states of central Asia it was undesirable to foster weakness if there was the slightest chance that radical Islamists would be able to exploit the situation. It was one of the reasons Russia supported dictatorships in the countries with Muslim majorities. From Tajikistan to Azerbaijan there had emerged ferocious regimes that annihilated political opposition and seized tight control of natural resources, but the judgement in Moscow was that this was of crucial assistance in preventing the contagion of jihadism spreading towards the borders of the Russian Federation. But, as in Chechnya, where Putin had turned a blind eye to the violence under Ramzan Kadyrov, the consequence was that rulers asserted themselves by declining to toe the Russian line with consistency. Kremlin leaders were frequently exasperated by events on the southern tier of Russia's frontiers.

They were even angrier about ex-Soviet republics along the western tier. As a stable and prosperous democracy Estonia was a constant irritant. Estonians bitterly remembered the chaos and privation of the 2007 cyber-attack, widely blamed on the Russian leadership. Meanwhile the Russian authorities continued to complain about the decision to remove the bronze statue erected in front of the National Library in Tallinn in 1946 to commemorate the Red Army's defeat of the Third Reich, and relocate it to a military cemetery on the outskirts.[3] This was the nub of the problem when it came to official remembrance: Russians, whether they lived in Russia or Estonia, wanted eternal reverence to be shown for the valour of Soviet forces in ending the Nazi occupation; Estonians declined to applaud the reoccupation of their country by a foreign foe, namely Stalin's USSR.

Absolute proof was lacking that Russian official agencies had conducted the cyber-attack – the source was traced back to private hackers in Russia – but circumstantial evidence pointed strongly that way. It was assumed the Kremlin's purpose was not only to knock out the Estonian network of communications but also to show the world what it could do – as well as to allow its disruptive specialists to conduct a real-life test of what became known as hybrid warfare. Without setting foot outside the Russian capital they could do enormous harm abroad. The Baltic countries felt particularly vulnerable: the Crimean annexation had shown that Kremlin rulers did not regard as sacrosanct the borders bequeathed by the USSR. The Russo-Estonian frontier near Narva was disputed, and there were other cities west of the long Russian frontier from the Baltic Sea down to the Black Sea where Russians lived in large numbers and, in several instances, complained about their treatment at the hands of their governments. Estonia, Latvia and Lithuania didn't help matters by each legislating for their native tongue to be recognized as the state language. Putin frequently spoke of his fears for his co-nationals outside the Russian Federation – and people remembered how zealously he had upheld the rights of Russians in Crimea even before 2014.

The NATO contingent in Estonia, small though it was, was a deterrent to the use of force by Russia. If a British trooper was killed in an incursion from Russia, there would be war in which the Estonians would not be alone and the use of firepower could rise unpredictably, perhaps even to the level of nuclear missiles. The wars of 2008 and 2014 had given politicians in all the bordering states food for thought. Not even Belarus could be completely confident about Russia's long-term trustworthiness. Vitebsk, the largest city in its north-east, had once belonged to the Russian Soviet republic, as Russian nationalists were just as capable as academic geographers of pointing out. Poland's former Defence Minister Radek Sikorski suggested that President Alyaksandr Lukashenka should keep an eye on the situation.[4]

Northern Kazakhstan is another zone about which Russian nationalist opinion has displayed a certain sensitivity. Russians are outnumbered by Kazakhs in the country, and Kazakhstan has steadily increased the Kazakh component of its ideology, politics and public appointments, which has in turn given rise to unease about the conditions imposed on the Russian minority. Thoughts have turned back to the circumstances in which Kazakhstan was established. Before 1936 it was an ethnic region inside the Russian Soviet republic; then Stalin gave it its own status as a Soviet republic, with the same rights and authority as the Russian one from which it had been detached. He and his successors also presided over an influx of Russians as new cities and economic enterprises were developed. The Kazakhs, most of whom had until the early 1930s lived an age-old nomadic existence, were forcibly moved to collective farms, where their task was to learn modern agricultural methods and increase cereal production. Tensions between Russians and Kazakhs were endemic, and in the late Soviet period riots had broken out. Just as Boris Yeltsin's expressions of concern for his compatriots had given rise to fears of eventual armed intervention, so Putin's words and actions evoked the same emotion from the Kazakh leadership. Nevertheless Russia's links stayed friendly enough for it to continue to use Baikonur in Kazakhstan as its space rocket launching base. The Kremlin, however, was less happy about the attitude to the Crimean annexation in the Kazakh capital, Astana – President Nazarbaev was understandably alarmed by the possibility that Putin might manufacture a political crisis and occupy northern Kazakhstan.

Putin had fewer grounds for worrying about Kyrgyzstan, but he could not fail to notice Kyrgyz criticisms of Ukraine's Yanukovych, whom Putin publicly supported. Uzbekistan, which refused to enter the Union, went further by declining to endorse the referendum to incorporate Crimea in the Russian Federation. In Belarus, Lukashenka ridiculed Yanukovych for his lack-lustre leadership in 2013–14. But shortly afterwards Lukashenka made overtures to the new Ukrainian president, Petro Poroshenko – hardly a sign that Belarusian policy unequivocally took Russia's side.[5]

The benefits that accrued to Russia from the end of empire were mixed. Ex-Soviet republics like Estonia, Latvia and Lithuania were hostile. Ukraine spent the 1990s and early 2000s tussling with the Russian government and from 2014 was confirmed in its enmity. All the other republics of the former USSR proved awkward about one thing or another. Without aiming to reconstitute the USSR, Putin and his ministers sought to exert pressure on each ex-Soviet republic, still considered a better policy than becoming entangled in the kind of local disputes, administrative costs and budgetary demands that had made things difficult for successive communist rulers.

The unspoken rule was that none of the new independent states – with the involuntary exceptions of Estonia, Latvia, Lithuania and latterly Ukraine – should try to subvert the political and economic requirements set out by the Kremlin. If a state wished to promote its nationhood and traditional faith, Russian rulers had no objection. If nearby foreign rulers engorged themselves with corruptly obtained riches, the Putin team saw nothing wrong because its own members did the same.

Yet there remained a desire to prevent foreign states beyond the borders of the ex-USSR from interfering with Russia's post-imperial machinations. Some were easy to deal with. Poland rarely strayed, with the exception of its intervention in the Ukrainian crisis of 2013–14, and, in the analysis of the Kremlin, in unhelpfully pushing NATO into increasing its foreign presence in eastern and east-central Europe. Turkey was involved in commercial links with Azerbaijan that cut across the purposes of Gazprom and Rosneft, and its premier, and latterly president, Recep Tayyip Erdoğan, expressed displeasure about the occupation of Crimea, though he subsequently let the matter drop. Iran had an ambition to spread its Shia Islamic faith abroad, but prudently decided to limit its activity in the former Soviet central Asia to distributing the Koran. Tehran wanted good relations with Moscow, particularly after the agreement on operations in the Syrian civil war.

Then there was the problem of Saudi Arabia. The Saudis, wanting to spread their faith and influence, had the opportunity to appeal to the many Sunni populations in the southern tier of the old USSR. But Riyadh caused less trouble than might have been expected. Putin's relations with the Saudi royal family steadily improved, and he gained its backing for Russia to acquire observer status at the Organization of the Islamic Conference from 2005. The two countries resolved to avoid conflict.

The whole region to the south of Russian frontiers down across the Middle East as far as the Arabian Gulf, Putin learned, was full of cross-cutting and jarring aspirations. However much Russia outmatched the other regional states in firepower, Saudi Arabia and the United Arab Emirates rivalled it in financial might. The Russians accepted the importance of negotiations as well as threats. By and large it succeeded in keeping the states of the 'outer abroad' out of Putin's zone of influence, namely the former USSR.

But America, in the eyes of the Kremlin, was tirelessly seeking to expand its influence in every part of the old USSR. Whenever Russian politicians or businessmen were baulked, the suspicion in the Kremlin was that an American hand was operating the levers. In 2001 Russia had not objected when the United States asked permission to use an air base in Uzbekistan for its bombers to attack the Taliban in Afghanistan. As relations with the Americans worsened, such friendliness ceased. Though the Americans were less active than they had been in the 1990s, nervousness remained among Russian leaders that America would find ways to infiltrate central Asia. President Karimov, the

Uzbek leader, Putin noted, subsequently alternated between favouring Russia and America so as to give himself a degree of freedom from Moscow's importunities. But by allowing Russian investment in Uzbek oil exploration and exploitation Karimov courted Putin's sympathy, and in 2014 the Russian Finance Ministry cancelled Uzbekistan's debts.

As we shall see later, even more intrusive was Chinese influence, as China pursued its Belt and Road Initiative. Russia sought to contain China's ambitions by embracing the Chinese as partners. Washington's ambitions in ex-Soviet central Asia were less grand than those of Beijing, but Moscow could not afford to express resentment of Chinese encroachment for fear of offending and losing its important friend in the East.

The Kremlin leadership tried to strengthen its position by building up regional organizations, chief among them the Commonwealth of Independent States and the Collective Security Treaty Organization. Neither had fulfilled Yeltsin's hopes of providing Russia with unconditional dominance, though, and in Putin's time their influence continued to disappoint. Georgia withdrew from the Commonwealth in 2008 after the Russian invasion; Ukraine, which had never agreed to more than associate membership, ended its link entirely in 2018, and Russia's aggression against them both severely reduced the trust of neighbouring countries in any military pact with the Kremlin leadership. The Collective Security Treaty Organization (CSTO) came under deeper suspicion. None of its member countries was willing to endorse the Russian armed intervention in Georgia. The Crimean annexation intensified their concerns, and CSTO Secretary Nikolai Bordyuzha had to issue a statement affirming that there would be no joint deployment in Ukraine.[6]

Putin concentrated his efforts on gathering support for a Eurasian Economic Union, which after years of negotiation was at last formed in January 2015. Treated as a pariah by the Western powers, the Kremlin aimed to extend its regional influence by drawing the neighbouring ex-Soviet republics into a single market with free movement of people, goods, capital and services. It fell a long way short of its objective. Initially the only other member states were Kazakhstan and Belarus. Though Armenia and Kyrgyzstan joined shortly afterwards, the list remained a disappointment to Russian leaders. The conspicuous omission was Ukraine, which had been courted assiduously since the idea had first occurred to Yeltsin and others. The Crimean annexation ruled this out permanently, and no aspiring Ukrainian political leader would be so imprudent as to suggest it again even as a way of balancing the European Union. The Baltic states of Estonia, Latvia and Lithuania had never been candidates at all. Georgia took the same approach. But several other former constituent republics of the USSR had also refused Putin's invitation. Moldova, Azerbaijan, Turkmenistan, Uzbekistan and Tajikistan all decided for their own reasons that it was better to ignore Russia's fishing expedition.

The Eurasian Economic Union was supposed to have no political agenda, distinguishing it from the European Union, which established a common parliament and a coordinating commission and aspired to pursue common foreign and defence policies. President Nursultan Nazarbaev demanded politics be kept out of the treaty. Despite Russia's efforts this has remained the case. The Union has no stated ideology or political goals, and the citizens of member countries do not hold Union passports.

With only 5 per cent of Russian exports going to its other members,[7] the Union cannot really be called a vibrant international phenomenon, and commercial progress has been racked by disputes. There have been 'meat wars' between Russia and Belarus, after Belarusian products were found to be falling below acceptable standards. Similar conflict arose between Kazakhstan and Kyrgyzstan over potatoes.[8] It was a turbulent baptism for the Union when, in December 2014, in retaliation for the Russian ban on Belarusian animal products, Belarus's Lukashenka restored customs posts. Russia subsequently raised gas prices for Belarus, which was totally reliant on the Russians for its fuel. In February 2017 Russia introduced its own border controls.[9] The Eurasian Economic Union had hardly been created when it succumbed to disputes that pulled it apart.

Problems were aggravated in 2015 when Kazakhstan, after years of negotiation, was granted accession to the World Trade Organization. On both agricultural and industrial products the agreed tariff levels were lower than Russia had set when it joined five years earlier. It did not pass unnoticed in Moscow that this would damage Russian interests when goods entered Russia via the lower barrier permitted in Kazakhstan. The government in Astana promised to set about renegotiating its World Trade Organization tariff levels to bring them up to the Eurasian Economic Union norms.[10]

A sign that Putin sees the need for tact when trying to attract countries into the Eurasian Economic Union is that, unlike many, he has ceased to use the condescending term 'near abroad' to refer to the rest of the ex-Soviet Union.[11] It was not always so. In August 2014 Putin referred dismissively to Kazakhstan's statehood by asserting that the country had not existed until Nazarbaev brought it to independence, and Kazakh opinion was affronted. Putin had commented in similar fashion about Ukrainian statehood at the Bucharest NATO summit in 2008, Kazakhs recalled – and now, just months after annexing Crimea, he cast a shadow over Kazakhstan. There was talk of sending Putin a history textbook. Nazarbaev declared that Kazakhstan reserved the right to withdraw from the Eurasian Economic Union if that independence was to be threatened. 'Our independence is our dearest treasure,' he said, 'for which our grandfathers fought.'[12] If Putin wanted to establish and expand the Eurasian Economic Union he would have to choose his words more carefully.

It seems that Kazakhstan decided in favour of the Eurasian Economic Union because it hoped to bind the Russians into a framework of peaceful commitments. A strictly economic motivation was not paramount: over half the country's exports went to the European Union, and only 10 per cent to Russia. But Nazarbaev, even before the Crimean annexation, wanted to reduce Russo-Kazakh tensions, and the Eurasian Economic Union Treaty appeared a good first step.

Armenia had originally been even more reluctant. Public opinion was deeply sceptical about Russia's purposes, with the sale of military equipment to Azerbaijan, the old enemy of the Armenians, exacerbating anti-Russian feelings. In 2013 President Serzh Sargsyan unexpectedly dropped his objections after a private discussion with Putin offered a number of commercial enticements, but what probably made up his mind was the promise of a Russian security guarantee. Behind the scenes, pressures of a non-economic nature were an ingredient.

For Kyrgyzstan it was a simpler matter. The Kyrgyz economy heavily depended on remittances from its migrants working in the Russian Federation. Membership of the Union would make it easier for Kyrgyz to find employment than Uzbeks and Tajiks.[13]

If Russia wants to be a regional economic power within a formal institutional structure, it cannot afford to humiliate its partners. Yeltsin understood this, but not all Putin's ministers and officials do. Nationalist opinion ascribed Russia's difficulties with its neighbours not to any recent fault of its own, or even to centuries of suspicion, but – for Putin's economics adviser Sergei Glazev, for example – to American machinations. Glazev saw the planet's widespread Russophobia as a 'mystification' sponsored by America. He looked back fondly to the Eurasian school of intellectual thought that arose in the 1920s and saw in the past a seamless record of inter-ethnic harmony under the Golden Horde, the Russian Empire and the USSR.[14] It is self-deception of staggering proportions when a public figure such as Glazev can so casually dismiss the historical reality and lasting effects of national and religious persecution. Ukrainians or Kazakhs whose parents or grand-parents starved in the 1930s did not need American propaganda to make them feel suspicious of Moscow.

One of the growing anxieties in Russian public opinion is economic migration, especially from central Asia. Putin, a Russian nationalist, has consistently spoken in favour of allowing Uzbeks and Kyrgyz to find work in the Russian Federation, even while admitting that free passage for people and goods from central Asia facilitates the illegal drugs trade – like many Russians, he notes that foreign migrants are widely involved in distributing and selling heroin and cocaine. But he sets his face against the introduction of a visa system. The Russian economy is heavily dependent on migrant labour, especially in manual jobs but also in small businesses. Russia also has to keep its frontiers open for citizens of the Eurasian Economic Union.

Azerbaijan showed a willingness to assert itself by carrying through its project to pipe oil from Baku directly to Erzurum in north-east Turkey, from where the supplies were to be sent to Europe, ignoring the Russian preference for their oil to use pipelines that crossed into Russia and drew in Russia's biggest hydrocarbon corporations as partners. The Azerbaijanis also had experience of the Kremlin's chronic failure to take Azerbaijan's side definitively against Armenia in the decades-old dispute over the Armenian-inhabited enclave on Azerbaijani territory. The Turkish connection gave Azerbaijan a degree of security from Russian pressure. Gazprom and Rosneft were huge businesses with ambitions to spread their operations widely around the world, but their closeness to the Kremlin made leaderships in the ex-USSR edgy about accepting their embrace. Russian assertiveness caused problems, especially when in January 2014 it suspended part of the oil pipeline between Baku and Novorossiisk on the Russian Black Sea coast.

When Moldova's government agreed to sign an association agree-ment with the European Union the Kremlin applied economic sanctions against it. Moldovan wine was banned from sale in Russia.[15] This only served to motivate the Moldovans to redouble their outreach to the West.

All the while Russian military and economic pressure on Ukraine intensified. The ceasefire introduced by the Minsk Accords of February 2015 quickly broke down. Russia's fighting contingents went on confronting the Ukrainian army in eastern Ukraine. Ukrainians in their vast majority supported Poroshenko in his defiance. Cities like Donetsk were subjected to the presence of fighters from both sides. Pleas by the United Nations were issued in vain. Though Gazprom continued to sell gas supplies to Ukraine, it raised its prices since Russia could no longer count on a friendly neighbour. The Russian navy blocked access to the Sea of Azov through the new Kerch Bridge for every ship until it had been inspected, a practice that allowed the Russians to discriminate against traffic out of Ukrainian ports and disrupted the economy of those parts of eastern Ukraine still held by the Ukrainian authorities. The Kremlin's economic sanctions were maintained. The message to Kyiv was that Russia had the patience and resources to make life difficult for Ukrainians while they continued with their choice of the European Union for their strategic partner, whatever the cost in lives and prosperity.

In 2018 the Trump administration took account of the Ukrainian plight by forwarding advanced lethal weaponry to improve Kyiv's defences against the Russians. Poroshenko countered Russian patience and violence with Ukrainian endurance. Nobody was left with the illusion that Ukraine was about to crumble. The great prize of Russian regional political and economic diplomacy after the fall of communism was kept beyond Russia's reach. Battered but unbowed, Ukraine was determined to stay free. Its sole state language was Ukrainian. Its school textbooks and Orthodox Church were Ukrainian. Its rulers, even those not brought up to speak the Ukrainian tongue, were proud of their Ukrainian nationality. Putin had lost the great game of the end of communism, and no amount of posturing about the acquisition of Crimea would disguise it. He had also made Russian ambitions visible to all the countries of the former USSR. Their edginess was understandable, and it was by no means obvious that Russia's geopolitical purposes benefited. For Russians with an imperial mentality this was bound to be a disappointment.

AMBITION

24. ECONOMIC SHOCK: WESTERN SANCTIONS AND THE OIL PRICE TUMBLE

Economic sanctions and the fall in oil and gas revenues were not the only afflictions suffered by the Russian economy in Putin's third and fourth presidential terms. The Crimean annexation itself was a costly venture. Kudrin complained that Moscow's direct support to the small peninsula in the first twelve months after the military operation cost $7 billion, and indirectly, according to him, over the next three to four years the government would have to set aside at least $150 billion and perhaps as much as $200 billion to prop up Crimea's economy and construct the necessary links with Russia.[1]

These Crimean costs attracted less attention abroad than the deluge of sanctions directed at those members of Putin's entourage considered complicit in framing, encouraging or implementing policy on Crimea. Their Western bank accounts were frozen, and they themselves were banned from travelling to America and its allies. Sanctions were also aimed at Russia's six largest banks, the four largest hydrocarbon companies and fourteen arms-exporting firms, which were prohibited from raising capital in America and associated countries, with the objective of cutting Russia off from funds to modernize its hydro-carbon and armaments sectors. Whether or not by design, this was the most damaging punishment: the business of extraction, refining and transporting Russian gas and oil was overdue a root-and-branch reno-vation. As the ruble tumbled in value Gazprom, Rosneft and other Russian corporations could no longer meet their debt repayments, and sanctions prevented them from raising new Western loans or extending old ones.[2]

At the same time the Western powers supplied financial assist-ance to the Ukrainian government. Immediately after the Crimean annexation the International Monetary Fund announced itself willing to lend $17 billion to Ukraine, and made $4.5 billion readily available as President Poroshenko sought to prevent economic collapse. By February 2015 agreement was reached to approve a conditional loan of $17.5 billion. The European Commission joined in, in May to December 2014 providing a €1.4 billion loan for macro-financial assistance, adding another €1.75 billion in 2015.[3] The loans came with strings attached: while the aim was to save the Ukrainian people from ruin, the Ukrainian authorities were also required to make the fundamental reforms necessary to gain associate membership of the European Union. This did not go unnoticed in Russia, whose leadership had been maintaining throughout 2013 that the West was plotting to grab control of Ukraine.

Meanwhile, Putin hastened to compensate targeted individuals for the material losses inflicted by the sanctions. Irritating as it was to be prevented from visiting Paris or New York, none of them was to suffer a loss of wealth: victims of Western action were to be treated as patriots who deserved national succour. The targeted companies and banks received protection from the Finance Ministry, which bailed them out with loan repayments and a line of ready credit. Putin's largesse, however, could not be unlimited or permanent. The sanctions forbade the provision of fresh loans that might be used to develop the key economic sectors, which meant financial institutions in Russia were suffering as well as individuals. The Vneshekonombank was sharply exposed after meeting loan requests from Russian corporations for the Sochi Olympics, for the Crimean annexation and for the fighting in eastern Ukraine. Pressed to pay off its own loans, the bank approached the government for a $20 billion bailout – and ministers obliged.[4]

On the few occasions Putin spoke about the Western sanctions he was defiant:

> In point of fact the history of Russia shows we as a rule lived under sanctions starting from the moment when Russia began to stand on its own feet and felt strong. When our partners in the world saw Russia as a serious rival, various restrictions were introduced on various pretexts. This has been the case throughout the course of our history. I'm not now talking about the Soviet period but rather this was the case even earlier, before the October Revolution. For that reason there is no surprise in all this.[5]

This was looking at the past through a distorting lens. Tsarist Russia had never suffered from foreign economic sanctions: quite the reverse – direct investment poured into the Russian Empire from abroad, with France and Belgium, closely followed by Britain and Germany, seeing a gleaming opportunity to make millions out of Russian factories and mines as the Russians made their bid to become an advanced economic power. Putin's portrait of a nation persistently singled out for malicious treatment by Johnny Foreigner is simply political paranoia. That he can spout such nonsense probably means he has begun to believe it.

In June 2017 Putin told viewers of the 'Direct Line' TV phone-in programme about Washington's moves to reinforce the sanctions. 'So that if it hadn't been Crimea or other problems,' he explained, 'they would still have invented something to act to contain Russia. It's always the same policy of containing Russia.'[6] Presidential spokesman Dmitri Peskov further demonstrated this pathological mistrust of Western intentions in arguing that the sanctions were a ploy to alienate the 'oligarchs' from Putin. If the country's biggest businessmen were kept out of international commerce, went this theory, they would withdraw their political support from him.[7]

But Western sanctions left a lot of room for the West's big corporations to continue to trade and invest in Russia, and in another interview in September 2016, this time with Bloomberg TV, Putin was claiming that they were aimed too narrowly to do fundamental harm to Russia:

> And it's totally clear that ten and certainly fifteen years ago we would not have been able to respond to the sanctions that have been imposed against Russia, with countermeasures in the agricultural sector, for example. We could not have closed our market in farm produce to the countries behaving in an unfriendly fashion against us, because we could not have satisfied the domestic market with our own produce at that time. But now we can.[8]

A month later he assured an audience of foreign visitors that the European Union was losing $60 billion in the value of exports as a result of its economic sanctions against Russia. The real losers, according to him, were the same countries in Europe that were applying them. Russia, he insisted, would survive and flourish.[9]

Despite lacking economic weapons of equal power, the Russians felt they should at least retaliate with harsh measures against Ukraine. Restrictions were therefore placed on Ukrainian exports of foodstuffs and industrial goods to Russia, and the government in Kyiv was put on notice that it would have to pay in advance for its gas supplies.[10] This was done even though it was America and its European allies, not Ukraine, who were imposing the main restrictions on Russian officials, corporations and banks. Russia's economy required Western industrial and technological imports to continue its course towards technological modernization and integration with global trade, and ministers had to be cautious in applying counter-sanctions if they wanted to avoid hardship or annoyance for the mass of Russian consumers. But they were determined to obtain for Crimea the status of a legitimate part of the Russian Federation, and placed a ban on Western IT companies bidding for Russian governmental contracts if they refused to do business in the peninsula. They also prohibited official institutions from using software such as Excel – a security precaution but also a commercial counter-sanction.[11]

The keenest of the counter-sanctions were centred on agricultural produce. In August 2014 the Kremlin prohibited farm imports from America and the countries that had joined them in imposing sanctions. America was little affected, with Obama receiving negligible pressure from its farming lobbies. Only 7 per cent of American poultry exports, for example, went to Russia. But the European Union would suffer, because Russia was the second-biggest purchaser of its food and drink exports.[12] The Moscow press publicized the banning of Roquefort and other French cheeses from the Russian market, and it was reported that vigilant patriots denounced those supermarket chains that continued to sell them.[13] The Kremlin was incensed, however, about the cracks in the wall of their counter-sanctions: Putin complained that Polish meat, vegetables and dairy products were continuing to enter the country,[14] when Poland had been one of the fiercest advocates of economic sanctions. Many Russian retailers were importing banned goods by getting them sent through Kazakhstan. Customs agencies on the Russian borders were ordered to tighten up supervision.

As a large country with one of the world's biggest economies, Russia would not languish as Iran had been doing under the America-led embargo that came into effect in the early 1980s:[15] indeed, speculated Putin, as foreign boycotts continued, Russian agriculture would benefit from domestic demand. He also boasted that Russia's industrial output had maintained its existing levels of production, and stressed that America's national debt was higher than its gross domestic product. It was Washington rather than Moscow, was the clear implication, that faced difficulties over its economic strategy.[16]

The balance sheet of sanctions and counter-sanctions is difficult to compute because it involves so much counterfactual calculus. What is certain, however, is that Russian manufacturing quickly expanded to fill gaps left by some traditional Western imports. The government enhanced the country's resilience through a strategic campaign of public procurement contracts and of pressure on Russia's finance houses to give support.[17] 'Import substitution' became both slogan and reality even though the new domestic output did not always match the standards achieved by the most successful foreign companies. Agriculture did even better than other sectors of the economy, but even for the farming sector it was not a unified picture. Pork and poultry products reported expansion, and cereal production continued to swell, but beef and dairy farms had not enjoyed the necessary capital investment and proved incapable of a rapid increase in output.[18] Nevertheless, sanctions had a weaker impact than the American administration had counted on, and indeed in some ways they acted to boost Russian economic independence. They also had the unintended effect of assisting those lobbying for the country's defence industrial sector. This was hardly the result that American politicians had sought.[19]

The greatest shock to the Kremlin's economic prospects, however, came from an entirely different quarter when, in mid-2014, the bubble of hydrocarbon revenues suddenly burst. The new 'fracking' technique, involving pumping water into stony deposits to release their petroleum and natural gas, revolutionized world hydrocarbon production, turning the United States into a leading exporter after years of importing its supplies. The growing global glut resulted in a collapse in prices. Crude oil – according to OPEC's records – dropped from $115 per barrel in June 2014 to around $50 in January 2015. This was not the lowest point: by January 2016 purchasers could buy a barrel for only $31.[20] This was a disaster for Russia's budget. No grandstanding by Putin and Medvedev could disguise the economic pain. Kudrin had warned for years about the need to prepare for the contingency of falling oil and gas receipts, and now suddenly it had come to pass, and the Finance Ministry had to find ways to cope at a time when it was already striving to shield the country from all the other pressures.

Rather than prop up the ruble's exchange rate by shovelling assets from the country's financial reserves, Finance Minister Siluanov let the currency float. In mid-2014 the US dollar cost 34 rubles. By the end of the year alone it had climbed to 59 rubles and rising.[21] Siluanov knew that if he tried to sustain the old rate, he would be pouring good money after bad, and was also glumly aware that Russian manufacturers, retailers and consumers would have to pay more for imported goods. A fall in the level of the standard of living was unavoidable.[22]

In the year after the Crimean annexation real wages fell by 8 per cent, retail sales by 10 per cent.[23] Gross national product plummeted by 3.8 per cent. Inflation soared to 15.5 per cent across the twelve months. The budget deficit gaped wider and wider, and the Finance Ministry had to make drastic cuts in its allocations.[24] Putin's chronic failure to do much to diversify the economy had had the consequence of mortgaging Russia's future to the vagaries in hydrocarbon prices, and now the debt was being abruptly called in. It was not as though he was unaware of the dangers of relying upon natural resources as the talisman of national regeneration: he had sounded the same alarm himself. By September 2016 the total assets in the Reserve Fund and a National Well-Being Fund had tumbled to $73 billion, as the government transferred money to deal with its welfare commitments rather than face the anger of those citizens who depended on state payments for utilities, transport and pensions. Putinism's grand bargain with the Russian people was under heightened strain.[25]

By November 2016 some other option had to be found, and the anti-liberal side of the leadership found its own increasing ascendancy was saddling it with the task of finding a solution. Since the turn of the millennium there had been an upward graph of state intervention, state control and state ownership. If the liberals were not allowed to go for growth by means of a comprehensive range of liberalizing policies, it was up to Rosneft's Igor Sechin and other anti-liberal leaders to offer an alternative of their own. This resulted in a splendid irony. In the interests of balancing the budget, Sechin agreed to the selling off of 19.5 per cent of the Rosneft shares that remained in the hands of the state, which at that time owned half the entire corporation – this was the kind of measure economic liberals like Kudrin might have proposed. In fact, Sechin's move had been planned for years, as a way of raising finance for investment. At a time of emergency, it helped rescue the entire Russian economy,[26] and Sechin's promise to increase the value of Rosneft by gobbling up Bashneft was probably one of the factors that in 2016 had turned Putin against Minister of Economic

Development Alexei Ulyukaev (who opposed the move) and towards accepting Sechin's demand to put him on trial.[27]

The sell-off of nearly a fifth of Rosneft took place without fanfare, perhaps because the government disliked admitting that foreign buyers Glencore and the Qatari Investment Fund were involved. Putin was renowned for having brought Russia's natural resources back under governmental tutelage: now he had to explain his about-face in allowing 50 per cent foreign ownership. He did so with chutzpah: 'Consequently, from the viewpoint of the interests of state, the ultimate interest of state and from the viewpoint of fiscal interests, we have, above all, a positive experience and not a negative one.'[28] Such complacency did not fool everyone. The opacity of the deal led to speculation that Sechin and others had ensured their own handsome pay-off. As with other matters of Russian high finance, it was hazarded that nothing was truly as it seemed.[29]

On 21 December 2017 Putin was upbeat when he met business leaders in the Kremlin: 'Now a few words about the economy. The period of recession has ended, this is obvious, as you and I can see.'[30] The businessmen listened respectfully before filing out. His former adviser Andrei Illarionov sceptically pointed out that though there had been an upturn in the first three quarters of 2017, this was followed by a fall – and a fall that, if continued into the following year, would indicate the resumption of recession. Manufacturing, mining, energy production, construction and even agriculture had declined, and Illarionov reckoned it was foolish to pretend that the prospects were rosy.[31] No one in government could seriously present the Rosneft share sale as any more than a palliative for the country's economic woes. A more fundamental revision of policy was required. Kudrin continued to demand this from outside the cabinet; Putin and Medvedev ignored him. Rather than devising a programme of reform, the authorities continued down the road of devouring existing financial assets. On 1 February 2018 the Reserve Fund was closed down and its remaining assets lodged with the National Well-Being Fund.[32] Welfare was not the sole drain on the sovereign wealth funds. The Finance Ministry also had to help with existing projects of national importance. Gazprom, Rosneft and other gigantic hydrocarbon corporations had been pushing ahead with costly projects to exploit new fields.

But it would be foolish to write off the Russian economy. Oil and gas continued to be exported abroad, including to countries such as Germany that were applying economic sanctions. Arms and other military equipment remained a huge source of profit for Russia's state-controlled factories, just as they had been in the Soviet period – and there was no downturn in the world market price for tanks, missiles and machine guns, unlike the hydrocarbon sector. Arms exports by 2013 gave Russia more than a quarter of the global market, with only the United States staying ahead of it.[33]

The Russian ruling group stuck to its usual economic practices without substantial amendment. Despite the straitened budget, ministers went on making generous loans to foreign countries. In 2017 the Finance Ministry's official in charge of international credit, Konstantin Vyshkovski, revealed that Russia had committed itself to $70 billion of such lending. On average, the country handed out $3 billion in new loans every year in the decade from 2007. Nine-tenths of the total amount in loans to foreign beneficiaries was committed to contracts for nuclear power stations. Next in line were defence contracts and the civil aviation business[34] – among the few branches of industry in which Russia excelled enough to find buyers beyond its borders. The Kremlin was doing what it could with its available resources. It wanted to show it still had a growing role to play in the world economy even after the juddering impact of Crimea and the hydrocarbon price collapse. Russian leaders were holding their heads high.

But Russia's financial assistance to other countries had been provided according to political criteria: not an entirely happy process. As the price of winning support in Venezuela, Russia had to forgo $900 million in failed repayments by 2017, and by early 2018 the political protest movement against Nicolás Maduro's administration was putting at risk billions of dollars of Russian investments in the country. Venezuela joined a line of hopeless debtors such as Cuba and North Korea, whose loans had had to be written off years ago. To avoid further losses in its international dealings the Finance Ministry revised its rules for future loans – and now the solvency of potential debtors is examined in advance.[35] The only surprise is that it has taken this long to introduce some common sense. Other credit operations have turned out more successfully, especially for the Rosatom nuclear agency's contracts to build civilian fuel plants in China and Hungary. Whereas the Chinese deal was struck in 1991, it was not until 2014 that Hungary accepted Moscow's offer of a thirty-year $11.7 billion loan to finance Rosatom's project to expand a Hungarian nuclear plant.[36]

The Russian leadership also aspires to an increase in foreign direct investment in Russia itself. Any commercial contract he has played a part in sealing makes Putin glow with pride, as happened in 2012 when the American Exxon Corporation signed an agreement with Rosneft for the expansion of the Russian oil industry. Putin personally endorsed the construction of factories by the Boeing Corporation, which buys Russia's aluminium for its aircraft production lines and employs many Russian citizens.[37]

After 2014 such investment plummeted, in the previous year having stood at a peak of $69.2 billion. Two years later it was down to $6.9 billion, a reduction of over 90 per cent.[38] The foreign companies that made most money in 2016 from operating inside the Russian Federation were led by the French retail giant Auchan. Metro Group came next, followed by Japan Tobacco Co., Philip Morris International, Toyota Motor Corporation and IKEA, Volkswagen, PepsiCo Holdings, Mercedes Benz, Leroy Merlin Procter and Gamble, and British–American Tobacco.[39] IKEA and Leroy Merlin built new mega-stores, and Mars, Pfizer and PepsiCo also expanded their operations.[40] Hypermarket chains from abroad have established a particularly strong hold in Moscow, St Petersburg and the biggest cities. Car manufacturing has grown in Russia, with German and Japanese firms leading the way – the American company General Motors had a presence until 2014, when it pulled its production facilities out of Russia as the recession deepened.[41]

The commercial risks of investing in the country are known in advance, and they are considerable. Boards of directors are told about them by their governmental ministries, even if they fail to read the sad stories that have appeared in the Western media ever since Russia rejected communism. They know the rule of law is only fitfully applied, and that the Russian government and Russian business lobbies frequently transgress legal procedure with impunity. Incoming companies have prior knowledge of the difficulties of red tape, bribery and corruption. Nor is most of the transport infrastructure up to high international standards. But the situation is improving: in 2012, according to the World Bank, Russia came 120th in its global ranking of the easiest countries in which to do business. By 2017 it had risen to 40th place. But for a country that has a pressing need for an influx of foreign firms and foreign investment, this was still not satisfactory.[42]

Most of the German companies stayed on if they had already made capital investment in Russia. They had spent their money, and hoped to see out the economic recession and international political tumult. In several regions the local Russian authorities made efforts to create a favourable climate for further business. Tatarstan and Kaluga actively courted the Germans with incentives that included special economic zones with land, buildings and tax concessions; they also promised to cut the usual red tape. The German Foreign Office lent support.[43] The result was that in 2015, according to the Russian-German Chamber of Foreign Trade, there were still 5,583 registered German companies operating in the Russian Federation, only 7 per cent fewer than in the previous year.[44] By June 2017 Putin was able to voice his pleasure that sanctions had failed to induce Germany's firms to pull out. While the Germans made big profits from Russian activities, the Russians in turn were benefiting from access to German technology: trade had risen by 40 per cent in the first quarter of the year. Putin asked why Germany would ever want to stop importing Russian fuel at a time when Norwegian and British hydrocarbon reserves were approaching the point of exhaustion – 'Well, where's it going to come from?' Russia had trillions of cubic metres of gas in the Yamal peninsula, and wanted to continue its 'absolutely natural partnership' with the Germans.[45]

Russian ministries and banks searched for new sources of finance to surmount the difficulties, but met with little readiness for cooperation in Shanghai, Hong Kong or Singapore. In 2015 only 10 per cent of foreign loans to Russia's businesses were raised in Asia.[46] The reasons were predictable. Creditors are wise to choose their largest debtors with caution. The long arm of the American legal system had been extended to act against those foreign commercial institutions that did business in both the United States and Iran in defiance of the American economic sanctions against the Iranians imposed in the 1980s and 1990s. Savage fines were levied by America's federal courts, and had to be paid on the nail if the accused banks wanted to continue dealing with American banking corporations or their overseas financial partners. Chinese and other east-Asian banks and investment firms were circumspect about the risk of attracting attention from America's judicial system.

Global finance was known for its lack of sentimentality. No Asian government had reason to feel sorry for Russia, anyway, for its record against Asian peoples was a bloody one, from the mid-nineteenth century in central Asia and China through to the war against Japan in 1904 and on to the invasion of Afghanistan in 1979. Though the Russian Empire and the USSR were no longer, memories remained of what the Russians had done. After 2014 the Asian political and financial response to Russia's overtures was implacable: the Kremlin had got its country into an impasse and would have to find its own way out. If Moscow's ruling elite were to reduce its readiness to deploy its armies abroad, Asian powers would have reason to celebrate.

Whereas the level of foreign investment in Russia has fallen, Russian trade with the outside world has risen; the sanctions and counter-sanctions applied since 2014 were not aimed at cutting all commercial ties, only those specified in decrees. American officials continually emphasized that Washington never introduced a comprehensive embargo. In December 2016 US Ambassador to Moscow John F. Tefft recounted the delight he took in enabling American companies to start operations in Russia.[47] Even so, the total volume of exports of goods from the United States to the Russian Federation in 2013 had been less than 0.1 per cent of America's gross domestic product. Aeroplanes and cars were the main items, followed by engineering products, medicines and medical instruments. In the same year the United States imported Russian goods – almost entirely raw materials – valued at only 0.2 per cent of America's gross domestic product. It was almost as if the USSR had not collapsed and the Cold War was still on. Russian private investors had largely steered away from investing in the United States: Americans held only $70 billion in long-term Russian securities and had only $14 billion in direct investments in Russia.[48]

This trend inevitably deepened with the introduction of economic sanctions. By 2016 Russia's bilateral trade with America amounted to only $20 billion, whereas the Sino-American total was $600 billion,[49] which meant that China headed Russia's import trade. Germany was still in second place, but fell back in total volume. Next came Belarus and the United States, at half even the German level. Exports from Russia the same year had the Netherlands at the top of the list. Close behind the Dutch were the Chinese, followed by Germans, Italians and Belarusians.[50] The breakdown of the Russian export trade in 2016 was as follows: Netherlands 10 per cent, China 9.8 per cent, Germany 5.8 per cent, Italy 4.9 per cent, Belarus 4.9 per cent, Japan 4.8 per cent, United States 4.2 per cent. This meant Europe as a whole, if Ukraine and Belarus were included, made up 52 per cent of the market for Russia's exports.[51]

In 2016 a gentle economic recovery began in Russia. There were people with ready cash despite the recession. With nearly 31 million new purchases of smartphones, Russians bought more of these than any other European nation. Samsung was the market leader, recording

22 per cent of sales, but Apple did well for itself, taking a third of the Russian smartphone market by value, thanks to the high price of its products. Chinese companies Huawei, ZTE and Lenovo had success with cheaper products.[52] After the turn of the millennium there was a steady rise in Russian steel production, whereas Britain's, France's and Italy's steadily fell away.[53] The general picture remained what it had been for decades: Russia sold natural resources such as petroleum, gas, coal and aluminium, while buying cars, medicines, computers and aircraft.[54]

But the impetus Kudrin and his supporters had provided for economic reform had faded. Objectives such as the rule of law, so important for commercial transactions, were honoured only in the breach – one of the fundamental reasons why foreign companies were not more active in Russia. But the ruling elite refrained from introducing the necessary reform. Years of huge hydrocarbon revenues had lulled the Kremlin into a state of complacency.

Inside the elite, however, there was growing nervousness. In June 2015 Sergei Ivanov, serving at the time as Putin's Chief of Staff, admitted to the *Financial Times* that 'in the 2000s, when we had very high oil prices, the motivation for carrying out structural reforms and diversifying the economy was not very high'.[55] After both Crimea and the oil price crash the incentive could not have been greater. In October 2015 Putin rejected the criticism that no progress was being made.

> Yes, this process is moving slowly. Is something positive happening there or not? Yes, it's happening, and here's something to illustrate this. Let's say that if the share of the oil and gas sector in Russia's gross national product five or seven years ago was 14 per cent, today the share of the oil and gas sector in the Russian Federation's gross national product, in the country's economy, is 9 per cent.

He contrasted Saudi Arabia and Venezuela and their failure to escape from the grip of hydrocarbon dependence.[56] Few independent economists agreed with his analysis. There was little sign of reform. The Russian leadership continued to sit tight and hope for better times ahead.

They were cheered when hydrocarbon prices began to rise again. From the lowest point at $27 a barrel for Brent crude oil in January 2016, there was a climb to $69 in September 2018 – still only half the peak price in 2008, but the easing of the Russian budget was very welcome. Inaugurated for his fourth presidential term in 2018, Putin issued a new set of May Decrees, which outstripped those of 2012 in their promises to improve life for everyone in the country. Now Putin wanted Russia to rise to the place of the world's fifth largest economic power, and be in the front rank of producers of information technology. National infrastructure was to be strengthened; so would welfare commitments be. He had said little about any of this during his election campaign, if only because he had not bothered to do any campaigning. These May Decrees were announced from on high by a ruler confident in his unchallengeable power. The historical resonances with communist party secretaries abruptly revealing ambitious programmes to transform conditions in the USSR were unmistakable.

Were the ambitious May Decrees simply impracticable? As Kudrin pointed out, everything depended on continued high prices for oil on the world market. Putin had brought back Kudrin to head the Audit Chamber, from where he could exercise financial oversight of the decrees. Kudrin did not mince his words. As the Eeyore of official policy, he warned that the tightening noose of sanctions foreclosed Russia's opportunities to raise external funds to renovate Russia's oil extraction and refining capacity.[57] Russia needed assistance for shale extraction as well as for deep-sea drilling and Arctic exploration, as the Siberian fields were approaching exhaustion, a source of anxiety for the Kremlin. In May 2014, not long after Obama announced his Crimean sanctions, Rosneft signed a deal with Exxon Mobil to look for sources beneath the bed of the Arctic Ocean. In America Exxon Mobil was fined $2 million, and by February 2018 had concluded that projects with Russian companies were no longer practicable. A bad result for the American corporation; an ill omen for Russia.[58]

In 2018 judicious analyses forecast a mere 1.5 per cent annual increase in gross national product in forthcoming years.[59] This would not turn Russia into an economic power of the first rank. In his end-of-year press conference Putin put a brave face on it. The sanctions, he said, had had the beneficial effect of compelling the country to use its own resources. Economic development had progressed. Agriculture had led the way, but industrial manufacturing was no longer far behind.[60] These were the usual official declarations of intent, but the outcomes were less conspicuous than the bragging.

25. TRAILING THE DRAGON: RUSSO-CHINESE RELATIONS

World politics have undergone a transformation since the mid-1970s, when the United States used China as a junior partner to counteract and threaten the USSR, while China welcomed America's economic and military assistance in building up its security against the Soviet threat. Now China is a superpower in the making and competes with the United States. The Chinese factor dominates Russian calculations in its Far Eastern policy, and Moscow views China as a helpful counterweight to America's global ambitions.

For years Russia's former prime minister Yevgeni Primakov had dwelt on the danger that America and China might strive to achieve a global condominium.[1] The obvious preventive measure, as he saw it, was for Russia to seal some kind of partnership with China. As well as seeking a counterbalance to America, this would neutralize the potential menace of the Chinese, who are Asia's greatest economic power and have nuclear weaponry. Putin's adviser Sergei Glazev puts the case most bluntly: Russia need not fear Western sanctions, because cooperation with China and the other BRICS countries offers a route to salvation and prosperity.[2] Russia has remained of importance to the Chinese because no other state in Eurasia matches its military power and natural resources.

Moscow's chances of a warm reception from the Chinese leadership only improved on America's announcement in 2011–12 of its strategic pivot towards the Pacific Rim, which resulted in a brief period of concern for the Beijing administration lasting at least until spring 2012, when American policy was redirected back to the Middle East and away from East Asia. Then the Ukrainian crisis in 2014 focused Obama's attention again on Europe, with the unplanned consequence of making Russia's need for partnership with China more imperative than China's quest for cooperation with Russia. The high bargaining cards had fallen to Xi Jinping, who had ascended to the Chinese presidency in November 2012 just months after Putin came back to the Kremlin for his third presidential term.

Xi reacted cautiously. The Chinese were far from happy about what the Russians had done to Crimea, and stated unequivocally that Ukrainian independence, sovereignty and territorial integrity should be respected. But they did this without direct criticism of Russia;[3] and when the Americans put forward a motion at the United Nations Security Council castigating the Russian land grab, China abstained. Russian leaders saw this as a signal that the Chinese were open to further overtures.

Moscow and Beijing had for a long time been united in annoyance at Washington's foreign-policy penchant for 'democracy promotion' and 'humanitarian intervention', with both Putin and successive Chinese leaders criticizing American military campaigns in Iraq, Libya and Syria. Although the Russians have usually been the more vociferous, both start from the same premise that the United States should cease to behave like a global policeman. They saw only danger in the calls by American leaders for foreign politicians to respect human rights in their countries. For Putin and Xi, America's ideas about democratization were a cover for its designs on global hegemony, and both Beijing and Moscow were alarmed at the possibility, however distant, that Washington might seek to interfere in their methods of running public affairs. It is of no concern to Xi Jinping that Putin maintains an authoritarian order: Xi's own order is politically even more repressive, and the Chinese communist ruling elite is unlikely to complain about fraudulent elections or economic corruption in Russia. Putin and Xi are comrades in an international authoritarian cause. In 2014 Xi Jinping had to deal with noisy street protests in Hong Kong at a time when Putin was handling the consequences of his policy towards Crimea. In Beijing and Moscow there was a shared ambition to restrict the opportunities for American interference.[4]

The official cordiality between Russia and China was signalled by the decision of newly elected President Xi to make Moscow the destination of his first foreign visit in 2013. Even though Xi's predecessor Hu Jintao had done the same in 2003, Putin appreciated this initiative: in the intervening years China had become one of the greatest economic powers, and Putin was effusive in praise of Xi, affirming that they had established 'very trusting, good relations' and adding that he thought he could say that they were friendly. This showed his fervour to build diplomatic bridges to the Chinese. It was not something he had ever done for Barack Obama or Angela Merkel – or even for George W. Bush or Tony Blair in the years when Putin's relationship with Western powers was at its warmest.[5] Neither Xi nor Putin has met any other national leader more often.[6]

They formed a close tie on first meeting. Their ease in each other's company was manifest in Putin's invitation to Xi to join his birthday party in Indonesia in 2013. It is said they swapped stories about the Second World War, as Putin described his father's experiences in the struggle against the Third Reich and Xi told of his father's part in the fight against Imperial Japan. In 2015 Xi was guest of honour at Moscow's seventieth-anniversary parade to commemorate the Soviet victory over the Third Reich, and several months later Putin went to Beijing's celebration of the defeat of Japan. Western powers boycotted both events in disapproval of the Crimean annexation and of China's growing military assertiveness in the Asia-Pacific region – South Korean President Park Geun-Hye was the only American ally to show up in Beijing.

The terms of the courtship between Moscow and Beijing have changed since the late Stalin and early Khrushchëv years. Back then, the Soviet Union helped Mao Zedong by shipping its manufactured products and technical specialists to a People's Republic in ruins after years of civil war. The reforms begun after Mao's death in 1976 – and the help rendered by an America that sought to build up Chinese industry and military strength as a counterweight to the USSR – have resulted in China's emergence as the world's largest industrial producer. Chinese factories churn out every kind of product with advanced technology. Long gone are the days when Soviet Party General Secretary Gorbachëv could say with inflated self-confidence that his Chinese counterpart Deng's reforms were a chimera. Now everyone knows China is an economic colossus. When Putin talks to Xi, he can offer few manufactured goods apart from equipment for the armed forces and civil nuclear technology, but what the Chinese want from Russia are its oil, gas and other natural resources. Putin's budgetary constraints have tightened since the collapse of the oil and gas prices in 2014: for the moment, there is a consonance between Chinese and Russian interests.

In May 2014 a deal was done between Gazprom and the Chinese National Petroleum Corporation to supply gas to the value of $400 billion. The pipelines running south into China were being completed, and the deal was touted in Moscow as the Russian government's triumph over

Western aggressive foreign policy. If America and Germany refused to play along with Russia, China offered an alternative foreign market.

While pleased about the export success for Gazprom, however, the Kremlin was disappointed by the size of Chinese investment in Russia. The exact figures are unknown, since finance can be channelled through places such as Hong Kong which are secretive about financial transactions. According to the Chinese Global Investment Tracker, though, the figure is only around 3 per cent of China's total overseas investments.[7] Nor are Chinese businessmen shy about entering markets at Russia's expense: in Ukraine, they have financed the dredging of the Black Sea coast near Odessa.[8] There was also, it is true, an encouraging willingness to support the modernization of Russia's railways and telecommunication sectors.[9] But this, noted the Ministry of Finances in Moscow, was the exception rather than the rule. Russian assurances did not dispel the wariness of China's banks and investment funds about legal trouble in the United States for breaching economic sanctions. BRICS countries, including even China, were not as invulnerable to American pressure as they liked to pretend. This was not the only reason for Chinese reluctance, however. Russia is a notoriously difficult place for foreign companies to set up business, and it would seem Chinese entrepreneurs know where their finance can be more productively employed. Russian bureaucracy and Russian corruption frustrated even the Chinese.[10]

Russia remains only sixteenth in the ranking of China's trading partners, whereas China's trade is easily the most important for the Russian economy after the European Union as a whole. If Putin ever aimed to make the Chinese dependent on oil and gas from Siberia, he was soon disappointed: Beijing has been careful to avoid reliance on a single supplier, so there is little prospect of Russia becoming able to use its hydrocarbon resources as a lever to constrain Beijing's activity in international relations.

China takes account of the Russian factor in its foreign policy, but not with the same intensity that Moscow looks on Beijing, and Xi Jinping makes a virtue of appearing calm and confident about his country's future. Yet the Moscow–Beijing ties have undeniably grown closer – Putin and Xi Jinping met five times in 2016 alone. Despite their divergent interests and ambitions, the Russians and Chinese have a common rival – even enemy – in the Americans. The map of geopolitics makes it obvious why the two leaderships think this way. China views with disquiet America's alliances with countries like Japan, South

Korea and the Philippines, while Russia suspects American intentions as leader of NATO. But there is certainly a difference in their diplomatic behaviour. Xi, like his recent predecessors, aims at putting pressure on the United States without undue public acrimony; Putin revels in increasing friction between Moscow and Washington. Both leaders see advantage in keeping friendly ties while each of them charts his chosen course towards a more powerful future for his country.

Russia and China head economic and security blocs they have built with countries around their borders. Each can use its regional influence as an incentive to the other to strengthen the Moscow–Beijing axis, a policy politicians and diplomats on both sides advocate as a sure route to bilateral progress. Currently the Eurasian Economic Union brings together Russia with Armenia, Belarus, Kazakhstan and Kyrgyzstan, and Russia can offer this as an enticement to China and the rest of the Shanghai Cooperation Organization, founded in 2001, whose other members include Tajikistan and Uzbekistan as well as Russia itself, Kazakhstan and Kyrgyzstan.

Such has been the attraction of the Shanghai Cooperation Organization, in fact, that in June 2017 both India and Pakistan opted to join. What initially brought them together were considerations of national security, and there was a notable desire in each to find ways to stabilize and protect its border regions.[11] China wanted to go further, and create a free-trade zone among the countries of the Shanghai Cooperation Organization, but Russia, nervous about Chinese economic might, has turned down the suggestion.[12] Security and controllable commerce are one thing, but the idea of unconditional exposure to China's capitalist expansiveness terrifies the Kremlin.

Nevertheless, Chinese ambitions are unquenched. In 2013 Xi announced his Belt and Road Initiative to link China directly with Europe, hailing it as the successor to the Silk Road of past centuries that would traverse the length of central Asia. Two years earlier American Secretary of State Hillary Clinton had made the same kind of suggestion, but the idea stirred little enthusiasm in the United States. Xi, however, was able to provide the political will and material resources, and China's success was impressive.

The Russians could do nothing to prevent the Belt and Road Initiative, since it was the Chinese authorities who were paying for it. At the turn of the millennium, China's trade with Kazakhstan, Uzbekistan, Turkmenistan, Kyrgyzstan and Tajikistan had been a mere twentieth of Russia's. In little more than a decade it became the leading commercial partner for all of them except Kazakhstan, and the leading foreign investor in ex-Soviet central Asia.[13] Putin tried to deal with the challenge by wrapping China in a collaborative relationship – better an embrace than a conflict. At their meeting in Moscow on 3–4 July 2017, Putin and Xi agreed to set about forming a 'broad Eurasian partnership' that would involve linking China's Belt and Road initiative with the Russia-led Eurasian Economic Union, something Putin had spoken keenly about at the Belt and Road Summit two months earlier. It means he has given up his aim of keeping the ex-Soviet republics of central Asia away from Chinese influence: even before the Crimean crisis of 2014 China had greater financial resources than Russia could muster. Now the plan is to create a vast economic space out of the Eurasian Economic Union and the Shanghai Cooperation Organization.[14]

As the Russian budgetary crisis continued, the Kremlin decided to drop some of its restrictions on military technological transfer, even though Russia maintained nuclear forces, tanks and air bases near to the long border with China, and Beijing remained a dangerous potential enemy. Now the Russian leadership accepted China's request to buy some of Russia's advanced military hardware, and in late 2016 it delivered the first four of two dozen Su-35 fighter jets to the Chinese. Moscow's financial concerns and geopolitical aims trumped security worries.[15]

Following discussions about military cooperation, Russia and China held joint exercises in September 2016, including a massive naval operation in the South China Sea involving submarines and fixed-wing aircraft as well as surface ships, and culminating in a simulated seizure of an island.[16] In July 2017 the Chinese navy joined a Russian military exercise in the Baltic. The two countries were giving a signal that NATO should no longer assume only Russia was willing to confront it. The Russians were pleased that an Asian power had agreed to deliver a joint challenge to American ambitions. Cooperation continued in summer 2018 when China accepted the Russian Defence Ministry's invitation to join its gigantic Vostok-2018 exercise in Siberia: 300,000 Russian troops were involved with 3,500 Chinese, as well as Mongolian forces. It was the biggest exercise on Russian territory since 1981, when the Chinese were among the USSR's enemies. Russia invited the Japanese prime minister Shinzo Abe to Vladivostok to allay his worries. The exercise demonstrated Russian military might and the Chinese rapprochement, and had the additional advantage of mitigating anxiety about China's intentions inside Russia's General Staff at a time when its main resources were focused on Ukraine.[17] Perhaps Moscow also wanted to show Beijing it could still, if necessary, cope with military action in its Asian territories. Times, the exercise proclaimed, had changed.

The warm embrace continued in other security sectors, and in his conversations with Oliver Stone Putin sternly denies that Russia spies on its Chinese ally. He presents this as though a code of honour, but it is hard to believe the Russian or the Chinese intelligence agencies behave with the self-restraint the Russians describe. What is more, not all Russians are comfortable about their Chinese neighbour. Russian companies show little enthusiasm for working with the Chinese, often finding them tricky and unfair in negotiations and deals. Some of Russia's commentators on national security have expressed alarm about China's purchases of advanced military hardware.[18]

There was also trepidation among many in Russia about the number of Chinese traders and workers coming over the border into southern Siberia. The newcomers' entrepreneurial prowess was feared to be pushing out existing local businesses, and the thought spread that such colonization by stealth could perhaps lead to war.[19] A poll conducted by Russia's Public Opinion Foundation in 2008 suggested about three-fifths of Russian people worried that the migration of Chinese to the Sino-Russian borderlands in eastern Siberia posed a menace to the country's territorial integrity. Two-fifths took the view that China's rise as a great power would injure Russia's interests. Russian people also felt some alarm about the spread of Chinese influence in the countries of 'the near abroad'. It was an attitude shared by the Kremlin authorities, who were reluctant to support Beijing's Belt and Road Initiative until 2014, when the clash with the West over Ukraine made Russia eager to make a closer friend of China.[20]

Putin dealt quietly with the latent threat China posed along the long Russian border in Siberia, knowing the Chinese had not forgotten about the 'unequal treaties' they had reluctantly signed in the nineteenth century. The Beijing communist leadership knew the Russian Empire had forced the cession of 600,000 square miles in the Siberian regions of Lake Baikal and the Amur and Ussuri rivers. Even if Putin had failed to read what Sinologists in Moscow's research institutes had written on the subject, ex-Soviet Foreign Affairs Minister Eduard Shevardnadze, by then living in Georgia, had told him about it in person. When Shevardnadze had travelled to China in early 1989, the focus had been on what needed to be done to improve Sino-Soviet relations, and barring some outbursts of rancour from Deng Xiao-Ping the visit had gone tolerably well. Shevardnadze had never forgotten Deng's words to the effect that when China fully recovered its strength, it would return to the question of the 'unequal treaties' and seek territorial revisions. 'There'll come a time,' Deng had casually remarked, 'when China will perhaps restore them to itself.'[21]

In public Putin brushes aside any suggestion that Russia has reason to worry about China's territorial aspirations. China and the USSR had had an unresolved dispute over the contested islands in the middle of the Ussuri river where it forms the border of the two countries, but instead of bristling with national assertiveness, Putin saw the sense in making concessions. A settlement was agreed in 2004 and ratified four years later by China's People's Congress and Russia's State Duma. Putin wants everyone to think he has eliminated all the tension that once existed, and that only a few small matters of disagreement remain, mainly pertaining to border management.[22] Apparently the Russian authorities have continued to have a problem with illegal fishing and migration as well as smuggling, but nobody in the Kremlin is inclined to make a fuss. Russia's leaders cannot afford a clash with Beijing. They can live with a degree of disorder across the long frontier.

The situation would be more reassuring for Russia if only China stopped bringing up the question of frontiers. In 2016 Chinese Deputy Foreign Affairs Minister Fu Ying remarked that some Chinese people think there is unfinished business in the 'Russian' Far East because of the territorial losses that the tsars forced on the ailing Chinese Empire in the second half of the nineteenth century.[23] This was no idle comment: China's history textbooks, she knew, had taught the same lesson for decades.[24] When the Beijing media revealed that Putin had agreed to adjusting the border by two square miles, tens of thousands of Chinese wrote accusing the Chinese government of failing to demand the restoration of all the 'lost territories'. This was not a passing phenomenon. On the occasion of President Xi's visit to Moscow in 2013, there was a flurry of demands by ordinary citizens for the frontier question to be raised with Putin and settled in China's favour.[25] But the Chinese authorities prefer to take their time – so long as the textbooks stress that China suffered unconscionable harm and humiliation at the hands of the Russian Empire, it is unlikely the Beijing leadership will forget. They can return to the matter in due course and be sure public opinion will be on their side.

In Russia over the past few decades there has appeared a profusion of books and articles on nineteenth-century history, but hardly any have discussed the importance and territorial details of those old treaties.[26] It is not hard to guess why public figures and historians are so chary of raising the subject: in the current state of world politics, Moscow has to keep Beijing sweet. In earlier decades the approved Soviet accounts held that the ministers of the tsars had negotiated with the Chinese on friendly terms and the Sino-Russian treaties were untainted by the threat of force or by imperialist intent, but if the Putin administration were to endorse such an analysis, it would find doors closed to it in Beijing. Acknowledging the unfairness underpinning the treaties, on the other hand, would present its own danger. Kremlin leaders have chosen reticence as the path of prudence.

Russia advertises the current diplomatic, economic and military deals with the People's Republic of China as proof that Russia can cope without America. In 2001 Putin and the then Chinese leader Jiang Zemin had signed a Treaty of Good Neighbourliness and Friendly Cooperation, followed by a number of agreements between the two great Asian powers, which the Russian authorities had presented as a story of triumph and resilience, avoiding mentioning that the Chinese treated the Russians as mere providers of natural resources. The net result of Moscow's diplomacy, however, served only to escalate the reliance on gas and oil exports. Russia's trump card is military power, but that has to be played with caution so as not to scare off the Chinese. Talks continued on economic diversification by means of a partnership with China, but remained just that: talk. In reality Russia was accepting a subordinate position in relation to its mighty neighbour across the long Siberian border. As the third decade of the twenty-first century draws nigh this seems unlikely to change.

26. FIGHTING ABROAD: THE SYRIAN INTERVENTION

The civil war in Syria had been going for four years when in September 2015 Russian war planes were dispatched to support the tottering Assad administration in Damascus. The action took the world by surprise just as the Crimean annexation had done a year and a half earlier.

Until then President Obama had been giving diplomatic and some financial support to the rebels while holding back from full-scale intervention, and President Assad appeared on the edge of defeat. Putin's move began to change the entire military picture. It also meant Russia was challenging the line of American foreign policy in the Middle East, which shocked foreign observers, coming so soon after the Russians had worked in agreement with America, the European Union and China between April and July to get Iran to abandon research that might be used to develop nuclear weaponry. In return the Iranians received a promise about the lifting of economic sanctions. Two years earlier, moreover, the Russians and Americans had agreed on measures to ensure the definitive destruction of Syria's stocks of chemical weapons. But Putin had made no secret of his opinion that America had taken the wrong side in Syria's civil war, and the orders he gave to his air force translated words into action.

The Americans received no advance alert from Moscow. When Secretary of State Kerry brought up the matter with Foreign Affairs Minister Lavrov – 'Sergei, you guys are now bombing in Syria and moving troops? What's up?' – Lavrov appeared taken aback, blanching and hurrying off to talk on his mobile phone. He had persistently said that military intervention in the Syrian civil war was a violation of the rules and policy of the United Nations Security Council.[1] Unless Lavrov was putting on a show of ignorance, Kerry concluded, the probability was that Putin had not chosen to inform him.[2] As with Crimea,

the Russian Foreign Ministry counted for little in Moscow when decisions of strategic consequence were made.

Putin and his confidants assumed that the risks were minimal. It
had never been easier for Russian armed forces to make an impact in
the Middle East: they had equipment no fighting force in Syria could
match, and Putin was keen to test out the General Staff's improvements
in planning and training. As important as anything else was that
Obama, shivering at the record of military interventions in Afghanistan, Iraq and Libya, was reluctant to extend American power any
further in the region. His predecessor in the White House, George
W. Bush, had left him with the task of managing the Iraqi situation
where American troops were garrisoned in numbers, which he had
dealt with by rushing through preparations for the Baghdad government to take full responsibility for the country and the withdrawal of
United States personnel, tanks and aircraft. Chaos and sectarian
disputes ensued, probably an inevitable consequence of Saddam
Hussein's overthrow: as democratic elections proceeded, the long-
persecuted Shia majority visited vengeance on the Sunni regions, and
Iraq collapsed into vicious civil war.

At the start of the 'Arab Spring' in Tunisia in December 2010,
Obama had reacted with a mixture of delight and trepidation. Country
after country in the Middle East subsided into political tumult. In
Libya, unlike Tunisia, the government reacted with brutality, and the
media around the world, including Russia, stirred up opinion in favour
of intervention against Muammar Gaddafi, whom nobody could deny
was a corrupt dictator who for decades had suppressed dissent with
unflinching cruelty. The French president Nicolas Sarkozy, followed by
British Prime Minister David Cameron, opted to send in air power
against government and police facilities, and Obama found himself
pushed into supplying military assistance in the form of signals intelligence. Gaddafi and his sons made bloodthirsty threats against the
Libyan rebels, and the Western powers, after the international recriminations that had ensued from the Iraq emergency in 2002–3, sought
endorsement from the United Nations.

As America, France and Britain stood together, in May 2011
President Medvedev indicated that his administration agreed with
them, though unlike them Moscow declined to break diplomatic
relations with Tripoli. But it also established links with some of the
diverse and fractious forces of rebellion, and Medvedev went along
with the conclusion reached at the G8 summit in Deauville that

'Gaddafi had lost legitimacy and had to go'.[3] The French and British bombing continued, disabling the Libyan government's capacity to operate, and in Benghazi and elsewhere the rebels grew in strength. Libya was breaking up; Gaddafi was pressed into a small Tripoli enclave. As the fighting in Tripoli descended into street warfare, the government fell apart and the Gaddafi family went into hiding. What followed was not an agreement on a new Libyan government but civil war. Regional divisions widened, and Gaddafi was trapped and lynched in the capital's streets before he could be put on trial. Western diplomatic and financial support was provided, but the mayhem continued.

The first sign that the troubles had spread to Syria came in January 2011. The protests in Damascus against the al-Assad administration were instantly suppressed, but they spread to the regions. In cities like Deraa, Aleppo and Homs, discontent intensified. As had taken place in Libya, there was a cycle of protest and repression. The Ba'ath administration had been in power since 1963, and its dictatorship was founded on the Alawite religious group, which was only a tiny minority of the Syrian population.

The American administration was nervous about pursuing a 'regime change' policy in Syria, but Obama, swayed by evidence of Assad's grievous assaults on civilians in the rebel-held cities, indicated that America would enter the conflict if the Syrian government were to cross specific 'red lines' of misconduct: any act of biological or chemical warfare, he warned, would constitute a casus belli. Yet in 2013 he moved away from his own 'red lines' for fear of bringing down the Ba'ath administration, seeing that Assad's removal would in all probability lead to a strengthening of the regional power of Sunni extremist factions, inspired and supported by Islamic State or Al-Qaida. Islamic State, having sprouted in Iraq after Saddam Hussein's overthrow in 2003, had spread like knotweed across the border in eastern Syria. In 2014 Obama ordered the bombing of Islamic State and Al-Qaida strongholds as well as some other anti-Assad rebel groups. But though he sent weapons to anti-Assad groups, he held back from supplying them in sufficient quantity to bring down Assad in Damascus, and even authorized the payment of compensation for a bombing raid that mistakenly hit Syria's government forces.

Throughout the Syrian civil war there was an opportunity for Obama to enforce a no-fly zone over the country. But he was scorched by the outcome of such decisions in Libya, where two of his NATO allies had pushed him into a more active policy than his instincts recommended. His goal for America was to end its role as the world's policeman. The undesired result was that Assad sent his bombers over rebel-held cities to carry out raids that caused thousands of civilian deaths. The world's broadcast and print media covered the devastation. But Obama held to his judgement that full-scale American intervention would have the effect of intensifying the civil war and creating ideal conditions for jihadi extremism. In the United Kingdom, Prime Minister Cameron was in favour of armed action but a majority of the House of Commons rejected it, mindful of how the chaotic military intervention in Iraq had given rise to Islamic State. NATO was still routinely condemned in the Kremlin as a bloodthirsty and rapacious war machine, but the truth was that America and its most powerful military allies were nervous about letting loose the dogs of war again.

Evidence grew about Assad's use of chemical weapons. For Obama, this was intolerable; Russia, though, was reluctant to give credence to the reports. Syrian official spokesmen said rebel forces had cynically carried out the attacks in order to besmirch the air force's reputation. After weeks of altercation, the Russians accepted the Americans' case and put pressure on Assad to renounce such methods of warfare. In return, Obama desisted from an all-out assault on Damascus. (In fact, as everyone knew, Obama had been reluctant to increase America's direct armed engagement anyway.)

In September 2015, after Bashar al-Assad lost several cities to the Syrian rebels, the Kremlin decided on direct armed intervention to prop up Syria's government and armed forces. Obama stayed out of Syria and confined American efforts to supplying the Kurdish armed units against Islamic State in Iraq. Increasingly reliant on Russian help, Assad agreed to Putin's proposal to develop Russia's naval facility at Tartus on the eastern edge of the Mediterranean, and also allowed the expansion of Russian signals intelligence capacity further north at Latakia. But Assad needed more than this to survive the civil war. Talks were held with Russia about increasing the scope of military assistance. Putin gave his consent, and from September 2015 the Russian air force began bombing rebel-held Syrian cities. As footage of mass carnage reached Western TV stations there was an international outcry, which Putin brushed aside. 'Our task', he publicly explained on the Rossia-1 television channel on 11 October, 'is to stabilize the legitimate government and establish conditions for the pursuit of political compromise.'[4]

The American administration replied that Russian bombs were falling on Syrian forces committed to democratizing the country and removing the Assad dictatorship, but Russia's answer was that four years of civil war had spawned the growth of jihadi groups associated with Al-Qaida and Islamic State, which also had a contempt for democracy and Syrian democrats. Putin's case was that the Arab Spring and the America-led reaction had fomented a disruption the jihadis were gratefully exploiting.

While refusing to be pessimistic about the prospects of peace in the Middle East, Putin guards against overconfidence, recalling that on one of his visits to Israel he had received the following advice from its prime minister Ariel Sharon: 'Mr President, right now you are in a region where no one can be trusted on any matter.'[5] What Putin wants for the Middle East is stability, and he is not worried about principles of human rights:

> On your question about whether Assad is or is not our ally and about what we want in Syria. You know, I'll tell you straight what we don't want: we don't want the situation in Syria to develop as it developed in Libya or Iraq.

Putin went on to endorse the military coup against President Mohammed Morsi of the Muslim Brotherhood in Egypt. The essential requirement was to eradicate all forms of religious fanaticism:

> Due credit should go to President el-Sisi in Egypt, as I've already said to him, because if he hadn't assumed the responsibility, shown courage and taken control of the country into his hand, then the same could have happened in Egypt as Libya. In my view, the need is to spare no effort in strengthening legitimate state power in the countries of the region.

Over the entire Middle East, as well as several other Muslim countries, there hung the terrible possibility of government by fanatics, unless foreign powers were willing to act:

> This applies to Syria. The need is to restore and strengthen the emerging structures of power in a country like Iraq or a country like Libya. To achieve stabilization in a country like Somalia, for example, and in other countries. To strengthen state power in Afghanistan. But this doesn't mean leaving everything as it is. Naturally it's necessary to carry through political reforms on the basis of this stabilization.[6]

About Assad himself, Putin was never effusive, telling NBC reporter Megyn Kelly at the St Petersburg International Economic Forum plenary session on 2 June 2017 that Russian foreign policy is aimed at preserving Syria's statehood rather than keeping Assad personally in power.[7] Putin also aimed to lever the United States out of the region and regain for Russia the presence and influence that the USSR had once enjoyed. His actions in Syria were part of his effort to confirm his country's status as a great power.

Around the world the talk was of Russian self-confidence and assertiveness, permitting Putin himself to express a note of caution. While ambitious to play an active role in Middle Eastern affairs, he was aware that Russia alone would be unable to bring the Syrian civil war to a halt. Ultimately the Russians would need partners, and Putin had some hope of enlisting support from the American, Saudi and Jordanian leaderships.[8] He did not mention the Turks and Iranians, even though he had both of them in his sights as possible diplomatic and military partners, and he repudiated the suggestion that he was aiming to complete the job solely through his alliance with Assad. He had told Assad, he revealed, that he intended to work with those Sunni tribes who were fighting against Islamic State – and this despite Assad's coalition of support inclining towards the Shia side.[9]

The *Admiral Kuznetsov* aircraft carrier caused a sensation on its long passage across the Mediterranean to the Syrian coast in summer 2017, but it looked less impressive on its return voyage, churning out thick smoke from its dilapidated fuel system. The British Defence Secretary, Michael Fallon, mocked the Russians by inviting the world to compare it with the UK's new carrier *Queen Elizabeth*. Such was Russian sensitivity that the London embassy then instantly and none too convincingly tweeted that the Defence Ministry in Moscow already had plans for the introduction by 2025 of a superb rival to the United States' gigantic vessels.[10] What was beyond doubt was Russia's return as a great power on land and in the air.

Russia's engagement with Turkey resulted from Recep Tayyip Erdoğan's search for new friends after seeing off the attempted military coup against him in 2016. But though the Turkish leader embraced Putin in Moscow, he still pursued goals that caused discomfort in the Kremlin. Ankara has specific national interests in the Syrian civil war that were disturbing for Russian policy: it was hostile to territorial concessions to the Kurds of Iraq and Syria, for fear of reanimating the Kurdish struggle for independence from Turkey. The Turks also had a horror of the kind of victory for Assad that might drive millions more Syrian refugees across the border onto Turkish soil. Turkey's foreign policy had also clashed for years with Russia over Karabagh, the Armenian-inhabited enclave of Azerbaijan, where the Turks consistently championed the Azerbaijani side against Armenia. More recently, in 2014, Turkey had espoused the cause of the Crimean Tatars and expressed displeasure about Crimea's annexation. Erdoğan had to bear in mind that public opinion in Turkey could turn hostile to Russia. His rapprochement with Putin had its potential pitfalls.[11]

Another problem, at least for Putin, was that Turkey and Iran have conflicting interests in the Middle East, which meant he could not be sure of holding his international coalition together. He learned quite soon not to take Iran's support for granted when, in autumn 2016, the Russian air force launched attacks on Syrian cities from Hamedan airport. Tehran lodged a protest, and Russia lost permission for military operations from the area. Leading a coalition is not the same thing as dominating it. The Iranians were a crucial component of the Assad regime, doing much of the fighting on the ground near to Damascus and financing the extension into Syria of Hezbollah's militia, a Shia religious and paramilitary organization based originally in Lebanon, with an insatiable zeal to help in suppressing Sunni jihadis and other rebels who confronted Assad.

A further complication was that Saudi Arabia was subsidizing Sunni jihadism, meaning Iran and the Saudis were locked in a proxy war on Syrian soil. The danger of widening their strategic duel was realized in their interventions in the Yemeni civil war on the Arabian peninsula which erupted in 2015, with the Saudis organizing bombing raids on cities held by the Houthi rebels. Russia stood apart from the conflict, seeking to avoid dispute with Saudi Arabia, which had enabled it to achieve observer status at the World Islamic Conference. Indeed, Russia's foreign policy was aimed at showing it to be the friend of Islam around the globe.

Moscow also wanted to preserve the good relations with Israel that had existed since the Gorbachëv period, even though Israeli policy was pugnaciously hostile to Iran, Hezbollah and – to a lesser degree – the Assad administration. The potential for a clash between Damascus and Tel Aviv caused regional disquiet. In 2010 Israeli scientists had released the Stuxnet computer virus to destroy Iran's uranium enrichment infrastructure, and in February 2018, anxious about Iran's rising influence in Syria and angered by an Iranian-produced drone flying into

Israeli air space, Israel's air force attacked and destroyed weapons storage depots at a base near Damascus. The Russians had to sit back and hope this would be the end of the conflict.

On 7 December 2017 Russia declared that the defeat of Islamic State in Syria was complete. But the trouble was only starting. In January 2018 Russia's entente with Turkey enabled Erdoğan to begin a full military assault on Kurdish rebel forces occupying the borderlands of northern Syria. Before the Russian involvement these Kurds, supplied and trained by the Americans, had been a crucial fighting force against Islamic State. For Erdoğan, however, they were an enemy who could threaten to establish a state of Kurdistan on his frontiers.

Russian forces were steadily withdrawn, but not to the point of leaving Assad exposed to any serious threat of rebel attack, and Russia's military installations and facilities were kept in place. Syrian aeroplanes, assisted by Russia-supplied technology, continued their bombing campaign. All the country's main cities except for Idlib in the north were reoccupied by the government. Aleppo, whose ancient centre had become a moonscape, was once again a stronghold for Assad. Putin was exultant, but understood he had to be cautious. The bulk of the foreign pro-Assad ground forces came from Tehran, whose interests had never fully coincided with those of Russia, and without the Iranians Assad would quickly find himself beleaguered again. The Kremlin, however, remembered the lesson learned by the Soviet army in Afghanistan: that once the body bags of dead Russian soldiers were flown back to the USSR, their mothers were capable of making their distress into a matter of public import. This was one of the reasons why the Russian authorities had been trying, albeit without complete success, to disguise the military occupations of men killed in the fighting of eastern Ukraine from 2014. The concern was that bereaved mothers might earn public sympathy by making a public fuss about why Russia's young servicemen were having to risk their lives in unnecessary wars.

From the standpoint of the Defence Ministry, however, the Syrian operations provided the scope to test the mettle of its forces after the weaknesses exposed in the 2008 Georgian war. Flight personnel in the Russian air force gained combat experience.[12] Putin knew his administration's prestige in Russia and abroad depended on success in the Middle East. In February 2018 Assad's forces discredited themselves again when, according to credible sources, they reverted to using chemical weapons on rebel-held cities, but Russia rejected the recriminations at the United Nations Security Council. In the continued absence of American intervention – President Trump was implicitly following the line of the Obama administration – Putin and Shoigu felt they had carte blanche in Syria.

Trump had come to power arguing that American troops and resources were to be reserved for other purposes, and he broke with this only occasionally. When evidence emerged in April 2018 of Syria's renewed use of chemical weapons, and the excruciating deaths of children, a scandalized Trump authorized retaliatory action by the US Air Force. But this was exceptional, and generally the Americans stood aside as Russian and Syrian warplanes pummelled rebel-held cities into rubble. At the end of the year Trump announced the intention of withdrawing the small number of American forces that were stationed in northern Syria, where they had been supporting the Kurds against Islamic State, reasoning that Islamic State was close to total defeat and America's objective had been achieved. Putin was delighted: this freed Russia to help the Assad administration bring more cities and territory under its control. Though the Syrian civil war was a long way from being ended, thoughts began to switch to the task of economic reconstruction and a political settlement. Russia by its own lights had worked to bring the bloodshed to an end. In the process it had confirmed its resurgence as a great power. But the Russian authorities were in no position to supply the external finance that the Syrians would need. Assad's expected victory was only the beginning of the end of war, and the entire Middle East crackled with fear and uncertainty.

27. JOSTLING AND EMBRACING: THE AMERICAN FACTOR

When Donald Trump won the American presidential election in November 2016, it seemed to many that the real victor was Putin. The Russian team of hackers and leakers had disrupted the campaign of Trump's main opponent, Democratic Party candidate Hillary Clinton. There were claims that Putin had some secret hold over Trump – that the Russians had personal information that, if disclosed to the media, would wreck Trump's career.[1]

The election caused a shock wave in American politics. In the summer, the opinion polls had Hillary Clinton as the front runner. Though Trump's campaign was dogged by scandalous revelations, he rejected them all as 'fake news'. Blustering and boasting, he attacked his own Republican Party's leaders with the same ferocity he turned on the Democrats, and presented himself as the only candidate with the will to challenge what he depicted as the cosy corruption in Washington. He threw away the standard political rulebook and ranted at the media, and made a virtue of never having been a professional politician.

As some of Trump's links with Russia came to light, his difficulties grew. Commentators noted how his statements often overlapped with allegations on the RT television channel about the fraudulent methods being used by the Clinton team. Another regular item on RT was Trump's charge that Obama had no right to be elected American president.[2] Into this melee flowed a leak by WikiLeaks of the Democratic National Committee's internal email traffic, which appeared to show that dirty tricks were played to undermine Clinton's Democrat rival contender Bernie Sanders. Clinton had a decidedly tough policy on Russia, and it was reasonably supposed that the Russian intelligence services were working to discredit her. Contacts were made between members of the Trump team and intermediaries of the Russian leadership, which had a distinct preference for Trump in the presidency. The feeling was mutual. On 27 October Trump showed his colours when he said of Clinton at a rally in Springfield, Ohio, 'She speaks very badly of Putin, and I don't think that's smart.'

Putin called on the West to face up to the reason why its societies had turned against their political establishment in recent elections and referendums:

> At first, these inconvenient results were hastily declared an anomaly or a fluke. When they started to be repeated, people said that society does not understand those at the summit of power and has not yet matured to the point of being able to assess the authorities' endeavours and concern for the public good. Or they become hysterical and declare it the result of foreign, usually Russian, propaganda.[3]

His point about popular disenchantment in America and Europe was well made, but typically he fudged the part that Moscow played in fomenting trouble.

Putin refrained from saying anything publicly that might encourage Trump's enemies to increase the pressure to investigate the Russian shenanigans. Already there were suspicions that the Trump team had colluded with intermediaries from Russia who fed his campaign with hacked data that would wound Clinton. Rumours spread that the FSB had a hold over Trump, either because of commercial deals he had done with Russians or because its agents had filmed him in sexually compromising circumstances on a visit to St Petersburg. On 15 December Obama indicated that practical measures would be put in hand to retaliate against Russian political interference.

In early January 2017, before Trump stepped into the White House, a dossier came to light that purported to summarize some sleazy past adventures involving Trump and Russian prostitutes in the Ritz Carlton in Moscow. Quite apart from the sexual allegations, there was an accusation that Trump on several visits to Russia had benefited from a cosy relationship with the Russian authorities, who had cultivated him as a person of influence. Trump had found a welcome in the Russian capital when hosting the 2013 Miss Universe 'pageant' in Moscow. There were also stories that the Russians had helped to bail out Trump's various financial difficulties over the years. The dossier went online too late to have an impact on the election, and Trump immediately rejected its claims as 'phony' and 'fake'. The author was revealed to be Christopher Steele, a former UK MI6 officer who was co-owner of a London-based business-intelligence firm. It was also revealed that Steele had collected the material on behalf of the Democratic Party in the months before the presidential election.[4]

Putin felt compelled to contribute to the discussion:

> This is firstly an adult and secondly a person who for many years, albeit not for his whole life, was engaged in organizing beauty contests and mingled with the world's most beautiful women. You know, I find it hard to imagine that he ran off to meet up with our own girls of reduced social responsibility – even though they are absolutely the best in the world. But I doubt that Trump fell for that.[5]

Trump's links with the Russian authorities before and during the electoral campaign were as yet a matter of speculation, but enough was known to make it likely Putin would pay a price for his mischief. If Clinton had beaten Trump to the White House, she would have initiated a systematic inquiry into Russian hacking of the Democratic National Committee email correspondence in summer 2016 – the leaked messages had disrupted the Clinton campaign for some weeks. She would also have ordered an investigation into allegations that Russians were responsible for anti-Clinton social media campaigns throughout the year. Trump's victory itself sparked investigations by the American media and both Democrats and Republicans in Congress. The result was a daily seepage of embarrassing material into the public domain which served to narrow Trump's scope to achieve his stated goal of an improved relationship with the Kremlin in foreign policy. Trump was distrusted in Russian affairs as much by his fellow Republicans in the Senate as by the Democrats. He had played hard and rough at electoral poker, and Putin had stood behind his chair and helped him to raise the stakes. Now he found the price of victory was not being able to cash in his chips.

Throughout his campaign Trump had been complimentary about Putin. In power, he now had to take care to avoid seeming to be Putin's catspaw. Putin, meanwhile, had to hope for the best. When asked about Russian interference in American politics, his reaction was either to feign offence at the question or to declare that Kremlin leaders had better ways of spending their time than leaking the emails of American public figures. Russian leaders bided their time: Lavrov spoke of having no illusions about settling Russia's difficulties with the United States,[6] an attitude widespread in Russia. By April 2017, according to a

VTsIOM survey, only a third of Russians felt optimistic about the course of Russo-American relations. Two out of five had a negative opinion about Trump.[7] Russian caution seemed justified when the new American president, a week after his inauguration, paid a visit to the Pentagon and signed an upgrade plan for America's nuclear weapons forces.[8]

The Russian leadership was in the dark about what Trump's next foreign policy moves would be. Putin revealed he had only one telephone conversation with Trump before his inauguration, and that the first one with the new president did not take place until 2 May 2017, when – according to the Russian account – they agreed to coordinate action against international terrorism and enable a 'real process of regulation' of the Syrian situation, as well as try to lower tensions in the Korean peninsula. The two presidents planned further contact by telephone in advance of the G20 summit in Hamburg in July.[9] The pair went onto first-name terms, though Putin did not yet use the familiar 'you' form when addressing him in Russian.[10]

Still Putin continued to suggest that America was a chronic offender against international law around the world, demanding that the American political leaders admit the reasonableness of Russia's security concerns. When a United States naval vessel with cruise missiles on board set out into the Black Sea, nobody in Washington seemed to understand the anxiety this caused in Moscow. But Romania had joined NATO back in 2004, and the Americans took it for granted that as allies they could conduct operations off the Romanian coast. To Russian eyes, it was provocative for the American navy to sail out into waters adjacent to Russia's coastline with ballistic missiles, and Russian warplanes were sent to 'buzz' the NATO ship. Far from being aggressive, Putin remarked, the Russians were exhibiting remarkable self-restraint.[11] Quite what he thought Russia had grounds for doing beyond buzzing American vessels, he omitted to make clear. His chief aim was to sound menacing.

Russo-American relations deteriorated when on 2 February 2017 Nikki Haley, the US Ambassador to the United Nations, called for an end to the Crimean occupation.[12] This was only the start of the Kremlin's irritation. On 15 February 2017 the ex-Soviet Baltic States signed an agreement to permit NATO troops of other countries to transit their territories. In Moscow, it was immediately greeted with annoyance that the governments in Tallinn, Riga and Vilnius were enabling America and its allies to reach the Russian border within hours. On 16 February

US Defense Secretary James Mattis added to Russian fears by stressing that America should deal with Russia from a position of strength.

On 20 March 2017 FBI Director James Comey came before the House Intelligence Committee to testify about 'Russian active measures' during the previous year. Accusing Putin of having a personal hatred for Hillary Clinton and encouraging a 'multifaceted campaign' to aid Donald Trump's presidential bid, he said the Russians were 'unusually loud' in their activities, as if they did not care about who noticed what they were doing. Allegedly they wanted to undermine the American democratic process and hoped for the break-up of the European Union. Putin, Comey went on to suggest, had a distinct preference for businessmen rather than career politicians to lead foreign countries. Why? Because supposedly he saw entrepreneurs as more amenable to compromise in pursuit of deals. Comey warned that Russia's secret services were likely to repeat their operations in forthcoming US elections.[13] There were strident demands in the US Congress for questions to be answered about the Trump–Putin connection, and under the Justice Department's aegis a special counsel investigation was announced in May 2017, to be headed by Robert Mueller, who had led the FBI until four years previously.

Comey made general remarks while omitting factual details; he was asking people to take his testimony on trust. He also mortified the president by continuing the FBI's inquiry into the links between Trump's electoral campaign team and the Kremlin. In May 2017 Trump's patience ran out and he fired Comey, tweeting that he was a 'showboat' and 'nut job', and fuelling the suspicion of collusion between Trump and the Russian authorities in 2016.

Putin grew fractious. He continued to argue for an agreed global protocol on cyber-warfare, stressing that he had submitted a draft proposal to the United States in autumn 2015 and claiming the Americans had not deigned to reply.[14] For years the Russian authorities had been accused of organizing the hacking of American email addresses and planting false news stories on America-based blogs, so Russia's draft protocol was an attempt to occupy the moral high ground. Its counter-case against Washington was that it is the Americans who have most aggressively interfered in foreign electoral campaigns, both by funding rallies and secretly subsidizing the Opposition. Putin drew attention again to the visit by Victoria Nuland to Kyiv in December 2013, when she openly supported the campaign against Ukrainian President Yanukovych.[15] While the American political establishment persisted with its accusations of interference, Putin decided to ask questions about America's own interfering.

On 23 May 2017 John Brennan, Obama's last CIA director, told the House Intelligence Committee that worries about Russian efforts to influence the result of the 2016 presidential election had led to a joint effort of the CIA, the National Security Agency and the FBI to investigate the scale of interference. Congressional leaders were briefed in August and Brennan himself contacted Alexander Bortnikov at the FSB to warn him off. When Bortnikov denied the charge, Brennan told him to tell Putin personally that further interference would have adverse consequences.

On 12 June 2017 the Senate voted by 98–2 to strengthen the sanctions regime against Russia, particularly to undermine international projects of American companies that involved Russian energy corporations. This would immediately disrupt agreements with Azerbaijan because of Lukoil's operation in its territories, and also jeopardize the Southern Corridor venture to supply Caspian gas to reach Europe without passing through Russia – not the result that US senators had in mind, but a sign of the strong will to maximize damage to Russian economic progress at any price short of direct armed conflict. Oil exports from Kazakhstan would also be affected. 'I think Russia is a global menace led by a man who is menacing,' said Paul Ryan, the Republican Speaker of the House. 'Vladimir Putin does not share our interests, he frustrates our interests . . . There's no secret here – Russia tried to meddle in our elections. This is why I'm a fan of sanctions. This is why I'm a Russia hawk and a Russia sceptic.'[16] Unity prevailed between Republicans and Democrats on the arguments for sanctions against Iran and North Korea as well as Russia.

The sanctions were cobbled together without consulting America's European allies. Making no pretence of altruism, senators stressed that further action against the Russians should give priority to 'the export of United States energy resources to create American jobs'. In Germany, France and Italy there was growing annoyance. Angela Merkel and her European partners could hardly endorse a policy that involved economic pain for Europe in the interest of America's employment statistics.[17] German commercial interests had already suffered significantly from Merkel's original decision in 2014 to join in the American-led sanctions. President Trump did nothing to alleviate Germany's anxiety by suggesting that the Germans could help themselves by purchasing American stocks of liquefied natural gas instead.

If this was an attempt at diplomacy, it fell at the first fence and disconcerted Moscow at the same time as annoying Berlin.

The new sanctions also targeted any company contributing to the
maintenance or upgrading of pipelines used for Russian hydrocarbon
exports, which included the project known as Nord Stream 2 to carry
natural gas from Russia under the Black Sea directly to Germany
without passing through Ukraine or Poland. Though Gazprom was the
chief owner of the project, European firms had substantial stakes. No
American investment was involved. President Donald Tusk of the
European Council, a former prime minister of Poland, was one of Nord
Stream 2's critics: as a Pole he was not enamoured of any sign of an
exclusive Russo-German embrace. But other European politicians,
notably Jean-Claude Juncker as President of the European Commission, were more intent on resisting American pressures. Juncker
objected to what he saw as Trump's national selfishness, and after
Trump had talked of introducing tariffs on steel imports, immediately
'threatened' the United States with commercial retaliation if European
interests were harmed. Juncker suggested the European Union should
consider blocking imports of American whiskey.[18]

Speaking to *Le Figaro* newspaper in Paris on 29 May 2017, Putin
said Russia was ready to bide its time and see how the Trump administration's policy would develop, noting that in American public affairs
it was possible for a defeated candidate to continue to exert influence.
(He didn't mention Hillary Clinton by name.) When asked whether in
a perfect world he would expect relations with America to improve, he
exploited the opportunity to purr that 'There is no such thing as a
perfect world, and there is no subjunctive mood in politics.' He went
on to criticize the continuing rise in American military expenditure,
already larger than the total expenditure of the rest of the world. He
also complained about NATO's eastward expansion and America's
withdrawal from the Anti-Ballistic Missile Treaty.[19] Putin regularly
took the political attack to the Americans, exclaiming to NBC's Megyn
Kelly in June 2017, 'Point your finger to any spot on the world's map:
everywhere you'll hear complaints that American officials interfere in
their political domestic processes.'[20]

At last Trump met Putin for the first time, on 8 July 2017 at the
G20 summit in Hamburg. Trump as usual made an inconsistent
impression. The day before, he had visited the Polish city of Gdansk,
where he delivered a rousing speech in which he warned Russia against
its unwarranted intervention in Ukraine, and recalled the illustrious

record of Solidarity in standing up to Soviet communism. The Poles greeted this with applause. They were also pleased with his endorsement of the principle of mutual military assistance embedded in NATO'S founding charter.

It came as a shock the next day in Germany, therefore, when Trump declared it an honour to make the acquaintance of Vladimir Putin: the same Putin who had annexed Ukrainian territory and excoriated NATO. Their conversation lasted much longer than scheduled, even though Melania Trump entered the room to alert her husband to the meetings he was about to miss. Trump was sitting with Secretary of State Tillerson, Putin with Foreign Affairs Minister Lavrov; no one else was in the room except for their interpreters. Tillerson had earlier implied that he expected an open agenda, to take shape as the conversation proceeded, which seemed a desultory way of planning. One positive result which pleased both presidents was a verbal agreement to stabilize the situation in south-west Syria. They also came to an understanding about counterterrorist operations. According to Tillerson, Trump brought up the allegations of Russian interference in the American electoral process, but when Putin rejected the charge, Trump recoiled and focused merely on securing agreement that no such interference would occur in the future.[21]

If Ukraine was a bone of contention, neither spoke about it afterwards. It was as if Trump assumed he had done enough with his speech in Poland. Small wonder that the Russian media, and not just the Putin-friendly TV channels, interpreted the encounter as Putin's triumph. Putin himself did not crow at his press conference, but instead emphasized how he and Trump had agreed to set up a working group to resolve contentious questions. Cyberspace was a burning topic, and the two of them had concurred on the desirability of a framework of mutual non-interference. Asked about Trump personally, he said:

> As regards personal relations, I think that they've been established. I don't know how this sounds but I'll tell you how I see it. The 'TV' Trump contrasts sharply with the real person. He's a down-to-earth person who absolutely, absolutely competently considers who he's talking to, quickly enough makes an analysis and gives his answers to the questions on the agenda or to any new factors that crop up in the course of discussion. For this reason it seems to me that if we go and construct relations on the basis of our conversation yesterday, there's every ground for

supposing that we'll be able to restore, even if only to a partial extent, the level of interaction that we need.[22]

Without dropping his earlier scepticism, Putin was pleased with how he'd found Trump.

Secretary of State Rex Tillerson preferred to follow the Trump-in-Poland line when on 9 July 2017 he flew from the G20 summit to Kyiv. Meeting with President Petro Poroshenko, Tillerson stipulated that Russia had to restore 'territorial integrity' to Ukraine before the United States would contemplate moving towards a fundamental improvement in relations with the Kremlin.[23] The feeling grew that Trump's administration was loosely organized to the point of chaos. Tillerson had been chosen for his openness to reconciliation with Russia – in 2013 he had received the Order of Friendship from Putin himself for his work for Exxon Mobil in partnership with Rosneft. But as Secretary of State Tillerson showed in Kyiv, he was no patsy for official Russia. Defence Secretary James Mattis, National Security Advisor H. R. McMaster and Trump's own Chief of Staff John Kelly were equally reluctant to indulge Putin; they became known as 'the grown-ups in the room', who discouraged Trump's preferences when they seemed injurious to the interests of America and its allies.

Russian leaders were disappointed by this cooling of the political weather. Their concern grew a day later, on 10 July 2017, when Poroshenko met with NATO Secretary-General Jens Stoltenberg and announced his country's ambition to achieve the alliance's membership requirements by 2020. Stoltenberg supported him, calling upon Russia to withdraw its forces from eastern Ukraine. A Ukrainian opinion poll in June 2017 indicated an immense tide of approval for Poroshenko's policy. Membership of NATO had become a goal endorsed by 69 per cent of Ukrainians, compared with 28 per cent in 2012. Poroshenko admitted that formal entry into the alliance would take several years, but the direction of intended travel was plainer than at any previous time. The tasks ahead for Ukraine were immense, involving fundamental reforms to eliminate corruption and impose the rule of law. It was also incumbent on a candidate country to settle its international disputes in advance – hardly an easy requirement while Russian troops remained on Ukrainian soil.[24]

On 25 July 2017 Kurt Volker, the United States' special envoy for efforts to end the fighting in eastern Ukraine, announced that Washington was thinking about delivering lethal weaponry to the Ukrainian armed forces, though only defensive equipment was under consideration. Even so, this would involve an upgrading of American support against Russia. Volker denied it would provoke Russian retaliation: 'First off, Russia is already in Ukraine, they are already heavily armed. There are more Russian tanks in there than [there are tanks] in western Europe.' President Poroshenko had long been asking for Javelin anti-tank missiles, if Russian military superiority was to be countered.[25]

In the same month there was a stream of revelations about contacts between the Kremlin's representatives, official or informal, and the Trump electoral campaign team. Trump's family and associates were loath to admit to any of it, but the investigative pressure from Senate and Congress as well as from the media was relentless. Donald Trump Jr's blurting out that he had met a Russian lawyer in summer of the previous year who offered to share damaging information about Hillary Clinton created a considerable controversy. That the Russian authorities interfered covertly and radically in the United States' general electoral process was hardly disputed: now everyone wanted to know the complicity of Trump's team and particularly Trump himself. It was becoming undeniable that Russians close to the Kremlin had interfered in domestic American politics just as they had provably done in European countries, to assist foreign politicians likely to enhance Russia's objectives. Candidate Trump was the American public figure who had come to fit this profile exactly.

Gradually President Trump was compelled to face up to the need for further precautions against military encroachment by Russia. He endorsed NATO's deployment of troops in Poland and the Baltic States without demur. When Vice-President Mike Pence visited Estonia in July 2017, he pledged unwavering American support; when he went on to Georgia, he castigated Russia for keeping forces in South Ossetia, which in international law remained Georgian territory. On 2 August 2017 Trump bowed to the inevitable, without much grace, and signed the Senate bill to reinforce American economic sanctions against Russia. In all but name, the United States was now engaged in an all-out trade war. On 24 August 2017 US and UK troops paraded in Kyiv in celebration of Ukraine's Independence Day. It was a signal of America's resolve to support the anti-Russian cause.

Strategic talks between Russia and America about their nuclear forces and about conventional arms in Europe stopped under Obama and have not been resumed. Instead Trump has accelerated the programme to develop new nuclear missiles; Putin was already committed to a similar objective. The ongoing mutual threats made by the United States and North Korea have served to reinforce the assumption of the world's political leaders that possession of rockets with nuclear warheads gives any country leverage in international relations. Neither Trump nor Putin has expressed a desire to reduce his forces. In a lecture at the General Staff Academy on 23 March 2017, Lavrov said that successive reductions in nuclear weapon stocks by Russia and America have reached their limit: the goal now, he contended, should only be strategic stability.[26] The implication is that Moscow and Washington should try to agree on a realistic agenda, with the vision of a 'nuclear-free world' expressed by Ronald Reagan and Mikhail Gorbachëv in the late 1980s having faded from the scene. When Putin made his annual address to the Federal Assembly on 1 March 2018, he boasted about the new nuclear weapons Russia had produced.

On 20 March 2018, just when the frost on Russo-American relations seemed unthawable, Trump picked up the phone to congratulate Putin on his re-election as president. He made no reference to the unfairness of the entire electoral process, nor did he allude to the recent Skripal affair. Trump said they talked about Syria, North Korea, Ukraine and arms control and agreed about the desirability of an early full summit.[27]

The Skripal poisoning had prompted additional British economic sanctions and the expulsion of several Russian intelligence officers from the London embassy. Trump was remarkably reticent about these events, but his administration supported the British position. Treasury Secretary Steven Mnuchin reinforced the American sanctions regime, citing not only Salisbury but also eastern Ukraine and Syria. Several tycoons who had flourished during Putin's tenure of high office, including Oleg Deripaska, Viktor Vekselberg, Alexei Miller and Suleiman Kerimov, were now refused the right to raise loans in the United States, with inevitable consequences for their financial dealings in other foreign markets. Twelve companies and seventeen senior governmental officials were also targeted. The impact was immediate. Deripaska's Rusal corporation, the biggest producer of aluminium in Russia, quickly lost 70 per cent in the value of its shares traded on the Hong Kong stock exchange.[28]

The difference from the sanctions of 2014 is stark. Obama introduced his by executive order, whereas Trump wanted an understanding with Putin, not confrontation, so the Senate bill of 2017, by leapfrog-ging the need to consult with the White House, had the capacity to increase the injury to the Russian economy regardless of what Trump might want. Sergei Lavrov called it 'genocide by sanctions'.[29]

In May 2018 the United Kingdom passed a law to punish money laundering, encouraging the British press to raise questions about the connivance of the big law and accountancy firms in easing Russian penetration of the City of London. The impact on the 'oligarchs' was minimal, but Roman Abramovich, the owner of Chelsea Football Club, had difficulty in procuring his normal entry visa from Russia, leading him to apply for Israeli citizenship, only to find this would still not enable him to conduct business regularly from his London base. In September his request for residence rights in a Swiss ski resort was met with refusal after a police report warned that he constituted a threat to national security. The warm welcome for Russian finance elsewhere in Europe had not come to an end, and Russian big business and its inter-mediaries continued to flourish in London. But while no Russian individual or company was charged with malpractice, the British parliament had at least begun the process of examining the sources of unexplained wealth.[30]

The Russian intention was to hit back with counter-sanctions, and a bill was drafted for the attention of the Duma. But at the last moment it was withdrawn because Putin saw he had an economic emergency on his hands. This time there would be no anti-American measures. Trump was rumoured to have told Putin his administration had no intention of intensifying its sanctions regime again, and there was talk of the two presidents visiting each other's capitals. While there was even a smidgen of a chance of ending the spat between Washington and Moscow, Putin called off his dogs.

The long-awaited summit between Trump and Putin took place in Helsinki in July 2018. It was the most secretive summit on record. Indeed, there were no transcripts of their conversation, since they met with only their interpreters present. When they came out of the meeting, neither said much about what had passed between them. This remained the position on the American side, giving rise to suspicions that Trump had made commitments he preferred to keep quiet about, and speculation that he had conceded on Crimea, eastern Ukraine and Syria. The Russians wrote of the summit as a national victory. Unlike the US State Department, the Russian Ambassador to Washington, Anatoli Antonov, divulged what had passed between the two presidents.

According to him, they had had productive talks on economic cooperation, Russian interference in the American election and America's anti-missile defence system, and also discussed Syria, medium- and short-range missiles reduction, nuclear arms non-proliferation, the Iranian nuclear arms deal and Russian gas transit across Ukraine.[31]

Antonov had avoided saying exactly what Putin and Trump had agreed: only what they had talked about. Trump in his tweets on 19 July was elated without being any more informative: 'The summit with Russia was a great success, except with the real enemy of the people, the Fake News Media . . . There are many answers,' he added, 'some easy and some hard, to these problems . . . but they can all be solved!' This did not satisfy Congress, which considered summoning Trump's interpreter to reveal the content of the discussion.

No further summit took place in 2018, and Putin's visit to Washington was postponed: Trump could not ignore public opinion. Nevertheless he did other things that pleased the Kremlin, particularly when in December he revealed his plan to pull out American forces from Syria and Afghanistan. Russia's leadership was also delighted by the worsening relations between America and China after Trump introduced trade tariffs in March to put pressure on the Chinese to lower their own tariffs and protect intellectual property rights. Though Putin could take comfort from signs of a weakening of America's global power, the American sanctions still caused difficulties. Elections to the House of Representatives in November 2018 gave a majority to the Democratic Party, and disappointed Trump's hopes of closing down the Mueller inquiry into the Trump team's Russian links. Campaign manager Paul Manafort, lawyer Michael Cohen and former National Security Advisor Michael Flynn were all found guilty of malpractice, and the cloud of suspicion thickened over Trump's claim to have received no assistance from the Russian authorities. Allegations of Trump's collusion with Putin in 2016 persisted, and the Democrats in Congress were not alone in suspecting that Putin had some kind of hold over Trump. Russo-American ties had never been more contentious.

Trump stuck to his own line in foreign policy, and there were changes to his administration. In March 2018 Rex Tillerson gave way to Mike Pompeo at the State Department, and John Bolton took the place of H. R. McMaster as National Security Advisor; in December James Mattis resigned from the Defense Department and John Kelly stepped down as Presidential Chief of Staff. But the newcomers were not Trump's yes-men – Bolton in particular had spent decades holding Russian leaders' feet to the fire. Not all the news, however, was bad for the Kremlin. In January 2019, the decision was taken to lift the sanctions against Rusal and other of Oleg Deripaska's companies.[32] This resulted from lobbying by Deripaska as well as from the disquiet of American industrial enterprises that had suffered from the fall-off in aluminium imports. The Trump administration, moreover, followed Russia in seeking talks with the Taliban in Afghanistan.[33] Trump repeated his wish to withdraw America's forces from Iraq and to shun 'foolish wars.'[34]

In March 2019 Trump received the glad news that the Mueller investigation had concluded with a recommendation for there to be no new indictments for collusion with the Russian authorities during the American presidential election three years earlier. The US president was cock-a-hoop, accusing his many accusers of having conducted a witch hunt against him.[35]

Although there could be no complacency in the Kremlin, Putin had reasons for cheer. In his address to the Federal Assembly in February 2019 he took pride in the national record. He noted that the government had paid off foreign debts so as to be able to cover the remainder from its own reserves if the need were to arise. He announced that the National Well-Being Fund had been able to make a substantial contribution to the state budget in the previous year. He warned that if short- or medium-range nuclear missiles were to be reinstalled on the European continent, Russians would bring back their own.[36] Without naming the Americans as the main enemy or rival, he made his message clear that Russia could face up to any challenge. And he continued to offer challenges of his own. In March 2019 a small Russian military contingent was flown to Venezuela to assist the tottering Maduro government. Maduro and Trump had for years engaged in mutual recriminations, and Putin's move was a signal to the United States that Russia had the capacity to meddle in the Americas just as the United States had done in Ukraine.

Trump called on Russia to withdraw its troops. The Russian authorities took delight in telling America to stay out of Venezuela. The harmony between Trump and Putin could no longer be taken as a given. The rest of the world watched and waited.

28. CHOICES: RUSSIA AND THE WEST

Russia's is a stunted democracy, malformed in the womb and maltreated after birth. Its people have negligible influence over who will occupy the presidency, premiership or cabinet. The security agencies assign their own personnel to official posts throughout the political and economic order. The Russian state eliminates serious opponents of the ruling group with methods ranging from electoral exclusion to murder. Parliamentary institutions have been neutered, and exert authority only when the leadership's internal divisions spill out into factional struggle in the State Duma. The courts are subservient to the rulers. The vertical machinery of command has been reconstructed from the debris of the USSR. It is true that the Kremlin's orders are frequently ignored, as they were in Soviet times, but when the Putin administration focuses efforts on particular objectives, it can trample down opposition. National pride is trumpeted. Sport and entertainment – as well as naked military power deployed beyond the Russian borders – are used as distractions. Patriotism, religion and traditional social values are promoted. Vladimir Putin is presented as the embodiment of everything that is good about Russia.

He and his associates boast of their successful expulsion of asset-snatching 'oligarchs' from political power, a process reminiscent of George Orwell's *Animal Farm*, where no sooner had the pig revolutionaries got rid of Mr Jones, the hated farmer, than they themselves lorded it over the other animals, dressing in splendid attire and gorging themselves on fine food and wine. Putin's appointees feasted on the benefits of high political office and cultivated relationships of mutual advantage with those 'oligarchs' who complied with the demand to stop interfering in politics. The powerful secured their power by ruthless means. The secret services operated with impunity and free of governmental or parliamentary supervision. Criminal gangs were employed to do dirty business. The political class passed on its privileges to families and friends. Bulging bank accounts were lodged abroad, including offshore in the Cayman Islands. Switzerland and the French Riviera became playgrounds for the Russian rich, and London was its counting house of convenience for money laundering, where British lawyers, accountants and some politicians made money as facilitators of business from the east.

Russian economic strength grew in line with rising hydrocarbon revenues, and the recovery of Moscow's confidence imprinted itself on Russia's behaviour abroad. Russian secret services were blamed for the assassination of Alexander Litvinenko and for the 2007 cyber-attack that afflicted Estonia and other countries to the west. In 2008 Russia's army and air force invaded Georgia.

In 2014, Crimea was occupied and annexed. This was followed by armed intervention in eastern Ukraine, an intervention that continues to this day as Russia's troops and equipment are covertly deployed to confront the Ukrainian armed forces. Russian armed forces entered the Syrian civil war to rescue the Assad administration, and Russia placed itself on the opposite side to the United States. The Kremlin interfered in politics in the European Union, consistently financing parties that sought to weaken its unity and prevent its expansion. Russian hackers and IT companies disrupted America's 2016 presidential election. As the Western powers retaliated with economic sanctions, Putin consolidated Russia's partnership with the People's Republic of China. Calling for multipolarity in world politics, he pinned his foreign policy on a challenge to American global power. His activity pointed in a single general direction while including a number of improvised moves.

But though Putin plans ahead, he has often been taken aback by unexpected reactions. Bush and Obama were temperate about Georgia, whereas Obama was stern on Crimea and became ever sterner. Putin's forward thinking lacked the flexibility demanded by the course of events.

His rule is not a silhouette in black and white but a canvas of diverse colours. The disorderliness of the 1990s has been surmounted. The old press and the new internet and newer social media have retained a limited space of freedom. People have privacy as a reality, not just as a formal right. Russians continue to travel abroad and to watch and listen to foreign broadcasts as never before in their history. Religious toleration is observed for the country's main faiths. Education, science and technology are promoted. Personal property is respected in the courts as long as high politics and big business have no dog in the fight. Capitalism flourishes. In every town, entrepreneurs are running businesses. Russia is integrated into the global economic system.

Some say we should celebrate rather than carp at the Russian transformation. Most commentators, at least in the West, are not so much pro-Kremlin as anti-anti-Kremlin. They allege Western bias, pointing out that the established democracies of Europe, North America and Asia took a long time to be consolidated, and are still far from being perfect expressions of the popular will. Russia endured a longer period of totalitarian rule than any other country, and had an inevitable legacy of problems from communism that will require many years to resolve. Every country, of course, has its own history and inclinations, and the Russian people are unlikely to accept a mould that others have made for their own different circumstances. One of the benefits of de-communization is that Russia can choose its new way of life. The anti-anti-Kremlin grouping contains some who are admirers of Putin. Why, they ask, do people fail to recognize what his leadership has achieved in the face of daunting difficulties?

Such queries are usually premised on denying that it was moral or sensible for NATO to expand its membership into the USSR's satellite countries, on the theory that every great power secures a zone of influence in nearby states. Russia, unlike Ukraine or Kazakhstan, it is also noted, is heir to the Soviet Union's arsenal of nuclear weapons and maintains the largest conventional forces in Europe. It is imprudent, say the anti-anti-Kremlin grouping, to tweak the tail of a bear.

Criticism is certainly heaped on Russia even though China's penal camps are more brutal. Beijing subjugates the press, internet and social media, and the Chinese Communist Party monopolizes power, but discussions in the West focus on Russian iniquity. A degree of racism is certainly involved, because less is expected of the Chinese than of the Russians. But foreigners are not alone in setting a different standard for Russia. Russian rulers have themselves often identified the country as quintessentially European. Gorbachëv dreamed of a 'common European home'; Yeltsin for a while refrained from speaking of 'the West' because he wanted the world to stop thinking of Russia as an outsider. Putin too started out by claiming Russia to be a part of European culture, but his commitment to 'European values' faded. Europe's own politics underwent change as Hungary and Poland pulled down the scaffolding of their own legal order and democratic procedures. As 'European' values and traditions became a matter of controversy,

Russia no longer seemed quite as peculiar as it once had done, and the Putin administration continues to express pride in Russia's idiosyncratic values, practices and 'civilization'.

When Russian disengagement from the West gathered momentum, Moscow's spokesmen put their stress on multipolarity as a way of counteracting America's alleged ambition to dominate the world as the sole hyperpower. Russia's challenge to American 'hegemony' was widely touted as both timely and justified. No great power has pursued an unblemished foreign policy in the past quarter-century, however, and the United States is no exception. That said, the charges of American misbehaviour at Russia's expense are overdrawn.

Although Gorbachëv had received some oral assurances about a reunified Germany, there was no such clarity about what was meant to happen in the former USSR and the ex-communist eastern Europe. During the 1990s a tornado of unpredicted events raged, and NATO and the European Union began their eastward expansion. The Western powers were tugged into the vortex of the wars in many parts of old Yugoslavia. The Americans led NATO forces in an aerial bombardment of Belgrade to free the Albanian majority in Kosovo from vicious ethnic persecution, and in the end judged Kosovan independence to be the only way to resolve the matter. But when Putin asks how this diverges from what he did later in Crimea, he ignores the conspicuous difference that Bill Clinton did not occupy and annex Kosovo: America still has only fifty states and Kosovo is not one of them. Russian recriminations do not stop there, but although there is some justification for Russians to say that economic sanctions from Soviet days persisted into the twenty-first century, the new sanctions were a reaction to the horrors that took place on Putin's watch, and would not have been applied had the Russian state behaved better.

As for the idea that America was responsible for the Chechen separatist insurgency, or that the West played midwife to the birth of the Russian business 'oligarchs', this is merely a way for the Kremlin to palm off Russian responsibility for what happened in Russia after the collapse of communism. It was Russians who caused most of their troubles. Putin is unconvincing when he attributes all ills to external interference.

Whenever Russian spokesmen fossick in historical annals for evidence of the sins of America, NATO and the West, they omit to consider why their neighbours continue to be fearful of and have suspicions about the motherland. The post-1945 suppression of national freedoms in all Europe to the east of the Elbe is lodged in the regional memory. Whereas Putin can fairly say that Russians suffered alongside other Soviet peoples under the USSR, the fact remains that it is primarily Russia that the societies in eastern and east-central Europe blame for imposing a brutal communist order. But the Russian government still holds to the idea that it has seigneurial rights over the region. Countries in eastern and east-central Europe formed an impatient queue of petitioners for entry into NATO and the European Union: they were not cudgelled into it by the United States. Their concerns appeared justified when, under Putin, Ukraine's gas supplies were cut off and Estonia fell victim to a nationwide cyber-attack.

Western economic investment has been thinner in Russia than in the countries on its western borders, and the fault lies chiefly with Russian rulers who failed to establish an accountable legal order. International sanctions are not the main reason why the Russian economy has failed to realize its full potential – and anyway Russia has coped adequately with the specific difficulties that the sanctions introduced after Magnitski, Crimea and Salisbury. But when Russia's politicians highlighted the history of Western economic attacks, they conveniently made no mention of the part they had played in provoking them and ignored entirely the damage caused by their failure to institute the rule of law.

Russian behaviour in world affairs worsened decisively after Putin returned to the presidency in 2012. The spirit of compromise with America disappeared again. The year 2014 marked another turning point and the devouring of Crimea and the battering of eastern Ukraine confirmed that Russia could no longer pretend to be the victim of external malefactors when it inflicted such harm on a vulnerable neighbour. The Syrian military intervention corroborated the stereotype of the wild, unpredictable bear. Russian agencies reinforced this image when they were found to have hacked the Democratic Party's email accounts in the 2016 American presidential election. Interference in European politics was widespread and systematically conducted on the side of parties hostile to European unity. In Syria, the Russians sided with Bashar al-Assad and indulged his use of chemical weaponry and other atrocities against rebel forces and cities. Russia's hooded subversion and naked military power were activated from the North Sea to the Mediterranean.

Other contenders for presidential office would have acted differently – or at least tried to. From Kasyanov and Nemtsov through to

Navalny, a less harsh way of governing Russia and handling the West was the likely result if only they had been able to mount an effective challenge to Putin. Instead, between 2008 and 2012 the country had a tepid interlude under Medvedev, who made promises of reform, of which few were realized and fewer still outlasted Putin's return to presidential office.

Putin reimposed his external and internal policies in a strengthened format. He had always been his own man, or at least someone formed by his background in the KGB, and he was not alone. In St Petersburg and other big cities in the 1990s there were several former security agency personnel in the city administration. This cohort shared the frustrations of many public officials who were angry about the business 'oligarchs' who strutted round on the political stage. The instabilities and unfairnesses in society annoyed most people, and there was a widespread yearning for Russia to move back to the centre of world affairs. This was the informal mandate that Putin received in 2000 when he first became president. He and his supporters were initially willing to test the possibility of mutual accommodation with America, but they had no intention of allowing a serious challenge to their power at home. As hydrocarbon prices soared and Russia achieved budgetary stability, they could turn their back on the Western powers. They did this with determination after the 'colour revolutions' in Ukraine and other nearby states in 2003–4. Democracy and the rule of law were never on Putin's true agenda – and this was going to be the situation regardless of what the West did.

Inside the Putin administration, ideas underwent ossification, reflecting Russia's post-imperial, post-superpower mindset. The benefits of a strong, orderly state under central control were emphasized. Nationalism was accentuated. Religious faith, especially the Christianity of the Russian Orthodox Church, was stimulated. The uniqueness of Russian values – including the notion of a distinct Russian civilization – was proclaimed. Social conservatism was promoted. Russia's right to influence nearby states was reasserted, culminating in the armed action in Crimea and eastern Ukraine. In Russia's name, Putin gleefully took on the role of Grand Disrupter in global politics. He threw away his chances to rinse the bad blood out of Russia's relations with the West. The result is that no Western leader – with the obvious exception of Donald Trump, and even he is far from a clear-cut case – is going to place trust in Putin again. The feeling is probably mutual – something the West has tended to overlook – because Putin has decided he cannot rely on the United States to abide by any compromise he might agree to.[1] Though President Trump called for reconciliation with Russia, his administration – and the American 'deep state' – has frequently moved in the opposite direction. Regardless of who is president in America and Russia, pressures persist that drive the countries apart, and Russia has little to offer that would tempt America to relax its posture.

The unfortunate likely consequence in the immediate future is that Ukraine's distress and peril will continue. If respite is to be achieved, it needs to be by way of cast-iron agreements with realistic penalty clauses. European security has to be a prerequisite for any deal. What adds to the grimness is that neither Putin nor his team is likely to choose a successor who would lessen the authoritarianism at home or the disruptiveness abroad. Nationalism has been inscribed in the Kremlin's codebook: Putin's vision has to have public appeal if it is to remain an asset for his administration. Russia, however, is not the only country where national feelings run high. Ukraine's people, in their vast majority, hate the Kremlin for what it has done to their country. Putin's actions since 2014 have had the unplanned effect of making it all but impossible for anyone to win the Ukrainian presidency without attacking Russian quasi-imperial pretensions. Meanwhile, Petro Poroshenko's administration became discredited for its failure to root out fraud and profiteering. Against him in the sensational presidential election of April 2019 stood the popular actor and comedian Volodymyr Zelensky. Like Poroshenko, he was committed to facing down Putin, but he also promised to put an end to the rampant corruption. Zelensky won a landslide electoral victory despite refusing to sketch out a programme of practical policies. On assuming power, he taunted that Ukraine, unlike Russia, was a free country with free elections, media and internet.[2]

Whereas the task of cleansing the Augean stables of Ukrainian public life may prove beyond Zelensky's strength, Ukraine's example of open politics fills Kremlin leaders with dread that it might be transferred to Russia. It is a situation laden with dangers for the wider world but also with possibilities for a degree of conciliation if chances are seized. Though Putin has persistently rejected the calls for him to moderate his disruptive objectives in foreign policy, there are two possible scenarios under which Russia and the West could reconverge, one positive and the other negative. The Middle East could become such an acute danger to world peace that the Western powers might welcome Russia as an intermediary. A second possibility is that Russian economic difficulties might become severe enough for a more moderate foreign policy to commend itself to the Kremlin leadership.

The West's options are limited. It would nevertheless be wrong to abandon the demand for the restoration of Ukraine's territorial integrity, including Crimea. This is not a cause for war, even a future war, but neither should the Crimean question be wiped off the slate. Nor should the slightest doubt be allowed to arise about the commitment of NATO and the European Union to the security of all their members. If this requires military reinforcement in countries that lie near to the Russian frontiers, so be it. The Russian authorities must also be put on credible notice that cyber-attacks will bring about retaliation. Economic sanctions have to be enforced more systematically until such time as Russia improves upon its record abroad. Channels of financial credit and technological transfer should be kept available to increase the pressure on Moscow. Russian money-laundering facilities have to be closed down in the City of London and elsewhere. Super-rich Russians close to Putin must be made to feel a pinch in their pockets.

Too often, Western politicians have levelled their charges exclusively against Putin. Though he bears ultimate liability for the ruling group's actions, he is the captive of the order that brought him to power. Though he has done far too little to reform that order, nobody should underestimate the difficulty of the task. Moreover, Putin does not and cannot know in advance everything done by the Russian authorities. He is the leader of a team with a shared strategy for external and internal affairs, but its members have their own ideas. Russia's ascendant politicians and businessmen are combative and ambitious. Putin is one of their kind, and he has to prove himself to fellow proponents of nationalist, authoritarian politics. But he and his team are also pragmatic, and have shown flexibility in the past: in 2000–3 Putin was open to compromise with the West, and in 2008 Medvedev unbolted some of the doors again. There is no such thing as an unchanging template of Russian governance.

The interests of peace and stability require that links between Russia and the West are maintained at all levels. Academic and cultural exchanges as well as business are useful ties. Sport helps, as do music, museum exchanges and literature. The broadcast media and internet websites can convey the message that a better way of life is available under the rule of law and with respect for principles of free competition in politics and business. But Russian hackers and fake news distributors are at an advantage in being able to attack open democratic elections. It was understandable but self-defeating when Obama indicated that retaliatory action might be taken quietly, out of the public gaze, because for it to work the Putin administration had to pay a demonstrable price for misconduct. International conflict by means of cyber-technology is complex and dangerous, but not all action needs to be confined to the shadows.

It remains a problem for the West that the Kremlin has a stranglehold on the Russian electoral process and television news services. Western policy-makers need to show that hostile measures are aimed not at the Russian people but at their rulers and leading associates in politics, administration and big business. And although their efforts to derail Putin and United Russia were ultimately unsuccessful, much more could have been done. An appeal has to be made to the Russian people's self-interest: most of them know something is wrong with how they are governed, and Western cable channels, internet outlets and magazines could do more to undermine the Kremlin's manicured image of official policies, practices and privileges. They could also focus on the activities of Westerners who aid and abet the Putin team. Consultants and spokesmen for so-called oligarchs must be exposed too; likewise the lawyers and accountants who protect them. And here is a small but heartfelt piece of advice: cartoonists, instead of portraying Putin as omniscient and omnipotent, should do what they usually do to politicians – scoff at him and his malpractices. He is not and never will be the demiurge of world affairs.

Change, when it comes to Russia, will be a project for Russian hands. Putin's image-builders have successfully disguised the fragilities of the ruling group, but street protests continue despite growing legal restrictions. Social media enables critics to argue their case and organize opposition. 'Colour revolutions' happened in Ukraine and Georgia earlier this century when public anger at oppression and corruption erupted, and the Kremlin leadership has been acutely sensitive to the potential for the same to happen in Russia. Although authoritarian controls have been tightened to prevent such an outcome, freedoms survive that are unimaginable in China, Saudi Arabia or North Korea. It is unclear whether Russians will be able to untie the country's political straitjacket and compel the introduction of reforms. The current economic problems, despite having roots in official policy, have not produced a crisis of public order, so if there is to be a political volte-face in the Kremlin, it will probably require serious fissures in the leadership.

This in turn means that dissension has to become open conflict, perhaps in the forthcoming struggle for the Kremlin succession. Currently this seems unlikely, but authoritarian states have in the past been particularly prone to sudden, unpredicted convulsions.

The consequence of Putin's political cult and his dominant style of leadership is that, as the Russian people increasingly object to official policies, his personal responsibility comes under scrutiny. It is not inconceivable that his team will find it advantageous to get rid of him and then heap the blame on him for the country's ills. Alternatively they could offer him an honourable retirement such as Yeltsin obtained from Putin.

Russian rulers have often shown a fondness for Lord Palmerston's remark in 1848 that England [sic] had no permanent allies, only permanent interests. In Russia's case, the position is rather bleaker. In the mid-nineteenth century, the United Kingdom had friendly allies and clients. In the 1990s the Russians came into a daunting bequest: when the Soviet Union was at its peak, it had many allies in eastern Europe, even though all of them were involuntary. Their peoples hated Russian domination and called communism a Russian plague. In all those countries, that dislike of Russia remains deeply embedded. The USSR had more willing allies in Cuba, Vietnam, parts of the Middle East and east Africa, and capitalist Russia, somewhat surprisingly, inherited some of them. Among the new states of the former Soviet Union, Ukraine was prized as a potential ally before it was subjected to war and partial conquest, but the others, except those in want of armed assistance, were wary of Russia's embrace. In eastern and east-central Europe the bitter memory of subjugation by the Red Army and the secret police has not faded. It makes diplomacy and business infinitely more difficult for the Kremlin.

Palmerston's words have been unduly exalted because they implied that everyone agreed on what constituted national interests. Just as the House of Commons then was regularly divided on the question, so Russia's politicians and commentators are constantly clashing, and there are several who challenge Putin's vision of the national destiny.

Russian liberals stuck to their argument that security and welfare would be enhanced through a smoother relationship, even a partnership, with the United States and the European Union. When Putin picked China as a partner, there was little direct public criticism. China is one of those factors that few Russian commentators choose to analyse in depth. This reticence is unhealthy and unlikely to last; the strong probability is that Putin, by exasperating Washington and relying on Beijing, made an unforced error that sooner or later will have to be corrected. He also merely promised to diversify the Russian economy and break the addiction to hydrocarbon exports, rather than actually delivering. The Opposition, from liberals through to communists, has been united in pointing out his failure. Even many supporters of the government have stressed the need for a fresh strategy to attract foreign investment and promote Russia's small businesses and start-ups. They also want to suspend the privileges that the security services enjoy, maintaining that the state's role in economic and social affairs must be reduced. Some add that the focus has to be widened from Moscow and St Petersburg to all regions of the Russian Federation, to give them an equal chance of prosperity.

Ultimately all Putin has done is steer the country further down a cul-de-sac. He leapt into the driver's seat of a limousine that was already moving in that direction in economics and politics. It may frighten passers-by, but under the bonnet it is less powerful than the manual proclaims. To remain a great power, Russia also has to become an international technological power, yet while it is an impressive producer and seller of armaments, in most other sectors it consistently lags behind America, China, Japan, Germany and South Korea. Present-day Russia is still only halfway down the cul-de-sac. Its passengers – the Russian people – are as talented and lively as they always have been. There is still time to reverse.

Internationally the situation is worse than at any time since the early 1980s, and it may deteriorate further, as UN Secretary General António Guterres told his Security Council on 13 April 2018: 'The cold war is back — with a vengeance, but with a difference. The mechanisms and the safeguards to manage the risks of escalation that existed in the past no longer seem to be present.'[3] Russian leaders have expressed no fixed opinion, sometimes accusing America of having started a new cold war, at others denying that such a war has begun.[4] The same, though, has been true of successive American leaderships. Words matter, because they have an impact on how we think and react, and it is important not to diminish the comprehensive conflict that consumed America and the USSR from the late 1940s to the mid-1980s, a conflict that was political, ideological, economic, social and cultural as well as military. Capitalism contested communism on a global scale. Superpower confronted super-power, each with alliances throughout the world.

The twenty-first century, however, has a number of great powers contending for authority. The current struggle involves values and prestige as well as influence and sovereignty, and today's contest between Russia and America is a vivid example. Democracy is at least a formal condition of membership of both NATO and the European Union, but the Kremlin flatly declines to be interested in the democratic credentials of countries, political parties or social movements willing to assist Russia's geopolitical objectives around the world; in fact, the Putin administration is openly sympathetic to rulers who suppress the freedoms of their peoples. Its basic goal is both to spread Russian influence and to shake the kaleidoscope of global politics. Putin set the theme at his Valdai conference in October 2017: 'Creative destruction: will a new world order emerge from conflicts?'[5] He was too canny to answer yes, or even admit that he aimed to destroy anything. But if one judges him by his actions, he seeks a redrawing of the rules of global politics in Russia's favour. He knows that tension with the United States is the unavoidable result.

There are unmistakable differences, however, between the current situation and the Soviet era up until the late 1980s. Since the end of communism the Russian leadership has adopted capitalist economics. Russia now fosters religious faith. Putin and his associates know that they have too much to lose from a total rupture with the United States and the European powers. They want to continue to enjoy the products and pleasures of the West. Though satisfied with their military operations in Crimea and eastern Ukraine, and engaging in another in Syria, they are not mad enough to risk the outbreak of a Third World War. Both they and the West have a vital interest in achieving security through nuclear arms reduction.

The geopolitical tension is likely to last for some years. Russian leaders are toughing it out, ruling a country with many chronic problems that they have hardly begun to solve. At New Year 2019 Putin wrote to Trump stressing that he was 'open to dialogue' on a broad agenda. He gave no clues as to what concessions he might put on offer or what demands he would make. Nevertheless fresh talks were certainly an urgent necessity, and it was not just the Russians who had an interest in taking them seriously. At the G20 summit in Osaka in June 2019 Trump and Putin behaved like old friends. At a joint press conference Trump wagged his finger in mirth when telling Putin not to meddle in the next American election, and Putin beamed with delight at the banter. On the summit sidelines he himself gave an extended interview to the *Financial Times* in which he derided the difficulties facing liberalism and its agenda around the world. He said that the West had harmed itself and other countries by promoting multiculturalism and omitting to control immigration. He traced the rise in populism in America and Europe to a refusal by Western elites to appreciate what their peoples really wanted and needed. Russians, he implied, are pleased to have a leader who understands them – and he expressed pride in the course that he has set for Russian foreign policy.

Putin's words could be a shock only to those who had not listened to him over the years. His message has a razor's sharpness. The Kremlin ruling group that he leads would like to receive plaudits in Russia and everywhere else but, whenever this is unforthcoming, it will settle for respect based on fear. This has been the firmly held objective ever since Putin returned to the presidency in 2012. A pattern underpins his thought and behaviour. Abroad he is a forceful disrupter, at home a forceful stabilizer. He has done little to settle the global atmosphere and much to render it more volatile, and Russia itself has fallen further and further into the shadows of unfreedom. It is a depressing situation. Not all the lights, however, have gone out and total pessimism is not yet called for. Change is still possible both in Russia and in world politics, even in the depths of a Kremlin winter.

Bibliography

Online sources

anticompromat.ru
archive.premier.gov.ru
atlas.media.mit.edu
auswaertiges-amt.de
bloomberg.com
clinton.presidentiallibraries.us
dassie2001.livejournal.com
data.worldbank.org
echo.msk.ru
gazeta.ru
interpretermag.com
intersectionproject.eu
lenta.ru
polit.ru
prezident.ru
ridl.io
ruleaks.net
Russkii WikiLeaks
skolesnikov.org
tass.com
unian.info
wikileaks.org
youtube.com

Periodicals

The Atlantic Monthly (Boston, MA)
Bild (Berlin)
Eurasia Daily Monitor (Jamestown)
Financial Times (London)
Foreign Affairs (New York)
Guardian (London)

Kommersant (Moscow)
Komsomolskaya pravda (Moscow)
Moskovskie novosti (Moscow)
Moskovskii komsomolets (Moscow)
New Statesman (London)
Nezavisimaya gazeta (Moscow)
New York Times (New York)
The New Yorker (New York)
Nouvel Observateur (Paris)
Novaya gazeta (Moscow)
Le Point (Paris)
Post-Soviet Affairs
Pravda (Moscow)
Rossiiskaya gazeta (Moscow)
Russkaya pravda (Kyiv)
Russkii Blok Sevastopolya (Sevastopol)
Sluzhba bezopasnosti (Moscow)
Time (New York)
Vedomosti (Moscow)
Washington Post (Washington DC)

Books and articles

A. Adamishin, *V raznye gody: vneshnepoliticheskie ocherki* (Ves' mir: Moscow, 2016)

D. Allan, 'Managed Confrontation: UK Policy Towards Russia After the Salisbury Attack', research paper, Chatham House, London, October 2018

R. Allison, 'Protective Integration and Security Policy Coordination: Comparing the SCO and CSTO', *Chinese Journal of International Relations*, no. 3 (2018)

———, 'Russia and the Post-2014 International Legal Order, Revisionism and Realpolitik', *International Affairs*, no. 3 (2017)

———, *Russia, the West and Military Intervention* (Oxford University Press: Oxford, 2013)

———, 'Russian "Deniable" Intervention in Ukraine, How and Why Russia Broke the Rules', *International Affairs*, no. 6 (2014)

A. Arutunyan, *The Putin Mystique: Inside Russia's Power Cult* (Skyscraper: Newbold on Stour, 2014)

A. Åslund, 'Sergei Glazyev and the Revival of Soviet Economics', *Post-Soviet Affairs*, no. 5 (2013)

R. D. Asmus, *A Little War that Shook the World: Georgia, Russia and the Future of the West* (Palgrave Macmillan: Basingstoke, 2010)

P. Aven (ed.), *Vremya Berezovskogo* (Korpus: Moscow, 2018)

H. Balzer, 'The Ukraine Invasion and Public Opinion', *Georgetown Journal of International Affairs*, no. 16/1 (2015), pp. 79–93

A. Barbashin, O. Irisova, F. Burkhardt and E. Wyciszkiewicz (eds), *A Successful Failure: Russia after Crime(a)* (Centre for Polish–Russian Dialogue and Understanding: Warsaw, 2017): http://intersectionproject.eu/sites/default/files/books/final_a_successful_failure_russia_after_crimea.pdf

A. Barbashin and H. Thoburn, 'Putin's Philosopher: Ivan Ilyin and the Ideology of Moscow's Rule', *Foreign Affairs*, 20 September 2015

S. Barsukova (ed.), *Reformy v Rossii v 2000-e gody: ot zakonodatel'stva k praktikam* (Vysshaya Shkola Ekonomiki: Moscow, 2016)

A. Baturo and J. Elkink, 'Dynamics of Regime Personalization and Patron-Client Networks in Russia, 1999–2014', *Post-Soviet Affairs*, no. 1 (2016)

S. Belkovskii and V. Golyshev, *Biznes Vladimira Putina* (Ultra-Kul'tura: Yekaterinburg, 2006)

M. Bennetts, *I'm Going to Ruin Their Lives: Inside Putin's War on Russia's Opposition*, extended edn (Oneworld: London, 2016)

M. Bodner, 'In Arms Trade, China is Taking Advantage of Russia's Desperation', *Moscow Times*, 1 November 2016

M. Boulègue, 'Five Things to Know About the Zapad-2017 Military Exercise', research paper, Chatham House, London, September 2017

R. Brooks, 'Looting with Putin', *Private Eye*, 5 October 2018

B. Browder, *Red Notice: How I Became Putin's No. 1 Enemy* (Bantam: London, 2015)

J. Browne, *Beyond Business: An Inspirational Memoir from a Visionary Leader* (Weidenfeld and Nicolson: London, 2010)

Z. Brzezinski, *The Grand Chessboard: American Primacy and Its Geostrategic Imperatives* (Basic Books: New York, 1997)

———, *Strategic Vision: America and the Crisis of Global Power* (Basic Books: New York, 2012)

O. Bullough, *Moneyland: Why Thieves and Crooks Now Rule the World and How to Take It Back* (Profile: London, 2018)

V. Bunce and A. Hozić, 'Diffusion-Proofing and the Russian Invasion of Ukraine', *Demokratizatsiya*, no. 4 (2016)

F. Burkhardt, 'Presidential Power in Putin's Third Term: Was Crimea a Critical Juncture in Domestic Politics?', in A. Barbashin, O. Irisova, F. Burkhardt and E. Wyciszkiewicz (eds), *A Successful Failure: Russia after Crime(a)* (Centre for Polish-Russian Dialogue and Understanding: Warsaw, 2017)

P. Chaisty, 'The Legislative Effects of Presidential Partisan Powers in Post-Communist Russia', *Government and Opposition*, no. 3 (2008)

P. Chaisty and S. Whitefield, 'Forward to Democracy or Backward to Authoritarianism? The Attitudinal Bases of Mass Support for the Russian Election Protests of 2011–2012', *Post-Soviet Affairs*, no. 29/5 (2013), pp. 387–403

S. Charap and T. J. Colton, *Everyone Loses: The Ukraine Crisis and the Ruinous Contest for Post-Soviet Eurasia* (Routledge: New York, 2016)

M. S. Chase, E. S. Medeiros, J. Stapleton Roy, E. B. Rumer, R. Sutter and R. Weitz, *Russia–China Relations: Assessing Common Ground and Strategic Fault Lines* (National Bureau of Asian Research, special report no. 66, July 2017)

A. Chelnokov, *Putinskii zastoi: Novoe Politbyuro Kremlya* (Yauza: Moscow, 2013)

D. Cheney and L. Cheney, *In My Time: A Personal and Political Memoir* (Simon and Schuster: New York, 2011)

H. R. Clinton, *Hard Choices: A Memoir* (Simon and Schuster: London 2014)

S. F. Cohen, *Soviet Fates and Lost Alternatives: From Stalinism to the New Cold War* (Columbia University Press: New York, 2011)

———, *War with Russia? From Putin and Ukraine to Trump and Russiagate* (Hot Books: New York, 2018)

R. Connolly, *Russia's Response to Sanctions: How Western Economic Statecraft is Reshaping Political Economy in Russia* (Cambridge University Press: Cambridge, 2018)

———, 'Troubled Times, Stagnation, Sanctions and the Prospects for Economic Reform in Russia', Chatham House research paper, London, February 2015

P. Conradi, *Who Lost Russia? How the World Entered a New Cold War* (Oneworld: London, 2017)

J. Cooper, 'The Development of Eurasian Economic Integration', in R. Dragneva and K. Wolczuk (eds), *Eurasian Economic Integration: Law, Policy and Politics* (Edward Elgar: Cheltenham, 2013)

E. Dąbrowska, 'The End of the Reserve Fund, the End of an Era', 4 April 2018: http://intersectionproject.eu/article/economy/end-reserve-fund-end-era

I. Danchenko and C. Gaddy, 'The Mystery of Vladimir Putin's Dissertation', The Brookings Institution, 30 March 2006: https://www.brookings.edu/wp-content/uploads/2012/09/Putin-Dissertation-Event-remarks-with-slides.pdf

C. Davis, 'The Ukraine Conflict, Economic-Military Power Balances and Economic Sanctions', *Post-Communist Economies*, no. 2 (2016)

K. Dawisha, *Putin's Kleptocracy: Who Owns Russia?* (Simon and Schuster: New York, 2014)

Defense Intelligence Agency [USA], *Russia Military Power: Building a Military to Support Great Power Aspirations* (Defense Intelligence Agency: Washington DC, 2017; available online at http://www.dia.mil/Military-Power-Publications)

R. Dragneva and K. Wolczuk, (eds), *Eurasian Economic Integration: Law, Policy and Politics* (Edward Elgar: Cheltenham, 2013)

———, 'The Eurasian Economic Union: Deals, Rules and the Exercise of Power', research paper, Chatham House, May 2017F.

Dragosei, *Stelle del Cremlino: L'Occidente deve temere la nuova Russia?* (Bompiano: Milan, 2009)

A. Dugin, *Chetvërtaya politicheskaya teoriya: Rossiya i politicheskie idei XXI veka* (Amfora: St Petersburg, 2009)

———, *Geopolitika* (Akademicheskii Proekt: Moscow, 2011)

———, *Putin vs Putin: Vladimir Putin Viewed from the Right* (Arktos Media: Budapest, 2014)

———, *Russkaya voina* (Algoritm: Moscow, 2015)

———, *Ukraina: moya voina. Geopoliticheskaya dnevnik* (Tsentropoligraf: Moscow, 2015)

J. B. Dunlop, *The Moscow Bombings of September 1999: Examinations of Russian Terrorist Attacks at the Onset of Vladimir Putin's Rule* (ibidem-Verlag: Stuttgart, 2012)

European Bank of Reconstruction and Development, *Transition Report 2009: Transition in Crisis* (EBRD: London, 2009)

A. B. Evans, Jr, 'Civil Society and Protest', in S. K. Wegren (ed.), *Return to Putin's Russia: Past Imperfect, Future Uncertain*, 5th edn (Rowman and Littlefield: Lanham, MD, 2013)

Federal State Statistical Service, *Russia In Figures* (Moscow, 2018)

J. Fedor, *Russia and the Cult of State Security: The Chekist Tradition, From Lenin to Putin* (Routledge: London, 2011)

P. Felgenhauer, 'Russia's Relations with the West Deteriorate as Military Prepares for "Resource Wars"', *Eurasia Daily Monitor*, 3 November 2016

N. Ferguson, 'In Decline, Russia is on Its Way to Global Irrelevance', *Newsweek*, 12 December 2011

A. Foxall, *Putin Sees and Hears It All: How Russia's Intelligence Agencies Menace the UK* (Henry Jackson Society: London, 2018)

T. Frye, S. Gehlbach, K. L. Marquardt and O. J. Reuter, 'Is Putin's Popularity Real?', *Post-Soviet Affairs*, no. 1 (2017)

Y. Fu, 'How China Sees Russia', *Foreign Affairs*, January/February 2016

A. Gabuev, 'Bol'she, da khuzhe. Kak Rossiya prevratila ShOS v klub bez interesov', Carnegie Center Moscow, 13 June 2017: http://carnegie.ru/commentary/71212

———, 'Friends With Benefits? Russian–Chinese Relations After the Ukraine Crisis', Carnegie Moscow Center, 29 June 2016: http://carnegie.ru/2016/06/29/friends-with-benefits-russian-chinese-relations-after-ukraine-crisis-pub-63953

———, 'Who's Afraid of Chinese Colonization?', Carnegie Moscow Center, 26 June 2015: http://carnegie.ru/ commentary/6051

G. Gaddy and B. Ickes, 'Ukraine: A Prize Neither Russia Nor the West Can Afford to Win', Brookings research article, 2014

M. Galeotti, 'Crimintern: How the Kremlin Uses Russia's Criminal Networks in Europe', *European Council on Foreign Relations Policy Brief*, April 2017

———, *The Vory: Russia's Super Mafia* (Yale University Press: New Haven, CT, 2018)

———, *We Need to Talk About Putin: Why the West Gets Him Wrong, and How to Get Him Right* (Ebury Press: London, 2019)

W. A. Galston, 'Dissecting Obama's Foreign Policy, America Self-Contained', *The American Interest*, no. 5 (May/June 2014)

R. M. Gates, *Duty: Memoirs of a Secretary at War* (Knopf: New York, 2014)

T. P. Gerber, 'Foreign Policy and the United States in Russian Public Opinion', *Problems of Post-Communism*, no. 2 (2015), pp. 98–111

M. Gessen, 'The Curious Case of the Television Star Running Against Vladimir Putin', *The New Yorker*, 12 February 2018

———, *The Future is History: How Totalitarianism Reclaimed Russia* (Granta: London, 2017)

G. Gill and J. Young (eds), *Routledge Handbook of Russian Politics and Society* (Routledge: London, 2012)

S. Glaz'ev, *Bitva za liderstvo v XXI veke: Rossiya-SShA-Kitai. Sem' variantov obozrimogo* (Knizhnyi mir: Moscow, 2017)

H. Goscillo (ed.), *Putin as Celebrity and Cultural Icon* (Routledge: London, 2013)

P. Gregory, 'Putin's Provocations Are Met With Ridicule in Ukraine', *The Hill*, 1 May 2019: https://thehill.com/opinion/international/441435-ridicule-is-a-sound-remedy-for-putins-provocations

H. E. Hale, 'The Myth of Mass Russian Support for Autocracy: The Public Opinion Foundations of a Hybrid Regime', *Europe-Asia Studies*, no. 8 (2011)

————, *Patronal Politics* (Cambridge University Press: Cambridge, 2014)

H. E. Hale, R. Sakwa and S. White, *Developments in Russian Politics* (Palgrave Macmillan: Basingstoke, 2018)

P. Hanson, 'Managing the Economy', in H. E. Hale, R. Sakwa and S. White, *Developments in Russian Politics* (Palgrave Macmillan: Basingstoke, 2018)

L. Harding, *Collusion: How Russia Helped Trump Win the White House* (Guardian Faber: London, 2017)

————, *Mafia State: How One Reporter Became an Enemy of the Brutal New Russia* (Guardian Books: London, 2011)

————, *A Very Expensive Poison: The Definitive Story of the Murder of Litvinenko and Russia's War with the West* (Guardian Books: London, 2016)

J. S. Henry, 'The Curious World of Donald Trump's Private Russian Connections', *The American Interest*, no. 4 (19 December 2016)

F. Hill and C. G. Gaddy, *Mr Putin: Operative in the Kremlin* (Brookings Institution: Washington DC, 2013)

G. Hosking, *Russia and the Russians: From Earliest Times to the Present Day* (Allen Lane: London, 2001)

House of Commons Foreign Affairs Committee, *Moscow's Gold: Russian Corruption in the UK* (House of Commons: London, 2018)

I. Il'in, *Filosofiya Gegelya kak uchenie o konkretnosti Boga i cheloveka* (Northwestern University Press: Evanston, IL, 2010)

M. Kantor, *Imperiya naiznanku: kogda zakonchitsya putinskaya Rossiya* (Algoritm: Moscow, 2015)

S. A. Karaganov, *Strategiya dlya Rossii: povestka dnya dlya prezidenta – 2000* (Sovet po inostrannoi i oboronnoi politike: Moscow, 2000)

V. Kara-Murza, 'After Years of Battling Nemtsov, the Kremlin Battles His Memory', *World Affairs*, 28 September 2017

————, 'Putin Unveils Memorial to Victims of Soviet Repression, While His Own Repression Continues', *World Affairs*, 30 October 2017

————, 'What Putin Isn't Learning from His Role Model, Czar Alexander III', *World Affairs*, 27 November 2017

E. Karasyuk, *Sberbank: The Rebirth of Russia's Financial Giant* (Glagoslav Publications: London, 2015)

S. Kardaś and I. Wiśniewska, 'The Ulyukaev Case: Tension Inside the Russian Elite', *OSW Commentary*, no. 255 (1 December 2017)

M. Kasyanov, *Bez Putina: politicheskie dialogi s Yevgeniem Kiselëvym* (Novaya gazeta: Moscow, 2009)

J. Kerry, *Every Day is Extra* (Simon and Schuster: New York, 2018)

S. Khazov, *'Spisok Magnitskogo': chego boitsya Putin* (Algoritm: Moscow, 2013)

A. Khinshtein and V. Medinskii, *Krizis* (Olma Media Grupp: Moscow, 2009)

V. Kirilenko, *Pravda pro NATO* (Nasha Ukraina: Kyiv, 2010)

H. Kissinger, 'To Settle the Ukraine Crisis, Start at the End', *Washington Post*, 14 March 2014

——, *World Order* (Penguin: New York, 2014)

A. Knight, *Orders to Kill: The Putin Regime and Political Murder* (Biteback: London, 2018)

——, *Spies Without Cloaks* (Princeton University Press: Princeton, NJ, 1996)

V. Kogan-Yasny, *Russia at the Crossroads and the Problems of Democracy* (RUDP Yabloko: Moscow, 2012)

A. Kolesnikov, *Prorab na galerakh: nablyudeniya zhurnalista iz-za stenki* (E: Moscow, 2017)

E. Korosteleva, 'The European Union and Russia', in D. Lane and V. Samokhvalov (eds), *The Eurasian Project and Europe: Regional Discontinuities and Geopolitics* (Palgrave Macmillan: Basingstoke, 2015)

V. Korovin, *Konets proekta 'Ukraina'* (Piter: Moscow, 2015)

A. Korzhakov, *Boris Yel'tsin, ot rassveta do zakata* (Interbuk: Moscow, 1997)

A. A. Kovalev and S. I. Levine, *Russia's Dead End: An Insider's Testimony from Gorbachev to Putin* (Potomac: New York, 2017)

S. Kremlëv, Yu. Nersesov, A. Burovskii, V. Dolgov and A. Raev, *Anti-Medinskii: oproverzhenie: kak partiya vlasti 'pravit' istoriyu* (Yauza-Press: Moscow, 2012)

Kremlin Echo: Three Views on Presidential Power, Law and the Economy; Interview with Andrei Illarionov, preface by Andrew Jack (Foreign Policy Centre: London, 2005)

R. Kupchinsky, 'The Strange Ties Between Semyon Mogilevich and Vladimir Putin', *Eurasia Daily Monitor*, 25 March 2009

V. Kuznechevskii, *Putin: kadrovaya politika* (Tsentropoligraf: Moscow, 2016)

D. Lane and V. Samokhvalov (eds), *The Eurasian Project and Europe: Regional Discontinuities and Geopolitics* (Palgrave Macmillan: Basingstoke, 2015)

S. V. Lavrov, *My – vezhlivye lyudi!: razmyshleniya o vneshnei politike* (Knizhnyi mir: Moscow, 2017)

A. Ledeneva, *Can Russia Modernize? Sistema, Power Networks and Informal Governance* (Cambridge University Press: Cambridge, 2013)

R. Legvold, *Return to Cold War* (Polity: London, 2016)

A. Lieven, 'The Dance of the Ghosts: A New Cold War with Russia Will Not Serve Western Interests', *Survival, Global Politics and Strategy*, no. 5 (2018)

A. Litvinenko, *LPG – Lubyanskaya Prestupnaya Gruppirovka. Ofitser FSB daët pokazaniya*, Interviews by Akram Murtazaev (Grani: New York, 2002)

B. Lo, *Axis of Convenience: Moscow, Beijing, and the New Geopolitics* (Royal Institute of International Affairs: London, 2008)

————, *A Wary Embrace: What the China–Russia Relationship Means for the World* (Penguin Random House Australia/Lowy Institute: Sydney, 2017)

B. Lo and L. Shevtsova, *A 21st Century Myth: Authoritarian Modernization in Russia and China* (Carnegie Moscow Center: Moscow, 2012)

E. Lucas, *Deception: Spies, Lies and How Russia Dupes the West* (Bloomsbury: London, 2012)

————, *The New Cold War: How the Kremlin Menaces both Russia and the West* (Bloomsbury: London, 2008)

R. Lyne, S. Talbott and K. Watanabe, *Engaging with Russia: The Next Phase. A Report to the Trilateral Commission* (The Trilateral Commission: Washington, Paris, Tokyo, 2006)

S. Malle, 'The All-Russia National Front – For Russia: A New Actor in the Political and Economic Landscape', *Post-Communist Economies*, no. 2 (2016)

V. I. Matvienko and S. E. Naryshkin (eds), *Neizvestnyi Primakov* (Airo-XXI: Moscow, 2016): vols. 1 (*Dokumenty*) and 2 (*Vospominaniya*)

V. Mau and Ya. I. Kuz'minov (eds), *Strategiya – 2020: Novaya model' rosta – novaya sotsial'naya politika*, vol. 1 (Delo: Moscow, 2013)

M. McFaul, *From Cold War to Hot Peace: An American Ambassador in Putin's Russia* (Houghton, Mifflin, Harcourt: New York, 2018)

————, *Russia's Unfinished Revolution: Political Change from Gorbachev to Putin* (Cornell University Press: Ithaca, NY, 2001)

J. J. Mearsheimer, 'Why the Ukraine Crisis is the West's Fault', *Foreign Affairs*, no. 5 (2015)

S. Medeiros and E. S. Chase, 'Chinese Perspectives on the Sino-Russian Relationship', in M. S. Chase, E. S. Medeiros, J. Stapleton Roy, E. B. Rumer, R. Sutter and R. Weitz, *Russia-China Relations: Assessing Common Ground and Strategic Fault Lines* (National Bureau of Asian Research, special report no. 66, July 2017)

V. Medinskii, *Osobennosti natsional'nogo piara: pravdivaya istoriya Rusi ot Ryurika do Petra* (Olma Media Grupp: Moscow, 2010)

————, *Voina, mify SSSR, 1939–1945* (Olma Media Grupp: Moscow, 2011)

S. Medvedev, *Park krymskogo perioda* (Individuum: Moscow, 2017)

A. Mel'nikov, *Ikh zvëzdnyi chas* (Rossiiskaya Ob"edinënnaya Demokraticheskaya Partiya 'Yabloko': Moscow, 2012)

R. Menon and E. Rumer, *Conflict in Ukraine: The Unwinding of the Post-Cold War World* (MIT Press: Cambridge, MA, 2015)

A. Michnik and A. Navalnyi, *Dialogi* (Novoe izdatel'stvo: Moscow, 2015)

A. Mikhailov, *Portret ministra v kontektse smutnogo vremeni: Sergei Stepashin* (Olma Press: Moscow, 2001)

C. Miller, *Putinomics: Power and Money in Resurgent Russia* (University of North Carolina Press: Chapel Hill, NC, 2018)

V. Milov, B. Nemtsov, V. Ryzhkov and O. Shorina (eds), *Nezavisimyi ekspertnyi doklad: Putin: korruptsiya*, vol. 2 (Partiya Narodnoi Svobody: Moscow, 2012)

Ye. Minchenko and K. Petrov, *Vladimir Putin's Big Government and the 'Politburo 2.0'* (Minchenko Consulting, 2012): http://minchenko.ru/netcat_files/File/Big%20Government%20and%20the%20Politburo%202_0.pdf

Ye. A. Mishina, *Dlinnye teni sovetskogo proshlogo* (Liberal'naya missiya: Moscow, 2014)

L. Mlechin, *Putin: Rossiya pered vyborom* (Piter: St Petersburg, 2012)

A. Monaghan, *Power in Modern Russia: Strategy and Mobilization* (Manchester University Press: Manchester, 2017)

A. A. Mukhin, *Kto est' mister Putin i kto s nim prishël? Dos'e na Prezidenta Rossii i ego spetssluzhby* (Gnom i D: Moscow, 2002)

A. Mukhin and A. Gafarova, *Naval'nyi: itogi* (Algoritm: Moscow, 2016)

A. A. Mukhin and Ya. Zdorovets, *Mikhail Kas'yanov: Moskovskii otvet 'Piterskim'* (Algoritm: Moscow, 2005)

S. L. Myers, *The New Tsar: The Rise and Reign of Vladimir Putin* (Simon and Schuster: London, 2015)

B. Nemtsov, *Ispoved' buntarya* (Partizan: Moscow, 2007)

B. Nemtsov and L. Martynyuk, *Nezavisimyi ekspertnyi doklad: Zimnyaya Olimpiada v subtropikakh* (Solidarnost'/RPR-Parnas: n.p., n.d.)

———, *Zhizn' raba na galerakh: Dvortsy, yakhty, avtomobili, samolëty i aksessuary* (n.p.: Moscow, 2012)

V. Nikonov, *Kod tsivilizatsii: chto zhdët Rossiyu v mire budushchego?* (E: Moscow, 2016)

———, *Sovremennyi mir i ego istoki* (Moscow University Press: Moscow, 2015)

B. Noble and E. Shulman, 'Not Just a Rubber Stamp, Parliament and Lawmaking', in D. Treisman (ed.), *The New Autocracy: Information, Politics, and Policy in Putin's Russia* (Brookings Institution: New York, 2018)

J. Norberg and F. Westerlund, 'Russia and Ukraine: Military-Strategic Options, and Possible Risks, for Moscow', RUFS Briefing no. 22 (April 2014)

A. Ostrovsky, *The Invention of Russia: The Journey from Gorbachev's Freedom to Putin's War* (Atlantic: London, 2015)

J. Ostrow (ed.), *The Consolidation of Dictatorship in Russia: An Inside View of the Demise of Democracy* (Praeger International: Westport, CT, 2007)

I. N. Panarin, *Russkii Krym i razval SShA* (Goryachaya liniya – Telekom: Moscow, 2016)

G. Pavlovskii (interview), 'Putin staraetsya, no on ustal', *Biznes Online*, 13 October 2017: https://www.business-gazeta.ru/article/360564

G. Pavlovsky, 'Putin's World Outlook: Interview With Tom Parfitt', *New Left Review*, July/August 2014

———, 'Russian Politics under Putin: The System Will Outlast the Master', *Foreign Affairs*, May–June 2016

R. Person, 'Potholes, Pensions, and Public Opinion: The Politics of Blame in Putin's Power Vertical', *Post-Soviet Affairs*, no. 5 (2015)

G. Petelin, 'Rossiyane stali sil'nee boyat'tsya yadernoi voiny', *Gazeta.ru*, 10 July 2015

T. Philips, *Beslan: The Tragedy of School No. 1* (Granta: London, 2007)

A. Piontkovskii, *Iskushenie Vladimira Putina* (Algoritm: Moscow, 2013)

P. Pomerantsev, *Nothing is True and Everything is Possible: Adventures in Modern Russia* (Faber and Faber: London, 2015)

V. V. Pribylovskii, *Vlast' – 2010: 60 biografii* (Tsentr 'Panorama': Moscow, 2010)

E. Primakov, *Blizhnii Vostok: na stsene i za kulisami* (Tsentropoligraf: Moscow, 2016)

————, *Gody v bol'shoi politike* (Sovershenno sekretno: Moscow, 1999)

————, *Rossiya: Nadezhdy i trevogi* (Tsentropoligraf: Moscow, 2015)

————, *Rossiya v sovremennom mire: proshloe, nastoyashchee, budushchee* (Tsentropoligraf: Moscow, 2018)

A. Prokhanov, *Chetyre tsveta Putina: kak Putinu obustroit' Rossiyu* (Algoritm: Moscow, 2013), pp. 220–2

A. K. Pushkov, *Putinskie kacheli: P. S. desyat' let v okruzhenii* (EKSMO-Algoritm: Moscow, 2009)

'Putin's Thesis (Raw Text)' (translated by Thomas Fennell), *The Atlantic*, 20 August 2008, pp. 1–17: https//www.theatlantic.com/daily-dish/archive/2008/08/putins-thesis-raw-text/212739/

P. Reddaway, *Russia's Domestic Security Wars: Putin's Use of Divide and Rule Against His Hardline Allies* (Palgrave Pivot: 2018)

J. Reuter, 'Regional Patrons and Hegemonic Party Electoral Performance in Russia', *Post-Soviet Affairs*, no. 2 (2013)

C. Rice, *Democracy: Stories from the Long Road to Freedom* (Twelve: New York, 2017)

————, *No Higher Honor: A Memoir of My Years in Washington* (Crown: New York, 2011)

B. Robertson, *The Politics of Protest in Hybrid Regimes: Managing Dissent in Post-Communist Russia* (Cambridge University Press: Cambridge, 2011)

N. Robinson, *Contemporary Russian Politics: An Introduction* (Polity: London, 2018)

C. Ross, 'Federalization and Defederalization in Russia', in G. Gill and J. Young (eds), *Routledge Handbook of Russian Politics and Society* (Routledge: London, 2012)

Rossiiskaya Ob"edinënnaya Demokraticheskaya Partiya 'Yabloko': politicheskii otchët. Dokumenty, 2008–2011 (Yabloko: Moscow, 2011)

Rossiya: metodologicheskie rekomendatsii po rabote s kartochkami dlya doshkol'nikov i mladshikh shkol'nikov (Karapuz: Moscow, 2016)

A. Roxburgh, *The Strongman: Vladimir Putin and the Struggle for Russia* (I. B. Tauris: London, 2012)

E. B. Rumer, 'Russia's China Policy: This Bear Hug Is Real', in M. S. Chase, E. S. Medeiros, J. Stapleton Roy, E. B. Rumer, R. Sutter and R. Weitz, *Russia–China Relations: Assessing Common Ground and Strategic Fault Lines* (National Bureau of Asian Research, special report no. 66, July 2017)

R. Sakwa, *Frontline Ukraine: Crisis in the Borderlands* (I. B. Tauris: London, 2016)

————, *Putin Redux: Power and Contradiction in Contemporary Russia* (Routledge: London, 2014)

————, *Russia Versus the West: The Post-Cold War Crisis of World Order* (Cambridge University Press: Cambridge, 2017)

R. Sakwa and P. Dutkiewicz (eds), *Eurasian Integration: the View from Within* (Routledge, Taylor and Francis: Abingdon, 2014)

S. Saradzhan, 'Is Russia Declining?', *Demokratizatsiya*, no. 3 (2016)

D. Satter, *The Less You Know, the Better You Sleep: Russia's Road to Terror and Dictatorship Under Yeltsin and Putin* (Yale University Press: New Haven, CT, 2016)

L. Savin, *Novye sposoby vedeniya voiny: kak Amerika stroit imperiyu* (Piter: St Petersburg, 2016)

J. Schubert, *New Eurasian Age: China's Silk Road and the EAEU in SCO Space*, Russian Economic Reform et al., August 2017: http://russianeconomicreform.ru/wp-content/uploads/2017/08/New-Eurasian-Age-with-Chinese-Silk-Road-and-EAEU-in-SCO-Space-Update.pdf

————, 'What Do Chinese Trade Investment People Think About Russia and Vice Versa?', Russian Economic Reform, 25 November 2014: http://russianeconomicreform.ru/2014/11/what-do-chinese-tradeinvestment-people-think-about-russia-and-vice-versa

I. Semenikhin, *Vladislav Surkov: Pro et Contra: Dialogi o suverennoi demokratii i istoricheskom vybore novoi Rossii* (SGU: Moscow, 2008)

V. Semënov, *Surkov i ego propaganda: fenomen glavnogo ideologa Kremlya* (Knizhnyi mir: Moscow, 2014)

R. Service, *The Penguin History of Modern Russia from Tsarism to the Twenty-First Century*, 4th edn (Penguin: London, 2015)

————, 'Putin's Czarist Folly', *New York Times*, 6 April 2014

————, *Russia and Its Islamic World* (Hoover Press: Stanford, CA, 2017)

————, *Russia: Experiment with a People* (Macmillan: London, 2002)

A. Shekhovtsev, *Russia and the Western Far Right: Tango Noir* (Routledge: London, 2018)

J. Sherr, *Hard Diplomacy and Soft Coercion* (Chatham House: London, 2013)

E. Shevardnadze, *Kogda rukhnul zheleznyi zanaves, vstrechi i vospominaniya* (Evropa: Moscow, 2009)

L. Shevtsova, 'Has The Russian System's Agony Begun?', *The American Interest*, 17 March 2016

————, *Lonely Power: Why Russia Has Failed to Become the West and the West is Weary of Russia* (Carnegie Endowment for International Peace: Washington DC, 2010)

————, *Russia – Lost in Transition: The Yeltsin and Putin Legacies* (Carnegie Endowment for International Peace: Washington DC, 2007)

R. Sikorski, *Polska może być lepsza* (Znak: Kraków, 2018)

M. Sixsmith, *The Litvinenko File: The Life and Death of a Russian Spy* (St Martin's Press: New York, 2007)

D. Skillen, *Freedom of Speech in Russia: Politics and Media from Gorbachev to Putin* (Routledge: London, 2016)

J. D. Smele, *The 'Russian' Civil Wars, 1916–1926: Ten Years That Shook the World* (Hurst and Co.: London, 2015)

T. Snyder, *The Road to Freedom: Russia, Europe, America* (Tim Duggan Books: New York, 2018)

A. Soldatov and I. Borogan, *The New Nobility: The Restoration of Russia's Security State and the Enduring Legacy of the KGB* (PublicAffairs: New York, 2010)

————, *The Red Web: The Kremlin's War on the Internet*, expanded edn (Public Affairs: New York, 2017)

————, 'Russia's Very Secret Services', *World Policy Journal*, no. 1 (2011)

O. Stone with V. Putin, *The Putin Interviews* (Hot Books: New York, 2017)

O. Stoun [O. Stone], *Interv'yu c Vladimirom Putinym: polnaya versiya* (Alpina: Moscow, 2017)

E. Strigin, *Vnedrenie v Kreml'* (Algoritm: Moscow, 2008)

V. Surkov, *Osnovnye tendentsii i perspektivy razvitiya sovremennoi Rossii* (SGU: Moscow, 2008)

D. Szakonyi, 'Governing Business: The State and Business in Russia', Foreign Policy Research Institute, 22 January 2018: https://www.fpri.org/wp-content/uploads/2018/01/Szakonyi-Final-Version.pdf

S. Talbott, *The Russia Hand: A Memoir of Presidential Diplomacy* (Random House: New York, 2002)

R. Taras, *Fear and the Making of Foreign Policy* (Edinburgh University Press: Edinburgh, 2015)

D. Taylor, *State Building in Putin's Russia: Policing and Coercion after Communism* (Cambridge: Cambridge University Press, 2011)

V. Tishkov, 'XXI vek priznaet prava bol'shinstva', *Russkii zhurnal*, 31 May 2011

D. Treisman (ed.), *The New Autocracy: Information, Politics, and Policy in Putin's Russia* (Brookings Institution: New York, 2018)

————, 'Why Putin Took Crimea: The Gambler in the Kremlin', *Foreign Affairs*, no 3 (2016)

D. Trenin, *Rossiya i mir v XXI veke* (E: Moscow, 2015)

P. Truscott, *Putin's Progress: A Biography of Russia's Enigmatic President, Vladimir Putin* (Simon and Schuster: London, 2004)

A. Tsygankov, 'Vladimir Putin's Last Stand: The Sources of Russia's Ukraine Policy', *Post-Soviet Affairs*, no. 4 (2015)

S. Udal'tsov, *Putin: vzglyad s Bolotnoi ploshchadi* (Algoritm: Moscow, 2012)

A. V. Ulyukaev: *V ozhidanii krizisa: khod i protivorechiya ekonomicheskikh reform v Rossii* (Strelets: Moscow, 1999)

M. van Herpen, *Putinism: The Rise of a Radical Right Regime in Russia* (Palgrave Macmillan: Basingstoke, 2013)

F. Varese, *The Russian Mafia: Private Protection in a New Market Economy* (Oxford University Press: Oxford, 2001)

V. Vasil'eva, *Aleksei Pichugin i pereput'ya: biograficheskii ocherk* (Human Rights Publishers: Moscow, 2011)

K. Voronkov, *Aleksei Naval'nyi: groza zhulikov i vorov* (Eksmo: Moscow, 2012)

J. M. Waller, *Secret Empire: The KGB in Russia Today* (Westview: Boulder, CO, 1994)

U. Walther, 'Russia's Failed Transformation: The Power of the KGB/FSB from Gorbachev to Putin', *International Journal of Intelligence and Counter-Intelligence*, no. 4 (2014)

J. R. Wedel, 'U.S. Assistance for Market Reforms, Foreign Aid Failures in Russia and the Former Soviet Bloc', *The Independent Review, A Journal of Political Economy*, no. 3 (2000), pp. 393–417

S. K. Wegren (ed.), *Return to Putin's Russia: Past Imperfect, Future Uncertain*, 5th edn (Rowman and Littlefield: Lanham, MD, 2013)

R. Weitz, 'Sino-Russian Security Ties', in M. S. Chase, E. S. Medeiros, J. Stapleton Roy, E. B. Rumer, R. Sutter and R. Weitz, *Russia–China Relations: Assessing Common Ground and Strategic Fault Lines* (National Bureau of Asian Research, special report no. 66, July 2017)

S. Wengle, 'The Domestic Effects of the Russian Food Embargo', *Demokratizatsiya*, no. 3 (2016)

———, 'Plentiful Harvests in Eurasia: Why Some Farms in Russia, Ukraine, Belarus, and Armenia are Thriving Despite Institutional Challenges', PONARS Policy Memo 490 (October 2017)

S. Wengle and M. Rasell, 'The Monetization of *L'goty*: Changing Patterns of Welfare Politics and Provision in Russia', *Europe-Asia Studies*, no. 5 (2008)

S. White (ed.), *Politics and the Ruling Group in Putin's Russia* (Palgrave Macmillan: Basingstoke, 2008)

S. White, R. Sakwa and H. E. Hale (eds), *Developments in Russian Politics* (Palgrave Macmillan: Basingstoke, 2010)

A. Wilson, *Ukraine Crisis* (Yale University Press: London, 2014)

———, *Virtual Politics, Faking Democracy in the Post-Soviet World* (Yale University Press: New Haven, CT, 2005)

A. Wood, 'Reflections on Russia and the West', Chatham House programme paper, 24 November 2008

T. Wood, *Without Putin: Money, Power and the Myths of the New Cold War* (Verso: London, 2018)

V. Yakunin, *The Treacherous Path* (Backbite: London, 2018)

I. Yashin, *A Threat to National Security*, Free Russian Foundation, 2016: http://www.4freerussia.org/wp-content/uploads/2016/03/A-Threat-to-National-Security.pdf

———, *Ulichnyi protest* (Galleya-Print: Moscow, 2005)

M. Zygar', *Vsya kremlëvskaya rat': kratkaya istoriya sovremennoi Rossii* (Intellektual'naya literatura: Moscow, 2016)

Notes

Introduction

1 For unconditionally hostile arguments about Putin, see K. Dawisha, *Putin's Kleptocracy: Who Owns Russia?*; E. Lucas, *The New Cold War: How the Kremlin Menaces both Russia and the West* and *Deception: Spies, Lies and How Russia Dupes the West*; A. Wilson, *Virtual Politics Faking Democracy in the Post-Soviet World* and *Ukraine Crisis*.

2 For anti-anti-Kremlin arguments, especially on foreign policy, see S. F. Cohen, *Soviet Fates and Lost Alternatives: From Stalinism to the New Cold War* and *War with Russia? From Putin and Ukraine to Trump and Russiagate*; R. Sakwa, *Putin Redux: Power and Contradiction in Contemporary Russia*, *Frontline Ukraine: Crisis in the Borderlands* and *Russia Versus the West: The Post-Cold War Crisis of World Order*; T. Wood, *Without Putin: Money, Power and the Myths of the New Cold War*.

Chapter 1: Father to the Nation: The Putin Cult

1 *Rossiya: metodologicheskie rekomendatsii po rabote s kartochkami dlya doshkol'nikov i mladshikh shkol'nikov.*

2 V. V. Putin, press conference (Hangzhou), 5 September 2016: http://kremlin.ru/catalog/countries/CN/events/52834

3 *The Putin Interviews*: Oliver Stone with Vladimir Putin, part 1 (12 June 2017): https://www.youtube.com/watch?v=QvlKSbYkTXI.

4 *The Putin Interviews* (book transcripts), p. 7.

5 Meeting of V. V. Putin and G. Zyuganov, 29 December 2015: http://kremlin.ru/catalog/persons/98/events/51030

6 *The Putin Interviews* (book transcripts), p. 11; V. V. Putin, interview with M. Kelly (NBC TV), 10 March 2018: http://kremlin.ru/events/president/news/57027; V. Yakunin, *The Treacherous Path*, p. 91.

7 V. V. Putin (interview), *Time*, 12 December 2007: http://kremlin.ru/events/president/transcripts/24735

8 V. V. Putin, remarks at the All-Russia Popular Front, 25 January 2016: http://kremlin.ru/events/president/news/51206

9 V. Yakunin, *The Treacherous Path*, p. 108.

10 V. V. Putin, interview with TASS, 24 November 2014: http://kremlin.ru/events/president/news/47054

11 V. V. Putin, visit to L. L. Matveev at home, 8 May 2017: http://kremlin.ru/events/president/news/54464

12 *The Putin Interviews*: Oliver Stone with Vladimir Putin, part 3 (14 June 2017): https://www.youtube.com/watch?v=QvlKSbYkTXI

13 *The Putin Interviews* (book transcripts), p. 87.

14 'Direct Line' multichannel TV interview with V. V. Putin, 15 June 2017: http://kremlin.ru/events/president/news/54790

15 V. V. Putin, interview with TASS, 24 November 2014: http://kremlin.ru/events/president/news/47054

16 'Direct Line' multichannel TV interview with V. V. Putin, 15 June 2017: http://kremlin.ru/events/president/news/54790

17 V. V. Putin, interview with TASS, 24 November 2014: http://kremlin.ru/events/president/news/47054

18 'Putin zhiv. Kreml' pokazal segodnyashnii photo prezidenta', *Korrespondent.net*, 13 March 2015.

19 *The Putin Interviews*: Oliver Stone with Vladimir Putin, part 2 (13 June 2017): https://www.youtube.com/watch?v=j01kF7UQr0Y

20 'Direct Line' multichannel TV interview with V. V. Putin, 14 April 2016: http://kremlin.ru/events/president/news/51716

21 A. Shamanska, 'Across Russia, a Scramble to Patch up Problems Aired in Putin Q&A', *RadioFreeEurope/Radio Liberty*, 15 April 2016.

22 *Izvestiya*, 22 October 2014.

23 V. V. Putin, Valdai International Discussion Club, 24 October 2014: http://kremlin.ru/events/president/news/46860

24 V. V. Putin, interview with TASS, 24 November 2014: http://kremlin.ru/events/president/news/47054

25 Ibid.

26 V. V. Putin, interview with TASS, 24 November 2014: http://kremlin.ru/events/president/news/47054

27 Valdai International Discussion Club, 24 October 2014: http://kremlin.ru/events/president/news/46860

28 *The Putin Interviews* (book transcripts), p. 21.

29 'Pokushavshiisya na Putina Osmaev rasskazal podrobnosti smerti svoei zheny', 31 October 2017: https://lenta.ru/news/2017/10/31/okueva

30 V. V. Putin, annual press conference, 14 December 2017: http://kremlin.ru/events/president/news/56378

31 K. Hille, 'Putin's Poll Rivals Gain a Platform But Cannot Win', *Financial Times*, 13 February 2018.

32 Candidates' debate, Rossiya-1 TV channel, 14 January 2018.

33 Luzhniki stadium pre-election rally, 3 March 2018: https://www.youtube.com/watch?v=caJso9aps14

34 V. V. Putin, presidential address to the Federal Assembly, 1 March 2018: http://kremlin.ru/events/president/news/56957

Chapter 2: Imagining Russia: A Vision for the Russians

1 V. V. Putin, presidential address to Federal Assembly, 25 April 2005: http://kremlin.ru/events/president/transcripts/22931

2 V. V. Putin, Valdai International Discussion Club, 19 September 2013: http://kremlin.ru/events/president/news/19243

3 V. V. Putin, annual presidential address to Federal Assembly, 12 December 2013: http://kremlin.ru/events/president/news/19825

4 Ibid.

5 Ibid.

6 V. V. Putin, presidential address to Federal Assembly, 25 April 2005: http://kremlin.ru/events/president/transcripts/22931

7 V. Putin, 'Rossiya, natsional'nyi vopros', Nezavisimaya gazeta, 23 January 2012.

8 V. V. Putin, Valdai International Discussion Club, 19 September 2013: http://kremlin.ru/events/president/news/19243

9 J. M. Barroso (interview with P. Spiegel), Financial Times, 4 November 2014.

10 V. Nikonov, Kod tsivilizatsii: chto zhdët Rossiyu v mire budushchego?, p. 618.

11 Ibid., pp. 282–3 and 301.

12 A. Dugin, Russkaya voina, pp. 53 and 260.

13 See A. Dugin, Chetvërtaya politicheskaya teoriya: Rossiya i politicheskie idei XXI veka, pp. 99–100, 112, 141 and 170.

14 Anna Nemtsova, 'Russia's Alt-Right Rasputin Says He's Steve Bannon's Ideological Soul Mate', The Daily Beast, 24 April 2017: http://www.thedailybeast.com/russias-alt-right-rasputin-says-hes-steve-bannons-ideological-soul-mate

15 V. V. Putin, presidential address to Federal Assembly, 25 April 2005: http://kremlin.ru/events/president/transcripts/22931

16 V. V. Putin, annual Moscow press conference, 23 December 2016: http://kremlin.ru/events/president/news/53573

17 C. Rice, No Higher Honor, p. 175.

18 The Putin Interviews: Oliver Stone with Vladimir Putin, part 1 (12 June 2017): https://www.youtube.com/watch?v=QvlKSbYkTXI

19 See T. Snyder, The Road to Freedom: Russia, Europe, America, p. 52.

20 The Putin Interviews: Oliver Stone with Vladimir Putin, part 2 (13 June 2017): https://www.youtube.com/watch?v=j01kF7UQr0Y

21 Ibid.

22 V. V. Putin, media interview, 19 January 2014: http://kremlin.ru/events/president/news/20080

23 V. V. Putin, Valdai International Discussion Club, 27 October 2016: http://kremlin.ru/events/president/news/53151

24 V. V. Putin, Valdai International Discussion Club, 24 October 2014: http://kremlin.ru/events/president/news/46860

25 V. V. Putin, Valdai International Discussion Club, 27 October 2016: http://kremlin.ru/events/president/news/53151

Chapter 3: Tsars, Commissars and After: The New Official Past

1 Confidential information to the author.
2 5 June 2007: http://kremlin.ru/events/president/news/40365
3 V. V. Putin, Valdai International Discussion Club, 19 September 2013: http://kremlin.ru/events/president/news/19243
4 V. V. Putin, annual presidential address to Federal Assembly, 12 December 2013: http://kremlin.ru/events/president/news/19825; V. V. Putin, annual presidential address to the Federal Assembly, 4 December 2014: http://kremlin.ru/events/president/news/47173
5 On Ilin's reinterment see S. Kishkovsky, 'Echoes of Civil War in Reburial of Russian', *New York Times*, 3 October 2005.
6 For a different interpretation, which postulates that Ilin has had an influence on Putin that predetermined his thinking and policies, see T. Snyder, *The Road to Freedom: Russia, Europe, America*, pp. 58–9.
7 V. V. Putin, Valdai International Discussion Club, 24 October 2014: http://kremlin.ru/events/president/news/46860
8 'Direct Line' multichannel TV interview with V. V. Putin, 16 April 2015: http://kremlin.ru/events/president/news/49261. Doubts have been expressed that Alexander III really spoke these words about the armed forces.
9 V. V. Putin, speech in the Livadia Palace park, 18 November 2017: http://kremlin.ru/events/president/news/56125
10 V. Kara-Murza, 'What Putin Isn't Learning from His Role Model, Czar Alexander III', World Affairs, 27 November 2017.
11 V. V. Putin, speech to State Duma, 5 October 2016: http://kremlin.ru/events/president/news/53027
12 V. V. Putin, annual presidential address to Federal Assembly, 12 December 2013: http://kremlin.ru/events/president/news/19825
13 V. V. Putin, annual presidential address to the Federal Assembly, 1 December 2016: http://kremlin.ru/events/president/transcripts/messages/53379
14 V. V. Putin, remarks at the All-Russia Popular Front, 25 January 2016: http://kremlin.ru/events/president/news/51206
15 Personal information given to the author at an FCO seminar, 9 February 2017.
16 V. V. Putin, remarks at the All-Russia Popular Front, 25 January 2016: http://kremlin.ru/events/president/news/51206
17 Ibid.
18 On the latest twist of fate of the White commanders, see J. D. Smele, *The 'Russian' Civil Wars, 1916–1926: Ten Years That Shook the World*, p. 239.
19 'Direct Line' multichannel TV interview with V. V. Putin, 25 April 2013: http://kremlin.ru/events/president/news/17976
20 'Direct Line' multichannel TV interview with V. V. Putin, 16 April 2015: http://kremlin.ru/events/president/news/49261
21 'Russia Unveils Controversial Yalta Monument Featuring Stalin', RFE/RL, 5 February 2015.

22 'Direct Line' multichannel TV interview with V. V. Putin, 16 April 2015: http://kremlin.ru/events/president/news/49261

23 'Direct Line' multichannel TV interview with V. V. Putin, 15 June 2017: http://kremlin.ru/events/president/news/54790

24 V. V. Putin, annual Moscow press conference, 23 December 2016: http://kremlin.ru/events/president/news/53573

25 *The Putin Interviews*: Oliver Stone with Vladimir Putin, part 4 (June 2017): https://www.youtube.com/watch?v=tMMakf1rvVM

26 V. Medinskii, *Osobennosti natsional'nogo piara, Pravdivaya istoriya Rusi ot Ryurika do Petra*.

27 S. Kremlëv, Yu. Nersesov, A. Burovskii, V. Dolgov and A. Raev, *Anti-Medinskii: oproverzhenie: kak partiya vlasti 'pravit' istoriyu*.

28 V. Medinskii, *Voina, mify SSSR, 1939–1945*, pp. 619–23.

29 V. V. Putin, remarks at the All-Russia Popular Front, 25 January 2016: http://kremlin.ru/events/president/news/51206

30 V. V. Putin (announcement), 15 February 2019: http://kremlin.ru/events/president/news/59843

31 V. V. Putin, presidential address to Federal Assembly: 25 April 2005: http://kremlin.ru/events/president/transcripts/22931. My thanks to Robin Milner-Gulland for emphasizing the specific context of Putin's remark.

32 V. V. Putin, Valdai International Discussion Club, 22 October 2015: http://kremlin.ru/events/president/news/50548. See also *The Putin Interviews*: Oliver Stone with Vladimir Putin, part 1 (16 June 2017): https://www.youtube.com/watch?v=QvlKSbYkTXI

33 V. V. Putin, presidential address to Federal Assembly, 25 April 2005: http://kremlin.ru/events/president/transcripts/22931

34 I owe this finding to my St Antony's and Hoover colleague Timothy Garton Ash, who met Putin in 1993. See his article 'Putin's Deadly Doctrine', *New York Times*, 18 July 2014.

35 See P. Goble, 'When a Western Leader Spoke the Truth Directly to Putin – and Putin Couldn't Take It', *Window on Eurasia – New Series*, 10 July 2017: http://windowoneurasia2.blogspot.com/2017/07/when-western-leader-spoke-truth.html. I owe this point to Neil Taylor.

36 V. V. Putin, presidential address to the Federal Assembly, 1 March 2018: http://kremlin.ru/events/president/news/56957

37 V. V. Putin (interview), *Time*, 12 December 2007: http://kremlin.ru/events/president/transcripts/24735. I have translated from the official Russian text because the magazine's text removes the crabbed language of Putin's words.

Chapter 4: Years of Hurt: Picturing National Humiliation

1 See A. Adamishin, *V raznye gody: vneshnepoliticheskie ocherki*, pp. 407–8.

2 Ibid.

3 V. V. Putin, Valdai International Discussion Club, 27 October 2016: http://kremlin.ru/events/president/news/53151

4 V. V. Putin, interview with TASS, 24 November 2014: http://kremlin.ru/events/president/news/47054

5 'Direct Line' multichannel TV interview with V. V. Putin, 16 April 2015: http://kremlin.ru/events/president/news/49261

6 V. V. Putin, Valdai International Discussion Club, 24 October 2014: http://kremlin.ru/events/president/news/46860

7 V. V. Putin, interview with *Bild* magazine, part 1, conducted on 5 January 2016 and printed on 11 January 2016: http://kremlin.ru/events/president/news/51154; V. V. Putin, interview with *Bild* magazine, part 2, conducted on 5 January 2016 and printed on 12 January 2016: http://kremlin.ru/events/president/news/51155

8 I am grateful to Roderic Lyne and Catherine Ashton for their emphatic information on this point. For the opposite viewpoint see T. Wood, *Without Putin: Money, Power and the Myths of the New Cold War*, p. 122.

9 Author's conversation with Toomas Hendrik Ilves, 1 August 2018 (Stanford).

10 Confidential communication to this book's author, 18 November 2017.

11 Author's conversation with Toomas Hendrik Ilves, 1 August 2018 (Stanford).

12 V. V. Putin, Valdai International Discussion Club, 24 October 2014: http://kremlin.ru/events/president/news/46860

13 S. Ivanov (interview): *Putin, Russia and the West: Taking Control* (producer N. Percy; BBC2, 19 January 2012).

14 V. V. Putin, presidential address, 4 September 2004: http://kremlin.ru/events/president/transcripts/22589. My thanks to Amir Weiner for discussing the wide-reaching importance of the Beslan outrage.

15 N. P. Patrushev (interview), *Sputnik International*, 1 November 2016: https://sputniknews.com/interviews/201611011046936463-patrushev-exclusive-interview/

16 V. V. Putin, Valdai International Discussion Club: 19 October 2017: http://kremlin.ru/events/president/news/55882

17 A. A. Kovalev and S. I. Levine, *Russia's Dead End: An Insider's Testimony from Gorbachev to Putin*, p. 308.

18 Ibid., p. 302.

19 S. Glaz'ev, *Bitva za liderstvo v XXI veke: Rossiya-SShA-Kitai. Sem' variantov obozrimogo*, pp. 82, 116 and 142.

20 Ibid., pp. 5 and 150.

21 Ibid., pp. 134–7.

22 See below, pp. 127–8.

23 M. McFaul, *From Cold War to Hot Peace: An American Ambassador in Putin's Russia*, pp. 106–7.

24 Ibid., p. 133.

25 See P. Conradi, *Who Lost Russia? How the World Entered a New Cold War*, p. 182.

26 V. V. Putin, Valdai International Discussion Club: 19 October 2017: http://kremlin.ru/events/president/news/55882

27 *The Putin Interviews*: Oliver Stone with Vladimir Putin, part 2 (13 June 2017): https://www.youtube.com/watch?v=j01kF7UQr0Y; The Putin Interviews: Oliver Stone with Vladimir Putin, part 1 (12 June 2017): https://www.youtube.com/watch?v=QvlKSbYkTXI

28 R. Lyne, S. Talbott and K. Watanabe, *Engaging with Russia: The Next Phase. A Report to the Trilateral Commission*, p. 112.

Chapter 5: Long Live Russia! Achievements and Prospects

1 M. Zygar', *Vsya kremlëvskaya rat': kratkaya istoriya sovremennoi Rossii*, p. 314.

2 V. Yakunin, *The Treacherous Path*, pp. 143–51.

3 M. Zygar', *Vsya kremlëvskaya rat': kratkaya istoriya sovremennoi Rossii*, p. 319; S. V. Lavrov, interview with *Komsomolskaya Pravda*, 31 May 2016; S. V. Lavrov, *My – vezhlivye lyudi: razmyshleniya o vneshnei politike*, pp. 170–2.

4 M. Zygar', *Vsya kremlëvskaya rat': kratkaya istoriya sovremennoi Rossii*, p. 320; A. Kolesnikov, 'Glavnaya noch' v Sochi', *Kommersant*, 7 February 2014.

5 'Tekstovaya translyatsiya *Novoi*' (online report), *Novaya gazeta*, 15 February 2014.

6 *Kommersant*, 16 February 2014.

7 See S. Medvedev, *Park krymskogo perioda*, pp. 187–9.

8 See A. Knight, *Orders to Kill: The Putin Regime and Political Murder*, pp. 262–3.

9 V. V. Putin, statement on the WADA report, 18 July 2017: http://kremlin.ru/events/president/news/52537

10 See B. Lo, *A Wary Embrace: What the China–Russia Relationship Means for the World*, p. 10.

11 Ibid.

12 E. M. Primakov, notes for meeting with V. V. Primakov, earlier than 3 September 2009: V. I. Matvienko and S. E. Naryshkin (eds), *Neizvestnyi Primakov*, vol. 1 (*Dokumenty*), p. 328.

13 Z. Brzezinski, *The Grand Chessboard: American Primacy and Its Geostrategic Imperatives*; Z. Brzezinski, *Strategic Vision: America and the Crisis of Global Power*; H. Kissinger, *World Order*.

14 V. V. Putin, speech at the 'Primakov Readings' International Forum, 30 November 2016: http://kremlin.ru/events/president/news/53361

15 *The Putin Interviews*: Oliver Stone with Vladimir Putin, part 2 (13 June 2017): https://www.youtube.com/watch?v=j01kF7UQr0Y

16 Ibid.

17 V. V. Putin, Valdai International Discussion Club: 19 October 2017: http://kremlin.ru/events/president/news/55882

18 *The Putin Interviews*: Oliver Stone with Vladimir Putin, part 3 (14 June 2017): https://www.youtube.com/watch?v=QvlKSbYkTXI

19 *The Putin Interviews* (book transcripts), p. 107.

20 Ibid., p. 112.

21 Ibid.

Chapter 6: Behind the Facade: Putin as Leader

1 See P. Reddaway, *Russia's Domestic Security Wars: Putin's Use of Divide and Rule Against His Hardline Allies*, p. 13.
2 *The Putin Interviews*: Oliver Stone with Vladimir Putin, part 3 (14 June 2017): https://www.youtube.com/watch?v=QvlKSbYkTXI
3 V. Yakunin, *The Treacherous Path*, p. 121.
4 G. Pavlovsky, 'Putin's World Outlook: Interview with Tom Parfitt', *New Left Review*, July/August 2014, p. 59.
5 Conversation between B. A. Berezovski and J. F. Collins (American embassy in Moscow), 5 February 1999: https://clinton.presidentiallibraries.us/items/show/36594
6 See the interview with former KGB Chairman L. Shebarshin, 'KGB idët vo vlast', *Vek*, no. 2 (2000).
7 *Sluzhba bezopasnosti*: Yu. M. Luzhkov, no. 3–4 (1998), p. 17 and V. A. Yakovlev, no. 5–6 (1998), p. 27. I am grateful to Amir Weiner for alerting me to the presence of this journal in the Hoover Institution Library.
8 V. I. Matvienko and S. E. Naryshkin (eds), *Neizvestnyi Primakov*, vol. 1 (*Dokumenty*), p. 362.
9 V. Yakunin, *The Treacherous Path*, pp. 88–9.
10 Conversation between B. A. Berezovski and J. F. Collins (American embassy in Moscow), 5 February 1999: https://clinton.presidentiallibraries.us/items/show/36594
11 Conversation between W. J. Clinton and B. N. Yeltsin, 20 June 1999 (Cologne): https://clinton.presidentiallibraries.us/items/show/16206
12 Meeting between Bill Clinton and Boris Yeltsin (Washington), 19 November 1999; phone conversation between them, 31 December 1999: https://clinton.presidentiallibraries.us/items/show/57569
13 See J. B. Dunlop, *The Moscow Bombings of September 1999: Examinations of Russian Terrorist Attacks at the Onset of Vladimir Putin's Rule*, pp. 35, 59–60, 62, 71 and 162. My thanks to John Dunlop for his advice on the onset of the war in Chechnya.
14 C. Rice, *Democracy: Stories from the Long Road to Freedom*, p. 124.
15 See chapters 9 and 10.
16 'Hacking at Defence', *International Herald Tribune*, 26 February 2013.
17 E. M. Primakov, *Rossiya: Nadezhdy i trevogi*, pp. 20–7 and 29.
18 M. McFaul, *From Cold War to Hot Peace*, pp. 225–7.
19 E. M. Primakov, *Rossiya: Nadezhdy i trevogi*, p. 30.
20 V. V. Putin, speech on a working visit to the Votkinsk missile factory, 21 March 2011: http://archive.premier.gov.ru/ru/events/news/1454/print/
21 G. Pavlovskii, 'Gosudarstvo Putina visit na voloske', *polit.ru*, 20 August 2012; M. McFaul, *From Cold War to Hot Peace*, p. 242.
22 Alexander Goldfarb (interview) in P. Aven (ed.), *Vremya Berezovskogo*, p. 553.
23 'Postanovil pered vyborami', *Vedomosti*, 13 July 2011; see the discussion by A. Arutunyan, *The Putin Mystique: Inside Russia's Power Cult*, note 161.

24 V. V. Putin, Q&A at the State Duma, November 1998: *Sluzhba bezopasnosti*, no. 1 (1999), pp. 32–3.

25 V. V. Putin, 'FSB protiv ekonomicheskikh prestuplenii', *Sluzhba bezopasnosti*, no. 1 (1999), p. 30.

26 V. V. Putin, Q&A at the State Duma, November 1998: *Sluzhba bezopasnosti*, no. 1 (1999), pp. 32–3.

27 Ibid.

28 M. Kasyanov, *Bez Putina: politicheskie dialogi s Yevgeniem Kiselëvym*, pp. 206–7. The suspicion has been raised that Putin plagiarized large parts of the text of his dissertation from the work of two American academics: see I. Danchenko and C. Gaddy, 'The Mystery of Vladimir Putin's Dissertation', The Brookings Institution, 30 March 2006: https://www.brookings.edu/wp-content/uploads/2012/09/Putin-Dissertation-Event-remarks-with-slides.pdf. I am assuming that even if Putin's authenticity as a writer is in doubt, he at least endorsed the argument of the dissertation. For a translation of the text see 'Putin's Thesis (Raw Text)' (translated by Thomas Fennell), *The Atlantic*, 20 August 2008, pp. 1–17: https://www.theatlantic.com/daily-dish/archive/2008/08/putins-thesis-raw-text/212739/

29 A. Roxburgh, *The Strongman: Vladimir Putin and the Struggle for Russia*, pp. 48–9.

30 A. Dubnov, 'Osoboe mnenie', *Ekho Moskvy*, 10 May 2017: http://echo.msk.ru/programs/personalno/1977880-echo

31 Ibid.

32 V. V. Putin, Valdai International Discussion Club, 22 October 2015: http://kremlin.ru/events/president/news/50548

33 Author's conversation with Michael McFaul, 9 August 2017 (Stanford, CA).

34 V. Yakunin, *The Treacherous Path*, p. 139.

35 G. W. Bush, *Decision Points*, p. 295.

36 I have this information from Timothy Nelson of the US State Department: 17 November 2017 (Washington DC).

37 G. W. Bush, *Decision Points*, p. 431.

38 *The Putin Interviews*: Oliver Stone with Vladimir Putin, part 3 (14 June 2017): https://www.youtube.com/watch?v=QvlKSbYkTXI

39 Author's conversation with Catherine Ashton, 20 February 2018.

40 G. Packer, 'The Quiet German', *New Yorker*, 1 December 2014.

41 *The Putin Interviews* (book transcripts), p. 23.

42 K. Gaaze and M. Fishman, 'Sluzhili dva tovarishcha', *Russkii Newsweek*, 24 December 2008.

43 V. V. Putin, press conference (Hangzhou), 5 September 2016: http://kremlin.ru/catalog/countries/CN/events/52834

44 See A. Ostrovsky, *The Invention of Russia: The Journey from Gorbachev's Freedom to Putin's War*, p. 247.

45 Meeting of V. V. Putin with 30 leading media figures, 18 January 2012: http://archive.premier.gov.ru/events/news/17798/print/

46 Author's conversation with Sir Roderic Lyne, 8 November 2017.

47 G. Pavlovsky, 'Putin's World Outlook: Interview with Tom Parfitt', *New Left Review*, July/August 2014, pp. 60–1. I heard similar accounts from diplomats about Putin's temporary depressed mental condition.

48 Oral information from Sir Roderic Lyne, 9 February 2017.

49 See A. Knight, 'Here's My President', *Times Literary Supplement*, 28 June 2017.

50 *The Putin Interviews*: Oliver Stone with Vladimir Putin, part 3 (14 June 2017): https://www.youtube.com/watch?v=QvlKSbYkTXI; O. Stoun [O. Stone], *Interv'yu c Vladimirom Putinym: polnaya versiya*, p. 211.

Chapter 7: Loyalty and Discipline: The Kremlin Team

1 C. Davis, 'The Ukraine Conflict, Economic-Military Power Balances and Economic Sanctions', *Post-Communist Economies*, no. 2 (2016), p. 176.

2 See R. Service, *The Penguin History of Modern Russia from Tsarism to the Twenty-First Century*, pp. xxxv, 235 and 252.

3 V. V. Cherkesov, 'Nevedomstvennye razmyshleniya o professii', *Komsomol'skaya Pravda*, 29 December 2004. On the struggle among the intelligence agencies, see P. Reddaway, *Russia's Domestic Security Wars: Putin's Use of Divide and Rule Against His Hardline Allies*, pp. 32–3.

4 'Tablo', *Zavtra*, 29 December 2006 reports a noisy meeting of veteran security officials where Putin was even accused of treason.

5 V. Yakunin, *The Treacherous Path*, p. 187.

6 Ibid., pp. 110 and 155.

7 Ibid., p. 177.

8 K. Gaaze and M. Fishman, 'Sluzhili dva tovarishcha', *Russkii Newsweek*, 24 December 2008.

9 Ibid.

10 Author's conversation with Michael McFaul, 9 August 2017 (Stanford, CA).

11 See below, pp. 183–4.

12 *The Putin Interviews*: Oliver Stone with Vladimir Putin, part 1 (12 June 2017): https://www.youtube.com/watch?v=QvlKSbYkTXI

13 V. Yakunin, *The Treacherous Path*, p. 18.

14 V. Milov, B. Nemtsov, V. Ryzhkov and O. Shorina (eds), *Nezavisimyi ekspertnyi doklad: Putin: korruptsiya*, vol. 2, p. 26.

15 M. Rostovskii, 'Gryzlova zamenit "mister obayanie"', *Moskovskii Komsomolets*, 18 December 2011.

16 A. Baturo and J. Elkink, 'Dynamics of Regime Personalization and Patron–Client Networks in Russia, 1999–2014', *Post-Soviet Affairs*, no. 1 (2016), pp. 88–9.

17 V. Yakunin recorded Kudrin's outburst in *The Treacherous Path*, p. 207.

18 M. Kasyanov, *Bez Putina: politicheskie dialogi s Yevgeniem Kiselëvym*, p. 125.

19 Ibid., pp. 122 and 126–7.

20 Ibid., pp. 128–9.

21 Ibid., pp. 130–1 and 132–3.

22 Ibid., p. 135.

23 Ibid., pp. 244–5.

24 Ibid., pp. 245–9.

25 Ibid., pp. 250.

26 Interview with A. L. Kudrin, *Novoe vremya*, no. 34 (1997).

27 See A. Chelnokov, *Putinskii zastoi: Novoe Politbyuro Kremlya*, p. 184.

28 'Kudrin Explains Decision to Resign', *Moscow Times*, 28 September 2011. For the background see R. Sakwa, *Putin Redux: Power and Contradiction in Contemporary Russia*, p. 114.

29 I am grateful to Carol Leonard and Ivan Lyubimov for information on the fate of Kudrin's report.

30 S. Glaz'ev, *Bitva za liderstvo v XXI veke: Rossiya-SShA-Kitai. Sem' variantov obozrimogo*, p. 119.

31 A. Åslund, 'Sergei Glazyev and the Revival of Soviet Economics', *Post-Soviet Affairs*, no. 5 (2013), pp. 376–8.

32 S. Glaz'ev, *Bitva za liderstvo v XXI veke: Rossiya-SShA-Kitai. Sem' variantov obozrimogo*, pp. 5–6 and 27.

33 Ibid., pp. 33, 35, 53, 67, 275 and 297–9.

34 Ibid., pp. 226 and 257.

35 See B. Lo and L. Shevtsova, *A 21st Century Myth: Authoritarian Modernization in Russia and China*, pp. 34–5.

36 A. Åslund, 'Sergei Glazyev and the Revival of Soviet Economics', *Post-Soviet Affairs*, no. 5 (2013), p. 379.

37 S. V. Lavrov, interview with *Komsomolskaya Pravda*, 31 May 2016; S. V. Lavrov, *My – vezhlivye lyudi: razmyshleniya o vneshnei politike*, pp. 170–2 and 176.

38 V. V. Putin, interview with Bloomberg TV, 5 September 2016: http://kremlin.ru/events/president/news/52830

39 'Vtoraya kholodnaya', *Rossiiskaya gazeta*, 15 October 2014.

40 Ibid.

41 Ibid.

42 S. A. Karaganov, *Strategiya dlya Rossii: povestka dnya dlya prezidenta – 2000*, p. 7.

43 Report by E. Surnachëva, 'V poiskakh mudrosti', *Kommersant Vlast'*, 20 January 2014.

44 V. Yu. Surkov, speech to the General Council of *Delovaya Rossiya*, 17 May 2005, reproduced in I. Semenikhin, *Vladislav Surkov: Pro et Contra: Dialogi o suverennoi demokratii i istoricheskom vybore novoi Rossii*, pp. 47–8.

Chapter 8: Life at the Top: No Embarrassment of Riches

1 See R. Service, *A History of Modern Russia from Nicholas II to Vladimir Putin*, p. 513.

2 S. Farolfi, L. Harding and S. Orphanides. 'Russian Oligarch Gets Cypriot Passport – and EU Citizenship', *Guardian*, 3 March 2018.

3 https://www.rt.com/business/russia-officials-foreign-assets-998

4 S. Grey, A. Kuzmin and E. Piper, *Reuters Investigates*, 10 November 2015: http://www.reuters.com/investigates/special-report/russia-capitalism-daughters

5 Declaration of Presidential income, 14 April 2017: http://kremlin.ru/events/security-council/54289

6 B. Nemtsov and L. Martynyuk, *Zhizn' raba na galerakh: Dvortsy, yakhty, avtomobili, samolëty i aksessuary*, p. 5.

7 Ibid, pp. 24 and 27.

8 Ibid, pp. 29–32.

9 S. V. Kolesnikov, open letter to D. A. Medvedev, 21 December 2010: http://skolesnikov.org/?page_id=92

10 S. Kolesnikov, 'Bor'ba s korruptsiei: prizrak dvortsa', *Vedomosti*, 25 April 2011.

11 S. Kolesnikov (interview by Tim Whewell), *Newsnight*, BBC1, 2 May 2012.

12 'Putin's Spokesman Dismisses Report of Palace on Black Sea', Sputnik International, 23 December 2010: https://sputniknews.com/russia/20101223161908045/

13 R. Oliphant, 'Friendly Oligarch Buys "Putin" Palace', *Moscow Times*, 3 March 2012.

14 A. Chelnokov, *Putinskii zastoi: Novoe Politbyuro Kremlya*, p. 7; V. Milov, B. Nemtsov, V. Ryzhkov and O. Shorina (eds), *Nezavisimyi ekspertnyi doklad: Putin: korruptsiya*, vol. 2, p. 20.

15 V. Milov, B. Nemtsov, V. Ryzhkov and O. Shorina (eds), *Nezavisimyi ekspertnyi doklad: Putin: korruptsiya, vol. 2*, pp. 19–25.

16 V. V. Putin, interview with TASS, 24 November 2014: http://kremlin.ru/events/president/news/47054

17 R. P. Spogli to the State Department and the White House, 26 January 2009: https://wikileaks.org/plusd/cables/09ROME97_a.html

18 P. di Caro, 'Berlusconi vola a festeggiare Putin: l'amicizia che resiste a governi e amori', *Corriere della Sera*, 7 October 2018. Present of a duvet with their handshake photo.

19 F. Dragosei, *Stelle del Cremlino: L'Occidente deve temere la nuova Russia?*, pp. 231–2.

20 S. Grey, A. Kuzmin and E. Piper, *Reuters Investigates*, 10 November 2015: http://www.reuters.com/investigates/special-report/russia-capitalism-daughters

21 V. Milov, B. Nemtsov, V. Ryzhkov and O. Shorina (eds), *Nezavisimyi ekspertnyi doklad: Putin: korruptsiya*, vol. 2, p. 27.

22 Ibid.

23 A. Navalnyi website, 9 December 2014: https://navalny.com/p/3954/

24 Fond Bor'by s Korruptsiei website, posted 15 September 2016: https://fbk.info/investigations/post/249

25 Fond Bor'by s Korruptsiei website, posted 15 September 2016: https://dimon.navalny.com/#rublevka

26 A. Navalnyi website, 27 March 2017: https://navalny.com/p/5306

27 A. Navalnyi presentation, 6 March 2018, 'Dvorets, na kotoryi zapreshcheno smotret": https://fbk.info/blog/post/408

28 V. Yakunin, *The Treacherous Path*, p. 89.

29 B. Nemtsov and L. Martynyuk, *Nezavisimyi ekspertnyi doklad: Zimnyaya Olimpiada v subtropikakh*, pp. 19–20.

30 N. Raibman, 'RZhD: Doklad Nemtsova pro Olimpiadu navredil reputatsiyu kompanii', *Vedomosti*, 10 October 2014.

31 V. V. Putin, interview with TASS, 24 November 2014: http://kremlin.ru/events/president/news/47054

32 'Direct Line' multichannel TV interview with V. V. Putin, 15 June 2017: http://kremlin.ru/events/president/news/54790

33 'Direct Line' multichannel TV interview with V. V. Putin, 15 June 2017: https://www.youtube.com/watch?v=kkQRF8YC--A

34 V. V. Putin, annual Moscow press conference, 23 December 2016: http://kremlin.ru/events/president/news/53573

35 Ibid.

36 'Sechin vyigral sud u "Vedomosti", i reshenie vstupilo v silu', *Vedomosti*, 18 November 2016.

37 E. M. Primakov, *Rossiya: nadezhdy i trevogi*, p. 26.

38 V. V. Putin, joint press conference with A. Merkel, 16 November 2012: http://kremlin.ru/events/president/transcripts/16852

39 M. Weiss, 'Corruption and Cover-Up in the Kremlin: The Anatoly Serdyukov Case', *The Atlantic Monthly*, 29 January 2013.

40 A. Sukhotin, 'Operatsiya "Vertikal"', *Novaya gazeta*, 18 August 2017.

41 O. Sapozhkov, 'Uvol'nenie nevolei', *Kommersant*, 30 December 2016.

42 See P. Reddaway, *Russia's Domestic Security Wars: Putin's Use of Divide and Rule Against His Hardline Allies*, p. 75.

43 O. Sapozhkov, 'Uvol'nenie nevolei', *Kommersant*, 30 December 2016.

44 See C. Miller, *Putinomics: Power and Money in Resurgent Russia*, p. 167.

45 A. V. Ulyukaev, *V ozhidanii krizisa: khod i protivorechiya ekonomicheskikh reform v Rossii*, pp. 163–4; V. Yakunin, *The Treacherous Path*, pp. 198–9.

46 A. Navalnyi, 'Ob Ulyukaeve: on na 100% zhulik, no sazhayut ego ne za eto', 15 November 2016: https://navalny.com/p/5131

47 K. Hille, 'Rosneft Chief Igor Sechin Refuses to Appear at Corruption Trial', *Financial Times*, 22 November 2017.

48 Twitter @aleksei_kudrin: 15 December 2017.

49 'Sechin nazval provokatsiei slukhi ob uchastii "Rosnefti" v obrushenii rublya', *Interfaks*, 16 December 2014: http://www.interfax.ru/business/413407

50 V. V. Putin, annual press conference, 14 December 2017: http://kremlin.ru/events/president/news/56378

Chapter 9: Economic Fist of State: Holding the 'Oligarchs' to Account

1 *Putin, Russia and the West: Taking Control* (producer N. Percy; BBC2, 19 January 2012).

2 See above, p. 71.

3 Interview with A. L. Kudrin, *Novoe vremya*, no. 34 (1997).

4 See above, p. 69.

5 See A. Arutunyan, *The Putin Mystique: Inside Russia's Power Cult*, p. 76.

6 United States Senate Judiciary Committee: interview of Glenn Simpson (Fusion GPS), 22 August 2017, pp. 46–7: https://www.feinstein.senate.gov/public/_cache/files/3/9/3974a291-ddbe-4525-9ed1-22bab43c05ae/934A35628 24CACA7BB4D915E97709D2F.simpson-transcript-redacted.pdf

7 Ibid., p. 161.

8 See S. Khazov, 'Spisok Magnitskogo'. *Chego boitsya Putin*, pp. 21–43; B. Browder, *Red Notice: How I Became Putin's No. 1 Enemy*, pp. 338–40.

9 Ibid., pp. 242–64.

10 V. V. Putin, Valdai International Discussion Club: 19 October 2017: http://kremlin.ru/events/president/news/55882

11 Yu. Felshtinskii (interview) in P. Aven (ed.), *Vremya Berezovskogo*, pp. 622–7.

12 I. Cobain, M. Taylor and (in Moscow) L. Harding, *Guardian*, 13 April 2007.

13 Ibid.

14 I was one of those witnesses, and can vividly recall the deliberate attempt that Berezovski, seated a few yards away and directly in front of the witness stand, made to stare down and intimidate witnesses.

15 B. Berezovski, open letter to Patriarch Kirill, 15 January 2012 (London): http://echo.msk.ru/blog/berezovski/849154-echo/

16 L. Harding, 'Humiliation for Boris Berezovsky in Battle of the Oligarchs', *Guardian*, 30 August 2012.

17 This evidence comes from P. Aven (pp. 22, 686), A. Goldfarb (p. 611), Ye. Gorbunova (pp. 644–5) and 'Darya K.', Berezovski's fiancée (p. 687) in P. Aven (ed.), *Vremya Berezovskogo*.

18 See P. Chaisty, *Legislative Politics and Economic Power in Russia*, pp. 126 and 136.

19 Vashukevich-Rybka was arrested in Thailand for prostitution. On release in January 2019 she flew to Belarus with a stopover at Moscow's Sheremetevo airport, where Russian police arrested her on a similar charge. She was released, reportedly on condition that she ceased to leak embarrassing information: '"Sex Trainer", Escort "Nastya Rybka", Released But Remains Suspect, Lawyer Says', RFE/RL, 22 January 2019.

20 A. Navalnyi, 'Yakhty, oligarkhi, devochki: okhotnitsa na muzhchin razoblachaet vzyatochnika', 8 February 2018: https://www.youtube.com/watch?v=RQZr2NgKPiU

21 Ibid.

22 'Vitse-prem'er Prikhod'ko zayavil o zhelanii otvetit' Naval'nomu po-muzhski',

RBK Politika, 9 February 2018: https://www.rbc.ru/politics/09/02/2018/5a7d-c6479a7947a4be81bebb

Chapter 10: Start and Stop Reforms: Perks for the Few, Costs for the Many

1 M. Kasyanov, *Bez Putina: politicheskie dialogi s Yevgeniem Kiselëvym*, pp. 127–8.
2 Ibid., p. 166.
3 Ibid.
4 Ibid., pp. 166–7.
5 Ibid., pp. 197–8.
6 Ibid.
7 See C. Miller, *Putinomics: Power and Money in Resurgent Russia*, pp. 47–8.
8 'Direct Line' multichannel TV interview with V. V. Putin, 25 April 2013: http://kremlin.ru/events/president/news/17976
9 *The Putin Interviews*: Oliver Stone with Vladimir Putin, part 3 (14 June 2017): https://www.youtube.com/watch?v=QvlKSbYkTXI
10 'Direct Line' multichannel TV interview with V. V. Putin, 25 April 2013: http://kremlin.ru/events/president/news/17976
11 V. Yakunin, *The Treacherous Path*, p. 177.
12 S. Glaz'ev, *Bitva za liderstvo v XXI veke: Rossiya-SShA-Kitai. Sem' variantov obozrimogo*, p. 204.
13 'Direct Line' multichannel TV interview with V. V. Putin, 25 April 2013: http://kremlin.ru/events/president/news/17976
14 P. Chaisty, 'The Legislative Effects of Presidential Partisan Powers in Post-Communist Russia', *Government and Opposition*, no. 3 (2008), pp. 446 and 449.
15 A. B. Evans Jr, 'Civil Society and Protest', in S. K. Wegren (ed.), *Return to Putin's Russia: Past Imperfect, Future Uncertain*, pp. 108–10; S. Wengle and M. Rasell, 'The Monetization of *L'goty*: Changing Patterns of Welfare Politics and Provision in Russia', *Europe-Asia Studies*, no. 5 (2008), p. 745; G. B. Robertson, *The Politics of Protest in Hybrid Regimes: Managing Dissent in Post-Communist Russia*, p. 187.
16 'Direct Line' multichannel TV interview with V. V. Putin, 25 April 2013: http://kremlin.ru/events/president/news/17976
17 Ibid.
18 *Kremlin Echo: Three Views on Presidential Power, Law and the Economy; Interview with Andrei Illarionov* (30 December 2004), p. 17.
19 'Putin: "K schast'yu, v VTO nas ne pustili"', 7 February 2009: https://www.pravda.ru/news/world/07-02-2009/301143-putin_barrozu-0
20 See S. Barsukova and C. Dufy, 'Doktrina prodovol'stvennoi bezopasnosti RF (2010 g.)', in S. Barsukova (ed.), *Reformy v Rossii v 2000-e gody: ot zakonodatel'stva k praktikam*, p. 37.

21 S. Wengle, 'Plentiful Harvests in Eurasia, Why Some Farms in Russia, Ukraine, Belarus, and Armenia are Thriving Despite Institutional Challenges', PONARS Policy Memo 490 (October 2017), pp. 6–7.

22 See S. Barsukova and C. Dufy, 'Doktrina prodovol'stvennoi bezopasnosti RF (2010 g.)', pp. 37–8.

23 *Kremlin Echo: Three Views on Presidential Power, Law and the Economy; Interview with Andrei Illarionov* (30 December 2004), pp. 16–17.

24 In Russian the names are 'Rezervnyi fond' and 'Fond natsional'nogo blagosostoyaniya'.

25 Ye. M. Primakov to N. P. Patrushev, 2010 (memo): V. I. Matvienko and S. E. Naryshkin (eds), *Neizvestnyi Primakov*, vol. 1 (*Dokumenty*), pp. 416–17, 418 and 420.

26 E. Dąbrowska, 'The End of the Reserve Fund, the End of an Era', 4 April 2018.

27 A. K. Pushkov, *Putinskie kacheli: P.S. desyat' let v okruzhenii*, p. 95.

28 See E. Dąbrowska, 'The End of the Reserve Fund, the End of an Era', 4 April 2018.

29 E. M. Primakov, *Rossiya: Nadezhdy i trevogi*, p. 115.

30 S. Glaz'ev, *Bitva za liderstvo v XXI veke: Rossiya-SShA-Kitai. Sem' variantov obozrimogo*, p. 273.

31 E. M. Primakov, *Rossiya: Nadezhdy i trevogi*, pp. 71–2.

32 See below, pp. 133–5.

33 European Bank of Reconstruction and Development, *Transition Report 2009: Transition in Crisis*, p. 27.

Chapter 11: Point of Decision: The Reaction to Revolution in Kyiv

1 *The Putin Interviews*: Oliver Stone with Vladimir Putin, part 3 (14 June 2017): https://www.youtube.com/watch?v=QvlKSbYkTXI

2 V. V. Putin, Valdai International Discussion Club: 19 October 2017: http://kremlin.ru/events/president/news/55882

3 E. M. Primakov, *Gody v bol'shoi politike*, p. 393. Please note, Primakov wrote this some years before the Crimean annexation

4 'Direct Line' multichannel TV interview with V. V. Putin, 25 April 2013: http://kremlin.ru/events/president/news/17976

5 V. V. Putin, Valdai International Discussion Club, 24 October 2014: http://kremlin.ru/events/president/news/46860

6 E. M. Primakov, *Gody v bol'shoi politike*, p. 393.

7 Russkii Blok programme, *Russkii Blok Sevastopolya*, no. 18, October 2010.

8 *Legendarnyi Sevastopol'*, no. 42, September 2010.

9 V. V. Putin, speech to Munich security conference, 10 February 2007: http://kremlin.ru/events/president/transcripts/24034

10 C. Rice, *No Higher Honor*, p. 683.

11 Ibid., p. 671.

12 W. J. Burns to US State Department (cable), 1 February 2008: https://wikileaks. org/plusd/cables/08MOSCOW265_a.html

13 C. Rice, *No Higher Honor*, pp. 671–2. I am grateful to Jean-Arthur Régibeau, Belgium's Moscow ambassador, for his exposition of the 2008 situation, 18 January 2018.

14 C. Rice, *No Higher Honor*, pp. 674–5.

15 R. Sikorski, *Polska może być lepsza*, p. 110.

16 Ibid., p. 111.

17 V. V. Putin, speech to the NATO Bucharest summit (2–4 April 2008): https:// www.unian.info/world/111033-text-of-putins-speech-at-nato-summit-bucharest-april-2-2008.html

18 R. Sikorski, *Polska może być lepsza*, pp. 111–12. I have used the Ukrainian publication of Putin's speech; see footnote 17 in this chapter.

19 R. Sikorski, *Polska może być lepsza*, p. 116.

20 J. M. Barroso (interview with P. Spiegel), *Financial Times*, 4 November 2014.

21 R. Sikorski, *Polska może być lepsza*, p. 25.

22 C. Rice, *No Higher Honor*, p. 532.

23 Ibid., pp. 685–6.

24 *The Putin Interviews*: Oliver Stone with Vladimir Putin, part 2 (13 June 2017): https://www.youtube.com/watch?v=j01kF7UQr0Y

25 See R. D. Asmus, *A Little War that Shook the World: Georgia, Russia and the Future of the West*, p. 5.

26 'Medvedev Gets Caught Telling the Truth', RFE/RL, 22 November 2011, http:// www.rferl. org/a/medvedev_gets_caught_telling_the_truth /24399004.html, accessed 19 April 2019.

27 See R. D. Asmus, *A Little War that Shook the World: Georgia, Russia and the Future of the West*, p. 201.

28 V. Jauvert, 'Histoire secrète d'un revirement, Sarko le Russe', *Nouvel Observateur*, 13 November 2008.

29 See R. D. Asmus, *A Little War that Shook the World: Georgia, Russia and the Future of the West*, pp. 212–14.

30 V. V. Putin, speech to the NATO Bucharest summit (2–4 April 2008): https:// www.unian.info/world/111033-text-of-putins-speech-at-nato-summit-bucharest-april-2-2008.html

31 V. V. Putin, interview with ARD TV, 29 August 2008: https://www.youtube. com/watch?v=30By6n3r_SQ

32 I owe this point to Paul Gregory.

33 'Sil'nyi Sevastopol' – Sil'naya Ukraina', 2010 flyer: Ukrainian Subject Collection, box 9.

34 A. Popova, 'Oligarkhi skupayut Krym', *Ponedel'nik*, 11 August 2003.

35 *Pervaya Krymskaya: informatsionnaya gazeta*, 5–11 November 2004: K. Bondarenko Papers (HIA), box 27.

36 R. Allison, 'Russian "Deniable" Intervention in Ukraine, How and Why Russia Broke the Rules', *International Affairs*, no. 6 (2014), p. 1270.

37 See P. Conradi, *Who Lost Russia?*, p. 262.

38 A. Roxburgh, 'Russia's Revenge: Why the West Will Never Understand the Kremlin', *New Statesman*, 27 March 2014.

39 *Russkaya Pravda* (Kyiv), no. 17, September 2010.

40 V. Kirilenko, *Pravda pro NATO*.

41 See C. Miller, *Putinomics: Power and Money in Resurgent Russia*, p. 144.

42 S. Lavrov, 'Russia–EU: Prospects for Partnership in the Changing World', *Journal of Common Market Studies Annual Review*, 14 August 2013: https://www.rusemb.org.uk/article/244

43 I. Shuvalov, 'Europe's Fear of Russia is a Rerun of Soviet Mistakes', *Financial Times*, 27 January 2014.

44 I. I. Shuvalov, public statement, 9 September 2013: http://www.interfax.com/newsinf.asp?id=442973

45 'Sergey Lavrov: The Interview', *National Interest*, 29 March 2017, p. 516.

46 J. M. Barroso (interview with P. Spiegel), *Financial Times*, 4 November 2014.

47 A. Tsygankov, 'Vladimir Putin's Last Stand: The Sources of Russia's Ukraine Policy', *Post-Soviet Affairs*, no. 4 (2015), p. 296.

48 'Sergey Lavrov: The Interview', *National Interest*, 29 March 2017.

49 *The Putin Interviews*: Oliver Stone with Vladimir Putin, part 3 (14 June 2017): https://www.youtube.com/watch?v=QvlKSbYkTXI

50 M. Zygar', *Vsya kremlëvskaya rat': kratkaya istoriya sovremennoi Rossii*, p. 337.

51 See H. Balzer, 'The Ukraine Invasion and Public Opinion', *Georgetown Journal of International Affairs*, no. 16/1 (2015), pp. 83–90.

52 See D. Treisman, 'Why Putin Took Crimea: The Gambler in the Kremlin', *Foreign Affairs*, no. 3 (2016), pp. 47–54.

53 V. V. Putin (press conference), 19 December 2013, 'Putin Denies That Troops Will Need to be Sent to Crimea': http://kremlin.ru/events/president/news/19859

54 *Novaya gazeta*, 24 February 2015.

55 J. R. Clapper (Director of National Intelligence), 'Statement for the Record: Worldwide Threat Assessment of the US Intelligence Community', United States Senate Select Committee on Intelligence, 29 January 2014, p. 24.

56 R. Sikorski, *Polska może być lepsza*, p. 29.

57 Ibid., pp. 32–3.

58 Agreement on the Ukrainian Political Crisis, Guardian (online), 21 February 2014: https://www.theguardian.com/world/2014/feb/21/agreement-on-the-settlement-of-crisis-in-ukraine-full-text

59 V. V. Putin, Valdai International Discussion Club, 24 October 2014: http://kremlin.ru/events/president/news/46860

60 Ibid.

61 Ibid.

Chapter 12: The Inseparable Peninsula:
The Annexation of Crimea

1 See http://kremlin.ru/events/president/news/20322
2 M. Zygar', *Vsya kremlëvskaya rat': kratkaya istoriya sovremennoi Rossii*, p. 336.
3 *Krym: put' na rodinu* (documentary film of Andrei Kondrashov), Rossiya-1 TV channel, 15 March 2015.
4 M. Zygar', *Vsya kremlëvskaya rat': kratkaya istoriya sovremennoi Rossii*, p. 336.
5 M. McFaul, *From Cold War to Hot Peace*, pp. 74–5.
6 M. McFaul, Elliott Lecture (St Antony's College, Oxford), 4 June 2018; M. McFaul, *From Cold War to Hot Peace*, p. 400; S. Rice: https://www.nbcnews.com/meet-the-press/meet-press-transcript-feb-23-2014-n36721
7 J. Heintz, 'Putin: Russia Prepared Raising Nuclear Readiness Over Crimea', Associated Press, 15 March 2015.
8 M. Zygar', *Vsya kremlëvskaya rat': kratkaya istoriya sovremennoi Rossii*, pp. 364–5; F. Burkhardt, 'Presidential Power in Putin's Third Term: Was Crimea a Critical Juncture in Domestic Politics?', in A. Barbashin, O. Irisova, F. Burkhardt and E. Wyciszkiewicz (eds), *A Successful Failure: Russia after Crime(a)*, p. 137.
9 See R. Allison, 'Russian "Deniable" Intervention in Ukraine, How and Why Russia Broke the Rules', *International Affairs*, no. 6 (2014), p. 1272.
10 Ibid., p. 1262.
11 S. V. Lavrov (press conference, Moscow), 26 January 2016 in S. V. Lavrov, *My – vezhlivye lyudi: razmyshleniya o vneshnei politike*, p. 37.
12 See R. Sakwa, *Frontline Ukraine: Crisis in the Borderlands*, p. 113.
13 See R. Allison, 'Russia and the Post-2014 International Legal Order: Revisionism and Realpolitik', *International Affairs*, no. 3 (2017), p. 531.
14 Ibid., p. 530.
15 O. Stoun [O. Stone], *Interv'yu c Vladimirom Putinym: polnaya versiya*, p. 94 (4 July 2015).
16 H. Kissinger, 'To Settle the Ukraine Crisis, Start at the End', *Washington Post*, 5 March 2014.
17 R. M. Gates, *Duty: Memoirs of a Secretary at War*, pp. 157–8.
18 V. V. Putin, Valdai International Discussion Club, 27 October 2016: http://kremlin.ru/events/president/news/53151
19 'Direct Line' multichannel TV interview with V. V. Putin, 17 April 2014: http://kremlin.ru/events/president/news/20796
20 I owe this insight to Paul Gregory.
21 A. Dugin, *Ukraina: moya voina. Geopoliticheskaya dnevnik*, p. 59 (7 March 2014).
22 See R. Sakwa, *Frontline Ukraine: Crisis in the Borderlands*, p. 196.
23 Ibid., p. 199.
24 YouTube. Cited by, Nicolai N. Petro, 'Timeline for Donbass Since the Signing of the Minsk Accords', unpublished paper. Nicolai N. Petro, https://www.youtube.com/watch?v=aHWHqj8g7Bk

25 http://vesti-ukr.com/strana/85885-poroshenko-ozvuchil-tri-beskompromissnyh-dlja-sebja-voprosa

26 V. V. Putin, Valdai International Discussion Club, 24 October 2014: http://kremlin.ru/events/president/news/46860

27 V. V. Putin, interview with TASS, 24 November 2014: http://kremlin.ru/events/president/news/47054

28 'Direct Line' multichannel TV interview with V. V. Putin, 16 April 2015: http://kremlin.ru/events/president/news/49261

29 V. V. Putin, Meeting with St Petersburg Mining University students, 26 January 2015: http://kremlin.ru/events/president/news/47519

30 V. V. Putin, interview with *Bild* magazine, part 1, conducted on 5 January 2016 and printed on 11 January 2016: http://kremlin.ru/events/president/news/51154

31 'Sergey Lavrov: The Interview', *National Interest*, 29 March 2017. See also Lavrov's interview with *Komsomol'skaya Pravda*, 31 May 2016: S. V. Lavrov, *My – vezhlivye lyudi: razmyshleniya o vneshnei politike*, p. 153.

32 L. Bershidsky, 'Russian Pensions Paid for Putin's Crimea Grab': https://www.bloomberg.com/opinion/articles/2014-06-26/russian-pensions-paid-for-putin-s-crimea-grab

33 M. Zygar', *Vsya kremlëvskaya rat': kratkaya istoriya sovremennoi Rossii*, p. 377.

34 G. Pavlovskii (interview), 'Putin staraetsya, no on ustal', *Biznes Online*, 13 October 2017: https://www.business-gazeta.ru/article/360564

35 V. V. Putin, annual presidential address to the Federal Assembly, 4 December 2014: http://kremlin.ru/events/president/news/47173

36 *The Putin Interviews*: Oliver Stone with Vladimir Putin, part 3 (14 June 2017): https://www.youtube.com/watch?v=QvlKSbYkTXI

37 'Vtoraya kholodnaya', *Rossiiskaya gazeta*, 15 October 2014.

38 N. P. Patrushev (interview), 'Voiny i miry', *Rossiiskaya gazeta*, 18 May 2017: https://rg.ru/2017/05/18/nikolaj-patrushev-ob-ukraine-i-ssha-kiberatakah-sirii.html

39 See R. Legvold, *Return to Cold War*, p. 137.

Chapter 13: Transatlantic Obsession: Troubles with America

1 J. Vinokur, 'Merkel is Dancing with a Bear', *New York Times*, 21 July 2011.

2 M. McFaul, *From Cold War to Hot Peace*, pp. 222–3.

3 N. von Twickel, 'Biden "Opposes" 3rd Putin Term', *Moscow Times*, 11 March 2011.

4 M. McFaul, *From Cold War to Hot Peace*, p. 262.

5 H. R. Clinton, remarks at Tolerance Centre (Vilnius), 6 December 2011: https://2009-2017.state.gov/secretary/20092013clinton/rm/2011/12/178313.htm

6 V. V. Putin, speech to Russian Popular Front's Coordinating Council, 8 December 2011: http://archive.premier.gov.ru/ru/events/news/17330/print/

7   H. R. Clinton, *Hard Choices: A Memoir*, p. 209.

8   V. Nuland, conversation with Ambassador Geoffrey Pyatt: https://www.youtube.com/watch?v=U0JVnYe7CzQ

9   *The Putin Interviews*: Oliver Stone with Vladimir Putin, part 1 (12 June 2017): https://www.youtube.com/watch?v=QvlKSbYkTXI

10 V. V. Putin (interview), *Le Figaro*, 31 May 2017: http://kremlin.ru/events/president/news/54638

11 *The Putin Interviews*: Oliver Stone with Vladimir Putin, part 2 (13 June 2017): https://www.youtube.com/watch?v=j01kF7UQr0Y

12 J. D. Goodman, 'Microphone Catches a Candid Obama', *New York Times*, 26 March 2012.

13 CNN interview with Wolf Blitzer, 26 March 2012: http://cnnpressroom.blogs.cnn.com/2012/03/26/romney-russia-is-our-number-one-geopolitical-foe/

14 J. McCain, 'Obama Has Made America Look Weak', *New York Times*, 15 March 2014.

15 'Wrestling with an Aging Arsenal', *New York Times*, 28 November 2014.

16 US Department of Defense Cyber Guard 16 Sheet, accessed 2 May 2016: https://www.defense.gov/Portals/1/features/2015/0415_cyber-strategy/Cyber-Guard-16-FactSheet-FINAL.pdf

17 W. J. Lynn, 'The End of the Military-Industrial Complex', *Foreign Affairs*, November/December 2014, p. 106.

18 W. A. Galston, 'Dissecting Obama's Foreign Policy, America Self-Contained', *The American Interest*, no. 5 (May/June 2014), p. 31.

19 NBC interview by Megyn Kelly, 2 June 2017: http://kremlin.ru/events/president/news/54688

20 *The Putin Interviews*: Oliver Stone with Vladimir Putin, part 1 (12 June 2017): https://www.youtube.com/watch?v=QvlKSbYkTXI

21 Author's conversation with Michael McFaul, 9 August 2017 (Stanford, CA).

22 *The Putin Interviews* (book transcripts), p. 39.

23 *The Putin Interviews*: Oliver Stone with Vladimir Putin, part 2 (13 June 2017): https://www.youtube.com/watch?v=j01kF7UQr0Y

24 Author's conversation with Michael McFaul, 9 August 2017 (Stanford, CA).

25 See below, pp. 239–40.

26 R. Sikorski, *Polska może być lepsza*, p. 99.

27 S. V. Lavrov, interview with *Komsomol'skaya Pravda*, 31 May 2016: S. V. Lavrov, *My – vezhlivye lyudi: razmyshleniya o vneshnei politike*, p. 160.

28 See, for example, S. V. Lavrov's lecture at General Staff Academy, 23 March 2017: ibid., p. 464.

29 H. Kissinger, 'To Settle the Ukraine Crisis, Start at the End', *Washington Post*, 5 March 2014.

30 V. V. Putin, meeting with H. Kissinger, 29 October 2013: http://kremlin.ru/events/president/news/19509

31 I have this information from State Department officials.

32 Author's conversation with Henry Kissinger in Washington DC, December 2017.

33 M. McFaul, 'To Beat Ukraine, Support Ukraine', *New York Times*, 8 August 2014.

34 S. V. Lavrov, Q&A in 'Government Hour' in State Duma, 25 January 2017: S. V. Lavrov, *My – vezhlivye lyudi: razmyshleniya o vneshnei politike*, p. 430.

35 V. V. Putin, interview with *Bild* magazine, part 2, conducted on 5 January 2016 and printed on 12 January 2016: http://kremlin.ru/events/president/news/51155

36 Ibid.

37 V. V. Putin, press conference, 18 December 2014: http://kremlin.ru/events/president/news/47250

38 Umberto Bacchi, 'Russia Issues Nuclear Threat over Crimea and Baltic States', *International Business Times*, 2 April 2015, in D. Satter, *The Less You Know, the Better You Sleep*, p. 163.

39 V. V. Putin, Valdai International Discussion Club, 24 October 2014: http://kremlin.ru/events/president/news/46860

40 Ibid.

41 N. P. Patrushev (interview), *Sputnik International*, 1 November 2016: https://sputniknews.com/interviews/201611011046936463-patrushev-exclusive-interview/

42 N. P. Patrushev (interview), *Moskovskii komsomolets*, 16 January 2016.

43 C. Cillizza, *Washington Post*, 6 September 2016.

Chapter 14: Continental Disruptions: Russia's Penetration of Europe

1 V. V. Putin, Valdai International Discussion Club, 22 October 2015: http://kremlin.ru/events/president/news/50548

2 O. Stoun [O. Stone], *Interv'yu c Vladimirom Putinym: polnaya versiya*, p. 58 (3 July 2015).

3 C. Rice, *No Higher Honor*, p. 530.

4 Ibid., p. 360.

5 V. V. Putin, interview with *Bild* magazine, part 1, conducted on 5 January 2016 and printed on 11 January 2016: http://kremlin.ru/events/president/news/51154

6 V. Yakunin, *The Treacherous Path*, p. 15.

7 M. Zygar', *Vsya kremlëvskaya rat': kratkaya istoriya sovremennoi Rossii*, p. 306.

8 F. A. Lukyanov, Valdai International Discussion Club: 19 October 2017: http://kremlin.ru/events/president/news/55882

9 E. Servettas, 'How to Avoid Sanctions Like Sergei Naryshkin', *The Interpreter*, 16 April 2014: http://www.interpretermag.com/how-to-avoid-sanctions-like-sergei-naryshkin

10 S. Naryshkin, 'Slabost' Bol'shoi Evropy', *Izvestiya*, 21 December 2015.

11 K. Willsher, 'France Looking for Warship Buyers After Cancelling Mistral Deal with Russia', *Guardian*, 5 August 2015.

12 O. Faye and B. Vitkine, 'La justice russe saisie sur le prêt bancaire consenti au Front National', *Le Monde*, 4 January 2017.

13 C. Bigg, 'French Far-Right Party Took Loan from Russian Bank', RFE/RL, 24 November 2014: https://www.rferl.org/a/russia-france-national-front-loan-le-pen/26707339.html

14 V. V. Putin and M. Le Pen (meeting), 24 March 2017: http://kremlin.ru/events/president/news/54102

15 Afternoon news item, *Rossiya-1* TV channel, 24 March 2017: https://www.1tv.ru/news/2017-03-24/322179-marin_le_pen_pribyla_s_vizitom_v_rossiyu_vstretilas_s_vladimirym_putinym_i_deputatami_gosdumy

16 V. V. Putin and M. Le Pen (meeting), 24 March 2017: http://kremlin.ru/events/president/news/54102

17 *Le Point*, 25 March 2017.

18 Ibid.

19 V. V. Putin, speech at the Katyn memorial meeting, 7 April 2010: https://dassie2001.livejournal.com/52206.html. This speech was once in the online record of Putin's statements as Prime Minister but has been taken down: a sign of subsequent official sensitivity about appearing concessive to neighbouring countries?

20 V. R. Medinskii, meeting of the 'Victory' organizational committee, 22 April 2017: http://kremlin.ru/events/president/transcripts/54347

21 Ye. Pismennaya and A. Andrianova, 'Russia's $70 Billion "Secret" Spending Lets Money Do the Talking', Bloomberg Politics, 25 July 2017: https://www.bloomberg.com/news/articles/2017-07-25/russia-s-70-billion-secret-spending-lets-money-do-the-talking

22 K. Than, 'Inside Hungary's $10.8 Billion Nuclear Deal with Russia', Reuters World News, 30 March 2015: https://www.reuters.com/article/us-russia-europe-hungary-specialreport/special-report-inside-hungarys-10-8-billion-nuclear-deal-with-russia-idUSKBN0MQ0MP20150330

23 *Financial Times*, 2 February 2017.

24 V. V. Putin, interview with *Bild* magazine, part 1, conducted on 5 January 2016 and printed on 11 January 2016: http://kremlin.ru/events/president/news/51154

25 V. V. Putin, press conference (Hangzhou), 5 September 2016: http://kremlin.ru/catalog/countries/CN/events/52834

26 M. Birnbaum, 'We Still Don't Know Who Will Lead Italy. But One Clear Winner is the Kremlin', *Washington Post*, 23 March 2018.

27 See A. Shekhovtsev, *Russia and the Western Far Right: Tango Noir*, pp. 187–9.

Chapter 15: Political Order: Parties, Elections, Parliaments

1 R. Person, 'Potholes, Pensions, and Public Opinion: The Politics of Blame in Putin's Power Vertical', *Post-Soviet Affairs*, no. 5 (2015), pp. 441.

2 See P. Chaisty, *Legislative Politics and Economic Power in Russia*, pp. 193–7.

3 See A. Wilson, *Virtual Politics: Faking Democracy in the Post-Soviet World*, pp. 260–5.

4 D. Orlov, 'Politicheskaya doktrina suverennoi demokratii', *Izvestiya*, 30 November 2006.

5 See V. Semënov, *Surkov i ego propaganda: fenomen glavnogo ideologa Kremlya*, pp. 89–90.

6 Ibid., p. 89.

7 'Prais-list loyal'nosti', *Novaya gazeta*, 12 April 2007.

8 See above, p. 55.

9 G. Pavlovsky, 'Putin's World Outlook: Interview with Tom Parfitt', *New Left Review*, July/August 2014, p. 57.

10 Ibid., p. 61.

11 Ibid.

12 C. Rice, *No Higher Honor*, p. 360.

13 See P. Chaisty, *Legislative Politics and Economic Power in Russia*, p. 127.

14 See B. Noble and E. Shulman, 'Not Just a Rubber Stamp, Parliament and Lawmaking' in D. Treisman (ed.), *The New Autocracy: Information, Politics, and Policy in Putin's Russia*, pp. 58 and 62–3.

15 See V. Semënov, *Surkov i ego propaganda: fenomen glavnogo ideologa Kremlya*, p. 105.

16 B. Noble and E. Shulman, 'Not Just a Rubber Stamp, Parliament and Lawmaking' in D. Treisman (ed.), *The New Autocracy: Information, Politics, and Policy in Putin's Russia*, pp. 54–6; M. Bennetts, *I'm Going to Ruin Their Lives: Inside Putin's War on Russia's Opposition*, p. 156.

17 D. A. Medvedev, report to the State Duma on governmental activity in the years 2012–2017 (11 April 2018): government.ru/news/32246

18 'Legislation to Limit Garlic Use', *Moscow Times*, 2 April 2013.

19 G. Pavlovskii (interview), 3 May 2018: https://newtimes.ru/articles/detail/160874

20 See V. Semënov, *Surkov i ego propaganda: fenomen glavnogo ideologa Kremlya*, p. 213.

21 V. V. Putin, Activities' Forum of the All-Russia Popular Front, 18 November 2014: http://kremlin.ru/events/president/news/47036

22 V. V. Putin, interview with TASS, 24 November 2014: http://kremlin.ru/events/president/news/47054

23 Ibid.

24 See D. Skillen, *Freedom of Speech in Russia: Politics and Media from Gorbachev to Putin*, pp. 317–18.

25 See L. Harding, *Mafia State: How One Reporter Became an Enemy of the Brutal New Russia*; K. Dawisha, *Putin's Kleptocracy: Who Owns Russia?*

26 P. Reddaway, *Russia's Domestic Security Wars: Putin's Use of Divide and Rule Against His Hardline Allies*, p. 14.

27 V. V. Putin, annual press conference, 14 December 2017: http://kremlin.ru/events/president/news/56378

Chapter 16: Media Pressures: TV, Press and the Internet

1 O. Stoun [O. Stone], *Interv'yu c Vladimirom Putinym: polnaya versiya*, p. 28 (3 July 2015).
2 See D. Skillen, *Freedom of Speech in Russia: Politics and Media from Gorbachev to Putin*, p. 295.
3 A. Dubnov, 'Osoboe mnenie', *Ekho Moskvy*, 10 May 2017: http://echo.msk.ru/programs/personalno/1977880-echo
4 See above, p. 25.
5 Meeting of V. V. Putin with 30 leading media figures, 18 January 2012: http://archive.premier.gov.ru/events/news/17798/print/
6 Ibid.
7 See D. Skillen, *Freedom of Speech in Russia: Politics and Media from Gorbachev to Putin*, p. 311.
8 Ibid., p. 307.
9 Ibid., p. 310.
10 Ibid., p. 70.
11 D. K. Kiselëv, 'Vesti nedeli', Rossiya-1 TV channel, 10 August 2013: www.youtube.com/watch?v=4KGVUhdqsMQ
12 See D. Skillen, *Freedom of Speech in Russia: Politics and Media from Gorbachev to Putin*, p. 70.
13 A. K. Pushkov, *Putinskie kacheli: P.S. desyat' let v okruzhenii*, p. 16.
14 https://in.reuters.com/video/2018/01/19/putin-strips-off-takes-dip-in-icy-waters?videoId=387166500
15 See http://kremlin.ru/events/president/news/53211
16 See D. Skillen, *Freedom of Speech in Russia: Politics and Media from Gorbachev to Putin*, p. 307.
17 Ibid., p. 332.
18 Ibid., p. 287.
19 'Doktrina informatsionnoi bezopasnosti Rossiiskoi Federatsii', *Rossiiskaya gazeta*, 6 December 2017: https://rg.ru/2016/12/06/doktrina-infobezopasnost-site-dok.html
20 See A. Soldatov and I. Borogan, *The Red Web: The Kremlin's War on the Internet*, p. 264.
21 V. V. Putin, Mediaforum plenary session, 24 April 2014: http://kremlin.ru/events/president/news/20858
22 M. Elder, 'Russia Threatens to Ban BuzzFfeed', 5 December 2014: https://www.buzzfeed.com/miriamelder/russia-threatens-to-ban-buzzfeed?utm_term=.kj2kl4GdwV#.luzW3k1e0Y
23 See A. Soldatov and I. Borogan, *The Red Web: The Kremlin's War on the Internet*, p. 272.
24 Ibid., p. 216.
25 Ibid., pp. 234–5.
26 Ibid., pp. 209–10.
27 Ibid., p. 211.

28 Ibid., p. 215.

29 'Russian Internet-Isolation Bill Advances, Despite Doubts in Duma', RFE/RL, 12 February 2019: https://www.rferl.org/a/russian-bill-on-autonomous-operation-of-internet-advances-in-duma/29765882.html

30 See V. Semënov, *Surkov i ego propaganda: fenomen glavnogo ideologa Kremlya*, p. 109.

31 I. Nagornykh, I. Safronov and Ye. Chernenko, 'S "tsvetnykh revolyutsii" khotyat snyat' kamuflyazh', *Kommersant*, 4 March 2015.

Chapter 17: Russian Soft Power: Global Charm Offensive

1 A. Roxburgh, *The Strongman: Vladimir Putin and the Struggle for Russia*, pp. xi–xii.

2 V. V. Putin, 'A Plea for Caution from Russia', *New York Times*, 12 September 2013.

3 Ibid.

4 A. Roxburgh, *The Strongman: Vladimir Putin and the Struggle for Russia*, pp. xii and 184–5.

5 Ibid., p. 185.

6 Ibid., p. 186.

7 Ibid., p. 190.

8 Ibid., pp. xii and 184–5.

9 I. Kottasova, 'Putin Drops His American PR Company', CNNMoney, 12 March 2015: https://money.cnn.com/2015/03/12/media/russia-putin-pr-ketchum/index.html

10 V. V. Putin, Valdai International Discussion Club, 27 October 2016: http://kremlin.ru/events/president/news/53151

11 V. V. Putin, Valdai International Discussion Club, 24 October 2014: http://kremlin.ru/events/president/news/46860

12 '"Valdai" prinyal zhelaemoe za deistvitel'nym', *Moskovskii komsomolets*, 13 November 2011.

13 Ibid.

14 V. V. Putin, Valdai International Discussion Club, 24 October 2014: http://kremlin.ru/events/president/news/46860

15 Ibid.

16 A. Roxburgh, *The Strongman: Vladimir Putin and the Struggle for Russia*, p. 195.

17 V. V. Putin, Valdai International Discussion Club, 24 October 2014: http://kremlin.ru/events/president/news/46860

18 A. Roxburgh, *The Strongman: Vladimir Putin and the Struggle for Russia*, p. 195.

19 R. Gray, 'Pro-Putin Think Tank Based in New York Shuts Down', BuzzFeed News, 30 June 2015: https://www.buzzfeednews.com/article/rosiegray/pro-putin-think-tank-based-in-new-york-shuts-down

20 M. Simonyan (Russia Today), meeting of the 'Victory' organizational committee, 22 April 2017: http://kremlin.ru/events/president/transcripts/54347

21 V. V. Putin, Valdai International Discussion Club, 27 October 2016: http://kremlin.ru/events/president/news/53151

22 J. Stubbs and G. Gibson, 'Russia's RT America Registers as "Foreign Agent" in U.S.', *Reuters*, 13 November 2017: https://www.reuters.com/article/us-russia-usa-media-restrictions-rt/russias-rt-america-registers-as-foreign-agent-in-u-s-idUSKBN1DD25B

23 P. Nikolskaya and A. Osborn, 'Russia to Amend Law to Classify U.S. Media "Foreign Agents"', *Reuters*, 10 November 2017: http://www.reuters.com/article/us-russia-usa-media-restrictions/russia-to-amend-law-to-classify-us-media-foreign-agents-idUSKBN1DA1HH

24 See the discussion in https://trendjackers.com/russia-today-provocative-adverts-london-underground/. I am grateful to Liz Teague for drawing this to my attention

25 Personal observation, Sheremetevo airport, 19 January 2018.

26 *The Putin Interviews*: Oliver Stone with Vladimir Putin, part 4 (June 2017): https://www.youtube.com/watch?v=tMMakf1rvVM

27 *The Putin Interviews*: Oliver Stone with Vladimir Putin, part 1 (16 June 2017): https://www.youtube.com/watch?v=QvlKSbYkTXI

Chapter 18: Public Opinion: The Potential for Unrest

1 See G. Hosking, *Russia and the Russians: From Earliest Times to the Present Day*; A. Ledeneva, *Can Russia Modernise? Sistema, Power Networks and Informal Governance*; R. Service, *Russia: Experiment with a People*, pp. 84–5 and 92.

2 'Direct Line' multichannel TV interview with V. V. Putin, 16 April 2015: http://kremlin.ru/events/president/news/49261

3 T. Frye, S. Gehlbach, K. L. Marquardt and O. J. Reuter, 'Is Putin's Popularity Real?', *Post-Soviet Affairs*, no. 1 (2017), pp. 8–15.

4 Levada Centre survey, 8 May 2018: https://www.levada.ru/en/2018/05/08/societal-problems. The survey was conducted on 19–23 January 2018 with the question: 'Which of the Following Societal Problems Worry You Most of All and Seem Most Severe to You?'

5 Levada Centre survey, 21 April 2017, https://www.levada.ru/en/2017/04/21/corruption. The survey was conducted between 2 and 7 March 2017

6 Levada Centre survey, 8 May 2018: https://www.levada.ru/en/2018/05/08/societal-problems. The survey was conducted on 19–23 January 2018 with the question: 'Which of the Following Societal Problems Worry You Most of All and Seem Most Severe to You?'

7 www.kremlin.ru/acts/bank/35260 through to 35270

8 Cabinet meeting, 12 September 2013: http://government.ru/news/4804. See

also A. Monaghan, *Power in Modern Russia: Strategy and Mobilisation*, pp. 61–2.

9   Levada Centre, November 2018: https://www.levada.ru/indikatory/odobrenie-organov-vlasti

10 VTsIOM survey, 8 February 2018, no. 2036: https://wciom.com/index.php?id=61&uid=1498. This survey was conducted between 29 January and 4 February 2018.

11 Levada Centre survey, 2 December 2016: https://www.levada.ru/en/2016/12/02/sanctions-4/

12 G. Petelin, 'Rossiyane stali sil'nee boyat'sya yadernoi voiny', *Gazeta.ru*, 10 July 2015.

13 A. L. Kudrin, 'Ustoichivyi ekonomicheskii rost: model' dlya Rossii', Gaidar Forum, 13 January 2017.

14 Federal State Statistical Service, *Russia in Figures*, p. 119.

15 See C. Miller, *Putinomics: Power and Money in Resurgent Russia*, p. 102.

16 Interview with M. A. Topilin, *Izvestiya*, 25 June 2018.

17 Levada Centre poll, 22–26 June 2018: https://www.levada.ru/2018/07/03/doverie-politikam

18 VTsIOM poll, 5 August 2018: https://wciom.ru/news/ratings/doverie_politikam

19 Levada Centre poll, 18–24 October 2018: https://www.levada.ru/2018/11/22/19281

20 VTsIOM poll, 5 August 2018: 'Ratings of State Institutions'.

21 VTsIOM poll, 5 August 2018: 'Electoral Rating of Political Parties'.

22 Levada Centre poll, 18–24 October 2018: https://www.levada.ru/2018/11/22/19281

23 E. Paneyakh, 'V Rossii poyavilsya zapros na chestnuyu vlast' i mirolyubie', *Vedomosti*, 27 December 2018.

24 V. V. Putin, address to citizens of Russia, 29 August 2018: http://kremlin.ru/events/president/news/58405

25 See H. E. Hale, 'The Myth of Mass Russian Support for Autocracy: The Public Opinion Foundations of a Hybrid Regime', *Europe-Asia Studies*, no. 8 (2011), pp. 1370–5.

26 VTsIOM poll, 5 August 2018: https://wciom.ru/news/ratings/doverie_politikam

27 VTsIOM poll, July 2018: 'Ratings of Social Institutions'.

Chapter 19: Knocking Down Skittles: The Flooring of the Political Opposition

1   'Tezisy po ekonomicheskomu krizisu v Rossii', 28 February 2009: *Rossiiskaya Ob"edinënnaya Demokraticheskaya Partiya 'Yabloko': Politicheskii otchët; Dokumenty, 2008–2011*, p. 16 in Russian Subject Collection (HIA), box 65.

2   Ibid., pp. 15–16 and 32.

3 Ibid.

4 B. Nemtsov, *Ispoved' buntarya*, p. 52.

5 B. Ye. Nemtsov to B. N. Yeltsin, n.d. but some time in 1995 after 14 June 1995: Vladimir Pribylovsky Papers (HIA), box 18, folder 9.

6 See A. Knight, *Orders to Kill: The Putin Regime and Political Murder*, p. 263.

7 See D. J. Smith, 'Russian Cyber Operations', *Potomac Institute Cyber Center*, July 2012, p. 4.

8 B. Ye. Nemtsov (selfie by unknown Ukrainian in Kyiv), April 2014: https://www.youtube.com/watch?v=YuMtk75UURc

9 V. Prokhorov, 'Where are the Organizers, Mr Putin? Did You Fail This Case?', *Institute of Modern Russia*, 14 December 2017: https://imrussia.org/en/opinions/2887-vadim-prokhorov-%E2%80%9Cwhere-are-the-organizers,-mr-putin-did-you-fail-this-case%E2%80%9D

10 Author's interview with Vadim Prokhorov, 18 October 2018.

11 See A. Knight, *Orders to Kill: The Putin Regime and Political Murder*, p. 265.

12 A. Naval'nyi, 'Ob ubiistve Borisa Nemtsova', 3 March 2015: https://navalny.com/p/4156

13 'Direct Line' multichannel TV interview with V. V. Putin, 16 April 2015: http://kremlin.ru/events/president/news/49261

14 G. Pavlovsky, 'Russian Politics Under Putin: The System Will Outlast the Master', *Foreign Affairs*, May–June 2016, pp. 10–17.

15 See A. Knight, *Orders to Kill: The Putin Regime and Political Murder*, p. 265.

16 A. Michnik and A. Navalnyi, *Dialogi*, p. 21.

17 See S. Medvedev, *Park krymskogo perioda*, p. 299.

18 V. Kara-Murza, 'After Years of Battling Nemtsov, the Kremlin Battles His Memory', *World Affairs*, 28 September 2017.

19 RT report, 28 February 2015: https://russian.rt.com/article/76831

20 V. Prokhorov, 'Where are the Organizers, Mr Putin? Did You Fail This Case?', *Institute of Modern Russia*, 14 December 2017: https://imrussia.org/en/opinions/2887-vadim-prokhorov-%E2%80%9Cwhere-are-the-organizers,-mr-putin-did-you-fail-this-case%E2%80%9D; author's interview with Vadim Prokhorov, 18 October 2018

21 I. Yashin, *Ulichnyi Protest*, pp. 9 and 11.

22 A. Navalnyi, 'Yakhty, oligarkhi, devochki: okhotnitsa na muzhchin razoblachaet vzyatochnika', 8 February 2018, observed on 8 April 2018: https://www.youtube.com/watch?v=RQZr2NgKPiU&feature=youtu.be

23 A. Michnik and A. Navalnyi, *Dialogi*, p. 101.

24 Interview with A. Navalnyi, in K. Voronkov, *Aleksei Naval'nyi: Groza zhulikov i vorov*, pp. 22–3.

25 Ibid., p. 28.

26 A. Mukhin and A. Gafarova, *Naval'nyi: itogi*, p. 15.

27 Ibid., p. 24.

28 Ibid., p. 20.

29 Russian Subject Collection (HIA), box 68.

30 A. Mukhin and A. Gafarova, *Naval'nyi: itogi*, p. 42.

31 Ibid., p. 97; M. Bennetts, *I'm Going to Ruin Their Lives: Inside Putin's War on Russia's Opposition*, pp. 244–7.

32 A. Mukhin and A. Gafarova, *Naval'nyi: itogi*, p. 97.

33 See A. Knight, *Orders to Kill: The Putin Regime and Political Murder*, p. 301.

34 A. Michnik and A. Navalnyi, *Dialogi*, p. 92.

35 A. Navalnyi, 'How to Punish Putin', *New York Times*, 20 March 2014.

36 A. Michnik and A. Navalnyi, *Dialogi*, p. 86.

37 A. Navalnyi, 'Sbityi focus' (interview), Ekho Moskvy, 15 October 2014: https://echo.msk.ru/programs/focus/1417522-echo.html

38 A. Michnik and A. Navalnyi, *Dialogi*, p. 92.

39 Ibid., p. 83.

40 Ibid., pp. 83–4.

41 Ibid., pp. 76–7.

42 Ibid., pp. 53–4.

43 Ibid., p. 78.

44 Ibid., p. 59.

45 Ibid., p. 58.

46 Ilya Azar, 'Ushchemlënnyi russkii' (interview of A. Navalnyi), 4 November 2011: https://lenta.ru/articles/2011/11/04/navalnyi

47 Ibid.

48 A. Michnik and A. Navalnyi, *Dialogi*, p. 73.

49 Ibid., p. 56.

50 Ibid., p. 57.

51 Ibid., p. 67.

52 Ibid., p. 72.

53 Ibid., p. 78.

54 'Naval'nyi vozglavil "Narodnyi al'yans"', 17 November 2013: http://www.interfax.ru/russia/341325

55 A. Michnik and A. Navalnyi, *Dialogi*, p. 47.

56 Ibid., pp. 76–7.

57 Ibid., p. 41.

58 'Aktsii protesta 26 marta i Navalny: Levada-Tsentr, 6 April 2017.

59 VTsIOM poll, 2 September 2018: https://wciom.ru/news/ratings/doverie_politikam

60 A. Michnik and A. Navalnyi, *Dialogi*, p. 64.

61 Ibid., p. 233.

Chapter 20: Eternal Vigilance: The Unbroken Rise of the Security State

1 See *Sluzhba bezopasnosti*, no. 1/2 (1994), pp. 7–14 and 55–9; no. 1/2 (1998), p. 74; no. 3/4 (1998), pp. 20–1.

2 Ibid., no. 1 (1999).

3 See J. Fedor, *Russia and the Cult of State Security: The Chekist Tradition, From Lenin to Putin*, p. 139.

4 V. V. Putin, speech, 30 October 2017: http://kremlin.ru/events/president/news/55948

5 V. Kara-Murza, 'Putin Unveils Memorial to Victims of Soviet Repression, While His Own Repression Continues', *World Affairs*, 31 October 2017.

6 V. V. Putin, expanded session of the FSB board, 16 February 2017: http://kremlin.ru/events/president/news/53883

7 Putin's meeting with permanent members of the Security Council, 8 November 2017: http://kremlin.ru/events/president/news/56021

8 M. Kasyanov, *Bez Putina: politicheskie dialogi s Yevgeniem Kiselëvym*, p. 165.

9 V. V. Putin, FSB Board meeting, 26 March 2015: http://kremlin.ru/events/president/news/49006

10 News item, 5 September 2017: https://www.nakanune.ru/news/2017/09/05/22481771

11 V. V. Putin (news conference), 19 December 2013: http://kremlin.ru/events/president/news/19859

12 I. Nagornykh, I. Safronov and Ye. Chernenko, 'S "tsvetnykh revolyutsii" khotyat snyat' kamuflyazh', *Kommersant*, 4 March 2015.

13 'Federal'nyi zakon Rossiiskoi Federatsii ot 6 marta g. N 35-FZ', *Rossiiskaya gazeta*, 10 March 2006 (available at http://www.rg.ru/2006/03/10/borba-terrorizm.html)

14 ITAR-TASS report, 28 June 2006.

15 Report in vesti-ru, 28 June 2006.

16 *Kommersant*, 12 July 2006.

17 *Moscow News*, 29 December 2006.

18 'Federal'nyi zakon Rossiiskoi Federatsii ot 27 iyulya 2006 g. N 148-FZ', *Rossiiskaya gazeta*, 29 July 2006 (available at http://www.rg.ru/2006/07/29/ekstremizm-protivodejstvie-dok.html)

19 'FSB Will Soon Run Operations Abroad', *Moscow Times*, 8 June 2006.

20 See L. Harding, *A Very Expensive Poison*, pp. 387–94; O. Bullough, *Moneyland: Why Thieves and Crooks Now Rule the World and How to Take It Back*, p. 207.

21 D. Allan, 'Managed Confrontation: UK Policy Towards Russia After the Salisbury Attack', pp. 2–5.

22 D. Trenin, *Rossiya i mir v XXI veke*, p. 174.

23 S. V. Lavrov (press conference, Moscow), 26 January 2016 in S. V. Lavrov, *My – vezhlivye lyudi: razmyshleniya o vneshnei politike*, p. 66.

24 V. V. Putin, press conference after Shanghai Cooperation Organisation summit in Qingdao, China, 10 June 2018: http://kremlin.ru/events/president/news/57719

25 V. V. Putin, press conference, 3 October 2018: https://tass.ru/politika/5632623

26 V. V. Putin, FSB Board meeting, 26 March 2015: http://kremlin.ru/events/president/news/49006

27 Ibid.

28 N. P. Patrushev (interview), 'Voiny i miry', *Rossiiskaya gazeta*, 18 May 2017:

https://rg.ru/2017/05/18/nikolaj-patrushev-ob-ukraine-i-ssha-kiberatakah-sirii.html

29 V. V. Putin, FSB Board meeting, 26 February 2016: http://kremlin.ru/events/president/news/51397

30 Ibid.

31 V. V. Putin, expanded session of the FSB board, 16 February 2017: http://kremlin.ru/events/president/news/53883

32 Ye. Milashina, 'Khalifat? Primanka dlya durakov!', *Novaya gazeta*, 29 July 2015.

33 M. Tsvetkova, 'How Russia Allowed Homegrown Radicals to Go and Fight in Syria', *Reuters Investigates*, 13 May 2016.

34 Putin, speech to Northern Fleet officers, 23 February 2017: http://kremlin.ru/events/president/news/53940

35 J. Schechtman, D. Volz and J. Stubbs, 'Under Pressure, Western Firms Bow to Russian Demands to Share Cyber Secrets', *Reuters*, 23 June 2017: http://www.reuters.com/article/uk-usa-russia-tech-insight-idUSKBN19E0XB

36 I. Murtazin, 'Troyanovskii kod', *Novaya gazeta*, 26 January 2017 and 'Komu shest' let "Shaltai"', *Novaya gazeta*, 2 February 2017.

37 'Full Transcript: Acting FBI Director McCabe and Others Testify Before the Senate Intelligence Committee', *Washington Post*, 11 May 2017.

38 ABC News, 24 May 2017: http://abcnews.go.com/Politics/classified-senate-briefing-expands-include-russian-cyber-firm/story?id=47619783

39 'Direct Line' multichannel TV interview with V. V. Putin, 17 April 2014: http://kremlin.ru/events/president/news/20796

40 See A. Soldatov and I. Borogan, *The Red Web: The Kremlin's War on the Internet*, pp. 207–8 and 221–2.

41 *The Putin Interviews*: Oliver Stone with Vladimir Putin, part 2 (13 June 2017): https://www.youtube.com/watch?v=j01kF7UQr0Y

42 Ibid.

43 *Komsomolskaya Pravda*, 20 December 2000.

44 A. Litvinenko, *LPG – Lubyanskaya Prestupnaya Gruppirovka. Ofitser FSB daët pokazaniya*, pp. 105–7.

45 Ibid., pp. 68 ff.

46 Ibid., p. 82.

47 http://www.telegraph.co.uk/news/uknews/law-and-order/11364900/Listen-Alexander-Litvinenkos-apparent-warning-before-his-death.html. See also A. Litvinenko's (undated) letter to the Italian parliamentary commission on the Mitrokhin dossier

48 See K. Dawisha, *Putin's Kleptocracy: Who Owns Russia?*, p. 329.

49 Ibid., pp. 135–41.

50 Confidential information from Louis Skyner: SSEES Conference, 5 November 2017.

51 See P. Reddaway, *Russia's Domestic Security Wars: Putin's Use of Divide and Rule Against His Hardline Allies*, pp. 43–62.

Chapter 21: Military Renewal: A Great Power Prepares

1 See R. Allison, 'Russian "Deniable" Intervention in Ukraine, How and Why Russia Broke the Rules', *International Affairs*, no. 6 (2014), p. 1272.

2 C. Davis, 'The Ukraine Conflict, Economic-Military Power Balances and Economic Sanctions', *Post-Communist Economies*, no. 2 (2016), p. 176.

3 Defense Intelligence Agency [USA], *Russia Military Power: Building a Military to Support Great Power Aspirations*: http://www.dia.mil/Military-Power-Publications, p. 20.

4 Ibid.

5 C. Davis, 'The Ukraine Conflict, Economic-Military Power Balances and Economic Sanctions', *Post-Communist Economies*, no. 2 (2016), tables 2 and 4.

6 Ibid., table 2.

7 S. K. Shoigu, Defence Ministry Board meeting, 22 December 2016: http://kremlin.ru/events/president/news/53571

8 Russian Military Doctrine (amended), 26 December 2014: http://www.scrf.gov.ru/security/military/document129/

9 V. V. Putin, speech to expanded board of the Defence Ministry, 19 December 2014: http://kremlin.ru/events/president/news/47257

10 Russian Military Doctrine (amended), 26 December 2014: http://www.scrf.gov.ru/security/military/document129/

11 V. V. Putin, interview with Radio Europe 1 and the TF1 TV channel, 4 June 2014: http://kremlin.ru/events/president/news/45832

12 V. V. Putin, interview with *Corriere della Sera*, 6 June 2015: http://kremlin.ru/events/president/news/49629. See also *The Putin Interviews* (book transcripts), p. 119.

13 Defense Intelligence Agency [USA], *Russia Military Power: Building a Military to Support Great Power Aspirations*: http://www.dia.mil/Military-Power-Publications, p. 31.

14 Ibid.

15 Russian Military Doctrine (amended), 26 December 2014: http://www.scrf.gov.ru/security/military/document129/

16 Federal law (Russia), 3 October 2016: http://asozd2.duma.gov.ru/addwork/scans.nsf/ID/C4294ACB989FB546432580410044CB71/$File/1186208-6_03102016_1186208-6.PDF?OpenElement. I am grateful to Michael Bernstam for drawing this law to my attention and discussing its implications and importance

17 P. Felgenhauer, 'Russia's Relations with the West Deteriorate as Military Prepares for "Resource Wars"', *Eurasia Daily Monitor*, vol. 13, no. 177 (3 November 2016).

18 I. Safronov, 'Esli ne skhod, to razval', *Kommersant*, 17 September 2016.

19 See P. Hanson, 'Managing the Economy', in H. E. Hale, R. Sakwa and S. White, *Developments in Russian Politics*, p. 145.

20 V. V. Putin, interview with *Corriere della Sera*, 6 June 2015: http://kremlin.ru/events/president/news/49629

21 S. K. Shoigu, Defence Ministry Board meeting, 22 December 2016: http, // kremlin.ru/events/president/news/53571

22 T. Batchelor, 'British Troops are Deployed in Estonia and Poland', *Independent on Sunday*, 5 February 2017.

23 M. Boulègue, 'Five Things to Know About the Zapad-2017 Military Exercise'.

24 R. Sikorski, interview with Zh. Nemtsova, Deutsche Welle, 10 October 2018.

25 M. Boulègue, 'Five Things to Know About the Zapad-2017 Military Exercise'.

26 The Vostok-2018 military exercise is dealt with below, pp. 293–4.

27 M. Gordon, 'Russia Deploys Missile, Violating Treaty and Challenging Trump', *New York Times*, 14 February 2017.

Chapter 22: Tranquillity of the Graveyard: Chechnya Under Kadyrov

1 I. Yashin, *A Threat to National Security*, p. 24.

2 Ibid., p. 23.

3 J. Longman, 'Mo Salah, Now Starring in Chechnya', *New York Times*, 11 June 2018.

4 V. V. Putin, presidential address to Federal Assembly, 25 April 2005: http://kremlin.ru/events/president/transcripts/22931

5 P. Baumgartner, 'Kadyrov's Snow Job', RFE/RL, 24 January 2018.

6 'Siluanov rasskazal, kak popolnyaetsya byudzhet Chechni', *Vedomosti*, 26 July 2018.

7 I. Yashin, *A Threat to National Security*, p. 23; *The Family* (Open Russia documentary film): https://www.khodorkovsky.com/the-family-a-film-about-ramzan-kadyrov

8 I. Yashin, *A Threat to National Security*, p. 25.

9 'Kadyrov poprosil uvelichit' federal'nye dotatsii Chechne iz-za rosta rozhdaemosti', *Vedomosti*, 27 September 2018.

10 Meeting of V. V. Putin and R. A. Kadyrov, 25 March 2016: http://kremlin.ru/catalog/persons/146/events/51567

11 Meeting of V. V. Putin and R. A. Kadyrov, 19 April 2017: http://kremlin.ru/catalog/persons/146/events/54342

12 'Direct Line' multichannel TV interview with V. V. Putin, 25 April 2013: http://kremlin.ru/events/president/news/17976

13 R. A. Kadyrov (interview): 'Putin – dar bozhii', *Kommersant Vlast'*, 18 June 2007.

14 I. Yashin, *A Threat to National Security*, p. 40.

15 Author's interview with Vadim Prokhorov, Navalnyi's former lawyer, 18 October 2018.

16 L. Fuller, 'Chechnya's Kadyrov, Rosneft Again at Odds', RFE/RL, 23 August 2017.

17 I. Yashin, *A Threat to National Security*, p. 12.

18 Ibid., p. 17.

19 See A. Knight, *Orders to Kill: The Putin Regime and Political Murder*, pp. 198 and 289.

20 Ibid., p. 289.

21 'Kadyrov Officially Sanctions Collective Responsibility for Families of Terrorists', *Open Caucasus Media*, 20 April 2017: http://oc-media.org/kadyrov-officially-sanctions-collective-responsibility-for-families-of-terrorists
22 L. Fuller, 'Analysis: Grozny Fatwa on "True Believers" Triggers Major Controversy', RFE/RL, 14 September 2016.
23 I. Yashin, *A Threat to National Security*, p. 17.
24 Ye. Milashina, 'Ubiistvo chesti', *Novaya gazeta*, 3 April 2017.
25 K. Hille, 'Chechen Ruler Hits Out at Russia Over Myanmar Policy', *Financial Times*, 4 September 2018.
26 Ye. Milashina, 'Nevol'nik mesti', *Nezavisimaya gazeta*, 6 August 2018.
27 K. Hille, 'How Chechnya's Ramzan Kadyrov Could Destabilize Russia', *Financial Times*, 23 August 2018.
28 I. Yashin, *A Threat to National Security*, p. 17.

Chapter 23: Imperial Instinct: Moscow and the 'Near Abroad'

1 A. L. Kudrin, 'Ustoichivyi ekonomicheskii rost: model' dlya Rossii', Gaidar Forum, 13 January 2017.
2 See N. Robinson, *Contemporary Russian Politics: An Introduction*, pp. 143–4 and 147. See also C. Ross, 'Federalisation and Defederalisation in Russia', in G. Gill and J. Young (eds), *Routledge Handbook of Russian Politics and Society*, pp. 143–4.
3 See N. Taylor, *Estonia: A Modern History*, p. 197.
4 R. Sikorski, *Polska może być lepsza*, p. 242.
5 R. Allison, 'Russia and the Post-2014 International Legal Order: Revisionism and Realpolitik', *International Affairs*, no. 3 (2017), pp. 532–3 and 538–9.
6 See R. Allison, 'Protective Integration and Security Policy Coordination: Comparing the SCO and CSTO', *Chinese Journal of International Relations*, no. 3 (2018), pp. 325, 328 and 330.
7 See R. Dragneva and K. Wolczuk, 'The Eurasian Economic Union: Deals, Rules and the Exercise of Power', p. 6.
8 Ibid., p. 20.
9 Ibid.
10 Ibid., pp. 21–2.
11 I base this finding on a trawl of Putin's speeches for the year 2018: http://kremlin.ru/events/president/news
12 'Nazarbaev zayavil o vozmozhnom vykhode Kazakhstana iz Evraziiskogo soyuza', newsru.com, 31 August 2014: https://www.newsru.com/world/31aug2014/nazarbaev.html
13 See R. Dragneva and K. Wolczuk, 'The Eurasian Economic Union: Deals, Rules and the Exercise of Power', p. 9.
14 S. Glaz'ev, *Bitva za liderstvo v XXI veke: Rossiya-SShA-Kitai. Sem' variantov obozrimogo*, pp. 284–5.
15 See C. Miller, *Putinomics: Power and Money in Resurgent Russia*, pp. 146–7.

Chapter 24: Economic Shock: Western Sanctions and the Oil Price Tumble

1 TASS Russian News Agency report, 31 March 2015.
2 See C. Miller, *Putinomics: Power and Money in Resurgent Russia*, p. 152.
3 C. Davis, 'The Ukraine Conflict, Economic-Military Power Balances and Economic Sanctions', *Post-Communist Economies*, no. 2 (2016), footnote 12.
4 See C. Miller, *Putinomics: Power and Money in Resurgent Russia*, pp. 154–5.
5 'Direct Line' multichannel TV interview with V. V. Putin, 15 June 2017: http://kremlin.ru/events/president/news/54790
6 Ibid.
7 *Washington Examiner*, 30 November 2017.
8 V. V. Putin, interview with Bloomberg TV, 5 September 2016: http://kremlin.ru/events/president/news/52830
9 V. V. Putin, Valdai International Discussion Club, 27 October 2016: http://kremlin.ru/events/president/news/53151
10 C. G. Gaddy and B. Ickes, 'Ukraine: A Prize Neither Russia Nor the West Can Afford to Win', *Brookings Research Articles* (Washington DC, 2014): https://www.brookings.edu/articles/ukraine-a-prize-neither-russia-nor-the-west-can-afford-to-win/
11 C. Davis, 'The Ukraine Conflict, Economic-Military Power Balances and Economic Sanctions', *Post-Communist Economies*, no. 2 (2016), p. 186.
12 See R. Sakwa, *Frontline Ukraine: Crisis in the Borderlands*, p. 195.
13 See S. Medvedev, *Park krymskogo perioda*, p. 199.
14 'Direct Line' multichannel TV interview with V. V. Putin, 16 April 2015: http://kremlin.ru/events/president/news/49261
15 Ibid.
16 Ibid.
17 See R. Connolly, *Russia's Response to Sanctions: How Western Economic Statecraft is Reshaping Political Economy in Russia*, pp. 69–73.
18 S. Wengle, 'The Domestic Effects of the Russian Food Embargo', *Demokratizatsiya*, no. 3 (2016), p. 283.
19 R. Connolly makes this case in *Russia's Response to Sanctions: How Western Economic Statecraft is Reshaping Political Economy in Russia*, pp. 192–4.
20 C. Davis, 'The Ukraine Conflict, Economic-Military Power Balances and Economic Sanctions', *Post-Communist Economies*, no. 2 (2016), p. 185.
21 https://www.currency-converter.org.uk/currency-rates/historical/table/USD-RUB.html
22 P. Hanson, 'Managing the Economy', in H. E. Hale, R. Sakwa and S. White, *Developments in Russian Politics*, p. 135.
23 Ibid.
24 C. Davis, 'The Ukraine Conflict, Economic-Military Power Balances and Economic Sanctions', *Post-Communist Economies*, no. 2 (2016), p. 175.
25 On the origins of these funds, see above, pp. 117–18.
26 https://uk.reuters.com/article/us-russia-rosneft-privatisation-idUKKBN1321V5

27 E. Stanovaya, 'Leadership and Bureaucracy in "Post-Crimean" Russia', in A. Barbashin, O. Irisova, F. Burkhardt and E. Wyciszkiewicz (eds), *A Successful Failure: Russia after Crime(a)*, p. 100.

28 V. V. Putin, interview with Bloomberg TV, 5 September 2016: http://kremlin. ru/events/president/news/52830

29 S. Kardaś and I. Wiśniewska, 'The Ulyukaev Case: Tension Inside the Russian Elite', *OSW Commentary*, no. 255 (1 December 2017), p. 4.

30 V. V. Putin, Kremlin meeting with big business leaders, 21 December 2017: http://kremlin.ru/events/president/news/56461

31 A. Illarionov, 22 December 2017: https://aillarionov.livejournal.com/2017/12/22

32 E. Dąbrowska, 'The End of the Reserve Fund, the End of an Era', 4 April 2018.

33 V. V. Putin, Meeting of the Commission for Military Technology Cooperation with Foreign Countries, 3 April 2013: http://kremlin.ru/events/president/news/17793

34 Ye. Pismennaya and A. Andrianova, 'Russia's $70 Billion "Secret" Spending Lets Money Do the Talking', Bloomberg Politics, 25 July 2017: https://www.bloomberg.com/news/articles/2017-07-25/russia-s-70-billion-secret-spending-lets-money-do-the-talking

35 Ibid.

36 Ibid.

37 Author's conversation with Michael McFaul, 9 August 2017 (Stanford, California).

38 World Bank Data: http://data.worldbank.org/indicator/BX.KLT.DINV.CD.WD?end=2016&locations=RU&start=1992&view=chart

39 '50 krupneishikh inostrannykh kompaniy v Rossii', *Forbes Magazine* (accessed online, 8 August 2017): http://www.forbes.ru/rating/50-krupneishikh-inostrannykh-kompanii-v-rossii-2016/2016#top10

40 I. Khrennikov, 'Big Western Companies are Pumping Cash into Russia', *Bloomberg*, 22 November 2016: https://www.bloomberg.com/news/articles/2016-11-23/bouncing-back-putin-s-shrunken-economy-lures-foreign-investors

41 Report in lenta.ru, 13 April 2017: http://getrussia.com/news/forbes_names_biggest_foreign_businesses_in_russia. (This report is no longer available online.)

42 D. Szakonyi, 'Governing Business: The State and Business in Russia', Foreign Policy Research Institute, 22 January 2018: https://www.fpri.org/wp-content/uploads/2018/01/Szakonyi-Final-Version.pdf, p. 2.

43 Auswärtiges Amt, general notification about Russian conditions, March 2017: http://www.auswaertiges-amt.de/EN/Aussenpolitik/Laender/Laenderinfos/01-Nodes/RussischeFoederation_node.html

44 TASS, 20 January 2016: http://tass.com/economy/850944

45 V. V. Putin (press conference), St Petersburg International Economic Forum, 1 June 2017: http://kremlin.ru/events/president/news/54650

46 R. Connolly, 'Western Financial Sanctions Won't Break Russia', *Moscow Times*, 28 June 2015.

47 J. L. Tefft, 'Why Russia–U.S. Trade Still Matters', *Moscow Times*, 22 December 2016.

48 United States Census Bureau, 'Trade in Goods with Russia' (July 2017); 'U.S.–Russian Trade Relationship? There Really Isn't One', *Fortune*, 18 March 2014; Observatory of Economic Complexity (MIT, Chicago), 8 August 2017: http://atlas.media.mit.edu/en/visualize/tree_map/hs92/export/usa/rus/show/2015

49 E. B. Rumer, 'Russia's China Policy, This Bear Hug is Real', in M. S. Chase, E. S. Medeiros, J. Stapleton Roy, E. B. Rumer, R. Sutter and R. Weitz, *Russia–China Relations: Assessing Common Ground and Strategic Fault Lines* (National Bureau of Asian Research, special report no. 66, July 2017), p. 22.

50 Observatory of Economic Complexity (MIT, Chicago), 6 August 2017: http://atlas.media.mit.edu/en/profile/country/rus

51 Observatory of Economic Complexity (MIT, Chicago), 8 August 2017: http://atlas.media.mit.edu/en/visualize/tree_map/hs92/import/rus/show/all/2015

52 'Russia Takes Lead on EMEA Smartphone Market', International Data Corporation (press release), 3 April 2017: https://www.idc.com/getdoc.jsp?containerId=prCEMA42443617. (This press release is no longer available online.)

53 See S. Saradzhan, 'Is Russia Declining?', *Demokratizatsiya*, no. 3 (2016), p. 416.

54 Observatory of Economic Complexity (MIT, Chicago), 6 August 2017: http://atlas.media.mit.edu/en/profile/country/rus

55 'Transcript, Interview with Sergei Ivanov', *Financial Times*, 21 June 2015.

56 V. V. Putin, Valdai International Discussion Club, 22 October 2015: http://kremlin.ru/events/president/news/50548

57 *Moscow Times*, 10 October 2018.

58 C. Krauss, 'Exxon Mobil Scraps a Russian Deal, Stymied by Sanctions', *New York Times*, 28 February 2018.

59 OECD report, 1 May 2018: http://www.oecd.org/eco/outlook/economic-forecast-summary-russia-oecd-economic-outlook.pdf

60 V. V. Putin, annual press conference, 21 December 2018: http://kremlin.ru/events/president/news/59455

Chapter 25: Trailing the Dragon: Russo-Chinese Relations

1 E. M. Primakov, notes for meeting with V. V. Putin, earlier than 3 September 2009, in V. I. Matvienko and S. E. Naryshkin (eds), *Neizvestnyi Primakov*, vol. 1 (*Dokumenty*), p. 328.

2 S. Glaz'ev, *Bitva za liderstvo v XXI veke: Rossiya-SShA-Kitai. Sem' variantov obozrimogo*, pp. 5–6.

3 Fu Ying, 'How China Sees Russia', *Foreign Affairs*, January/February 2016, pp. 100–2.

4 E. S. Medeiros and M. S. Chase, 'Chinese Perspectives on the Sino-Russian Relationship', in M. S. Chase, E. S. Medeiros, J. Stapleton Roy, E. B. Rumer, R. Sutter and R. Weitz, *Russia–China Relations: Assessing Common Ground and*

Strategic Fault Lines (National Bureau of Asian Research, special report no. 66, July 2017), p. 8.

5 V. V. Putin, press conference (Hangzhou), 5 September 2016: http://kremlin. ru/catalog/countries/CN/events/52834

6 See B. Lo, *A Wary Embrace: What the China–Russia Relationship Means for the World*, pp. 19–20.

7 J. Schubert, *New Eurasian Age: China's Silk Road and the EAEU in SCO Space*, p. 17.

8 J. Brooke, 'With Russia on the Sidelines, China Moves Aggressively into Ukraine', *Atlantic Council*, January 5, 2018.

9 E. S. Medeiros and M. S. Chase, 'Chinese Perspectives on the Sino-Russian Relationship', in M. S. Chase, E. S. Medeiros, J. Stapleton Roy, E. B. Rumer, R. Sutter and R. Weitz, *Russia–China Relations: Assessing Common Ground and Strategic Fault Lines* (National Bureau of Asian Research, special report no. 66, July 2017), p. 19.

10 J. Schubert, *New Eurasian Age: China's Silk Road and the EAEU in SCO Space*, p. 12.

11 Ibid., p. 52.

12 Ibid., p. 54.

13 See B. Lo, *A Wary Embrace: What the China–Russia Relationship Means for the World*, p. 41.

14 J. Schubert, *New Eurasian Age: China's Silk Road and the EAEU in SCO Space*, pp. 3–5; A. Gabuev, 'Friends With Benefits? Russian–Chinese Relations After the Ukraine Crisis', Carnegie Moscow Center, 29 June 2016: http://carnegie. ru/2016/06/29/friends-with-benefits-russian-chinese-relations-after-ukraine-crisis-pub-63953

15 E. S. Medeiros and M. S. Chase, 'Chinese Perspectives on the Sino-Russian Relationship', in M. S. Chase, E. S. Medeiros, J. Stapleton Roy, E. B. Rumer, R. Sutter and R. Weitz, *Russia–China Relations: Assessing Common Ground and Strategic Fault Lines* (National Bureau of Asian Research, special report no. 66, July 2017), p. 8.

16 Ibid., p. 18.

17 J. Norberg and F. Westerlund, 'Russia and Ukraine: Military-Strategic Options, and Possible Risks, for Moscow', RUFS Briefing No. 22 (April 2014), p. 2.

18 M. Bodner, 'In Arms Trade, China is Taking Advantage of Russia's Desperation', *Moscow Times*, 1 November 2016.

19 A. Gabuev, 'Who's Afraid of Chinese Colonization?', Carnegie Moscow Center, 26 June, 2015: http://carnegie.ru/commentary/60515

20 R. Weitz, 'Sino-Russian Security Ties', in M. S. Chase, E. S. Medeiros, J. Stapleton Roy, E. B. Rumer, R. Sutter and R. Weitz, *Russia–China Relations: Assessing Common Ground and Strategic Fault Lines* (National Bureau of Asian Research, special report no. 66, July 2017), p. 41.

21 E. Shevardnadze, *Kogda rukhnul zheleznyi zanaves, vstrechi i vospominaniya*, p. 115.

22 V. V. Putin, press conference (Hangzhou), 5 September 2016: http://kremlin. ru/catalog/countries/CN/events/52834

23 Fu Ying, 'How China Sees Russia', *Foreign Affairs*, January/February 2016, pp. 100–2.

24 See B. Lo, *A Wary Embrace: What the China–Russia Relationship Means for the World*, p. 4.

25 Miles Yu, 'Storm Over Russia Border Rages', *Washington Times*, 12 November 2015.

26 This paragraph benefits from advice from Bobo Lo.

Chapter 26: Fighting Abroad: The Syrian Intervention

1 A. Anishchuk, 'Russia Warns Against Military Intervention in Syria', Reuters, 26 August 2013.

2 J. Kerry, *Every Day is Extra*, pp. 548–9.

3 D. A. Medvedev, news conference after the G8 summit, 27 May 2011: http://kremlin.ru/events/president/transcripts/11374

4 V. V. Putin interviewed by V. R. Solovëv, Rossiya 1 TV, 11 October 2015: https://www.youtube.com/watch?v=9NvwB6pmDoc

5 *The Putin Interviews*: Oliver Stone with Vladimir Putin, part 3 (14 June 2017): https://www.youtube.com/watch?v=QvlKSbYkTXI

6 V. V. Putin, interview with *Bild* magazine, part 2, conducted on 5 January 2016 and printed on 12 January 2016: http://kremlin.ru/events/president/news/51155

7 V. V. Putin, St Petersburg International Economic Forum plenary session, 2 June 2017: http://kremlin.ru/events/president/news/54667

8 *The Putin Interviews*: Oliver Stone with Vladimir Putin, part 3 (14 June 2017): https://www.youtube.com/watch?v=QvlKSbYkTXI

9 Ibid.

10 *The Times*, 29 June 2017.

11 D. Trenin, *Rossiya i mir v XXI veke*, pp. 227–8.

12 S. K. Shoigu, Defence Ministry Board meeting, 22 December 2016: http, // kremlin.ru/events/president/news/53571

Chapter 27: Jostling and Embracing: The American Factor

1 See L. Harding, *Collusion: How Russia Helped Trump Win the White House*, pp. 84 and 103.

2 Testimony of Clinton Watts, ex-FBI agent and senior fellow of the George Washington Center for Cyber and Homeland Security, to the United States Intelligence Committee, C-Span3, 27 May 2017.

3 V. V. Putin, Valdai International Discussion Club, 27 October 2016: http://kremlin.ru/events/president/news/53151

4 See L. Harding, *Collusion: How Russia Helped Trump Win the White House*, pp. 27–32. The original BuzzFeed publication appeared at: https://www.buzzfeed-

news.com/article/kenbensinger/these-reports-allege-trump-has-deep-ties-to-russia

5 Joint press conference of V. V. Putin and President I. N. Dodon of Moldova, 17 January 2017: http://kremlin.ru/events/president/news/53744

6 S. V. Lavrov, Q&A in 'Government Hour' in State Duma, 25 January 2017: S. V. Lavrov, *My – vezhlivye lyudi: razmyshleniya o vneshnei politike*, p. 436.

7 VTsIOM survey no. 3352, 17 April 2017.

8 Presidential Memorandum on Rebuilding the U.S. Armed Forces, 27 January 2017: https://www.whitehouse.gov/presidential-actions/presidential-memorandum-rebuilding-u-s-armed-forces

9 Telephone conversation between V. V. Putin and D. J. Trump, 2 May 2017: http://kremlin.ru/events/president/news/54441; *The Putin Interviews*: Oliver Stone with Vladimir Putin, part 3 (14 June 2017): https://www.youtube.com/watch?v=QvlKSbYkTXI

10 V. V. Putin, annual press conference, 14 December 2017: http://kremlin.ru/events/president/news/56378

11 *The Putin Interviews*: Oliver Stone with Vladimir Putin, part 3 (14 June 2017): https://www.youtube.com/watch?v=QvlKSbYkTXI

12 See R. Allison, 'Russia and the Post-2014 International Legal Order: Revisionism and Realpolitik', *International Affairs*, no. 3 (2017), p. 525.

13 J. Comey (testimony), House Intelligence Committee hearing, 20 March 2017: https://www.youtube.com/watch?v=fwkw_b2-K80

14 *The Putin Interviews*: Oliver Stone with Vladimir Putin, part 3 (14 June 2017): https://www.youtube.com/watch?v=QvlKSbYkTXI

15 Ibid.

16 PONARS Eurasia, 'Why Trump's Bid to Improve U.S.–Russian Relations Backfired in Congress': http://www.ponarseurasia.org/ru/node/9595

17 W. Ischinger, 'Why Europeans Oppose the Russian Economic Sanctions', *Wall Street Journal*, 17 July 2017.

18 S. Erlanger and N. MacFarquhar, 'E.U. is Uneasy, and Divided, About U.S. Sanctions on Russia', *New York Times*, 25 July 2017.

19 V. V. Putin (interview), *Le Figaro*, 31 May 2017: http://kremlin.ru/events/president/news/54638

20 NBC interview by Megyn Kelly, 2 June 2017: http://kremlin.ru/events/president/news/54688

21 D. Philipov, D. Paletta and A. Phillip, 'Putin Denies Election Hacking After Trump Pressed Him, Tillerson Says', *Washington Post*, 8 July 2017.

22 V. V. Putin, G20 press conference (Hamburg), 8 July 2017: http://kremlin.ru/events/president/news/55017

23 *New York Times*, 10 July 2017

24 Reuters World News, 10 July 2017: https://www.reuters.com/article/us-ukraine-nato-idUSKBN19V12V

25 'New Envoy Volker Says U.S. Considering Sending Arms to Ukraine', RFE/RL, 25 July 2017: https://www.rferl.org/a/ukraine-volker-sending-arms-russia-conflict/28637079.html

26 S. V. Lavrov, lecture at General Staff Academy, 23 March 2017: S. V. Lavrov, *My – vezhlivye lyudi: razmyshleniya o vneshnei politike*, p. 462.

27 J. Johnson and A. Troianovski, 'Trump Congratulates Putin on His Reelection, Discusses U.S.–Russian "Arms Race"', *Washington Post*, 20 March 2018.

28 I. Arkhipov and E. Pismennaya, 'Putin Still Wants Deal with Trump, Even After Sanctions, Syria Attack', *Bloomberg*, 18 April 2018: https://www.bloomberg.com/news/articles/2018-04-18/putin-said-to-seek-trump-deal-even-after-sanctions-syria-attack

29 *Hard Talk* (with S. Sackur), BBC News Channel, 16 April 2018.

30 D. Allan, 'Managed Confrontation: UK Policy Towards Russia After the Salisbury Attack', p. 11.

31 'Posol Rossii v SShA rasskazal o dogovorënnostyakh Putina i Trampa', *Izvestiya*, 18 July 2018.

32 *Guardian*, 27 January 2019.

33 *Washington Post*, 28 January 2019.

34 G. Trush, 'Trump's State of the Union Address', *New York Times*, 5 February 2019.

35 S. LaFraniere and K. Benner, 'Mueller Delivers Report', *New York Times*, 23 March 2019.

36 V. V. Putin, address to the Federal Assembly, 20 February 2019: http://kremlin.ru/events/president/news/59863

Chapter 28: Choices: Russia and the West

1 Conversation with Henry Kissinger, 11 December 2017. I am grateful to Dr Kissinger for sharing this impression on the basis of his discussions with Vladimir Putin.

2 Interfax-Ukraine, 29 April 2019: https://en.interfax.com.ua/news/general/584679.html. See also P. Gregory, 'Putin's Provocations Are Met With Ridicule in Ukraine', *The Hill*, 1 May 2019: https://thehill.com/opinion/international/441435-ridicule-is-a-sound-remedy-for-putins-provocations

3 A. Guterres, UN Security Council, 13 April 2018: https://www.un.org/press/en/2018/sgsm18986.doc.htm

4 'Sergey Lavrov: The Interview', *National Interest*, 29 March 2017, p. 516.

5 V. V. Putin, Valdai International Discussion Club: 19 October 2017: http://kremlin.ru/events/president/news/55882

Index